An Introduction to
SOCIAL
PSYCHOLOGY

William McDougall

DOVER PUBLICATIONS, INC.
Mineola, New York

Bibliographical Note

This Dover edition, first published in 2003, is an unabridged republication of the 1936 revised edition of the work first published in 1908 by Methuen & Co. Ltd., London.

Library of Congress Cataloging-in-Publication Data

McDougall, William, 1871-1938.
    An introduction to social psychology / by William McDougall.
      p. cm.
    Originally published: London : Methuen, 1908.
    Includes index.
    ISBN 0-486-42711-0 (pbk.)
      1. Social psychology. I. Title.

HM1033.M357 2003
302—dc21

2003043532

Manufactured in the United States of America
Dover Publications, Inc., 31 East 2nd Street, Mineola, N.Y. 11501

PREFACE TO THE FOURTEENTH EDITION

IN this little book I have attempted to deal with a
difficult branch of psychology in a way that shall
make it intelligible and interesting to any cultivated
reader, and that shall imply no previous familiarity with
psychological treatises on his part ; for I hope that the
book may be of service to students of all the social sciences,
by providing them with the minimum of psychological
doctrine that is an indispensable part of the equipment for
work in any of these sciences. I have not thought it
necessary to enter into a discussion of the exact scope
of social psychology and of its delimitation from sociology
or the special social sciences ; for I believe that such
questions may be left to solve themselves in the course of
time with the advance of the various branches of science
concerned. I would only say that I believe social psychology to offer for research a vast and fertile field, which
has been but little worked hitherto, and that in this book
I have attempted to deal only with its most fundamental
problems, those the solution of which is a presupposition
of all profitable work in the various branches of the
science.

If I have severely criticised some of the views from

which I dissent, and have connected these views with the names of writers who have maintained them, it is because I believe such criticism to be a great aid to clearness of exposition and also to be much needed in the present state of psychology ; the names thus made use of were chosen because the bearers of them are authors well known for their valuable contributions to mental science. I hope that this brief acknowledgment may serve as an apology to any of them under whose eyes my criticisms may fall. I owe also some apology to my fellow-workers for the somewhat dogmatic tone I have adopted. I would not be taken to believe that my utterances upon any of the questions dealt with are infallible or incapable of being improved upon ; but repeated expressions of deference and of the sense of my own uncertainty would be out of place in a semi-popular work of this character and would obscure the course of my exposition.

Although I have tried to make this book intelligible and useful to those who are not professed students of psychology, it is by no means a mere dishing up of current doctrines for popular consumption ; and it may add to its usefulness in the hands of professional psychologists if I indicate here the principal points which, to the best of my belief, are original contributions to psychological doctrine.

In Chapter II. I have tried to render fuller and clearer the conceptions of instinct and of instinctive process, from both the psychical and the nervous sides.

In Chapter III. I have elaborated a principle, briefly enunciated in a previous work, which is, I believe, of the first importance for the understanding of the life of emotion and action—the principle, namely, that all emotion is the affective aspect of instinctive process. The adoption of this principle leads me to define emotion more strictly and narrowly than has been done by other writers ; and I have used it as a guide in attempting to distinguish the more important of the primary emotions.

In Chapter IV. I have combated the current view that imitation is to be ascribed to an instinct of imitation ; and I have attempted to give greater precision to the conception of suggestion, and to define the principal conditions of suggestibility. I have adopted a view of the most simple and primitive form of sympathy that has been previously enunciated by Herbert Spencer and others, and have proposed what seems to be the only possible theory of the way in which sympathetic induction of emotion takes place. I have then suggested a modification of Professor Groos's theory of play, and in this connection have indulged in a speculation as to the peculiar nature and origin of the emulative impulse.

In Chapter V. I have elaborated the conception of a " sentiment " which is a relatively novel one. Since this is the key to all the constructive, as contrasted with the more purely analytical, part of the book, I desire to state as clearly as possible its relations to kindred conceptions of other authors. In the preface to the first edition of this book I attributed the conception of the sentiments which was expounded in the text to Mr. A. F. Shand. But on the publication of his important work on *The Foundations of Character* in the year 1914, I found that the conception I had developed differed very importantly from his as expounded at length in that work. I had to some extent misinterpreted the very brief statements of his earlier publications, and had read into them my own meaning. Although I still recognise that Mr. Shand has the merit of having first clearly shown the need of psychology for some such conception, I must in the interests of truth point out that my conception of the sentiment and its relation to the emotion is so different from his as to be in reality a rival doctrine rather than a development of it. Looking back, I can now see that the germ of my conception was contained in and derived by me from Professor Stout's chapter on " Emotions " in his *Manual of Psychology*. At the time of writing the book I was not acquainted with the work of Freud and Jung and the other psycho-analysts. And I have been gratified to find that the workers of this important school, approaching psychological problems from the point of view of mental pathology, have independently arrived at a conception which is almost identical with my notion of the sentiment. This is the conception of the " complex " which now occupies a position of great importance in psycho-analytic literature. Arrived at and still used mainly in the attempt to understand the processes at work in the minds of neurotic patients, it has been recognised by some recent writers on mental pathology (notably Dr. Bernard Hart) that the " complex," or something very like it, is not a feature of mental structure confined to the minds of neurotic patients, and they are beginning to use the term in this wider sense as denoting those structural features of the normal mind which I have called sentiments. It would, I venture to suggest, contribute to the development of our psychological terminology if it could be agreed to restrict the term

" complex " to those pathological or morbid sentiments in connection with which it was first used, and to use " sentiment " as the wider more general term to denote all those acquired conjunctions of ideas with emotional-conative tendencies or dispositions the acquisition and operating of which play so great a part both in normal and morbid mental development.

In Chapter V. I have analysed the principal complex emotions in the light of the conception of the sentiment and of the principle laid down in Chapter II. respecting the relation of emotion to instinct.   The analyses reached are in many respects novel ; and I venture to think that, though they may need much correction in detail, they have the merit of having been achieved by a method very much superior to the one commonly pursued, the latter being that of introspective analysis unaided by any previous determination of the primary emotions by the comparative method.

In Chapters VI., VII., VIII., and IX. I have applied the doctrine of the sentiments and the results reached in the earlier chapters to the description of the organisation of the life of emotion and impulse, and have built upon these foundations an account which is more definite than any other with which I am acquainted.   Attention may be drawn to the account offered of the nature of active or developed sympathy ; but the principal novelty contained in these chapters is what may, perhaps, without abuse of the phrase, be called a theory of volition, and a sketch of the development of character conceived as consisting in the organisation of the sentiments in one harmonious system.

Of the heterogeneous assortment of ideas presented in the second section of the book I find it impossible to say what and how much is original. No doubt almost all of them derive from a moderately extensive reading of anthropological and sociological literature.

Since the original publication of this book I have added three supplementary chapters, one on " Theories of Action " to the fifth edition in 1912, one " On the Sex Instinct " to the eighth edition in 1914, and the third on " The Derived Emotions " to the present edition. These additional chapters give the work, I think, more the character of a complete treatise on the active side of man's nature, a character at which I had not aimed in the first instance ; for I aimed chiefly at setting out my own views so far as they seemed to me to be novel and original. I feel now that yet another chapter is required to complete the work, namely one on habit, and I hope to attempt this as soon as I may achieve some degree of clearness on the subject in my own mind. Since the first publication of this book, there have appeared several books dealing in part with the same topics and offering some criticism of my views. Of these I have found three especially inter- esting, namely Mr. Shand's *Foundations of Character*, Professor Thorndike's *Original Nature of Man*, and Dr. J. Drever's *Instinct in Man*. With Mr. Shand's aims and with his ransacking of the poets for psychological evidence I have much sympathy, but I find myself at variance with him over many matters of fundamental importance for the understanding of character. He regards the emotions as highly complex innate disposi- tions, within which the instincts are organised as merely so many sensory-motor dispositions to particular bodily movements. A second important difference is that he regards the sentiments as innately organised systems of emotional dispositions ; thus for him both love and hate are innate sentiments, and each of them consists of the dispositions of four emotions, joy, sorrow, anger, and fear, linked together to form one system. In my view the sentiments are acquired through individual experience, and where two or more emotional dispositions become conjoined in the structure of one sentiment, as when fear and anger are combined in the sentiment of hate, we have to regard these two dispositions as connected, not directly with one another, but only indirectly through the association of each with the particular object of this particular sentiment of hatred. Those are, I think, the most deep-lying differences between his view and mine ; but there are many others which cannot be discussed here. Some of these differences have been set out and discussed in a symposium on " Instinct and the Emotions," published in the *Proceedings of the Aristotelian Society* for 1914. Those readers who are interested in contrasting these views may find some assistance there. Other differences are discussed at some length in the new chapter which I have added to the present edition of this book.

Mr. Thorndike's view of the constitution of man differs from mine in the opposite way from Mr. Shand's. While I postulate a few great primary instincts, each capable, like those of the animals, of prompting and sustaining long trains of thought and action ; and while Mr. Shand postulates still more complex systems of

innate dispositions, such as preformed sentiments of love
and hate, each comprising an array of emotional dispositions and many instincts (in his sense of the word),
Mr. Thorndike, on the other hand, lays it down that our
innate constitution consists of nothing more than a vast
number of simple reflex tendencies. How we are to
conceive character and intellect as being built up from
such elements I utterly fail to grasp. This multitude of
reflexes corresponds to Mr. Shand's many instincts; these
two authors, then, agree in postulating a great number
of very simple instinctive or reflex motor tendencies as
given in the innate constitution; they differ in that for
Mr. Thorndike they are a mere unorganised crowd of
discrete unconnected tendencies to movement; while for
Mr. Shand they are somehow subordinated to and organised within vast systems of emotional dispositions and
still more comprehensive systems of innate sentiments.

I am encouraged to find that my own position is
midway between these extreme views, that which postulates vastly complex innate organisations comprising many
emotional and conative dispositions, and that which denies
all but the most rudimentary conative reflexes to our
innate constitution. And I am further encouraged to
believe that my scheme of our innate conative endowment
approximates to the truth by Dr. Drever's recent essay on
Instinct in Man. For Dr. Drever has given us a careful
historical survey of this question, and, after critically
considering the various views that have been put forward,
comes to the conclusion that the one set out in this book
is the most acceptable. He is not content with it in
certain particulars; for example, he would prefer to

class as appetites certain of the tendencies which I have
classed with the instincts, such as the sex and the food-
seeking tendencies ; but I am not convinced that it is
possible to draw any clear line of separation, and I would
prefer to continue to regard instinct as the comprehensive
class, or genus, of which the appetites are one species.
The distinction that Dr. Drever would have us sharply
draw may seem to be fairly clear in the human species ;
but it seems to me to break down when we attempt to
apply it at all rigidly to animal life. What shall we say,
for example, of the nest-building, the brooding, and the
migratory tendencies of birds ? Are these instincts or
appetites ? I am glad to note that Dr. Drever agrees
with me also in respect of the other most fundamental
feature of this book, namely, he approves and accepts
the conception of the sentiment that I have attempted
to develop. He, however, makes in this connection a
suggestion which I am unable to accept. I have proposed as the essential distinction between an instinct and
a sentiment the view that in the instinct the connection
between the cognitive and the conative dispositions is
innate, while in the sentiment this connection is acquired
through individual experience. Dr. Drever proposes
to substitute for this the distinction that " the instinct
' disposition ' is perceptual, that is, involves only perceptual consciousness, while the sentiment ' disposition '
is ideational, and is a sentiment because it is ideational."
I cannot accept this for two good reasons. First, I
believe and have argued elsewhere that some instincts
(for example, some of the complex nest-building instincts
of birds) are ideational. Secondly, some animals which

seem to be incapable of ideation or representation seem nevertheless capable of acquiring through experience connections between particular perceptions and certain conative-affective dispositions, as when they acquire a lasting fear of an object towards which they are natively indifferent. Such an acquired tendency is essentially of the nature of a sentiment, and I cannot see why we should refuse to class it as a very simple perceptual sentiment.

Yet another of Dr. Drever's suggestions I am unable to accept, namely, that " the instinct-emotion is not an invariable accompaniment of instinctive activity, but that the instinct interest is ; that the instinct-emotion is due to what we previously called ' tension,' that is, in the ordinary case, to arrest of the impulse, to the denying of immediate satisfaction to the interest." In maintaining this thesis Dr. Drever seems to be putting forward independently a view which Professor Dewey has long taught. But I have never felt that Dewey's reasoning carried any conviction to my mind, nor can I see that Drever has added anything to it. If the instinctive disposition is so constituted as to be capable of generating the appropriate emotion when its impulse is denied immediate satisfaction, it is difficult to see any theoretical ground for denying it this capacity when its activity is unobstructed ; nor does inspection of the facts seem to me to yield any more evidence in support of this view than the theoretical consideration of the possibilities. Surely, it is merely a matter of degree of intensity of the emotional excitement ! Some of Dr. Drever's criticisms I am happy to be able to accept. Especially I have to admit that he has con-

victed me of injustice to some of the philosophers of the
Scottish school, notably Dugald Stewart and Hutcheson,
who had in many respects anticipated me in my view of
the place of instinct in human nature.   In my defence I
can only plead sheer ignorance, and I may attempt to
throw off the blame for this by saying that I had fallen
a victim to the recent English fashion of over-rating the
German schools of philosophy and psychology at the
expense of our British predecessors.   I am grateful to
Dr. Drever for having corrected me in this matter.

In this part of psychology it is only by the consensus
of opinion of competent psychologists that any view or
hypothesis can be established or raised to the status of a
theory that may confidently be taught or used as a basis
for further constructive work.   And the only method of
verification open to us is the application of our hypothesis
to the control and guidance of human conduct, especially
in the two great fields of education and medicine.   I am
therefore much encouraged by the fact that in both these
fields my sketch of the active side of human nature and
its development in the individual has been found useful
Several writers on educational psychology have acknowledged its value, and some of them have incorporated the
essence of it in books written for students of education.
I have noticed above that the doctrines of the psycho-
analytic school contain much that coincides with my views.
This school has realised the fundamental importance of
instincts in human nature ; and though it has devoted an
excessive, and in some cases an almost exclusive, attention
to the sex instinct, it recognises the existence of other
human instincts and is realising more fully that they, as

well as the sex instinct, may play a part in the genesis of the psycho-neuroses. Other workers in this field have applied, and in various degrees approved, my sketch, notably Dr. Morton Prince, who in his important work, *The Unconscious*, published in 1914, has made large use of it and furnished new evidence in support of it. In spite of these encouraging indications that the substance of this book presents an approximation towards the truth, it can by no means be claimed that it has secured general acceptance. The greater number of the more influential of psychologists seem still to give a very small place to instinct in human nature, admitting as instinct at most only some simple and rudimentary tendencies to particular forms of movement, such as the crawling, sucking, and lalling of the infant. I may perhaps be allowed to testify that during five years of military service, devoted almost wholly to the care of cases of psycho-neurosis among soldiers and their treatment by the various methods of psycho-therapy, I have found no reason to make any radical alterations in my view of the innate constitution of man.

Some critics have complained of this book that it hardly begins to treat of social psychology. One writes : " He seems to do a great deal of packing in preparation for a journey on which he never starts." I confess that the title of the book lays me open to this charge. It should rather have been called " Propædeutic to Social Psychology," for it was designed to prepare the way for a treatise on Social Psychology. When I came to attempt the writing of such a treatise, I found that the psychology of the active and emotional side of our nature was in so backward a condition that it was impossible to go on without first attempting to attain to some clear and generally acceptable account of the innate tendencies of human nature and of their organisation under the touch of individual experience to form the characters of individual men. I hoped that this book would provide such an agreed basis for Social Psychology. In that I have been disappointed. Its substance was more remote from contemporary opinion than I had supposed. However, in spite of this, I have decided at last to start on the journey for which I have done my packing as thoroughly as my powers permit, and I am glad to report that I have now in the press a book entitled *The Group Mind*, which does actually make some attempt to deal with a part of the large field of Social Psychology

W. McD.

OXFORD, *September* 1919

PREFACE TO THE TWENTIETH EDITION

IT is natural that, in the seventeen years that have elapsed since the first publication of this book, my views have undergone certain changes. These changes have not been of any radical kind ; they have rather been of a nature to supplement, consolidate, and define more clearly the views expounded in the first edition. Some of these changes have been expressed in the three supplementary chapters that have been added at intervals to the book. I have felt that the plan of adding such chapters, embodying such further understanding as I seem to have attained, would be more instructive to the reader than any rewriting of the chapters previously published. In pursuance of this plan I now add two further chapters. They contain a further supplementation of the account of the human instincts contained in earlier editions, and a brief review of the present state of opinion upon the problems of instinct. Although the book as first written made no pretence to ennumerate and describe all the instinctive tendencies of the human species, it has been widely regarded as attempting that task. I feel, therefore, under some obligation to attempt to respond to that expectation. The most important of the instincts now discussed for the first time in this volume is the instinct of laughter ; the section on this topic presents in very concise form a new theory of laughter and of humour which I have propounded else- where. I have added a few comments on the bearing of recent advances in psychology on other of the principal topics discussed in this volume.

W. McD.

HARVARD COLLEGE,
December 1925

PREFACE TO THE TWENTY-SECOND EDITION

IN accordance with the plan followed in earlier editions of this book I have added a supplementary chapter without making any other substantial change. The new chapter, entitled " The Hormic Psychology," is reprinted from the volume *Psychologies of 1930*, pub- lished by the Clark University Press, and I have to thank Dr. Carl Murchison, the editor of that volume, for his permission to reproduce the chapter. The chapter should help the reader to understand the relations of the views expressed in this book to psychologies of other types, and may, I hope, make new friends for those views and confirm the good opinion of them implied by the demand for a new edition.

I have adopted the descriptive title " Hormic Psy- chology," and regret that I did not do so at the first publication. For such a title might have led to a more general recognition of the fact that this book propounds the essentials of a psychology of distinctive type, a general view of mind and personality radically different from the views and theories prevalent at the date of its first publication.

Since the whole field that belongs to psychology has been cultivated by schools of widely divergent principles and theories, and seems likely to continue to be so cultivated for some considerable time, it is of very great advantage to any one of these schools to have a distinctive banner under which it may march, to which its recruits may repair, and which they may use as their badge. I hope that henceforth the title " Hormic Psychology " or " Hormicism " may serve as such a banner and badge, and thus do something to consolidate the adherents of this way of thinking into a coherent school that may then play its part more effectively in the war of schools that seems to be the inevitable road of progress.

The chapter, having been written for an American volume, contains some special criticisms of American authors, but since their works are well known in Great Britain, it has not seemed advisable to excise these passages.

W. McD.

Duke University, N.C.
1931

PREFACE TO THE TWENTY-THIRD EDITION

IT is now nearly thirty years since I wrote this book, and it is time that I made my bow to the public which has so greatly encouraged me by demanding successive new impressions. Messrs. Methuen tell me that some sixty-two thousand copies of the English language edition have been disposed of, as well as various editions in foreign languages. I am duly grateful to the public, and feel the weight of the responsibility that is mine. In this edition I endeavour to live up to that responsibility by adding yet another supplementary chapter, in which my account of Instinct is rectified in certain particulars, and a gap in my account of the active side of our nature is filled by the section on Tastes and Distastes.

Since the only one of my books to find a larger public than this one has done is a small book in a popular series, the verdict of the public would seem to be that this is the best of my books. And I am convinced that in this the public is right. My knowledge and my critical power are very much greater than when this book was written, in my thirty-sixth year. But I have never again reached the same level of original productivity. The substance of this book will continue to be my best contribution to psychology. It is therefore very gratifying that I can now report further convergence of various schools and groups and individuals towards the type of psychology here put forward. The Psycho-analysts, the Gestaltists, the Behaviourists, the Connectionists, the Character-ologists, the Social Psychologists of America, the cautious middle-of-the-road men, all these have moved further towards the acceptance of the principles first clearly propounded in the first edition of this book. But we are still very far from a general agreement.

For myself I am more than ever convinced that these principles are valid, and that, after the lapse of some few years, when my name shall have been entirely forgotten, these principles will be generally accepted as main pillars of a psychology which will serve as the indispensable basis of all the social sciences—provided, of course, that our civilization shall contrive to endure for so long a period.

W. McD.

Duke University, N.C.
October 1936

CONTENTS

CHAPTER I

The position of psychology at the basis of all the social sciences now theoretically recognised but practically ignored—Historical explanation of this anomalous state of affairs—Illustrations of the need of the social sciences for better psychological foundations — Ethics — Economics — Political science—Philosophy of history—Jurisprudence.

SECTION I

THE MENTAL CHARACTERS OF MAN OF PRIMARY IMPORTANCE FOR HIS LIFE IN SOCIETY

CHAPTER II

The vagueness of current conceptions of instinct—The lack of agreement as to the rôle of instincts in the human mind—Instinctive process is truly mental, and involves knowing and feeling as well as doing—The physiological conception of an instinct as an innate disposition, having three parts corresponding to these three functions—The modification of instincts on their afferent and efferent sides—The relation of instinct to emotion—Instincts the prime movers of all human activity.

CHAPTER VI

Sentiments of three principal types : love, hate, and respect —The genesis of hate—Parental love as a type of highly complex sentiment—Active sympathy and its rôle in the genesis of the sentiment of affection between persons.

CHAPTER VII

Illustration of behaviour unregulated by self-regarding sentiment—The problem of moral conduct defined—Genesis of ideas of self and of other selves—Why are we so much influenced by praise and blame ?—This is the crucial problem for the theory of morals—The solution furnished by the study of the growth of the self-regarding sentiment under the moulding influences of the social environment—Regulation of conduct by regard for praise and blame implies only egoistic motives—Complication of these motives by certain pseudo-altruistic motives and by quasi-altruistic motives springing from the extended self-regarding sentiment.

CHAPTER VIII

Defects of public opinion as supreme sanction of conduct—Moral judgments are of two kinds, original and imitative—The relation of emotion to moral judgment—The moral sentiments and their relation to the moral tradition—The influence of admired personalities—The influence of native disposition on the growth of moral sentiments—The synthesis of the abstract moral sentiments and the self-regarding sentiment—The rôle of æsthetic admiration.

SECTION II

THE OPERATION OF THE PRIMARY TENDENCIES OF THE HUMAN MIND IN THE LIFE OF SOCIETIES

CHAPTER X

CHAPTER XI

CONTENTS

CONTENTS

SUPPLEMENTARY CHAPTER VII

SUPPLEMENTARY CHAPTER VIII

An Introduction to
SOCIAL
PSYCHOLOGY

SOCIAL PSYCHOLOGY

CHAPTER I

INTRODUCTION

AMONG students of the social sciences there has always been a certain number who have recognised the fact that some knowledge of the human mind and of its modes of operation is an essential part of their equipment, and that the successful development of the social sciences must be dependent upon the fulness and accuracy of such knowledge These propositions are so obviously true that any formal attempt to demonstrate them is superfluous. Those who do not accept them as soon as they are made will not be convinced of their truth by any chain of formal reasoning. It is, then, a remarkable fact that psychology, the science which claims to formulate the body of ascertained truths about the constitution and working of the mind, and which endeavours to refine and to add to this knowledge, has not been generally and practically recognised as the essential common foundation on which all the social sciences— ethics, economics, political science, philosophy of history, sociology, and cultural anthropology, and the more special social sciences, such as the sciences of religion, of law, of education, and of art—must be built up. Of the workers in these sciences, some, like Comte, and, at the present time, M. Durkheim, repudiate the claim of psychology to such recognition. Some do lip service to psychology, but in practice ignore it, and will sit down to write a treatise on morals or economics, or any other of the social sciences, cheerfully confessing that they know nothing of psychology. A certain number, perhaps the majority, of recent writers on social topics recognise the true position of psychology, but in practice are content to take as their psychological foundations the vague and extremely misleading psychology embodied in common speech, with the addition of a few hasty assumptions about the mind made to suit their particular purposes. There are signs, however, that this regrettable state of affairs is about to pass away, that psychology will before long be accorded in universal practice the position at the base of the social sciences which the more clear-sighted have long seen that it ought to occupy.

Since this volume is designed to promote this change of practice, it is fitting that it should open with a brief inquiry into the causes of the anomalous state of affairs at present obtaining and with some indication of the way in which it is hoped that the change may be brought about For there can be no question that the lack of practical recognition of psychology by the workers in the social sciences has been in the main due to its deficiencies, and that the only way of establishing it in its true place is to make good these deficiencies. What, then, are these deficiencies, and why have they so long persisted ? We may attempt very briefly to indicate the answers to these questions without presuming to apportion any blame for the long continuance of these deficiencies between the professed psychologists and the workers in the social sciences.

The department of psychology that is of primary importance for the social sciences is that which deals with the springs of human action, the impulses and motives that sustain mental and bodily activity and regulate conduct ; and this, of all the departments of psychology, is the one that has remained in the most backward state, in which the greatest obscurity, vagueness, and confusion still reign. The answers to such problems as the proper classification of conscious states, the analysis of them into their elements, the nature of these elements and the laws of the compounding of them, have but little bearing upon the social sciences ; the same may be said of the range of problems connected with the relations of soul and body, of psychical and physical process, of consciousness and brain processes ; and also of the discussion of the more purely intellectual processes, of the way we arrive at the perception of relations of time and place or of likeness and difference, of the classification and description of the intellectual processes of ideation, conception, comparison, and abstraction, and of their relations to one another. Not these processes themselves, but only the results or products of these processes—the knowledge or system of ideas and beliefs achieved by them, and the way in which these ideas and beliefs regulate conduct and determine social institutions and the relations of men to one another in society, are of immediate importance for the social sciences. It is the mental forces, the sources of energy, which set the ends and sustain the course of all human activity—of which forces the intellectual processes are but the servants, instruments, or means—that must be clearly defined, and whose history in the race and in the individual must be made clear, before the social sciences can build upon a firm psychological foundation. Now, it is with the questions of the former classes that psychologists have chiefly concerned themselves and in regard to which they have made the most progress towards a consistent and generally acceptable body of doctrine : and they have unduly neglected these more socially important problems.

This has been the result of several conditions, a result which we, looking back upon the history of the sciences, can see to have been inevitable. It was inevitable that, when men began to reflect upon the complex phenomena of social life, they should have concentrated their attention upon the problems immediately presented, and should have sought to explain them deductively from more or less vaguely conceived principles that they entertained they knew not why or how, principles that were the formulations of popular conceptions, slowly grown up in the course of countless generations and rendered more explicit, but hardly less obscure, by the labours of theologians and metaphysicians. And when, in the eighteenth century and the early part of the nineteenth century, the modern principles of scientific method began to be generally accepted and to be applied to all or most objects of human speculation, and the various social sciences began to be marked off from one another along the modern lines, it was inevitable that the workers in each department of social science should have continued in the same way, attempting to explain social phenomena from proximate principles which they falsely conceived to be fundamental, rather than to obtain a deeper knowledge of the fundamental constitution of the human mind. It was not to be expected that generations of workers, whose primary interest it was to lay down general rules for the guidance of human activity in the great fields of legislation, of government, of private and public conduct, should have deliberately put aside the attempt to construct the sciences of these departments of life, leaving them to the efforts of after-coming generations, while they devoted themselves to the preparatory work of investigating the individual mind, in order to secure the basis of psychological truth on which the labours of their successors might rear the social sciences. The problems confronting them were too urgent ; customs, laws, and institutions demanded theoretical justification, and those who called out for social reform sought to strengthen their case with theoretical demonstrations of its justice and of its conformity with the accepted principles of human nature.

And even if these early workers in the social sciences had made this impossible self-denying ordinance, it would not have been possible for them to achieve the psychology that was needed. For a science still more fundamental, one whose connection with the social phenomena they sought to explain or justify was still more remote and obscure, had yet to be created—namely, the science of biology. It is only a comparative and evolutionary psychology that can provide the needed basis ; and this could not be created before the work of Darwin had convinced men of the continuity of human with animal evolution as regards all bodily characters, and had prepared the way for the quickly following recognition of the similar continuity of man's mental evolution with that of the animal world.

Hence the workers in each of the social sciences, approaching their social problems in the absence of any established body of psychological truth and being compelled to make certain assumptions about the mind, made them *ad hoc* ; and in this way they provided the indispensable minimum of psychological doctrine required by each of them. Many of these assumptions contained sufficient truth to give them a certain plausibility ; but they were usually of such a sweeping character as to leave no room for, and to disguise the need for, more accurate and detailed psychological analysis. And not only were these assumptions made by those who had not prepared themselves for the task by long years of study of the mind in all its many aspects and by the many possible avenues of approach, but they were not made with the single-hearted aim of discovering the truth ; rather they were commonly made under the bias of an interest in establishing some normative doctrine ; the search for what is was clogged and misled at every step by the desire to establish some preconceived view as to what ought to be. When, then, psychology began very slowly and gradually to assert its status as an independent science, it found all that part of its province which has the most immediate and important bearing on the social sciences already occupied by the fragmentary and misleading psychological assumptions of the workers in these sciences ; and these workers naturally resented all attempts of psychology to encroach upon the territory they had learned to look upon as their own ; for such attempts would have endangered their systems.

The psychologists, endeavouring to define their science and to mark it off from other sciences, were thus led to accept a too narrow view of its scope and methods and applications. They were content for the most part to define it as the science of consciousness, and to regard introspection as its only method ; for the introspective analysis and description of conscious states was a part of the proper work of psychology that had not been undertaken by any other of the sciences. The insistence upon introspection as the one method of the science tended to prolong the predominance of this narrow and paralysing view of the scope of the science ; for the life of emotion and the play of motives is the part of our mental life which offers the least advantageous field for introspective observation and description. The cognitive or intellectual processes, on the other hand, present a rich and varied content of consciousness which lends itself well to introspective discrimination, analysis, and description ; in comparison with it, the emotional and conative consciousness has but little variety of content, and that little is extremely obscure and elusive of introspection

Then, shortly after the Darwinian ideas had revolutionised the biological sciences, and when it might have been hoped that psychologists would have been led to take a wider view of their science and to assert its rights to its whole field, the introduction of the experimental methods of introspection absorbed the energies of a large proportion of the workers in the re-survey, by the new and more accurate methods, of the ground already worked by the method of simple introspection.

Let us note some instances of the unfortunate results of this premature annexation of the most important and obscure region of psychology by the sciences which should, in the logical order of things, have found the fundamental psychological truths ready to their hands as a firm basis for their constructions.

Ethics affords perhaps the most striking example ; for any writer on this subject necessarily encounters psychological problems on every hand, and treatises on ethics are apt to consist very largely of amateur psychologising. Among the earlier moralists the lack of psychological insight led to such doctrines as that of certain Stoics, to the effect that the wise and good man should seek to eradicate the emotions from his bosom ; or that of Kant, to the effect that the wise and good man should be free from desire. Putting aside, however, these quaint notions of the earlier writers, we may note

that in modern times three false and hasty assumptions
of the kind stigmatised above have played leading rôles
and have furnished a large part of the matter with which
ethical controversy has been busied during the nineteenth
century. First in importance perhaps as a topic for
controversy was the doctrine known as psychological
hedonism, the doctrine that the motives of all human
activity are the desire of pleasure and the aversion to
pain. Hand in hand with this went the false assumption that happiness and pleasure are synonymous terms.
These two false assumptions were adopted as the psychological foundation of utilitarianism; they rendered
that doctrine repugnant to many of the best minds and
drove them to fall back upon vague and mystical conceptions. Of these the old conception of a special faculty
of moral intuition, a conscience, a moral sense or instinct,
was the most important; and this was the third of the
trio of false psychological assumptions on which ethical
systems were based. Many of those who adopted some
form of this last assumption were in the habit of supplementing it by similar assumptions hastily made to afford
explanations of any tendencies they noted in human
conduct which their master principle was inadequate
to meet; they postulated strange instincts of all kinds
as lightly and easily as a conjurer produces eggs from
a hat or a phrenologist discovers bumps on a head.

It is instructive to note that as recently as the year
1893 the late Professor H. Sidgwick, one of the leaders
of the ethical thought of his time, still inverted the problem; like his predecessors he assumed that moral or
reasonable action is normal and natural to man in virtue
of some vaguely conceived principle, and in all seriousness wrote an article [1] to prove that " unreasonable
action " is possible and is actually achieved occasionally,
and to explain if possible this strange anomalous fact.
He quotes Bentham's dictum that " on the occasion
of every act he exercises every human being is led to
pursue that line of conduct which, according to his
view of the case, taken by him at the moment, will be

[1] " Unreasonable Action," *Mind*, N.S., vol. iii.

in the highest degree contributory to his own greatest happiness." He points out that, although J. S. Mill admitted certain exceptions to this principle, his general view was that " to desire anything, except in proportion as the idea of it is pleasant, is a physical impossibility." So that, according to this school, any action of an individual that does not tend to produce for him the maximum of pleasure can only arise from an error of judgment as to the relative quantities of pleasure that will be secured by different lines of action. And, since, according to this school, all actions ought to be directed to securing a maximum of pleasure, action of any other kind is not only unreasonable action, but also immoral action ; for it is action in a way other than the way in which the individual knows he ought to act. Sidgwick then goes on to show that the doctrine that unreasonable action (or wilful action not in accordance with what the individual knows that he ought to do) is exceptional, paradoxical, or abnormal is not peculiar to the utilitarians, but is common also to their opponents ; he takes as an example T. H. Green, who " still lays down as broadly as Bentham that every person in every moral action, virtuous or vicious, presents to himself some possible state or achievement of his own as for the time his greatest good, and acts for the sake of that good, and that this is how he ought to act." So that Green only differs from Bentham and Mill in putting good in the place of pleasure, and for the rest makes the same grotesquely false assumption as they do Sidgwick then, instead of attacking and rejecting as radically false the conception of human motives common to both classes of his predecessors, goes on in all seriousness to offer a psychological explanation of the paradox that men do *sometimes* act unreasonably and otherwise than they ought to act. That is to say, Sidgwick, like those whom he criticises, accepts the doctrine that men normally and in the vast majority of cases act reasonably and as they ought to act, in virtue of some unexplained principle of their constitution, and defines as a problem for solution the fact that they sometimes act otherwise But the truth is that men are moved

by a variety of impulses whose nature has been determined through long ages of the evolutionary process
without reference to the life of men in civilised societies ;
and the psychological problem we have to solve, and with
which this book is mainly concerned, is—How can we
account for the fact that men so moved ever come to act
as they ought, or morally and reasonably ?

One is driven to suppose that the minds of the moral
philosophers who maintain these curious views as to the
sources and nature of human conduct are either consti-
tutionally devoid of the powerful impulses that so often
move ordinary men to actions which they know to be
morally wrong and against their true interests and destructive of their happiness, or so completely moralised
by strict self-discipline that these powerful impulses are
completely subordinated and hardly make themselves
felt.   But if either alternative is true, it is unfortunate
that their peculiar constitutions should have led these
philosophers to base the social sciences on profoundly
fallacious psychological doctrines.

Political economy suffered hardly less from the crude
nature of the psychological assumptions from which it
professed to deduce the explanations of its facts and its
prescriptions for economic legislation.   It would be a
libel, not altogether devoid of truth, to say that the
classical political economy was a tissue of false conclusions drawn from false psychological assumptions.
And certainly the recent progress in economic doctrine
has largely consisted in, or resulted from, the recognition
of the need for a less inadequate psychological basis.
An example illustrating these two facts will be not out
of place   The great assumption of the classical political
economy was that man is a reasonable being who always
intelligently seeks his own good or is guided in all his
activities by enlightened self-interest;   and this was
usually combined with the psychological hedonism which
played so large a part in degrading utilitarian ethics ;
that is to say, good was identified with pleasure.   From
these assumptions, which contained sufficient truth to
be plausible, it was deduced, logically enough, that free

competition in an open market will secure a supply of goods at the lowest possible rate. But mankind is only a little bit reasonable and to a great extent very un-intelligently moved in quite unreasonable ways. The economists had neglected to take account of the suggesti-bility of men which renders the arts of the advertiser, of the "pushing" of goods generally, so profitable and effective. Only on taking this character of men into account can we understand such facts as that sewing-machines, which might be sold at a fair profit for £5, find a large sale at £12, while equally good ones are sold in the same market at less than half the price. The same deduction as to competition and prices has been signally falsified by those cases in which the establishment by trusts or corporations of virtual monopolies in articles of universal consumption has led to a reduction of the market prices of those commodities ; or again, by the fact that so enormous a proportion of the price paid for goods goes into the pockets of small shopkeepers and other economically pernicious middlemen.

As an example of the happy effect of the recent intro-duction of less crude psychology into economic discussions, it will suffice to mention Mrs. Bosanquet's work on *The Standard of Life*.

In political science no less striking illustrations may be found. What other than an error due to false psycho-logical assumptions was the cosmopolitanism of the Manchester school, with its confident prophecy of the universal brotherhood of man brought about by en-lightened self-interest assigning to each region and people the work for which it was best suited ? This prophecy has been notoriously falsified by a great out-burst of national spirit which has played the chief part in shaping European history during the last half-century.

Again, in the philosophy of history we have the same method of deduction from hasty, incomplete, and mis-leading, if not absolutely false, assumptions as to the human mind. We may take as a fair example the assumptions that V. Cousin made the foundation of his philosophy of history. Cousin, after insisting strongly upon the fundamental importance of psychological analysis for the interpretation of history, proceeds as follows : [1] " The various manifestations and phases of social life are all traced back to tendencies of human nature from which they spring, from five fundamental wants each of which has corresponding to it a general idea. The idea of the useful gives rise to mathematical and physical science, industry, and political economy ; the idea of the just to civil society, the State, and jurisprudence ; the idea of the beautiful to art ; the idea of God to religion and worship ; and the idea of truth in itself, in its highest degree and under its purest form, to philosophy. These ideas are argued to be simple and indecomposable, to coexist in every mind, to constitute the whole foundation of humanity, and to follow in the order mentioned." No better illustration of the truth of the foregoing remarks could be found. We have here the spectacle of a philosopher, who exerted a great influence on the thought of his own country, and who rightly conceived the relation of psychology to the social sciences, but who, in the absence of any adequate psychology, contents himself with concocting on the spur of the moment the most flimsy substitute for it in the form of these five assumptions

As for the philosophies of history that make no pretence of a psychological foundation, they are sufficiently characterised by M. Fouillée who, when writing of the development of sociology, says : " Elle est née en effet d'une étude en grande partie mythique ou poétique : je veux parler de la philosophie de l'histoire telle que les metaphysiciens ou les théologiens l'ont d'abord conçue, et qui est à la sociologie positive ce que l'alchimie fut à la chimie, l'astrologie à l'astronomie." [2]

From the science of jurisprudence we may take, as a last illustration, the retributive doctrine of punishment, which is still held by a considerable number of writers. This barbarous conception of the grounds on which

[1] I quote from Professor Flint's *History of the Philosophy of History*, p. 456.
[2] *La Science Sociale Contemporaine*, p. 380. Paris, 1904.

punishment is justified arises naturally from the doctrine of free will; to any one who holds this doctrine in any thoroughgoing form there can be no other rational view of punishment than the retributive; for since, according to this assumption, where human action is concerned, the future course of events is not determined by the present, punishment cannot be administered in the forward-looking attitude with a view to deterrence or to moral improvement, but only in the backward-looking vengeful attitude of retribution. The fuller becomes our insight into the springs of human conduct, the more impossible does it become to maintain this antiquated doctrine; so that here, too, progress depends upon the improvement of psychology.

One might take each of the social sciences in turn and illustrate in each case the great need for a true doctrine of human motives. But, instead of doing that, I will merely sum up on the issue of the work of the nineteenth century as follows : During the last century most of the workers in the social sciences were of two parties—those on the one hand who with the utilitarians reduced all motives to the search for pleasure and the avoidance of pain, and those on the other hand who, recoiling from this hedonistic doctrine, sought the mainspring of conduct in some vaguely conceived intuitive faculty variously named the conscience, the moral faculty, instinct, or sense. Before the close of the century the doctrines of both of these parties were generally seen to be fallacious ; but no satisfactory substitute for them was generally accepted, and by the majority of psychologists nothing better was offered to fill the gap than a mere word, " the will," or some such phrase as " the tendency of ideas to self-realisation." On the other hand, Darwin, in the *Descent of Man* (1871), first enunciated the true doctrine of human motives, and showed how we must proceed, relying chiefly upon the comparative and natural history method, if we would arrive at a fuller understanding of them. But Darwin's own account suffered from the deference he paid, under protest, to the doctrine of psychological hedonism, still dominant at that time; and his lead has been followed by comparatively few psychologists, and but little has yet been done to carry forward the work he began and to refine upon his first rough sketch of the history of human motives.

Enough has been said to illustrate the point of view from which this volume has been written, and to enforce the theme of this introductory chapter, namely, that psychologists must cease to be content with the sterile and narrow conception of their science as the science of consciousness, and must boldly assert its claim to be the positive science of the mind in all its aspects and modes of functioning, or, as I would prefer to say, the positive science of conduct or behaviour.[1] Psychology must not regard the introspective description of the stream of consciousness as its whole task, but only as a preliminary part of its work. Such introspective description, such " pure psychology," can never constitute a science, or at least can never rise to the level of an explanatory science ; and it can never in itself be of any great value to the social sciences. The basis required by all of them is a comparative and physiological psychology relying largely on objective methods, the observation of the behaviour of men and of animals of all varieties under all possible conditions of health and disease. It must take the largest possible view of its scope and functions, and must be an evolutionary natural history of mind. Above all, it must aim at providing a full and accurate account of those most fundamental elements of our constitution, the innate tendencies to thought and action that constitute the native basis of the mind.

Happily this more generous conception of psychology is beginning to prevail. The mind is no longer regarded as a mere *tabula rasa* or magic mirror whose function it is passively to receive impressions from the outer world or to throw imperfect reflections of its objects—" a row of moving shadow-shapes that come and go." Nor are we any longer content to supplement this Lockian conception of mind with only two principles of intrinsic

[1] This definition of psychology was proposed in my *Primer of Physiological Psychology*. London, 1905.

activity, that of the association and reproduction of ideas, and that of the tendency to seek pleasure and to avoid pain. The discovery is being made that the old psychologising was like the playing of *Hamlet* with the Prince of Denmark left out, or like describing steam-engines while ignoring the fact of the presence and fundamental rôle of the fire or other source of heat. On every hand we hear it said that the static, descriptive, purely analytic psychology must give place to a dynamic, functional, voluntaristic view of mind.

A second very important advance of psychology towards usefulness is due to the increasing recognition of the extent to which the adult human mind is the product of the moulding influence exerted by the social environment, and of the fact that the strictly individual human mind, with which alone the older introspective and descriptive psychology concerned itself, is an abstraction merely and has no real existence.

It is needless to attempt to describe the many and complex influences through which these changes are being effected. It suffices to note the happy fact and briefly to indicate the way in which this book aims to contribute its mite towards the building up of a psychology that will at last furnish the much-needed basis of the social sciences and of the comprehensive science of sociology. The first section begins with the elucidation of that part of the native basis of the mind which is the source of all our bodily and mental activity. In Chapter II. I have attempted to render as clear and definite as possible the conception of an instinct, and to make clear the relation of instinct to mental process and the fundamental importance of the instincts ; in the third chapter I have sought to enumerate and briefly to define the principal human instincts ; and in the fourth I have defined certain general functional tendencies which, though they are sometimes classed with the instincts, are of a different nature. I have not thought it necessary to make any elaborate criticism of psychological hedonism, as that doctrine is now sufficiently exploded. In the following chapters of this section I have attempted to describe in general terms the way in which these native tendencies of our constitution co-operate to determine the course of the life of emotion and action ; to show how, under the influence of the social environment, they become gradually organised in systems of increasing complexity, while they remain unchanged as regards their most essential attributes ; to show that, although it is no longer easy to trace to their source the complex manifestations of human character and will, it is nevertheless possible to sketch in rough outline the course of this development and to exhibit human volition of the highest moral type as but a more complex conjunction of the mental forces which we may trace in the evolutionary scale far back into the animal kingdom.

This first section of the book deals, then, with the characters of the individual mind that are of prime importance for the social life of man. Of this section it might be said that it is not properly a part of a social psychology. Nevertheless, it is an indispensable preliminary of all social psychology, and, since no consistent and generally acceptable scheme of this kind has hitherto been furnished, it was necessary to attempt it. It may even be contended that it deals with the fundamental problem of social psychology. For social psychology has to show how, given the native propensities and capacities of the individual human mind, all the complex mental life of societies is shaped by them and in turn reacts upon the course of their development and operation in the individual. And of this task the primary and most essential part is the showing how the life of highly organised societies, involving as it does high moral qualities of character and conduct on the part of the great mass of men, is at all possible to creatures that have been evolved from the animal world, whose nature bears so many of the marks of this animal origin, and whose principal springs of activity are essentially similar to those of the higher animals. For, as Dr. Rashdall well says, " the raw material, so to speak, of Virtue and Vice is the same—*i.e.*, desires which in themselves, abstracted from their relation to the higher self, are not either moral or immoral but simply non-moral." [1]   That is to say, the fundamental problem of social psychology is the moralisation of the individual by the society into which he is born as a creature in which the non-moral and purely egoistic tendencies are so much stronger than any altruistic tendencies.   This moralisation or socialisation of the individual is, then, the essential theme of this section.

In Section II. I have briefly indicated some of the ways in which the principal instincts and primary tendencies of the human mind play their parts in the lives of human societies ; my object being to bring home to the reader the truth that the understanding of the life of society in any or all of its phases presupposes a knowledge of the constitution of the human mind, a truth which, though occasionally acknowledged in principle, is in practice so frequently ignored.

[1] *The Theory of Good and Evil*, vol. ii. p. 73.   Oxford, 1907.

SECTION I

THE MENTAL CHARACTERS OF MAN OF PRIMARY IMPORTANCE FOR HIS LIFE IN SOCIETY

CHAPTER II

THE NATURE OF INSTINCTS AND THEIR PLACE IN THE CONSTITUTION OF THE HUMAN MIND

THE human mind has certain innate or inherited tendencies which are the essential springs or motive powers of all thought and action, whether individual or collective, and are the bases from which the character and will of individuals and of nations are gradually developed under the guidance of the intellectual faculties. These primary innate tendencies have different relative strengths in the native constitutions of the individuals of different races, and they are favoured or checked in very different degrees by the very different social circumstances of men in different stages of culture ; but they are probably common to the men of every race and of every age. If this view, that human nature has everywhere and at all times this common native foundation, can be established, it will afford a much-needed basis for speculation on the history of the development of human societies and human institutions. For so long as it is possible to assume, as has often been done, that these innate tendencies of the human mind have varied greatly from age to age and from race to race, all such speculation is founded on quicksand and we cannot hope to reach views of a reasonable degree of certainty.

The evidence that the native basis of the human

mind, constituted by the sum of these innate tendencies, has this stable unchanging character is afforded by comparative psychology. For we find, not only that these tendencies, in stronger or weaker degree, are present in men of all races now living on the earth, but that we may find all of them, or at least the germs of them, in most of the higher animals. Hence there can be little doubt that they played the same essential part in the minds of the primitive human stock, or stocks, and in the pre-human ancestors that bridged the great gap in the evolutionary series between man and the animal world.

These all-important and relatively unchanging tendencies, which form the basis of human character and will, are of two main classes :

(1) The specific tendencies or instincts ;

(2) The general or non-specific tendencies arising out of the constitution of mind and the nature of mental process in general, when mind and mental process attain a certain degree of complexity in the course of evolution.

In the present and seven following chapters I propose to define the more important of these specific and general tendencies, and to sketch very briefly the way in which they become systematised in the course of character-formation ; and in the second section of this volume some attempt will be made to illustrate the special importance of each one for the social life of man.

Contemporary writers of all classes make frequent use of the words " instinct " and " instinctive," but, with very few exceptions, they use them so loosely that they have almost spoilt them for scientific purposes. On the one hand, the adjective " instinctive " is commonly applied to every human action that is performed without deliberate reflection ; on the other hand, the actions of animals are popularly attributed to instinct, and in this connection instinct is vaguely conceived as a mysterious faculty, utterly different in nature from any human faculty, which Providence has given to the brutes because the higher faculty of reason has been denied them. Hundreds of passages might be quoted from contemporary authors, even some of considerable philosophical culture, to illustrate how these two words are used with a minimum of meaning, generally with the effect of disguising from the writer the obscurity and incoherence of his thought. The following examples will serve to illustrate at once this abuse and the hopeless laxity with which even cultured authors habitually make use of psychological terms. One philosophical writer on social topics tells us that the power of the State " is dependent on the instinct of subordination, which is the outcome of the desire of the people, more or less distinctly conceived, for certain social ends " : another asserts that ancestor-worship has survived amongst the Western peoples as a " mere tradition and instinct " : a medical writer has recently asserted that if a drunkard is fed on fruit he will " become instinctively a teetotaler " : a political writer tells us that " the Russian people is rapidly acquiring a political instinct " : from a recent treatise on morals by a distinguished philosopher two passages, fair samples of a large number, may be taken; one describes the " notion that blood demands blood " as an " inveterate instinct of primitive humanity " ; the other affirms that " punishment originates in the instinct of vengeance " : another of our most distinguished philosophers asserts that " popular instinct maintains " that " there is a theory and a justification of social coercion latent in the term ' self-government.' " As our last illustration we may take the following passage from an avowedly psychological article in a recent number of the *Spectator* : " The instinct of contradiction, like the instinct of acquiescence, is inborn. . . . These instincts are very deep-rooted and absolutely incorrigible, either from within or from without. Both springing as they do from a radical defect, from a want of original independence, they affect the whole mind and character." These are favourable examples of current usage, and they justify the statement that these words " instinct " and " instinctive" are commonly used as a cloak for ignorance when a writer attempts to explain any individual or collective action that he fails, or has not tried, to understand. Yet there can be no understanding of the development of individual character or of individual and collective conduct unless the nature of instinct and its scope and function in the human mind are clearly and firmly grasped.

It would be difficult to find any adequate mention of instincts in treatises on human psychology written before the middle of last century. But the work of Darwin and of Herbert Spencer has lifted to some extent the veil of mystery from the instincts of animals, and has made the problem of the relation of instinct to human intelligence and conduct one of the most widely discussed in recent years.

Among professed psychologists there is now fair agreement as to the usage of the terms " instinct " and " instinctive." By the great majority they are used only to denote certain innate specific tendencies of the mind that are common to all members of any one species, racial characters that have been slowly evolved in the process of adaptation of species to their environment and that can be neither eradicated from the mental constitution of which they are innate elements nor acquired by individuals in the course of their lifetime. A few writers, of whom Professor Wundt is the most prominent, apply the terms to the very strongly fixed, acquired habits of action that are more commonly and properly described as secondarily automatic actions, as well as to the innate specific tendencies. The former usage seems in every way preferable and is adopted in these pages.

But, even among those psychologists who use the terms in this stricter sense, there are still great differences of opinion as to the place of instinct in the human mind. All agree that man has been evolved from pre-human ancestors whose lives were dominated by instincts ; but some hold that, as man's intelligence and reasoning powers developed, his instincts atrophied, until now in civilised man instincts persist only as troublesome vestiges of his pre-human state, vestiges that are comparable to the vermiform appendix, and which, like the latter, might with advantage be removed by the surgeon's knife, if that were at all possible. Others assign them a more prominent place in the constitution of the human mind ;

for they see that intelligence, as it increased with the evolution of the higher animals and of man, did not supplant and so lead to the atrophy of the instincts, but rather controlled and modified their operation ; and some, like G. H. Schneider [1] and William James,[2] maintain that man has at least as many instincts as any of the animals, and assign them a leading part in the determination of human conduct and mental process. This last view is now rapidly gaining ground ; and this volume, I hope, may contribute in some slight degree to promote the recognition of the full scope and function of the human instincts ; for this recognition will, I feel sure, appear to those who come after us as the most important advance made by psychology in our time.

Instinctive actions are displayed in their purest form by animals not very high in the scale of intelligence. In the higher vertebrate animals few instinctive modes of behaviour remain purely instinctive—*i.e.*, unmodified by intelligence and by habits acquired under the guidance of intelligence or by imitation. And even the human infant, whose intelligence remains but little developed for so many months after birth, performs few purely instinctive actions ; because in the human being the instincts, although innate, are, with few exceptions, undeveloped in the first months of life, and only ripen, or become capable of functioning, at various periods throughout the years from infancy to puberty.

Insect life affords perhaps the most striking examples of purely instinctive action. There are many instances of insects that invariably lay their eggs in the only places where the grubs, when hatched, will find the food they need and can eat, or where the larvæ will be able to attach themselves as parasites to some host in a way that is necessary to their survival. In such cases it is clear that the behaviour of the parent is determined by the impressions made on its senses by the appropriate objects or places : *e.g.*, the smell of decaying flesh leads the carrion-fly to deposit its eggs upon it ; the sight or odour of some

---

[1] *Der Tierische Wille.*   Leipzig, 1880.
[2] *Principles of Psychology.*   London, 1891.

particular flower leads another to lay its eggs among the ovules of the flower, which serve as food to the grubs. Others go through more elaborate trains of action, as when the mason-wasp lays its eggs in a mud-nest, fills up the space with caterpillars, which it paralyses by means of well-directed stings, and seals it up ; so that the caterpillars remain as a supply of fresh animal food for the young which the parent will never see and of whose needs it can have no knowledge or idea.

Among the lower vertebrate animals also instinctive actions, hardly at all modified by intelligent control, are common. The young chick runs to his mother in response to a call of peculiar quality and nestles beneath her ; the young squirrel, brought up in lonely captivity, when nuts are given him for the first time, opens and eats some and buries others with all the movements characteristic of his species ; the kitten in the presence of a dog or a mouse assumes the characteristic feline attitudes and behaves as all his fellows of countless generations have behaved. Even so intelligent an animal as the domesticated dog behaves on some occasions in a purely instinctive fashion ; when, for example, a terrier comes across the trail of a rabbit, his hunting instinct is immediately aroused by the scent ; he becomes blind and deaf to all other impressions as he follows the trail, and then, when he sights his quarry, breaks out into the yapping which is peculiar to occasions of this kind. His wild ancestors hunted in packs, and, under those conditions, the characteristic bark emitted on sighting the quarry served to bring his fellows to his aid ; but when the domesticated terrier hunts alone, his excited yapping can but facilitate the escape of his quarry ; yet the old social instinct operates too powerfully to be controlled by his moderate intelligence.

These few instances of purely instinctive behaviour illustrate clearly its nature. In the typical case some sense-impression, or combination of sense-impressions, excites some perfectly definite behaviour, some movement or train of movements which is the same in all individuals of the species and on all similar occasions ; and in general the behaviour so occasioned is of a kind either to promote the welfare of the individual animal or of the community to which he belongs, or to secure the perpetuation of the species.[1]

In treating of the instincts of animals, writers have usually described them as innate tendencies to certain kinds of action, and Herbert Spencer's widely accepted definition of instinctive action as compound reflex action takes account only of the behaviour or movements to which instincts give rise. But instincts are more than innate tendencies or dispositions to certain kinds of movement. There is every reason to believe that even the most purely instinctive action is the outcome of a distinctly mental process, one which is incapable of being described in purely mechanical terms, because it is a psycho-physical process, involving psychical as well as physical changes, and one which, like every other mental process, has, and can only be fully described in terms of, the three aspects of all mental process—the cognitive, the affective, and the conative aspects; that is to say, every instance of instinctive behaviour involves a knowing of some thing or object, a feeling in regard to it, and a striving towards or away from that object.

We cannot, of course, directly observe the threefold psychical aspect of the psycho-physical process that issues in instinctive behaviour; but we are amply justified in assuming that it invariably accompanies the process in the nervous system of which the instinctive movements are the immediate result, a process which, being initiated on stimulation of some sense organ by the physical impressions received from the object, travels up the sensory nerves, traverses the brain, and descends as an orderly or co-ordinated stream of nervous impulses along efferent nerves to the appropriate groups of muscles and other executive organs. We are justified in assuming the cognitive aspect of the psychical process, because the

[1] In many cases an instinct is excitable only during the prevalence of some special organic condition (*e.g.*, the nest-building and mating instincts of birds, the sitting instinct of the broody hen); and some writers have given such organic conditions an undue prominence while neglecting the essential part played by sense-impressions.

nervous excitation seems to traverse those parts of the brain whose excitement involves the production of sensations or changes in the sensory content of consciousness ; we are justified in assuming the affective aspect of the psychical process, because the creature exhibits unmistakable symptoms of feeling and emotional excitement ; and, especially, we are justified in assuming the conative aspect of the psychical process, because all instinctive behaviour exhibits that unique mark of mental process, a persistent striving towards the natural end of the process. That is to say, the process, unlike any merely mechanical process, is not to be arrested by any sufficient mechanical obstacle, but is rather intensified by any such obstacle and only comes to an end either when its appropriate goal is achieved, or when some stronger incompatible tendency is excited, or when the creature is exhausted by its persistent efforts.

Now, the psycho-physical process that issues in an instinctive action is initiated by a sense-impression which, usually, is but one of many sense-impressions received at the same time ; and the fact that this one impression plays an altogether dominant part in determining the animal's behaviour shows that its effects are peculiarly favoured, that the nervous system is peculiarly fitted to receive and to respond to just that kind of impression. The impression must be supposed to excite, not merely detailed changes in the animal's field of sensation, but a sensation or complex of sensations that has significance or meaning for the animal ; hence we must regard the instinctive process in its cognitive aspect as distinctly of the nature of perception, however rudimentary. In the animals most nearly allied to ourselves we can, in many instances of instinctive behaviour, clearly recognise the symptoms of some particular kind of emotion such as fear, anger, or tender feeling ; and the same symptoms always accompany any one kind of instinctive behaviour, as when the cat assumes the defensive attitude, the dog resents the intrusion of a strange dog, or the hen tenderly gathers her brood beneath her wings. We seem justified in believing that each kind of instinctive behaviour is always attended by some such emotional excitement, however faint, which in each case is specific or peculiar to that kind of behaviour. Analogy with our own experience justifies us, also, in assuming that the persistent striving towards its end, which characterises mental process and distinguishes instinctive behaviour most clearly from mere reflex action, implies some such mode of experience as we call conative, the kind of experience which in its more developed forms is properly called desire or aversion, but which, in the blind form in which we sometimes have it and which is its usual form among the animals, is a mere impulse, or craving, or uneasy sense of want. Further, we seem justified in believing that the continued obstruction of instinctive striving is always accompanied by painful feeling, its successful progress towards its end by pleasurable feeling, and the achievement of its end by a pleasurable sense of satisfaction.

An instinctive action, then, must not be regarded as simple or compound reflex action if by reflex action we mean, as is usually meant, a movement caused by a sense-stimulus and resulting from a sequence of merely physical processes in some nervous arc. Nevertheless, just as a reflex action implies the presence in the nervous system of the reflex nervous arc, so the instinctive action also implies some enduring nervous basis whose organisation is inherited, an innate or inherited psycho-physical disposition, which, anatomically regarded, probably has the form of a compound system of sensori-motor arcs.

We may, then, define an instinct as an inherited or innate psycho-physical disposition which determines its possessor to perceive, and to pay attention to, objects of a certain class, to experience an emotional excitement of a particular quality upon perceiving such an object, and to act in regard to it in a particular manner, or, at least, to experience an impulse to such action.

It must further be noted that some instincts remain inexcitable except during the prevalence of some temporary bodily state, such as hunger. In these cases we must suppose that the bodily process or state determines the stimulation of sense-organs within the body, and that nervous currents ascending from these to the psychophysical disposition maintain it in an excitable condition.[1]

[1] Most definitions of instincts and instinctive actions take account only of their conative aspect, of the motor tendencies by which the instincts of animals are most clearly manifested to us, and it is a common mistake to ignore the cognitive and the affective aspects of the instinctive mental process. Some authors make the worse mistake of assuming that instinctive actions are performed unconsciously. Herbert Spencer's definition of instinctive action as compound reflex action was mentioned above. Addison wrote of instinct that it is " an immediate impression from the first Mover and the Divine Energy acting in the creatures." Fifty years ago the entomologists, Kirby and Spence, wrote : " We may call the instincts of animals those faculties implanted in them by the Creator, by which, independent of instruction, observation, or experience, they are all alike impelled to the performance of certain actions tending to the well-being of the individual and the preservation of the species." More recently Dr. and Mrs. Peckham, who have observed the behaviour of wasps so carefully, have written : " Under the term ' instinct ' we place all complex acts which are performed previous to experience, and in a similar manner by all members of the same sex and race." One modern authority, Professor Karl Groos, goes so far as to say that " the idea of consciousness must be rigidly excluded from any definition of instinct which is to be of practical utility." In view of this persistent tendency to ignore the inner or psychical side of instinctive processes, it seems to me important to insist upon it, and especially to recognise in our definition its cognitive and affective aspects as well as its conative aspect. I would reverse Professor Groos's dictum and would say that any definition of instinctive action that does not insist upon its psychical aspect is useless for practical purposes, and worse than useless because misleading. For, if we neglect the psychical aspect of instinctive processes, it is impossible to understand the part played by instincts in the development of the human mind and in the determination of the conduct of individuals and societies ; and it is the fundamental and all-pervading character of their influence upon the social life of mankind which alone gives the consideration of instincts its great practical importance.

The definition of instinct proposed above does not insist, as do many definitions, that the instinctive action is one performed without previous experience of the object ; for it is only when an instinct is exercised for the first time by any creature that the action is prior to experience, and instinctive actions may continue to be instinctive even after much experience of their objects. The nest-building or the migratory flight of birds does not cease to be instinctive when these actions are repeated year after year, even though the later performances show improvement through experience, as the instinctive actions of the higher animals commonly do. Nor does our definition insist, as some do, that the instinctive action is performed without awareness of the end towards which it tends, for this too is not essential ; it may be, and in the case of the lower animals, no doubt, often is, so performed, as also by the very young child ; but in the case of the higher animals

The behaviour of some of the lower animals seems to be almost completely determined throughout their lives by instincts modified but very little by experience; they perceive, feel, and act in a perfectly definite and invariable manner whenever a given instinct is excited—*i.e.*, whenever the presence of the appropriate object coincides with the appropriate organic state of the creature. The highest degree of complexity of mental process attained by such creatures is a struggle between two opposed instinctive tendencies simultaneously excited. Such behaviour is relatively easy to understand in the light of the conception of instincts as innate psycho-physical dispositions.

While it is doubtful whether the behaviour of any animal is wholly determined by instincts quite unmodified by experience, it is clear that all the higher animals learn in various and often considerable degrees to adapt their instinctive actions to peculiar circumstances; and in the long course of the development of each human mind, immensely greater complications of the instinctive processes are brought about, complications so great that they have obscured until recent years the essential likeness of the instinctive processes in men and animals. These complications of instinctive processes are of four principal kinds, which we may distinguish as follows :

(1) The instinctive reactions become capable of being initiated, not only by the perception of objects of the kind which directly excite the innate disposition, the natural or native excitants of the instinct, but also by ideas of such objects, and by perceptions and by ideas of objects of other kinds :

(2) The bodily movements in which the instinct finds expression may be modified and complicated to an indefinitely great degree :

(3) Owing to the complexity of the ideas which can

some prevision of the immediate end, however vague, probably accompanies an instinctive action that has often been repeated ; *e.g.*, in the case of the dog that has followed the trail of game many times, we may properly regard the action as instinctive, although we can hardly doubt that, after many kills, the creature has some anticipation of the end of his activity.

bring the human instincts into play, it frequently happens that several instincts are simultaneously excited; when the several processes blend with various degrees of intimacy:

(4) The instinctive tendencies become more or less systematically organised about certain objects or ideas.

The full consideration of the first two modes of complication of instinctive behaviour would lead us too far into the psychology of the intellectual processes, to which most of the text-books of psychology are mainly devoted. It must suffice merely to indicate in the present chapter a few points of prime importance in this connection. The third and fourth complications will be dealt with at greater length in the following chapters, for they stand in much need of elucidation.

In order to understand these complications of instinctive behaviour we must submit the conception of an instinct to a more minute analysis. It was said above that every instinctive process has the three aspects of all mental process—the cognitive, the affective, and the conative. Now, the innate psycho-physical disposition, which is an instinct, may be regarded as consisting of three corresponding parts—an afferent, a central, and a motor or efferent part—whose activities are the cognitive, the affective, and the conative features respectively of the total instinctive process. The afferent or receptive part of the total disposition is some organised group of nervous elements or neurones that is specially adapted to receive and to elaborate the impulses initiated in the sense-organ by the native object of the instinct; its constitution and activities determine the sensory content of the psycho-physical process. From the afferent part the excitement spreads over to the central part of the disposition; the constitution of this part determines in the main the distribution of the nervous impulses, especially of the impulses that descend to modify the working of the visceral organs, the heart, lungs, blood-vessels, glands, and so forth, in the manner required for the most effective execution of the instinctive action; the nervous activities of this central part are the correlates of the affective or emotional aspect or feature of the total psychical process.[1]   The excitement of the efferent or motor part reaches it by way of the central part ; its constitution determines the distribution of impulses to the muscles of the skeletal system by which the instinctive action is effected, and its nervous activities are the correlates of the conative element of the psychical process, of the felt impulse to action.

Now, the afferent or receptive part and the efferent or motor part are capable of being greatly modified, independently of one another and of the central part, in the course of the life-history of the individual ; while the central part persists throughout life as the essential unchanging nucleus of the disposition.   Hence in man, whose intelligence and adaptability are so great, the afferent and efferent parts of each instinctive disposition are liable to many modifications, while the central part alone remains unmodified : that is to say, the cognitive processes through which any instinctive process may be initiated exhibit a great complication and variety ; and the actual bodily movements by which the instinctive process achieves its end may be complicated to an indefinitely great extent ; while the emotional excitement, with the accompanying nervous activities of the central part of the disposition, is the only part of the total instinctive process that retains its specific character and remains common to all individuals and all situations in which the instinct is excited.   It is for this reason that authors have commonly treated of the instinctive actions of animals on the one hand, and of the emotions of men on the other hand, as distinct types of mental process, failing to see that each kind of emotional excitement is always an indication of, and the most constant feature of, some instinctive process.

Let us now consider very briefly the principal ways in which the instinctive disposition may be modified on

---

[1] It is probable that these central affective parts of the instinctive dispositions have their seat in the basal ganglia of the brain.   The evidence in favour of this view has been greatly strengthened by the recent work of Pagano (*Archives Italiennes de Biologie,* 1906).

its afferent or receptive side; and let us take, for the
sake of clearness of exposition, the case of a particular
instinct, namely, the instinct of fear or flight, which is
one of the strongest and most widely distributed instincts
throughout the animal kingdom. In man and in most
animals this instinct is capable of being excited by any
sudden loud noise, independently of all experience of
danger or harm associated with such noises. We must
suppose, then, that the afferent inlet, or one of the afferent
inlets, of this innate disposition consists in a system of
auditory neurones connected by sensory nerves with the
ear. This afferent inlet to this innate disposition is but
little specialised, since it may be excited by any loud
noise. One change it may undergo through experience
is specialisation; on repeated experience of noises of
certain kinds that are never accompanied or followed by
hurtful effects, most creatures will learn to neglect them; [1]
their instinct of flight is no longer excited by them; they
learn, that is to say, to discriminate between these and
other noises ; this implies that the perceptual disposition,
the afferent inlet of the instinct, has become further
specialised.

More important is the other principal mode in which
the instinct may be modified on its afferent or cognitive
side. Consider the case of the birds on an uninhabited
island, which show no fear of men on their first appearance on the island. The absence of fear at the sight of
man implies, not that the birds have no instinct of fear,
but that the instinct has no afferent inlet specialised for
the reception of the retinal impression made by the
human form. But the men employ themselves in shoot-
ing, and very soon the sight of a man excites the instinct
of fear in the birds, and they take to flight at his approach.
How are we to interpret this change of instinctive behaviour brought about by experience ? Shall we say
that the birds observe on one occasion, or on several or
many occasions, that on the approach of a man one of
their number falls to the ground, uttering cries of pain ;

[1] As in the case of wild creatures that we may see from the windows
of a railway train browsing undisturbed by the familiar noise.

that they infer that the man has wounded it, and that
he may wound and hurt them, and that he is therefore
to be avoided in the future ? No psychologist would
now accept this anthropomorphic interpretation of the
facts. If the behaviour we are considering were that
of savage men, or even of a community of philosophers
and logicians, such an account would err in ascribing
the change of behaviour to a purely intellectual process.
Shall we, then, say that the sudden loud sound of the gun
excites the instinct of fear, and that, because the perception of this sound is constantly accompanied by the
visual perception of the human form, the idea of the latter
becomes associated with the idea of the sound, so that
thereafter the sight of a man reproduces the idea of the
sound of the gun, and hence leads to the excitement of
the instinct by way of its innately organised afferent inlet,
the system of auditory neurones ? This would be much
nearer the truth than the former account ; some such
interpretation of facts of this order has been offered by
many psychologists and very generally accepted.[1] Its
acceptance involves the attribution of free ideas, of the
power of representation of objects independently of sense-
presentation, to whatever animals display this kind of
modification of instinctive behaviour by experience—
that is to say, to all the animals save the lowest ; and
there are good reasons for believing that only man and
the higher animals have this power. We are therefore
driven to look for a still simpler interpretation of the facts,
and such a one is not far to seek. We may suppose that
since the visual presentation of the human form repeatedly
accompanies the excitement of the instinct of fear by
the sound of the gun, it acquires the power of exciting
directly the reactions characteristic of this instinct, rather
than indirectly by way of the reproduction of the idea
of the sound ; *i.e.*, we may suppose that, after repetition
of the experience, the sight of a man directly excites the
instinctive process in its affective and conative aspects
only ; or we may say, in physiological terms, that the

[1] It is, *e.g.*, the interpretation proposed by G. H. Schneider in his
work, *Der Tierische Wille* ; it mars this otherwise excellent book.

visual disposition concerned in the elaboration of the retinal impression of the human form becomes directly connected or associated with the central and efferent parts of the instinctive disposition, which thus acquires, through the repetition of this experience, a new afferent inlet through which it may henceforth be excited independently of its innate afferent inlet.

There is, I think, good reason to believe that this third interpretation is much nearer the truth than the other two considered above. In the first place, the assumption of such relative independence of the afferent part of an instinctive disposition as is implied by this interpretation is justified by the fact that many instincts may be excited by very different objects affecting different senses, prior to all experience of such objects. The instinct of fear is the most notable in this respect, for in many animals it may be excited by certain special impressions of sight, of smell, and of hearing, as well as by all loud noises (perhaps also by any painful sense-impression), all of which impressions evoke the emotional expressions and the bodily movements characteristic of the instinct. Hence, we may infer that such an instinct has several innately organised afferent inlets, through each of which its central and efferent parts may be excited without its other afferent inlets being involved in the excitement.

But the best evidence in favour of the third interpretation is that which we may obtain by introspective observation of our own emotional states. Through injuries received we may learn to fear, or to be angered by, the presence of a person or animal or thing towards which we were at first indifferent ; and we may then experience the emotional excitement and the impulse to the appropriate movements of flight or aggression, without recalling the nature and occasion of the injuries we have formerly suffered ; *i.e.*, although the idea of the former injury may be reproduced by the perception, or by the idea, of the person, animal, or thing from which it was received, yet the reproduction of this idea is not an essential step in the process of re-excitement of the instinctive reaction in its affective and conative aspects ;

for the visual impression made by the person or thing leads directly to the excitement of the central and efferent parts of the innate disposition. In this way our emotional and conative tendencies become directly associated by experience with many objects to which we are natively indifferent ; and not only do we not necessarily recall the experience through which the association was set up, but in many such cases we cannot do so by any effort of recollection.[1]

Such acquisition of new perceptual inlets by instinctive dispositions, in accordance with the principle of association in virtue of temporal contiguity, seems to occur abundantly among all the higher animals and to be the principal mode in which they profit by experience and learn to adapt their behaviour to a greater variety of the objects of their environment than is provided for by their purely innate dispositions. In man it occurs still more abundantly, and in his case the further complication ensues that each sense-presentation that thus becomes capable of arousing some emotional and conative disposition may be represented, or reproduced in idea ; and, since the representation, having in the main the same neural basis as the sense-presentation, induces equally well the same emotional and conative excitement, and since it may be brought to mind by any one of the intellectual processes, ranging from simple associative reproduction to the most subtle processes of judgment and inference, the ways in which any one instinctive disposition of a developed human mind may be excited are indefinitely various.

There is a second principal mode in which objects other than the native objects of an instinct may lead to the excitement of its central and efferent parts. This is similar to the mode of reproduction of ideas known as the reproduction by similars ; a thing, or sense-

[1] In this way some particular odour, some melody or sound, some phrase or trick of speech or manner, some peculiar combination of colour or effect of light upon the landscape, may become capable of directly exciting some affective disposition, and we find ourselves suddenly swept by a wave of strong emotion for which we can assign no adequate cause.

impression, more or less like the specific excitant of an instinct, but really of a different class, excites the instinct in virtue of those features in which it resembles the specific object. As a very simple instance of this, we may take the case of a horse shying at an old coat left lying by the roadside. The shying is, no doubt, due to the excitement of an instinct whose function is to secure a quick retreat from any crouching beast of prey, and the coat sufficiently resembles such a crouching form to excite the instinct. This example illustrates the operation of this principle in the crudest fashion. In the human mind it works in a much more subtle and wide-reaching fashion. Very delicate resemblances of form and relation between two objects may suffice to render one of them capable of exciting the emotion and the impulse which are the appropriate instinctive response to the presentation of the other object ; and, in order that this shall occur, it is not necessary that the individual shall become explicitly aware of the resemblance between the two objects, nor even that the idea of the second object shall be brought to his consciousness ; though this, no doubt, occurs in many cases. The wide scope of this principle in the human mind is due, not merely to the subtler operation of resemblances, but also to the fact that through the working of the principle of temporal contiguity, discussed on the foregoing page, the number of objects capable of directly exciting any instinct becomes very considerable, and each such object then serves as a basis for the operation of the principle of resemblance ; that is to say, each object that in virtue of temporal contiguity acquires the power of exciting the central and efferent parts of an instinct renders possible the production of the same effect by a number of objects more or less resembling it. The conjoint operation of the two principles may be illustrated by a simple example : a child is terrified upon one occasion by the violent behaviour of a man of a peculiar cast of countenance or of some special fashion of dress ; thereafter not only does the perception or idea of this man excite fear, but any man resembling him in face or costume may do so without the idea of the original occasion of fear, or of the terrifying individual, recurring to consciousness.

As regards the modification of the bodily movements by means of which an instinctive mental process achieves,[1] or strives to achieve, its end, man excels the animals even to a greater degree than as regards the modification of the cognitive part of the process. For the animals acquire and use hardly any movement-complexes that are not natively given in their instinctive dispositions and in the reflex co-ordinations of their spinal cords. This is true of even so intelligent an animal as the domestic dog. Many of the higher animals may by long training be taught to acquire a few movement-complexes—a dog to walk on its hind legs, or a cat to sit up ; but the wonder with which we gaze at a circus-horse standing on a tub, or at a dog dancing on hind legs, shows how strictly limited to the natively given combinations of movements all the animals normally are.

In the human being, on the other hand, a few only of the simpler instincts that ripen soon after birth are displayed in movements determined purely by the innate dispositions ; such are the instincts of sucking, of wailing, of crawling, of winking and shrinking before a coming blow. Most of the human instincts ripen at relatively late periods in the course of individual development, when considerable power of intelligent control and imitation of movement has been acquired ; hence the motor tendencies of these instincts are seldom manifested in their purely native forms, but are from the first modified, controlled, and suppressed in various degrees. This is the case more especially with the large movements of trunk and limbs ; while the subsidiary movements, those which Darwin called serviceable associated movements, such as those due to contractions of the facial muscles, are less habitually controlled, save by men of certain races and countries among whom control of facial

[1] It would, of course, be more correct to say that the creature strives to achieve its end under the driving power of the instinctive impulse awakened within it, but, if this is recognised, it is permissible to avoid the repeated use of this cumbrous phraseology.

movement is prescribed by custom. An illustration may indicate the main principle involved : One may have learnt to suppress more or less completely the bodily movements in which the excitement of the instinct of pugnacity naturally finds vent ; or by a study of pugilism one may have learnt to render these movements more finely adapted to secure the end of the instinct ; or one may have learnt to replace them by the habitual use of weapons, so that the hand flies to the sword-hilt or to the hip-pocket, instead of being raised to strike, whenever this instinct is excited. But one exercises but little, if any, control over the violent beating of the heart, the flushing of the face, the deepened respiration, and the general redistribution of blood - supply and nervous tension which constitute the visceral expression of the excitement of this instinct and which are determined by the constitution of its central affective part. Hence in the human adult, while this instinct may be excited by objects and situations that are not provided for in the innate disposition, and may express itself in bodily movements which also are not natively determined, or may fail to find expression in any such movements owing to strong volitional control, its unmodified central part will produce visceral changes, with the accompanying emotional state of consciousness, in accordance with its unmodified native constitution ; and these visceral changes will usually be accompanied by the innately determined facial expression in however slight a degree ; hence result the characteristic expressions or symptoms of the emotion of anger which, as regards their main features, are common to all men of all times and all races.

All the principal instincts of man are liable to similar modifications of their afferent and motor parts, while their central parts remain unchanged and determine the emotional tone of consciousness and the visceral changes characteristic of the excitement of the instinct.

It must be added that the conative aspect of the psychical process always retains the unique quality of an impulse to activity, even though the instinctive activity has been modified by habitual control ; and this felt impulse, when it becomes conscious of its end, assumes the character of an explicit desire or aversion.

Are, then, these instinctive impulses the only motive powers of the human mind to thought and action ? What of pleasure and pain, which by so many of the older psychologists were held to be the only motives of human activity, the only objects or sources of desire and aversion ?

In answer to the former question, it must be said that in the developed human mind there are springs of action of another class, namely, acquired habits of thought and action. An acquired mode of activity becomes by repetition habitual, and the more frequently it is repeated the more powerful becomes the habit as a source of impulse or motive power. Few habits can equal in this respect the principal instincts ; and habits are in a sense derived from, and secondary to, instincts ; for, in the absence of instincts, no thought and no action could ever be achieved or repeated, and so no habits of thought or action could be formed. Habits are formed only in the service of the instincts.[1]

The answer to the second question is that pleasure and pain are not in themselves springs of action, but at the most of undirected movements ; they serve rather to modify instinctive processes, pleasure tending to sustain and prolong any mode of action, pain to cut it short ; under their prompting and guidance are effected those modifications and adaptations of the instinctive bodily movements which we have briefly considered above.[2]

---

[1] I am now disposed to question the view that habits or acquired motive dispositions can be properly regarded as springs of conative energy. Cf. my article on " Motives in the Light of Recent Discussion," in *Mind*, N.S., vol. xxix.

[2] None of the doctrines of the associationist psychology was more profoundly misleading and led to greater absurdities than the attempt to exhibit pleasure and pain as the source of all activities. What could be more absurd than Professor Bain's doctrine that the joy of a mother in her child, her tender care and self-sacrificing efforts in its behalf, are due to the pleasure she derives from bodily contact with it in the maternal embrace ? Or what could be more strained and opposed to hundreds of familiar facts than Herbert Spencer's doctrine that the emotion of fear provoked by any object consists in faint revivals, in some strange cluster, of ideas of all the pains suffered in the past upon contact with, or in the presence of, that object ? (cf. Bain's

We may say, then, that directly or indirectly the instincts are the prime movers of all human activity ; by the conative or impulsive force of some instinct (or of some habit derived from an instinct), every train of thought, however cold and passionless it may seem, is borne along towards its end, and every bodily activity is initiated and sustained. The instinctive impulses determine the ends of all activities and supply the driving power by which all mental activities are sustained ; and all the complex intellectual apparatus of the most highly developed mind is but a means towards these ends, is but the instrument by which these impulses seek their satisfactions, while pleasure and pain do but serve to guide them in their choice of the means.

Take away these instinctive dispositions with their powerful impulses, and the organism would become incapable of activity of any kind ; it would lie inert and motionless like a wonderful clockwork whose mainspring had been removed or a steam-engine whose fires had been drawn. These impulses are the mental forces that maintain and shape all the life of individuals and societies, and in them we are confronted with the central mystery of life and mind and will.[1]

The following chapters, I hope, will render clearer, and will give some support to, the views briefly and somewhat dogmatically stated in the present chapter.

Emotions and the Will, chap. vi. ; and H. Spencer's *Principles of Psychology*, vol. i. part iv. chap. viii. 3rd edition).

[1] For a further discussion of the nature of instinct the reader may be referred to *The British Journal of Psychology*, vol. iii., which contains papers contributed to a symposium on Instinct and Intelligence by Messrs. C. S. Myers, Lloyd Morgan, Wildon Carr, G. F. Stout, and the author.

CHAPTER III

THE PRINCIPAL INSTINCTS AND THE PRIMARY EMOTIONS OF MAN

BEFORE we can make any solid progress in the understanding of the complex emotions and impulses that are the forces underlying the thoughts and actions of men and of societies, we must be able to distinguish and describe each of the principal human instincts and the emotional and conative tendencies characteristic of each one of them. This task will be attempted in the present chapter ; in Chapter V. we shall seek to analyse some of the principal complex emotions and impulses, to display them as compounded from the limited number of primary or simple instinctive tendencies ; [1] and in the succeeding chapters of this

[1] It has often been remarked that the emotions are fluid and indefinable, that they are in perpetual flux and are experienced in an infinite number of subtle varieties. This truth may be used as an argument against the propriety of attempting to exhibit all the many varieties of our emotional experience as reducible by analysis to a small number of distinct primary emotions. But such an objection would be ill-taken. We may see an instructive parallel in the case of our colour-sensations. The colour-sensations present, like the emotions, an indefinitely great variety of qualities shading into one another by imperceptible gradations ; but this fact does not prevent us regarding all these many delicate varieties as reducible by analysis to a few simple primary qualities from which they are formed by fusion, or blending, in all proportions. Rather it is the indefinitely great variety of colour qualities, their subtle gradations, and the peculiar affinities between them, that justify us in seeking to exhibit them as fusions in many different proportions of a few primary qualities. And the same is true of the emotions.

Of course, if the James-Lange theory of the emotions is true, then each of the primary emotions is in principle not an elementary affection of consciousness or mode of experience, but a complex of organic sensations and feeling tone. But in that case the conception of a primary emotion, and the propriety of regarding each complex emotion

section we shall consider the way in which these tendencies become organised within the complex dispositions
that constitute the sentiments.

In the foregoing chapter it was said that the instinctive
mental process that results from the excitement of any
instinct has always an affective aspect, the nature of
which depends upon the constitution of that most stable
and unchanging of the three parts of the instinctive
disposition, namely, the central part.   In the case of the
simpler instincts, this affective aspect of the instinctive
process is not prominent;   and though, no doubt, the
quality of it is peculiar in each case, yet we cannot readily
distinguish these qualities and we have no special names
for them.   But, in the case of the principal powerful
instincts, the affective quality of each instinctive process
and the sum of visceral and bodily changes in which it
expresses itself are peculiar and distinct;   hence language
provides special names for such modes of affective experience, names such as anger, fear, curiosity;   and the
generic name for them is "emotion."   The word
"emotion" is used of course in popular speech loosely
and somewhat vaguely, and psychologists are not yet
completely consistent in their use of it.   But all psychological terms that are taken from common speech have to
undergo a certain specialisation and more rigid definition
before they are fit for scientific use;   and in using the
word "emotion" in the restricted sense which is indicated
above, and which will be rigidly adhered to throughout
these pages, I am but carrying to its logical conclusion
a tendency displayed by the majority of recent English
writers on psychology.
    Each of the principal instincts conditions, then, some
one kind of emotional excitement whose quality is specific
or peculiar to it;   and the emotional excitement of specific
quality that is the affective aspect of the operation of any

as a fusion of two or more primary emotions, are not invalidated.
For the primary emotion must be regarded (according to that theory)
as a complex of organic sensation and feeling tone which is constant
and specific in character, its nature having been determined and fixed
by the evolutionary process at a very remote pre-human period.

one of the principal instincts may be called a primary emotion. This principle, which was enunciated in my little work on physiological psychology, proves to be of very great value when we seek to analyse the complex emotions into their primary constituents. Several writers have come very near to the recognition of this principle, but few or none of them have stated it clearly and explicitly, and, what is more important, they have not systematically applied it in any thoroughgoing manner as the guiding principle on which we must chiefly rely in seeking to define the primary emotions and to unravel the complexities of our concrete emotional experiences.[1]

In adapting to scientific use a word from popular speech, it is inevitable that some violence should be done to common usage ; and, in adopting this rigid definition of emotion, we shall have to do such violence in refusing to admit joy, sorrow, and surprise (which are often re-garded, even by writers on psychology, as the very types of emotions) to our list whether of simple and primary or of complex emotions. Some arguments in justification of this exclusion will be adduced later. At this stage I will only point out that joy and sorrow are not emotional

---

[1] *A Primer of Physiological Psychology*, 1905. That the principle is not generally recognised is shown by the fact that in Baldwin's *Dictionary of Philosophy and Psychology* (1901) no mention is made of any intimate relation between emotion and instinct ; we are there told that no adequate psychological definition of instinct is possible, since the psychological state involved is exhausted by the terms " sensa-tion " (and also " perception "), " instinct," " feeling," and " im-pulse " ; and instinct is defined as " an inherited reaction of the sensori-motor type, relatively complex and markedly adaptive in character, and common to a group of individuals." Professor James, who treats of the instincts and the emotions in successive chapters, comes very near to the recognition of the principle laid down above, without, however, explicitly stating it. Others who have recognised—more or less explicitly—this relation between instinct and emotion are Schneider (*Der Tierische Wille*), Ribot (*Psychologie des Sentiments*), and Rutgers Marshal (*Pain, Pleasure, and Æsthetics*, and *Instinct and Reason*).

Mr. Shand (chapter xvi., Stout's *Groundwork of Psychology*) has rightly insisted upon the impossibility of analysing the complex emotions by unaided introspection, and has laid down the principle that we must rely largely on the observation of their motor tendencies. But he has not combined this sound methodological suggestion with the recognition of the above-mentioned guiding principle. It is on this combination that I rely in the present chapter.

states that can be experienced independently of the true emotions, that in every case they are qualifications of the emotions they accompany, and that in strictness we ought rather to speak always of a joyful or sorrowful emotion— e.g., a joyful wonder or gratitude, a sorrowful anger or pity.

In considering the claim of any human emotion or impulse to rank as a primary emotion or simple instinctive impulse, we shall find two principles of great assistance. First, if a similar emotion and impulse are clearly displayed in the instinctive activities of the higher animals, that fact will afford a strong presumption that the emotion and impulse in question are primary and simple ; on the other hand, if no such instinctive activity occurs among the higher animals, we must suspect the affective state in question of being either a complex composite emotion or no true emotion. Secondly, we must inquire in each case whether the emotion and impulse in question occasionally appear in human beings with morbidly exaggerated intensity, apart from such general hyper-excitability as is displayed in mania. For it would seem that each instinctive disposition, being a relatively independent functional unit in the constitution of the mind, is capable of morbid hypertrophy or of becoming abnormally excitable, independently of the rest of the mental dispositions and functions. That is to say, we must look to comparative psychology and to mental pathology for confirmation of the primary character of those of our emotions that appear to be simple and unanalysable.[1]

---

[1] That the emotion as a fact of consciousness may properly be distinguished from the cognitive process which it accompanies and qualifies is, I think, obvious and indisputable. The propriety of distinguishing between the conative element in consciousness, the impulse, appetite, desire, or aversion, and the accompanying emotion is not so obvious. For these features are most intimately and constantly associated, and introspective discrimination of them is usually difficult. Nevertheless, they show a certain degree of independence of one another ; e.g., with frequent repetition of a particular emotional situation and reaction, the affective aspect of the process tends to become less prominent, while the impulse grows stronger.

The Instinct of Flight and the Emotion of Fear

The instinct to flee from danger is necessary for the survival of almost all species of animals, and in most of the higher animals the instinct is one of the most powerful. Upon its excitement the locomotory apparatus is impelled to its utmost exertions, and sometimes the intensity and long duration of these exertions is more than the visceral organs can support, so that they are terminated by utter exhaustion or death. Men also have been known to achieve extraordinary feats of running and leaping under this impulse ; there is a well-known story of a great athlete who, when pursued as a boy by a savage animal, leaped over a wall which he could not again " clear " until he attained his full stature and strength. These locomotory activities are accompanied by a characteristic complex of symptoms, which in its main features is common to man and to many of the higher animals, and which, in conjunction with the violent efforts to escape, constitutes so unmistakable an expression of the emotion of fear that no one hesitates to interpret it as such ; hence popular speech recognises the connection of the emotion with the instinct that determines the movements of flight in giving them the one name *fear*. Terror, the most intense degree of this emotion, may involve so great a nervous disturbance, both in men and animals, as to defeat the ends of the instinct by inducing general convulsions or even death. In certain cases of mental disease the patient's disorder seems to consist essentially in an abnormal excitability of this instinct and a consequent undue frequency and intensity of its operation ; the patient lives perpetually in fear, shrinking in terror from the most harmless animal or at the least unusual sound, and surrounds himself with safeguards against impossible dangers.

In most animals this instinct may be excited by a variety of objects and sense-impressions prior to all experience of hurt or danger ; that is to say, the innate disposition has several afferent inlets. In some of the more timid creatures it would seem that every unfamiliar

sound or sight is capable of exciting it.[1]   In civilised
man, whose life for so many generations has been more
or less sheltered from the dangers peculiar to the natural
state, the instinct exhibits (like all complex organs and
functions that are not kept true to the specific type by
rigid selection) considerable individual differences, especially on its receptive side.   Hence it is difficult to discover
what objects and impressions were its natural excitants in
primitive man.   The wail of the very young infant has
but little variety ; but mothers claim to be able to distinguish the cries of fear, of anger, and of bodily discomfort, at a very early age, and it is probable that these three
modes of reaction become gradually differentiated from a
single instinctive impulse, that of the cry, whose function
is merely to signal to the mother the need for her ministrations.   In most young children unmistakable fear is
provoked by any sudden loud noise (some being especially
sensitive to harsh deep-pitched noises even though of low
intensity), and all through life such noise remains for
many of us the surest and most frequent excitant of the
instinct.   Other children, while still in arms, show fear if
held too loosely when carried downstairs, or if the arms
that hold them are suddenly lowered.   In some, intense
fear is excited on their first introduction at close quarters
to a dog or cat, no matter how quiet and well-behaved the
animal may be ; and some of us continue all through
life to experience a little thrill of fear whenever a dog
runs out and barks at our heels, though we may never
have received any hurt from an animal and may have
perfect confidence that no hurt is likely to be done us.[2]

[1] It may be noted in passing that this is one of a class of facts
which offers very great difficulty to any attempt to account for instinctive action on purely mechanical principles.

[2] Lest any reader should infer, from what is said above of the
immediate and often irrational character of our emotional responses
upon the reception of certain sense-impressions, that I accept the
James-Lange theory of emotion in the extreme form in which it is
stated by Professor James, I would point out that the acceptance of
the theory is by no means implied by my treatment of emotion.   In
the course of the discussion of instinct in the preceding chapter, it was
expressly stated that the instinctive process is not to be regarded as
merely a compound reflex, initiated by crude sensation, but that its
first stage always involves distinct cognition, which, in the case of

In other persons, again, fear is excited by the noise of a high wind, and though they may be in a solidly built house that has weathered a hundred storms, they will walk restlessly to and fro throughout every stormy night.

In most animals instinctive flight is followed by equally instinctive concealment as soon as cover is reached, and there can be little doubt that in primitive man the instinct had this double tendency. As soon as the little child can run, his fear expresses itself in concealment following on flight ; and the many adult persons who seek refuge from the strange noises of dark nights, or from a thunderstorm, by covering their heads with the bedclothes, and who find a quite irrational comfort in so doing, illustrate the persistence of this tendency. It is, perhaps, in the opposed characters of

purely instinctive action, is always a sense-perception. That is to say, the sense-impressions must undergo the psychical elaboration and synthesis implied by the word " perception " ; but such perceptual elaboration is in every case only rendered possible by the activities of a preformed psycho-physical disposition, which in the case of the purely instinctive action is innately organised. Professor Ward has effectively criticised the James-Lange theory (art. " Psychology " in supplementary volumes of *Encyclopædia Britannica*, 9th edition), and I would in the main endorse that criticism, though I think Professor Ward does not sufficiently recognise that our emotional responses are bound up with, and in many cases are immediately determined by, simple perceptions. He writes : " Let Professor James be confronted first by a chained bear and next by a bear at large : to the one object he presents a bun, and to the other a clean pair of heels." This passage seems by implication to ignore the truth I wish especially to insist upon, namely, the immediacy with which the emotional response follows upon perception, if the perceptual disposition involved is a part of the instinctive disposition, or if it has become connected with its central part as an acquired afferent inlet in the way discussed in Chapter II. There is a world of difference between, on the one hand, the instinctive response to the object that excites fear, and, on the other hand, running away because one judges that discretion is the better part of valour. I well remember standing in the zoological garden at Calcutta before a very strong cage in which was a huge Bengal tiger fresh from the jungle. A low-caste Hindu sweeper had amused himself by teasing the monster, and every time he came near the cage the tiger bounded forward with an awful roar. At each of many repetitions of this performance a cold shudder of fear passed over me, and only by an effort could I restrain the impulse to beat a hasty retreat. Though I knew the bars confined the brute more securely than any chain, it was not because the emotion of fear and the corresponding impulse were lacking that I did not show a " clean pair of heels."

these two tendencies, both of which are bound up with the emotion of fear, that we may find an explanation of the great variety of, and variability of, the symptoms of fear. The sudden stopping of heart-beat and respiration, and the paralysis of movement in which it sometimes finds expression, are due to the impulse to concealment; the hurried respiration and pulse, and the frantic bodily efforts, by which it is more commonly expressed, are due to the impulse to flight.[1]

That the excitement of fear is not necessarily, or indeed usually, the effect of an intelligent appreciation or anticipation of danger, is especially well shown by children of four or five years of age, in whom it may be induced by the facial contortions or playful roarings of a familiar friend. Under these circumstances, a child may exhibit every symptom of fear even while he sits upon his tormentor's lap and, with arms about his neck, beseeches him to cease or to promise not to do it again. And many a child has been thrown into a paroxysm of terror by the approach of some hideous figure that he knew to be but one of his playfellows in disguise.

Of all the excitants of this instinct the most interesting, and the most difficult to understand as regards its mode of operation, is the unfamiliar or strange as such. Whatever is totally strange, whatever is violently opposed to the accustomed and familiar, is apt to excite fear both in men and animals, if only it is capable of attracting their attention. It is, I think, doubtful whether an eclipse of the moon has ever excited the fear of animals, for the moon is not an object of their attention; but for savage men it has always been an occasion of fear. The well-known case of the dog described by Romanes, that was terrified by the movements of an object jerked forward by an invisible thread, illustrates the fear-exciting powers of the unfamiliar in the animal world. The following incident is instructive in this respect: A courageous

---

[1] It is worth noting that, if the emotional accompaniment of these two very different sets of bodily symptoms seems to have essentially the same quality in the two cases and to be unmistakably fear, this fact is very difficult to reconcile with the James-Lange theory of emotion interpreted in a literal fashion.

child of five years, sitting alone in a sunlit room, suddenly screams in terror, and, on her father hastening to her, can only explain that she saw something move. The discovery of a mouse in the corner of the room at once explains and banishes her fear, for she is on friendly terms with mice. The mouse must have darted across the peripheral part of her field of vision, and this unexpected and unfamiliar appearance of movement sufficed to excite the instinct. This avenue to the instinct, the unfamiliar, becomes in man highly diversified and intellectualised, and it is owing to this that he feels fear before the mysterious, the uncanny, and the supernatural, and that fear, entering as an element into the complex emotions of awe and reverence, plays its part in all religions.

Fear, whether its impulse be to flight or to concealment, is characterised by the fact that its excitement, more than that of any other instinct, tends to bring to an end at once all other mental activity, riveting the attention upon its object to the exclusion of all others; owing, probably, to this extreme concentration of attention, as well as to the violence of the emotion, the excitement of this instinct makes a deep and lasting impression on the mind. A gust of anger, a wave of pity or of tender emotion, an impulse of curiosity, may co-operate in supporting and reinforcing mental activities of the most varied kinds, or may dominate the mind for a time and then pass away, leaving but little trace. But fear, once roused, haunts the mind; it comes back alike in dreams and in waking life, bringing with it vivid memories of the terrifying impression. It is thus the great inhibitor of action, both present action and future action, and becomes in primitive human societies the great agent of social discipline through which men are led to the habit of control of the egoistic impulses.

The Instinct of Repulsion and the Emotion of Disgust

The impulse of this instinct is, like that of fear, one of aversion, and these two instincts together account probably for all aversions, except those acquired under the influence of pain. The impulse differs from that of fear in that, while the latter prompts to bodily retreat from its object, the former prompts to actions that remove or reject the offending object. This instinct resembles fear in that under the one name we, perhaps, commonly confuse two very closely allied instincts whose affective aspects are so similar that they are not easily distinguishable, though their impulses are of different tendencies. The one impulse of repulsion is to reject from the mouth substances that excite the instinct in virtue of their odour or taste, substances which in the main are noxious and evil-tasting ; its biological utility is obvious. The other impulse of repulsion seems to be excited by the contact of slimy and slippery substances with the skin, and to express itself as a shrinking of the whole body, accompanied by a throwing forward of the hands. The common shrinking from slimy creatures with a " creepy " shudder seems to be the expression of this impulse. It is difficult to assign any high biological value to it (unless we connect it with the necessity of avoiding noxious reptiles), but it is clearly displayed by some children before the end of their first year ; thus in some infants furry things excite shrinking and tears at their first contact. In others the instinct seems to ripen later, and the child that has handled worms, frogs, and slugs with delight suddenly evinces an unconquerable aversion to contact with them.

These two forms of disgust illustrate in the clearest and most interesting manner the intellectualisation of the instincts and primary emotions through extension of the range of their objects by association, resemblance, and analogy. The manners or speech of an otherwise presentable person may excite the impulse of shrinking in virtue of some subtle suggestion of sliminess. Or what we know of a man's character—that it is noxious, or, as we significantly say, is of evil odour—may render the mere thought of him an occasion of disgust ; we say, " It makes me sick to think of him " ; and at the same time the face exhibits in some degree, however slight, the expression produced by the act of rejection of some evil-tasting substance from the mouth. In these cases we may see very clearly that this extension by resemblance or analogy does not take place in any roundabout fashion ; it is not that the thought of the noxious or " slippery " character necessarily reproduces the idea of some evil-tasting substance or of some slimy creature. Rather, the apprehension of these peculiarities of character excites disgust directly, and then, when we seek to account for, and to justify, our disgust, we cast about for some simile and say, " He is like a snake," or " He is rotten to the core ! " The common form of emotion serves as the link between the two ideas.

The Instinct of Curiosity and the Emotion of Wonder

The instinct of curiosity is displayed by many of the higher animals, although its impulse remains relatively feeble in most of them. And, in fact, it is obvious that it could not easily attain any considerable strength in any animal species, because the individuals that displayed a too strong curiosity would be peculiarly liable to meet an untimely end. For its impulse is to approach and to examine more closely the object that excites it—a fact well known to hunters in the wilds, who sometimes by exciting this instinct bring the curious animal within the reach of their weapons. The native excitant of the instinct would seem to be any object similar to, yet perceptibly different from, familiar objects habitually noticed. It is therefore not easy to distinguish in general terms between the excitants of curiosity and those of fear ; for we have seen that one of the most general excitants of fear is whatever is strange or unfamiliar. The difference seems to be mainly one of degree, a smaller element of the strange or unusual exciting curiosity, while a larger and more pronounced degree of it excites fear. Hence the two instincts, with their opposed impulses of approach and retreat, are apt to be excited in animals and very young children in rapid alternation, and simultaneously in ourselves. Who has not seen a horse, or other animal, alternately approach in curiosity, and flee in fear from, some such object as an old coat upon the ground ? And who has not experienced a fearful curiosity in penetrating some dark cave or some secret chamber of an ancient castle ? The behaviour of animals under the impulse of curiosity may be well observed by any one who will lie down in a field where sheep or cattle are grazing and repeat at short intervals some peculiar cry. In this way one may draw every member of a large flock nearer and nearer, until one finds onself the centre of a circle of them, drawn up at a respectful distance, of which every pair of eyes and ears is intently fixed upon the strange object of their curiosity.

In the animals nearest to ourselves, namely, the monkeys, curiosity is notoriously strong, and them it impels not merely to approach its object and to direct the senses attentively upon it, but also to active manipulation of it. That a similar impulse is strong in children, no one will deny. Exception may perhaps be taken to the use of wonder as the name for the primary emotion that accompanies this impulse ; for this word is commonly applied to a complex emotion of which this primary emotion is the chief but not the sole constituent.[1] But, as was said above, some specialisation for technical purposes of words in common use is inevitable in psychology, and in this instance it is, I think, desirable and justifiable, owing to the lack of any more appropriate word.

This instinct, being one whose exercise is not of prime importance to the individual, exhibits great individual differences as regards its innate strength ; and these differences are apt to be increased during the course of life, the impulse growing weaker for lack of use in those in whom it is innately weak, stronger through exercise in those in whom it is innately strong. In men of the latter type it may become the main source of intellectual energy and effort ; to its impulse we certainly owe most of the purely disinterested labours of the highest types of intellect. It must be regarded as one of the principal roots of both science and religion.

[1] A form of admiration in which curiosity (or wonder in the sense in which the word is here used) predominates (see Chapter V.).

The Instinct of Pugnacity and the Emotion of Anger

This instinct, though not so nearly universal as fear, being apparently lacking in the constitution of the females of some species, ranks with fear as regards the great strength of its impulse and the high intensity of the emotion it generates. It occupies a peculiar position in relation to the other instincts, and cannot strictly be brought under the definition of instinct proposed in the first chapter. For it has no specific object or objects the perception of which constitutes the initial stage of the instinctive process. The condition of its excitement is rather any opposition to the free exercise of any impulse, any obstruction to the activity to which the creature is impelled by any one of the other instincts.[1] And its impulse is to break down any such obstruction and to destroy whatever offers this opposition. This instinct thus presupposes the others ; its excitement is dependent upon, or secondary to, the excitement of the others, and is apt to be intense in proportion to the strength of the obstructed impulse. The most mean-spirited cur will angrily resent any attempt to take away its bone, if it is hungry ; a healthy infant very early displays anger, if his meal is interrupted ; and all through life most men find it difficult to suppress irritation on similar occasions. In the animal world the most furious excitement of this instinct is provoked in the male of many

---

[1] It may be objected that, if a man strikes me a sudden and unprovoked blow, my anger is effectually and instantaneously aroused, even when I am at the moment not actively engaged in any way ; for it may be said that in this case the blow does not obstruct or oppose any impulse working within me at the moment. To raise this objection would be to ignore my consciousness of the personal relation and my personal attitude towards the striker. The impulse, the thwarting of which in this case provokes my anger, is the impulse of self-assertion, which is habitually in play during personal intercourse. That this is the case we may see on reflecting that anger would not be aroused if the blow came from a purely impersonal source—if, for example, it came from a falling branch, or if the blow received from a person were clearly quite accidental and unavoidable under the circumstances. Anger at the stupidity of others might also be quoted as an instance not conformable to the law ; but it is only when such stupidity hinders the execution of some plan that the normal man is angered by it.

species by any interference with the satisfaction of the
sexual impulse ; since such interference is the most
frequent occasion of its excitement, and since it commonly comes from other male members of his own species,
the actions innately organised for securing the ends of
this instinct are such actions as are most effective in
combat with his fellows.　Hence, also, the defensive
apparatus of the male is usually, like the lion's or the
stallion's mane, especially adapted for defence against
the attacks of his fellows.　But the obstruction of every
other instinctive impulse may in its turn become the
occasion of anger.　We see how among the animals even
the fear-impulse, the most opposed in tendency to the
pugnacious, may on obstruction give place to it ; for the
hunted creature when brought to bay—*i.e.*, when its
impulse to flight is obstructed—is apt to turn upon its
pursuers and to fight furiously, until an opportunity
for escape presents itself.

Darwin has shown the significance of the facial
expression of anger, of the contracted brow and raised
upper lip ; and man shares with many of the animals
the tendency to frighten his opponent by loud roars or
bellowings.　As with most of the other human instincts,
the excitement of this one is expressed in its purest form
by children.　Many a little boy has, without any example
or suggestion, suddenly taken to running with open
mouth to bite the person who has angered him, much to
the distress of his parents.　As the child grows up, as
self-control becomes stronger, the life of ideas richer,
and the means we take to overcome obstructions to our
efforts more refined and complex, this instinct ceases to
express itself in its crude natural manner, save when most
intensely excited, and becomes rather a source of increased
energy of action towards the end set by any other instinct ;
the energy of its impulse adds itself to and reinforces that
of other impulses and so helps us to overcome our difficulties.　In this lies its great value for civilised man.　A
man devoid of the pugnacious instinct would not only
be incapable of anger, but would lack this great source
of reserve energy which is called into play in most of us

by any difficulty in our path.   In this respect also it is the opposite of fear, which tends to inhibit all other impulses than its own.

The Instincts of Self-abasement (or Subjection) and of Self-assertion (or Self-display), and the Emotions of Subjection and Elation (or Negative and Positive Self-feeling)

These two instincts have attracted little attention, and the two corresponding emotions have, so far as I know, been adequately recognised by M. Ribot alone,[1] whom I follow in placing them among the primary emotions. Ribot names the two emotions negative and positive self-feeling respectively, but since these names are awkward in English, I propose, in the interests of a consistent terminology, to call them the emotions of subjection and elation.   The clear recognition and understanding of these instincts, more especially of the instinct of self-display, is of the first importance for the psychology of character and volition, as I hope to show in a later chapter. At present I am only concerned to prove that they have a place in the native constitution of the human mind.

The instinct of self-display is manifested by many of the higher social or gregarious animals, especially, perhaps, though not only, at the time of mating.   Perhaps among mammals the horse displays it most clearly.   The muscles of all parts are strongly innervated, the creature holds himself erect, his neck is arched, his tail lifted, his motions become superfluously vigorous and extensive, he lifts his hoofs high in air, as he parades before the eyes of his fellows.   Many animals, especially the birds, but also some of the monkeys, are provided with organs of display that are specially disposed on these occasions. Such are the tail of the peacock and the beautiful breast of the pigeon.   The instinct is essentially a social one, and is only brought into play by the presence of spectators. Such self-display is popularly recognised as implying pride ; we say " How proud he looks ! " and the peacock

[1] *Psychology of the Emotions*, p. 240.

has become the symbol of pride. By psychologists pride is usually denied the animals, because it is held to imply self-consciousness, and that, save of the most rudimentary kind, they probably have not. But this denial arises from the current confusion of the emotions and the sentiments. The word " pride " is no doubt most properly to be used as the name of one form of the self-regarding sentiment, and such sentiment does imply a developed self-consciousness such as no animal can be credited with. Nevertheless, popular opinion is, I think, in the right in attributing to the animals in their moments of self-display the germ of the emotion that is the most essential constituent of pride. It is this primary emotion which may be called positive self-feeling or elation, and which might well be called pride, if that word were not required to denote the sentiment of pride. In the simple form, in which it is expressed by the self-display of animals, it does not necessarily imply self-consciousness.

Many children clearly exhibit this instinct of self-display ; before they can walk or talk the impulse finds its satisfaction in the admiring gaze and plaudits of the family circle as each new acquirement is practised ; [1] a little later it is still more clearly expressed by the frequently repeated command, " See me do this," or " See how well I can do so-and-so " ; and for many a child more than half the delight of riding on a pony, or of wearing a new coat, consists in the satisfaction of this instinct, and vanishes if there be no spectators. A little later, with the growth of self-consciousness the instinct may find expression in the boasting and swaggering of boys, the vanity of girls ; while, with almost all of us, it becomes the most important constituent of the self-regarding sentiment and plays an all-important part in the volitional control of conduct, in the way to be discussed in a later chapter.

The situation that more particularly excites this

---

[1] One of my boys, who learnt to walk when eighteen months old, delighted in the applause that greeted his first steps, and, every time that one of his many excursions across the room failed to evoke it, he threw himself prone upon the floor with loud cries of anger and displeasure.

instinct is the presence of spectators to whom one feels oneself for any reason, or in any way, superior, and this is perhaps true in a modified sense of the animals ; the " dignified " behaviour of a big dog in the presence of small ones, the stately strutting of a hen among her chicks, seem to be instances in point. We have, then, good reason to believe that the germ of this emotion is present in the animal world, and, if we make use of our second criterion of the primary character of an emotion, it answers well to the test. For in certain mental diseases, especially in the early stages of that most terrible disorder, general paralysis of the insane, exaggeration of this emotion and of its impulse of display is the leading symptom. The unfortunate patient is perpetually in a state of elated self-feeling, and his behaviour corresponds to his emotional state ; he struts before the world, boasts of his strength, his immense wealth, his good looks, his luck, his family, when, perhaps, there is not the least foundation for his boastings.

As regards the emotion of subjection or negative self-feeling, we have the same grounds for regarding it as a primary emotion that accompanies the excitement of an instinctive disposition. The impulse of this instinct expresses itself in a slinking, crestfallen behaviour, a general diminution of muscular tone, slow restricted movements, a hanging down of the head, and sidelong glances. In the dog the picture is completed by the sinking of the tail between the legs. All these features express submissiveness, and are calculated to avoid attracting attention or to mollify the spectator. The nature of the instinct is sometimes very completely expressed in the behaviour of a young dog on the approach of a larger, older dog ; he crouches or crawls with legs so bent that his belly scrapes the ground, his back hollowed, his tail tucked away, his head sunk and turned a little on one side, and so approaches the imposing stranger with every mark of submission.

The recognition of this behaviour as the expression of a special instinct of self-abasement and of a corresponding primary emotion enables us to escape from a much-discussed difficulty. It has been asked, " Can animals and young children that have not attained to self-consciousness feel shame ? " And the answer usually given is, " No ; shame implies self-consciousness." Yet some animals, notably the dog, sometimes behave in a way which the popular mind interprets as expressing shame. The truth seems to be that, while fully-developed shame, shame in the full sense of the word, does imply self - consciousness and a self - regarding sentiment, yet in the emotion that accompanies this impulse to slink submissively we may see the rudiment of shame ; and, if we do not recognise this instinct, it is impossible to account for the genesis of shame or of bashfulness.

In children the expression of this emotion is often mistaken for that of fear ; but the young child sitting on his mother's lap in perfect silence and with face averted, casting sidelong glances at a stranger, presents a picture very different from that of fear.

Applying, again, our pathological test, we find that it is satisfied by this instinct of self-abasement. In many cases of mental disorder the exaggerated influence of this instinct seems to determine the leading symptoms. The patient shrinks from the observation of his fellows, thinks himself a most wretched, useless, sinful creature, and, in many cases, he develops delusions of having performed various unworthy or even criminal actions ; many such patients declare they are guilty of the un-pardonable sin, although they attach no definite meaning to the phrase—that is to say, the patient's intellect en-deavours to justify the persistent emotional state, which has no adequate cause in his relations to his fellow-men.

The Parental Instinct and the Tender Emotion

As regards the parental instinct and tender emotion, there are wide differences of opinion. Some of the authors who have paid most attention to the psychology of the emotions, notably Mr. A. F. Shand, do not recognise tender emotion as primary ; [1] others, especially Mr. Alex. Sutherland [2] and M. Ribot,[3] recognise it as a true primary and see in its impulse the root of all altruism ; Mr. Sutherland, however, like Adam Smith and many other writers, has confused tender emotion with sympathy, a serious error of incomplete analysis, which Ribot has avoided.

The maternal instinct, which impels the mother to protect and cherish her young, is common to almost all the higher species of animals. Among the lower animals the perpetuation of the species is generally provided for by the production of an immense number of eggs or young (in some species of fish a single adult produces more than a million eggs), which are left entirely unprotected, and are so preyed upon by other creatures that on the average but one or two attain maturity. As we pass higher up the animal scale, we find the number of eggs or young more and more reduced, and the diminution of their number compensated for by parental protection. At the lowest stage this protection may consist in the provision of some merely physical shelter, as in the case of those animals that carry their eggs attached in some way to their bodies. But, except at this lowest stage, the protection afforded to the young always involves some instinctive adaptation of the parent's behaviour. We may see this even among the fishes, some of which deposit their eggs in rude nests and watch over them, driving away creatures that might prey upon them. From this stage onwards protection of offspring becomes increasingly psychical in character, involves more profound modification of the parent's behaviour and a more prolonged period of more effective guardianship. The highest stage is reached by those species in which each female produces at a birth but one or two young and protects them so efficiently that most of the young born reach maturity ; the maintenance of the species thus

[1] See his chapter on the emotions in Professor Stout's *Groundwork of Psychology*.
[2] *Origin and Growth of the Moral Instinct*.
[3] *Op. cit.*

becomes in the main the work of the parental instinct
In such species the protection and cherishing of the young
is the constant and all-absorbing occupation of the mother,
to which she devotes all her energies, and in the course
of which she will at any time undergo privation, pain,
and death. The instinct becomes more powerful than
any other, and can override any other, even fear itself ;
for it works directly in the service of the species, while
the other instincts work primarily in the service of the
individual life, for which Nature cares little. All this
has been well set out by Sutherland, with a wealth of
illustrative detail, in his work on *The Origin and Growth
of the Moral Instinct.*

When we follow up the evolution of this instinct to
the highest animal level, we find among the apes the
most remarkable examples of its operation. Thus in
one species the mother is said to carry her young one
clasped in one arm uninterruptedly for several months,
never letting go of it in all her wanderings. This instinct
is no less strong in many human mothers, in whom, of
course, it becomes more or less intellectualised and
organised as the most essential constituent of the sentiment of parental love. Like other species, the human
species is dependent upon this instinct for its continued
existence and welfare. It is true that reason, working
in the service of the egoistic impulses and sentiments,
often circumvents the ends of this instinct and sets up
habits which are incompatible with it. When that occurs
on a large scale in any society, that society is doomed to
rapid decay. But the instinct itself can never die out,
save with the disappearance of the human species itself ;
it is kept strong and effective just because those families
and races and nations in which it weakens become rapidly
supplanted by those in which it is strong.

It is impossible to believe that the operation of this,
the most powerful of the instincts, is not accompanied
by a strong and definite emotion ; one may see the
emotion expressed unmistakably by almost any mother
among the higher animals, especially the birds and the
mammals—by the cat, for example, and by most of

the domestic animals ; and it is impossible to doubt that this emotion has in all cases the peculiar quality of the tender emotion provoked in the human parent by the spectacle of her helpless offspring. This primary emotion has been very generally ignored by the philosophers and psychologists ; that is, perhaps, to be explained by the fact that this instinct and its emotion are in the main decidedly weaker in men than in women, and in some men, perhaps, altogether lacking. We may even surmise that the philosophers as a class are men among whom this defect of native endowment is relatively common.

It may be asked, How can we account for the fact that men are at all capable of this emotion and of this disinterested protective impulse ? For in its racial origin the instinct was undoubtedly primarily maternal. The answer is that it is very common to see a character, acquired by one sex to meet its special needs, transmitted, generally imperfectly and with large individual variations, to the members of the other sex. Familiar examples of such transmission of sexual characters are afforded by the horns and antlers of some species of sheep and deer. That the parental instinct is by no means altogether lacking in men is probably due in the main to such transference of a primarily maternal instinct, though it is probable that in the human species natural selection has confirmed and increased its inheritance by the male sex.

To this view, that the parental tenderness of human beings depends upon an instinct phylogenetically continuous with the parental instinct of the higher animals, it might be objected that the very widespread prevalence of infanticide among existing savages implies that primitive man lacked this instinct and its tender emotion. But that would be a most mistaken objection. There is no feature of savage life more nearly universal than the kindness and tenderness of savages, even of savage fathers, for their little children. All observers are agreed upon this point. I have many a time watched with interest a bloodthirsty head-hunter of Borneo spending a day at home tenderly nursing his infant in his arms. And it is a rule, to which there are few exceptions among savage

peoples, that an infant is only killed during the first hours
of its life. If the child is allowed to survive but a few
days, then its life is safe ; the tender emotion has been
called out in fuller strength and has begun to be organised
into a sentiment of parental love that is too strong to be
overcome by prudential or purely selfish considerations.[1]

The view of the origin of parental tenderness here
adopted compares, I think, very favourably with other
accounts of its genesis. Bain taught that it is generated
in the individual by the frequent repetition of the intense
pleasure of contact with the young ; though why this
contact should be so highly pleasurable he did not explain.[2]
Others have attributed it to the expectation by the parent
of filial care in his or her old age. This is one form of
the absurd and constantly renewed attempt to reveal all
altruism as arising essentially out of a more or less subtle
regard for one's own welfare or pleasure. If tender
emotion and the sentiment of love really arose from a
disguised selfishness of this sort, how much stronger
should be the love of the child for the parent than that
of the parent for the child! For the child is for many
years utterly dependent on the parent for his every
pleasure and the satisfaction of his every need ; whereas
the mother's part—if she were not endowed with this
powerful instinct—would be one long succession of sacrifices and painful efforts on behalf of her child. Parental
love must always appear an insoluble riddle and paradox
if we do not recognise this primary emotion, deeply rooted
in an ancient instinct of vital importance to the race.
Long ago the Roman moralists were perplexed by it.
They noticed that in the Sullan prosecutions, while many
sons denounced their fathers, no father was ever known to
denounce his son ; and they recognised that this fact was
inexplicable by their theories of conduct. For their doctrine was like that of Bain, who said explicitly : " Tender
feeling is as purely self-seeking as any other pleasure,
and makes no inquiry as to the feelings of the beloved

[1] Cf. chapter xvii. of E. Westermarck's *Origin and Development of
the Moral Ideas.* London, 1906.
[2] *Emotions and the Will,* p. 82.

personality. It is by nature pleasurable, but does not necessarily cause us to seek the good of the object farther than is needful to gratify ourselves in the indulgence of the feeling." And again, in express reference to maternal tenderness, he wrote : " The superficial observer has to be told that the feeling in itself is as purely self-regarding as the pleasure of wine or of music. Under it we are induced to seek the presence of the beloved objects and to make the requisite sacrifices to gain the end, looking all the while at our own pleasure and to nothing beyond." [1] This doctrine is a gross libel on human nature, which is not so far inferior to animal nature in this respect as Bain's words imply. If Bain, and those who agree with his doctrine, were in the right, everything the cynics have said of human nature would be justified ; for from this emotion and its impulse to cherish and protect spring generosity, gratitude, love, pity, true benevolence, and altruistic conduct of every kind ; in it they have their main and absolutely essential root without which they would not be.[2]

Like the other primary emotions, the tender emotion cannot be described ; a person who had not experienced it could no more be made to understand its quality than a totally colour-blind person can be made to understand the experience of colour-sensation. Its impulse is prim-arily to afford physical protection to the child, especially by throwing the arms about it ; and that fundamental impulse persists in spite of the immense extension of the range of application of the impulse and its incorporation in many ideal sentiments.[3]

Like all the other instinctive impulses, this one, when its operation meets with obstruction or opposition, gives place to, or is complicated by, the pugnacious or com-

[1] *Op. cit.* p. 80.

[2] There are women, happily few, whose attitude towards their children shows them to be devoid of the maternal instinct. Reflection upon the conduct of such a woman will discover that her conduct in all relations proceeds from purely selfish motives.

[3] It is, I think, not improbable that the impulse to kiss the child, which is certainly strong and seems to be innate, is a modification of the maternal impulse to lick the young which is a feature of the maternal instinct of so many animal species.

bative impulse directed against the source of the obstruction ; and, the impulse being essentially protective, its
obstruction provokes anger perhaps more readily than
the obstruction of any other.   In almost all animals that
display it, even in those which in all other situations are
very timid, any attempt to remove the young from the
protecting parent, or in any way to hurt them, provokes
a fierce and desperate display of all their combative
resources.   By the human mother the same prompt
yielding of the one impulse to the other is displayed on the
same plane of physical protection, but also on the higher
plane of ideal protection ; the least threat, the smallest
slight or aspersion (*e.g.*, the mere speaking of the baby as
" it," instead of as " he " or " she "), the mere suggestion
that it is not the most beautiful object in the world, will
suffice to provoke a quick resentment.

This intimate alliance between tender emotion and
anger is of great importance for the social life of man,
and the right understanding of it is fundamental for a
true theory of the moral sentiments ; for the anger
evoked in this way is the germ of all moral indignation,
and on moral indignation justice and the greater part of
public law are in the main founded.   Thus, paradoxical
as it may seem, beneficence and punishment alike have
their firmest and most essential root in the parental
instinct.   For the understanding of the relation of this
instinct to moral indignation, it is important to note
that the object which is the primary provocative of tender
emotion is, not the child itself, but the child's expression
of pain, fear, or distress of any kind, especially the child's
cry of distress ; further, that this instinctive response is
provoked by the cry, not only of one's own offspring,
but of any child.   Tender emotion and the protective
impulse are, no doubt, evoked more readily and intensely
by one's own offspring, because about them a strongly
organised and complex sentiment grows up.   But the
distress of any child will evoke this response in a very
intense degree in those in whom the instinct is strong.
There are women—and men also, though fewer—who
cannot sit still, or pursue any occupation, within sound

of the distressed cry of a child ; if circumstances compel them to restrain their impulse to run to its relief, they yet cannot withdraw their attention from the sound, but continue to listen in painful agitation.

In the human being, just as is the case in some degree with all the instinctive responses, and as we noticed especially in the case of disgust, there takes place a vast extension of the field of application of the maternal instinct. The similarity of various objects to the primary or natively given object, similarities which in many cases can only be operative for a highly developed mind, enables them to evoke tender emotion and its protective impulse directly—*i.e.*, not merely by way of associative reproduction of the natively given object. In this way the emotion is liable to be evoked, not only by the distress of a child, but by the mere sight or thought of a perfectly happy child ; for its feebleness, its delicacy, its obvious incapacity to supply its own needs, its liability to a thousand different ills, suggest to the mind its need of protection. By a further extension of the same kind the emotion may be evoked by the sight of any very young animal, especially if in distress ; Wordsworth's poem on the pet lamb is the celebration of this emotion in its purest form ; and indeed it would be easy to wax enthusiastic in the cause of an instinct that is the source of the only entirely admirable, satisfying, and perfect human relationship, as well as of every kind of purely disinterested conduct.

In a similar direct fashion the distress of any adult (towards whom we harbour no hostile sentiment) evokes the emotion ; but in this case it is more apt to be complicated by sympathetic pain, when it becomes the painful, tender emotion we call pity ; whereas the child, or any other helpless and delicate thing, may call it out in the pure form without alloy of sympathetic pain. It is amusing to observe how, in those women in whom the instinct is strong, it is apt to be excited, owing to the subtle working of similarity, by any and every object that is small and delicate of its kind—a very small cup or chair, or book, or what not.

Extension takes place also through association in

virtue of contiguity ; the objects intimately connected
with the prime object of the emotion—such objects as the
clothes, the toys, the bed, of the beloved child—become
capable of exciting the emotion directly.

But the former mode of direct extension of the field
of application is in this case the more important. It is
in virtue of such extension to similars that, when we
see, or hear of, the ill-treatment of any weak, defenceless
creature (especially, of course, if the creature be a child)
tender emotion and the protective impulse are aroused
on its behalf, but are apt to give place at once to the anger
we call moral indignation against the perpetrator of the
cruelty ; and in bad cases we are quite prepared to tear
the offender limb from limb, the tardy process of the law
with its mild punishments seeming utterly inadequate to
afford vicarious satisfaction to our anger.[1]

How is this great fact of wholly disinterested anger or
indignation to be accounted for, if not in the way here
suggested ? The question is an important one ; it supplies
a touchstone for all theories of the moral emotions and
sentiments. For, as was said above, this disinterested
indignation is the ultimate root of justice and of public
law ; without its support law and its machinery would be
most inadequate safeguards of personal rights and liberties ; and, in opposition to the moral indignation of a
majority of members of any society, laws can only be very
imperfectly enforced by the strongest despotism, as we
see in Russia at the present time. Those who deny any
truly altruistic motive to man and seek to reduce apparent
altruism to subtle and far-sighted egoism, must simply
deny the obvious facts, and must seek some far-fetched
unreal explanations of such phenomena as the anti-slavery

[1] It is a fair question whether, among those nations who pride
themselves upon having attained so high a state of civilisation that
they can no longer inflict capital punishment, the greater clemency of
the law should not be attributed to a relative deficiency in the strength
of the parental instinct in the mass of the people, and to a consequent
relative incapacity for moral indignation. At the present moment the
moral indignation of a large section of the French people is clamouring
for the death of a wretch who has been convicted of cruelly maltreating a child, and to whom, it is thought, the presidential clemency
may be extended.

and Congo-reform movements, the anti-vivisection crusade, and the Society for the Prevention of Cruelty to Children. Let us examine briefly the way in which Bain sought to account for ostensibly disinterested emotion and action. As we have seen above, he regarded tender emotion as wholly self-seeking, and, like many other authors, he attributed such actions as we are considering to sympathy. He wrote : " From a region of the mind quite apart from the tender emotion arises the principle of sympathy, or the prompting to take on the pleasures and pains of other beings, and act on them as if they were our own. Instead of being a source of pleasure to us, the primary operation of sympathy is to make us surrender pleasures and to incur pains. This is a paradox of our constitution to be again more fully considered." [1]

Here he has clearly committed himself to a position that needs much explanation. But, when we seek his fuller consideration of this paradox, all we find is a passage of a few lines in his section on moral disapprobation. This passage tells us that when another's conduct inspires a feeling of disapprobation as violating the maxims recognised to be binding, " It is to be supposed that the same sense of duty that operates upon one's own self, and stings with remorse and fear in case of disobedience, should come into play when some other person is the guilty agent. The feeling that rises up towards that person is a strong feeling of displeasure or dislike, proportioned to the strength of our regard to the violated duty. There arises a moral resentment, or a disposition to inflict punishment upon the offender." [2] That is to say, according to Bain, the source of all disinterested moral indignation is the reflection, " If I had done that, I should have been punished ; therefore he must be punished." Now, this attitude is not uncommon, especially in the nursery, and it plays some small part, no doubt, in securing equal distribution of punishments ; but it is surely wholly inadequate to account for that paradox of our constitution previously recognised by Bain. In order to realise how far from the truth this

[1] *Op. cit.* p. 83.   [2] *Op. cit.* p. 291.

doctrine is, we have only to consider what kinds of conduct provoke our moral indignation most strongly. If we hear of a man robbing a bank, holding up a mail train, or killing another in fair fight, we may agree that he should be punished ; for we recognise intellectually that the interests of society demand that such things shall not be done too frequently, and we ourselves might shrink from similar conduct; but our feeling towards the criminal may be one of pity, or perhaps merely one of amusement dashed with admiration for his audacity and skill. But let the act be one inflicting pain on a helpless creature—an act of cruelty to a horse, a dog, or, above all, to a child—and our moral indignation blazes out, even though the act be one for which the law prescribes no punishment Bain's explanation of his "paradox" of sympathy is then utterly inadequate, and a closer examination of his statement of the principle of sympathy shows that it is false, and that any plausibility it may seem to possess depends upon the vague and rhetorical language in which it is made His statement is that sympathy is the prompting to take on the pains and pleasures of another being, and to endeavour to abolish that other's pain and to prolong his pleasure. But, if we use more accurate language, we shall have to say that the sympathetic pain or pleasure we experience is immediately evoked in us by the spectacle of pain or of pleasure, and that we then act on it because it is our own pain or pleasure ; and the action we take (so long as no other principle is at work) is directed to cut short our own pain and to prolong our own pleasure, quite regardless of the feelings of the other person Now, the easiest and quickest way of cutting short sympatheti- cally induced pain is to turn our eyes and our thoughts away from the suffering creature ; and this is the way invariably followed by all sensitive natures in which the tender emotion and its protective impulse are weak. They pass by the sick and suffering with averted gaze, and resolutely banish all thoughts of them, surrounding themselves as far as possible with gay and cheerful faces. No doubt the spectacle of the poor man who fell among thieves was just as distressing to the priest and the Levite, who passed by on the other side, as to the good Samaritan who tenderly cared for him.   They may well have been exquisitely sensitive souls, who would have fainted away if they had been compelled to gaze upon his wounds. The great difference between them and the Samaritan was that in him the tender emotion and its impulse were evoked, and that this impulse overcame, or prevented, the aversion naturally induced by the painful and, perhaps, disgusting spectacle.[1]

Our susceptibility to sympathetically induced pain or pleasure, operating alone, simply inclines us, then, to avoid the neighbourhood of the distressed and to seek the company of the cheerful ; but tender emotion draws us near to the suffering and the sad, seeking to alleviate their distress.   It is to be noted also that the intensity of the emotion and the strength of its impulse to cherish and protect, and also the violence of the anger we feel against him who inflicts pain on any weak and defenceless creature—all these bear no constant relation to the intensity of our sympathetically induced pain.   There are natures so strong and so happily constituted that they hardly know pain ; yet they may be very tender-hearted and easily aroused to anger by the spectacle of cruelty. Again, the mere threat of injury to a feeble creature may provoke an instantaneous anger ; and it would be absurd to suppose that in such a case one first pictures the suffering of the creature that would result if the threat were executed, then sympathetically experiences the pain, and then, putting oneself in the place of the prospectively injured, goes on to feel anger against him who threatens.   The response is as direct and instantaneous as the mother's emotion at the cry of her child or her impulse to fly to its defence ; and it is essentially the same process.

In no other way than that here proposed is it possible to account for disinterested beneficence and moral indignation.   If this view is rejected, they remain a paradox and a miracle—tendencies, mysteriously implanted in the human breast, that have no history in the evolutionary

[1] For fuller discussion of sympathy see Chapters IV. and VI.

process, no analogy and no intelligible connection with, no resemblance to, any of the other features of our mental constitution.

The importance of establishing the place of tender emotion among the primary emotions necessitates in this place a brief criticism of Mr. Shand's treatment of it, although this criticism may be more easily understood after reading Chapters V. and VI., in which the organisation of the sentiments is discussed.

According to Mr. Shand,[1] tender emotion is always complex, and into its composition there enter always both joy and sorrow. He arrives at this view in the following way : Accepting the traditional view that joy and sorrow are primary emotions, he says that joy is a diffusive emotion that has no specific tendency (for he has not accepted the guiding principle followed in these pages, namely, that each primary emotion accompanies the excitement of an instinctive disposition of specific tendency) ; and sorrow, he says, has two impulses, namely, to cling to its object and to restore it, to repair the injury done to it that is the cause of the sorrow. He then takes pity as the simplest type of tender emotion, and finds that it has the fundamental impulses of sorrow, to restore and to cling to its object ; but pity is not pure sorrow, because it has an element of sweetness ; which element he identifies with joy. Hence pity, the simplest variety of tender emotion, is, he says, a fusion of joy and sorrow.

Mr. Shand does not attempt to account for sorrow, or to trace its history in the race, or to show how it gets its disinterested impulse to restore and do good to its object. And this is the all-important question, for this impulse of tender emotion is, as has been said, the source of all altruistic conduct. He simply begs the question in assuming sorrow to be a primary emotion having this impulse. Further, in the course of his discussion Shand recognises the existence of a kind of sorrow or grief that has no impulse to restore its object—the hard, bitter variety of grief ; and in doing that he implicitly admits that

[1] Professor Stout's *Groundwork of Psychology*, chap. xvi.

sorrow is complex and derived from simpler elements. He makes also this significant admission : " The tenderness of pity seems to come from the ideas and impulses that go out to relieve suffering." Now, that is just the point I wish to insist upon—that there is in pity as one element this impulse to cherish and protect, with its accompanying tender emotion ; and that this is present also in sorrow proper, but that it is not in itself painful —as sorrow is—and therefore is not sorrow, but is one of the primary elements of which sorrowful emotion is compounded.

According to the view here adopted, the element of pain in pity is sympathetically induced pain,[1] and the element of sweetness is the pleasure that attends the satisfaction of the impulse of the tender emotion. That this view is truer than the other is, I think, shown by the fact that pity may be wholly devoid of this element of sweetness without losing its essential character—namely, in the case of pity evoked by some terrible suffering that we are powerless to relieve ; in this case the pain of the obstructed tender impulse is added to the sympathetic pain, and our pity is wholly painful.

Another good reason for refusing to regard sorrow as one of the primary emotions is the fact that sorrowful emotion of every kind presupposes the existence of an organised sentiment, and is, in fact, the tender emotion developed within the sentiment of love and rendered painful either by sympathetically induced pain—as in the case of injury to the beloved object, or by the baffling of its impulse—as in the case of the loss of that object. If, as seems to me indisputable, sorrow presupposes the organised sentiment of love, it clearly cannot be regarded as a primary emotion.

Some other Instincts of less well-defined Emotional Tendency

The seven instincts we have now reviewed are those whose excitement yields the most definite of the primary

[1] See Chapter IV.

emotions ; from these seven primary emotions together with feelings of pleasure and pain (and perhaps also feelings of excitement and of depression) are compounded all, or almost all, the affective states that are popularly recognised as emotions, and for which common speech has definite names. But there are other human instincts which, though some of them play but a minor part in the genesis of the emotions, have impulses that are of great importance for social life ; they must therefore be mentioned.

Of these by far the most important is the sexual instinct or *instinct of reproduction*. It is unnecessary to say anything of the great strength of its impulse or of the violence of the emotional excitement that accompanies its exercise. One point of interest is its intimate connection with the parental instinct. There can, I think, be little doubt that this connection is an innate one, and that in all (save debased) natures it secures that the object of the sexual impulse shall become also the object in some degree of tender emotion.[1] The biological utility of an innate connection of this kind is obvious. It would prepare the way for that co-operation between the male and female in which, even among the animals, a lifelong fidelity and mutual tenderness is often touchingly displayed.

This instinct, more than any other, is apt in mankind to lend the immense energy of its impulse to the sentiments and complex impulses into which it enters, while its specific character remains submerged and unconscious. It is unnecessary to dwell on this feature, since it has been dealt with exhaustively in many thousands of novels.[2] From the point of view of this section the chief importance of this instinct is that it illustrates, in a manner that must convince the most obtuse, the continuity and the essential similarity of nature and function between the human and the animal instincts.

In connection with the instinct of reproduction a

---

[1] In so far, of course, as the impulse is not completely thwarted.
[2] See Supplementary Chapter II. at the end of this volume, which contains a fuller discussion of the sex instinct.

few words must be said about *sexual jealousy* and *female coyness*. These are regarded by some authors as special instincts, but perhaps without sufficiently good grounds. Jealousy in the full sense of the word is a complex emotion that presupposes an organised sentiment, and there is no reason to regard the hostile behaviour of the male animal in the presence of rivals as necessarily implying any such complex emotion or sentiment. The assumption of a specially intimate innate connection between the instincts of reproduction and of pugnacity will account for the fact that the anger of the male, both in the human and in most animal species, is so readily aroused in an intense degree by any threat of opposition to the operation of the sexual impulse ; and perhaps the great strength of the sexual impulse sufficiently accounts for it.

The coyness of the female in the presence of the male may be accounted for in similar fashion by the assumption that in the female the instinct of reproduction has specially intimate innate relations to the instincts of self-display and self-abasement, so that the presence of the male excites these as well as the former instinct.

The desire for food that we experience when hungry, with the impulse to seize it, to carry it to the mouth, to chew it and swallow it, must, I think, be regarded as rooted in a true instinct. In many of the animals the movements of feeding exhibit all the marks of truly instinctive behaviour. But in ourselves the instinct becomes at an early age so greatly modified through experience, on both its receptive and its executive sides, that little, save the strong impulse, remains to mark the instinctive nature of the process of feeding.

The *gregarious instinct* is one of the human instincts of greatest social importance, for it has played a great part in moulding societary forms. The affective aspect of the operation of this instinct is not sufficiently intense or specific to have been given a name. The instinct is displayed by many species of animals, even by some very low in the scale of mental capacity. Its operation in its simplest form implies none of the higher qualities of mind, neither sympathy nor capacity for mutual aid.

Mr. Francis Galton has given the classical description of the operation of the crude instinct. Describing the South African ox in Damaraland,[1] he says he displays no affection for his fellows, and hardly seems to notice their existence, so long as he is among them ; but, if he becomes separated from the herd, he displays an extreme distress that will not let him rest until he succeeds in rejoining it, when he hastens to bury himself in the midst of it, seeking the closest possible contact with the bodies of his fellows. There we see the working of the gregarious instinct in all its simplicity, a mere uneasiness in isolation and satisfaction in being one of a herd. Its utility to animals liable to the attacks of beasts of prey is obvious.

The instinct is commonly strongly confirmed by habit ; the individual is born into a society of some sort and grows up in it, and the being with others and doing as they do becomes a habit deeply rooted in the instinct. It would seem to be a general rule, the explanation of which is to be found in the principle of sympathetic emotion to be considered later, that the more numerous the herd or crowd or society in which the individual finds himself the more complete is the satisfaction of this impulse. It is probably owing to this peculiarity of the instinct that gregarious animals of so many species are found at times in aggregations far larger than are necessary for mutual protection or for the securing of any other advantage. Travellers on the prairies of North America in the early days of exploration have told how the bison might sometimes be seen in an immense herd that blackened the surface of the plain for many miles in all directions: In a similar way some kinds of deer and of birds gather together and move from place to place in vast aggregations.

Although opinions differ widely as to the form of primitive human society, some inclining to the view that it was a large promiscuous horde, others, with more probability, regarding it as a comparatively small group of near blood relatives, almost all anthropologists agree

[1] *Inquiries into Human Faculty*, p. 72.

that primitive man was to some extent gregarious in his habits ; and the strength of the instinct as it still exists in civilised men lends support to this view.

The gregarious instinct is no exception to the rule that the human instincts are liable to a morbid hypertrophy under which their emotions and impulses are revealed with exaggerated intensity. The condition known to alienists as agoraphobia seems to result from the morbidly intense working of this instinct—the patient will not remain alone, will not cross a wide empty space, and seeks always to be surrounded by other human beings. But of the normal man also it is true that, as Professor James says : " To be alone is one of the greatest of evils for him. Solitary confinement is by many regarded as a mode of torture too cruel and unnatural for civilised countries to adopt. To one long pent up on a desert island the sight of a human footprint or a human form in the distance would be the most tumultuously exciting of experiences." [1]

In civilised communities we may see evidence of the operation of this instinct on every hand. For all but a few exceptional, and generally highly cultivated, persons the one essential condition of recreation is the being one of a crowd. The normal daily recreation of the population of our towns is to go out in the evening and to walk up and down the streets in which the throng is densest— the Strand, Oxford Street, or the Old Kent Road ; and the smallest occasion—a foreign prince driving to a railway station or a Lord Mayor's Show—will line the streets for hours with many thousands whose interest in the prince or the show alone would hardly lead them to take a dozen steps out of their way. On their few short holidays the working classes rush together from town and country alike to those resorts in which they are assured of the presence of a large mass of their fellows. It is the same instinct working on a slightly higher plane that brings tens of thousands to the cricket and football grounds on half-holidays. Crowds of this sort exert a greater fascination and afford a more complete satisfaction to

[1] *Principles of Psychology.*

the gregarious instinct than the mere aimless aggregations of the streets, because all their members are
simultaneously concerned with the same objects, all
are moved by the same emotions, all shout and applaud
together.   It would be absurd to suppose that it is merely
the individuals' interest in the game that brings these
huge crowds together   What proportion of the ten
thousand witnesses of a football match would stand for
an hour or more in the wind and rain, if each man were
isolated from the rest of the crowd and saw only the
players ?

Even cultured minds are not immune to the fascination of the herd.   Who has not felt it as he has stood at
the Mansion House crossing or walked down Cheapside ?
How few prefer at nightfall the lonely Thames Embank-
ment, full of mysterious poetry as the barges sweep slowly
onward with the flood-tide, to the garish crowded Strand
a hundred yards away !   We cultivated persons usually
say to ourselves, when we yield to this fascination, that
we are taking an intelligent interest in the life of the
people   But such intellectual interest plays but a small
part, and beneath works the powerful impulse of this
ancient instinct.

The possession of this instinct, even in great strength,
does not necessarily imply sociability of temperament.
Many a man leads in London a most solitary, unsociable
life, who yet would find it hard to live far away from
the thronged city.   Such men are like Mr. Galton's
oxen, unsociable but gregarious ; and they illustrate the
fact that sociability, although it has the gregarious instinct
at its foundation, is a more complex, more highly developed,
tendency.   As an element of this more complex tendency
to sociability, the instinct largely determines the forms
of the recreations of even the cultured classes, and is the
root of no small part of the pleasure we find in attendance
at the theatre, at concerts, lectures, and all such enter-
tainments.   How much more satisfying is a good play
if one sits in a well-filled theatre than if half the seats are
empty ; especially if the house is unanimous and loud
in the expression of its feelings !   But this instinct has

in all ages produced more important social effects that
must be considered in a later chapter.

Two other instincts of considerable social importance
demand a brief mention. The impulse to collect and
hoard various objects is displayed in one way or another
by almost all human beings, and seems to be due to a
true instinct ; it is manifested by many animals in the
blind, unintelligent manner that is characteristic of crude
instinct. And, like other instinctive impulses of man,
it is liable to become morbidly exaggerated, when it
appears, in a mild form, as the collecting mania and,
in greater excess, as miserliness and kleptomania. Like
other instincts, it ripens naturally and comes into play
independently of all training. Statistical inquiry among
large numbers of children has shown that very few attain
adult life without having made a collection of objects of
one kind or another, usually without any definite purpose ;
such collecting is no doubt primarily due to the ripening
of an *instinct of acquisition*.

We seem to be justified in assuming in man an *instinct
of construction*. The playful activities of children seem
to be in part determined by its impulse ; and in most
civilised adults it still survives, though but little scope
is allowed it by the circumstances of the majority. For
most of us the satisfaction of having actually made something is very real, quite apart from the value or usefulness
of the thing made. And the simple desire to make something, rooted in this instinct, is probably a contributing
motive to all human constructions from a mud-pie to a
metaphysical system or a code of laws.

The instincts enumerated above, together with a
number of minor instincts, such as those that prompt
to crawling and walking, are, I think, all that we can
recognise with certainty in the constitution of the human
mind. Lightly to postulate an indefinite number and
variety of human instincts is a cheap and easy way to
solve psychological problems, and is an error hardly less
serious and less common than the opposite error of ignoring all the instincts. How often do we not hear of the
religious instinct ! Renan asserted that the religious

instinct is as natural to man as the nest-building instinct is to birds, and many authors have written of it as one of the fundamental attributes of the human mind.[1]   But, if we accept the doctrine of the evolution of man from animal forms, we are compelled to seek the origin of religious emotions and impulses in instincts that are not specifically religious.   And consideration of the conditions, manifestations, and tendencies of religious emotions must lead to the same search.   For it is clear that religious emotion is not a simple and specific variety, such as could be conditioned by any one instinct; it is rather a very complex and diversified product of the co-operation of several instincts, which bring forth very heterogeneous manifestations, differing from one another as widely as light from darkness, according to the degree and kind of guidance afforded by imagination and reason.

Much has been written in recent years of instincts of imitation, of sympathy, and of play, and the postulation of these instincts seems to have been allowed to pass without challenge.   Yet, as I shall show in the following section, there is no sufficient justification for it; for all the behaviour attributed to these three supposed instincts may be otherwise accounted for.

Professor James admits an instinct of emulation or rivalry, but the propriety of this admission is to my mind questionable.   It is possible that all the behaviour which is attributed to this instinct may be accounted for as proceeding from the instincts of pugnacity and of self-display or self-assertion.   It would, I think, be difficult to make out any good case for the existence of such an instinct in the animal world.   But a suggestion as to the peculiar position and origin of a human instinct of emulation will be made in the next chapter

[1] Cf. p. 260.

CHAPTER IV

SOME GENERAL OR NON-SPECIFIC INNATE
TENDENCIES

IN this chapter we have to consider certain innate tendencies of the human mind of great importance for social life which are sometimes ascribed to special instincts, but which are more properly classed apart from the instinctive tendencies. For we have seen that an instinct, no matter how profoundly modified it may be in the developed human mind as regards the conditions of its excitement and the actions in which it manifests itself, always retains unchanged its essential and permanent nucleus ; this nucleus is the central part of the innate disposition, the excitement of which determines an affective state or emotion of specific quality and a native impulse towards some specific end. And the tendencies to be considered in this chapter have no such specific characters, but are rather of a many-sided and general nature. Consider, for example, the tendency to imitate—the modes of action in which this tendency expresses itself and the accompanying subjective states are as various as the things or actions that can be imitated.

Sympathy or the Sympathetic Induction of the Emotions

The three most important of these pseudo-instincts, as they might be called, are suggestion, imitation, and sympathy. They are closely allied as regards their effects, for in each case the process in which the tendency manifests itself involves an interaction between at least two individuals, one of whom is the agent, while the other is the person acted upon or patient ; and in each case the result of the process is some degree of assimilation of the actions and mental state of the patient to those of the agent. They are three forms of mental interaction of fundamental importance for all social life, both of men and animals. These processes of mental interaction, of impression and reception, may involve chiefly the cognitive aspect of mental process, or its affective or its conative aspect. In the first case, when some presentation, idea, or belief of the agent directly induces a similar presentation, idea, or belief in the patient, the process is called one of suggestion ; when an affective or emotional excitement of the agent induces a similar affective excitement in the patient, the process is one of sympathy or sympathetic induction of emotion or feeling ; when the most prominent result of the process of interaction is the assimilation of the bodily movements of the patient to those of the agent, we speak of imitation.

Now, M. Tarde [1] and Professor Baldwin [2] have singled out imitation as the all-important social process, and Baldwin, like most contemporary writers, attributes it to an instinct of imitation. But careful consideration of the nature of imitative actions shows that they are of many kinds, that they issue from mental processes of a number of different types, and that none are attributable to a specific instinct of imitation, while many are due to sympathy and others to suggestion. We must therefore first consider sympathy and suggestion, and, after defining them as precisely as possible, go on to consider the varieties of imitative action.

Sympathy is by some authors ascribed to a special instinct of sympathy, and even Professor James has been misled by the confused usage of common speech and has said " sympathy is an emotion." [3] But the principles maintained in the foregoing chapter will not allow us to accept either of these views. The word " sympathy," as popularly used, generally implies a tender regard for the person with whom we are said to sympathise. But

[1] *Les Lois de l'Imitation.* Paris, 1904.
[2] *Mental Development,* and *Social and Ethical Interpretations.*
[3] *Op. cit.* vol. ii. p. 410.

such sympathy is only one special and complex form of sympathetic emotion, in the strict and more general sense of the words The fundamental and primitive form of sympathy is exactly what the word implies, a suffering with, the experiencing of any feeling or emotion when and because we observe in other persons or creatures the expression of that feeling or emotion.[1]

Sympathetic induction of emotion is displayed in the simplest and most unmistakable fashion by many, probably by all, of the gregarious animals ; and it is easy to understand how greatly it aids them in their struggle for existence One of the clearest and commonest examples is the spread of fear and its flight-impulse among the members of a flock or herd Many gregarious animals utter when startled a characteristic cry of fear ; when this cry is emitted by one member of a flock or herd, it immediately excites the flight-impulse in all of its fellows who are within hearing of it ; the whole herd, flock, or covey takes to flight like one individual Or again, one of a pack of gregarious hunting animals, dogs or wolves, comes upon a fresh trail, sights the prey, and pursues it, uttering a characteristic yelp that excites the instinct of pursuit in all his fellows and brings them yelping behind him Or two dogs begin to growl or fight, and at once all the dogs within sound and sight stiffen themselves and show every symptom of anger. Or one beast in a herd stands arrested, gazing in curiosity on some unfamiliar object, and presently his fellows also, to whom the object may be invisible, display curiosity and come up to join in the examination of the object In all these cases we observe only that the behaviour of one animal, upon the excitement of an instinct, immediately evokes similar behaviour in those of his fellows who perceive his expressions of excitement But we can hardly doubt that in each case the instinctive behaviour is accompanied by the appropriate emotion and felt impulse

Sympathy of this crude kind is the cement that binds

---

[1] This truth has been clearly expressed by Herbert Spencer (*Principles of Psychology*, vol. ii. p. 563), and Bain recognised it, although, as we have seen, he failed to hold it consistently.

animal societies together, renders the actions of all members of a group harmonious, and allows them to reap some of the prime advantages of social life in spite of lack of intelligence.

How comes it that the instinctive behaviour of one animal directly excites similar behaviour on the part of his fellows ? No satisfactory answer to this question seems to have been hitherto proposed, although this kind of behaviour has been described and discussed often enough. Not many years ago it would have seemed sufficient to answer, It is due to instinct. But that answer will hardly satisfy us to-day. I think the facts compel us to assume that in the gregarious animals each of the principal instincts has a special perceptual inlet (or recipient afferent part) that is adapted to receive and to elaborate the sense-impressions made by the expressions of the same instinct in other animals of the same species—that, *e.g.*, the fear-instinct has, besides others, a special perceptual inlet that renders it excitable by the sound of the cry of fear, the instinct of pugnacity a perceptual inlet that renders it excitable by the sound of the roar of anger.

Human sympathy has its roots in similar specialisations of the instinctive dispositions on their afferent sides. In early childhood sympathetic emotion is almost wholly of this simple kind ; and all through life most of us continue to respond in this direct fashion to the expressions of the feelings and emotions of our fellow-men. This sympathetic induction of emotion and feeling may be observed in children at an age at which they cannot be credited with understanding of the significance of the expressions that provoke their reactions. Perhaps the expression to which they respond earliest is the sound of the wailing of other children. A little later the sight of a smiling face, the expression of pleasure, provokes a smile. Later still, fear, curiosity, and, I think, anger, are communicated readily in this direct fashion from one child to another. Laughter is notoriously infectious all through life, and this, though not a truly instinctive expression, affords the most familiar example of sympathetic induction of an affective state. This immediate and unrestrained responsiveness to the emotional expressions of others is one of the great charms of childhood. One may see it particularly well displayed by the children of some savage races (especially perhaps of the negro race), whom it renders wonderfully attractive.

Adults vary much in the degree to which they display these sympathetic reactions, but in few or none are they wholly lacking. A merry face makes us feel brighter ; a melancholy face may cast a gloom over a cheerful company ; when we witness the painful emotion of others, we experience sympathetic pain ; when we see others terror-stricken or hear their scream of terror, we suffer a pang of fear though we know nothing of the cause of their emotion or are indifferent to it ; anger provokes anger ; the curious gaze of the passer-by stirs our curiosity ; and a display of tender emotion touches, as we say, a tender chord in our hearts.[1] In short, each of the great primary emotions that has its characteristic and unmistakable bodily expression seems to be capable of being excited by way of this immediate sympathetic response. If, then, the view here urged is true, we must not say, as many authors have done, that sympathy is due to an instinct, but rather that sympathy is founded upon a special adaptation of the receptive side of each of the principal instinctive dispositions, an adaptation that renders each instinct capable of being excited on the perception of the bodily expressions of the excitement of the same instinct in other persons.

[1] Shortly after writing these lines I was holding a child in my arms, looking out of window on a dark night. There came a blinding flash of lightning and, after some seconds, a crash of thunder. The child was pleased by the lightning, but at the first crack of thunder she screamed in terror ; immediately upon hearing the scream, I experienced, during a fraction of a second, a pang of fear that could not have been more horrible had I been threatened with all the terrors of hell. I am not at all disturbed by thunder when alone. This incident illustrates very well two points—first the sympathetic induction of emotion by immediate instinctive reaction to the expression of emotion by another ; secondly, the specific character of loud noises as excitants of fear. Regarded as merely a sensory stimulus, the flash of lightning was far more violent than the thunder ; yet it provoked no fear in the child.

It has been pointed out on a previous page that this primitive sympathy implies none of the higher moral qualities. There are persons who are exquisitely sympathetic in this sense of feeling with another, experiencing distress at the sight of pain and grief, pleasure at the sight of joy, who yet are utterly selfish and are not moved in the least degree to relieve the distress they observe in others or to promote the pleasure that is reflected in themselves. Their sympathetic sensibility merely leads them to avoid all contact with distressful persons, books, or scenes, and to seek the company of the careless and the gay. And a too great sensibility of this kind is even adverse to the higher kind of conduct that seeks to relieve pain and to promote happiness ; for the sufferer's expressions of pain may induce so lively a distress in the onlooker as to incapacitate him for giving help. Thus in any case of personal accident, or where surgical procedure is necessary, many a woman is rendered quite useless by her sympathetic distress.[1]

Suggestion and Suggestibility

" Suggestion " is a word that has been taken over from popular speech and been specialised for psychological use. But even among psychologists it has been used in two rather different senses. A generation ago it was used in a sense very similar to that which it has in common speech ; one idea was said to suggest another. But this purpose is adequately served by the word " reproduction," and there is a growing tendency to use " suggestion " only in a still more technical and strict manner, and it is in this stricter sense that it is used in these pages. Psychologists have only in recent years begun to realise the vast scope and importance of suggestion and suggestibility in social life. Their attention was directed to the study of suggestion by the recognition that the phenomena of hypnotism, so long disputed and derided, are

[1] This is very noticeable in the case of vomiting. A tender mother will sometimes turn away from a vomiting child with an irresistible impulse of repulsion.

genuine expressions of a peculiar abnormal condition of the mind, and that the leading symptom of this condition of hypnosis is the patient's extreme liability to accept with conviction any proposition submitted to him. This peculiar condition was called one of suggestibility, and the process of communication between agent and patient which leads to the latter's acceptance of any proposition was called suggestion. There was for some time a tendency to regard suggestibility as necessarily an abnormal condition and suggestion as a psychological curiosity. But very quickly it was seen that there are many degrees of suggestibility, ranging from the slight degree of the normal educated adult to the extreme degree of the deeply hypnotised subject, and that suggestion is a process constantly at work among us, the understanding of which is of extreme importance for the social sciences.

It is difficult to find a definition of suggestion which will include all varieties and will yet mark it off clearly from other processes of communication ; and there is no sharp line to be drawn, for in many processes by which conviction is produced there is a more or less strong element of suggestion co-operating with logical processes. The following definition will, I think, cover all varieties : *Suggestion is a process of communication resulting in the acceptance with conviction of the communicated proposition in the absence of logically adequate grounds for its acceptance.* The measure of the suggestibility of any subject is, then, the readiness with which he thus accepts propositions. Of course, the proposition is not necessarily communicated in formal language, it may be implied by a mere gesture or interjection. The suggestibility of any subject is not of the same degree at all times ; it varies not only according to the topic and according to the source from which the proposition is communicated, but also with the condition of the subject's brain from hour to hour. The least degree of suggestibility is that of a wide-awake, self-reliant man of settled convictions, possessing a large store of systematically organised knowledge which he habitually brings to bear in criticism of all statements made to him.

Greater degrees of suggestibility are due in the main to conditions of four kinds : (1) Abnormal states of the brain, of which the relative dissociation obtaining in hysteria, hypnosis, normal sleep, and fatigue, is the most important ; (2) deficiency of knowledge or convictions relating to the topic in regard to which the suggestion is made, and imperfect organisation of knowledge ; (3) the impressive character of the source from which the suggested proposition is communicated; (4) peculiarities of the character and native disposition of the subject.

Of these the first need not engage our attention, as it has but little part in normal social life. The operation of the other three conditions may be illustrated by an example. Suppose a man of wide scientific culture to be confronted with the proposition that the bodies of the dead will one day rise from their graves to live a new life. He does not accept it, because he knows that dead bodies buried in graves undergo a rapid and complete decomposition, and because the acceptance of the proposition would involve a shattering of the whole of his strongly and systematically organised knowledge of natural processes. But the same proposition may be readily accepted by a child or a savage for lack of any system of critical belief and knowledge that would conflict with it. Such persons may accept almost any extravagant proposition with primitive credulity. But, for the great majority of civilised adults of little scientific culture, the acceptance or rejection of the proposition will depend upon the third and fourth of the conditions enumerated above. Even a young child or a savage may reject such a proposition with scorn if it is made to him by one of his fellows ; but, if the statement is solemnly affirmed by a recognised and honoured teacher, supported by all the prestige and authority of an ancient and powerful Church, not only children and savages, but most civilised adults, will accept it, in spite of a certain opposition offered by other beliefs and knowledge that they possess. Suggestion mainly dependent for its success on this condition may be called *prestige suggestion*.

But not all persons of equal knowledge and culture

are equally open to prestige suggestion. Here the fourth factor comes into play, namely, character and native disposition. As regards the latter the most important condition determining individual suggestibility seems to be the relative strengths of the two instincts that were discussed in Chapter III. under the names "instincts of self-assertion" and "subjection" Personal contact with any of our fellows seems regularly to bring one or other, or both, of these two instincts into play. The presence of persons whom we regard as our inferiors in the particular situation of the moment evokes the impulse of self-assertion ; towards such persons we are but little or not at all suggestible. But, in the presence of persons who make upon us an impression of power or of superiority of any kind, whether merely of size or physical strength, or of social standing, or of intellectual reputation, or, perhaps, even of tailoring, the impulse of submission is brought into play, and we are thrown into a submissive, receptive attitude towards them ; or, if the two impulses are simultaneously evoked, there takes place a painful struggle between them and we suffer the complex emotional disturbance known as bashful feeling.[1] In so far as the impulse of submission predominates we are suggestible towards the person whose presence evokes it. Persons in whom this instinct is relatively strong will, other things being the same, be much subject to prestige suggestion ; while, on the other hand, persons in whom this impulse is weak and the opposed instinct of self-assertion is strong will be apt to be self-confident, "cocksure" persons, and to be but little subject to prestige suggestion. In the course of character-formation by social intercourse, excessive strength of either of these impulses may be rectified or compensated to some extent ; the able, but innately submissive, man may gain a reasonable confidence ; the man of self-assertive disposition may, if not stupid, learn to recognise his own weaknesses ; and in so far as these compensations are effected, liability to prestige suggestion will be diminished or increased.

Children are, then, inevitably suggestible, firstly,

[1] See p. 126, for bashfulness.

because of their lack of knowledge and lack of systematic organisation of such knowledge as they have ; secondly, because the superior size, strength, knowledge, and reputation of their elders tend to evoke the impulse of submission and to throw them into the receptive attitude. And it is in virtue largely of their suggestibility that they so rapidly absorb the knowledge, beliefs, and especially the sentiments, of their social environment. But most adults also remain suggestible, especially towards mass-suggestion and towards the propositions which they know to be supported by the whole weight of society or by a long tradition. To the consideration of the social importance of suggestion we must return in a later chapter.

This brief discussion may be concluded by the repudiation of a certain peculiar implication attached to the word " suggestion " by some writers. They speak of " suggestive ideas " and of ideas working suggestively in the mind, implying that such ideas and such working have some peculiar potency—a potency that would seem to be almost of a magical character ; but they do not succeed in making clear in what way these ideas and their operations differ from others. The potency of the idea conveyed by suggestion seems to be nothing but the potency of conviction ; and convictions produced by logical methods seem to have no less power to determine thought and action, or even to influence the vital processes, than those produced by suggestion ; the principal difference is that by suggestion conviction may be produced in regard to propositions that are insusceptible of logical demonstration, or even are opposed to the evidence of perception and inference.

A few words must be said about *contra-suggestion*. By this word it is usual to denote the mode of action of one individual on another which results in the second accepting, in the absence of adequate logical grounds, the contrary of the proposition asserted or implied by the agent. There are persons with whom this result is very liable to be produced by any attempt to exert suggestive influence, or even by the most ordinary and casual utterance. One remarks to such a person that

it is a fine day, and, though, up to that moment, he may
have formulated no opinion about the weather, and have
been quite indifferent to it, he at once replies, "Well, I
don't agree with you.   I think it is perfectly horrid
weather."   Or one says to him, "I think you ought to
take a holiday," and, though he had himself contemplated this course, he replies, "No, I don't need one,"
and becomes more immovably fixed in this opinion and
the corresponding course of action the more he is urged
to adopt their opposites.   Some children display this
contra-suggestibility very strongly for a period and
afterwards return to a normal degree of suggestibility.
But in some persons it becomes habitual or chronic ;
they take a pride in doing and saying nothing like other
people, in dressing and eating differently, in defying all
the minor social conventions.   Commonly, I believe,
such persons regard themselves as displaying great
strength of character and cherish their peculiarity.   In
such cases the permanence of the attitude may have
very complex mental causes ; but in its simpler instances,
and probably at its inception in all instances, contra-
suggestion seems to be determined by the undue dominance of the impulse of self-assertion over that of submission, owing to the formation of some rudimentary
sentiment of dislike for personal influence resulting from
an unwise exercise of it—a sentiment which may have
for its object the influence of some one person or personal
influence in general.

Imitation

This word has been used by M. Tarde in his well-
known sociological treatises to cover processes of sympathy and suggestion as well as the processes to which
the name is more usually applied, and, since the verb
" to suggest " can be applied only to the part of the
agent in the process of suggestion, and since we need
some verb to describe the part of the patient, it is perhaps
legitimate to extend the meaning of the word " imitate "
in this way, so as to make it cover the process of accepting
a suggestion

But in the more strict sense of the word " imitation,"
it is applicable only to the imitation or copying by one
individual of the actions, the bodily movements, of
another. Imitation and imitativeness in this narrower
sense of the words are usually ascribed to an instinct.
Thus James writes : " This sort of imitativeness is
possessed by man in common with other gregarious
animals, and is an instinct in the fullest sense of the
term." [1] Baldwin also uses the phrase " instinct of
imitation " and its equivalents,[2] but applies the word
" imitation " to so great a variety of processes that it
can hardly be supposed he means to attribute all of them
to the operation of this assumed instinct.

The reasons for refusing to recognise an instinct of
imitation may be stated as follows : Imitative actions
are extremely varied, for every kind of action may be
imitated ; there is therefore nothing specific in the nature
of the imitative movements and in the nature of the
sense-impressions by which the movements are excited
or guided. And this variety of movement and of sense-
impression is not due to complication of a congenital
disposition, such as takes place in the case of all the true
instincts ; for this variety characterises imitative movements from the outset. More important is the fact that,
underlying the varieties of imitative action, there is no
common affective state and no common impulse seeking
satisfaction in some particular change of state. And we
have seen reason to regard such a specific impulse, prompting to continued action until its satisfaction is secured,
as the most essential feature of every truly instinctive
process. Further, if we consider the principal varieties
of imitative action, we find that all are explicable without
the assumption of a special instinct of imitation. Imitative
actions of at least three, perhaps of five, distinct classes
may be distinguished, according to the kind of mental
process of which they are the outcome.

   1. The expressive actions that are sympathetically

---

[1] *Principles of Psychology*, vol. ii. p. 408.
[2] *Mental Development, Methods and Processes,* 3rd edition, p. 281
New York, 1906.

excited in the way discussed under the head of " sympathy " form one class of imitative actions.   Thus, when a child responds to a smile with a smile, when he cries on hearing another child cry, or when he runs to hide himself on seeing other children running frightened to shelter, he may be said to be imitating the actions of others.   If we were right in our conclusions regarding the responses of primitive sympathy, these outwardly imitative actions are instinctive, and are due, not to an instinct of imitation, but to special adaptations of the principal instinctive dispositions on their sensory sides, and they are secondary to the sympathetic induction of the emotions and feelings they express.   Imitative actions of this sort are displayed by all the gregarious animals, and they are the only kind of which most of the animals seem capable.   They are displayed on a great scale by crowds of human beings and are the principal source of the wild excesses of which crowds are so often guilty.

2. Imitative actions of a second class are simple ideo-motor actions.   The clearest examples are afforded by subjects in hypnosis and in certain other abnormal conditions.   Many hypnotised subjects will, if their attention is forcibly drawn to the movements of the hypnotiser, imitate his every action.   A certain proportion of the people of the Malay race are afflicted with a disorder known as *làtah*,[1] which renders them liable to behave like the hypnotic subject in this respect.   And all of us, if our attention is keenly concentrated on the movements of another person, are apt to make, at least in a partial incipient fashion, every movement we observe—*e.g.*, on watching a difficult stroke in billiards, the balancing of a tight-rope walker, the rhythmic swaying of a dancer In all these cases the imitative movement seems to be due to the fact that the visual presentation of the movement of another is apt to evoke the representation of a similar movement of one's own body, which, like all motor representations, tends to realise itself immediately in

[1] An excellent account of this peculiar affliction may be found in Sir Hugh Clifford's *Studies in Brown Humanity*, as also in Sir F. A. Swettenham's *Malay Sketches*.

movement. Many of the imitative movements of children
are of this class. Some person attracts a child's curious
attention, by reason perhaps of some unfamiliar trait ;
the child becomes absorbed in watching him and presently
imitates his movements. It seems to be in virtue of
this simp'e ideo-motor imitation that a child so easily
picks up, as we say, the peculiarities of gesture, and the
facial expressions and deportment generally, of those
among whom he lives. This kind of imitation may be in
part voluntary and so merges into a third kind—deliberate, voluntary, or self-conscious imitation.

3. Some person, or some kind of skilled action,
excites our admiration, and we take the admired person
for our model in all things or deliberately set ourselves
to imitate the action.

Between the second and third kinds is a fourth kind
of imitation allied to both, and affording for the child a
transition from the one to the other. In cases of this
fourth type the imitator, a child say, observes a certain
action, and his attention is concentrated, not on the
movements, but on the effects produced by the movements.
When the child again finds himself in a situation similar
to that of the person he has observed, the idea of the
effect observed comes back to mind and perhaps leads
directly to action. For example, a child observes an elder
person throw a piece of paper on the fire ; then, when on
a later occasion the child finds himself in the presence of
fire and paper, he is very apt to imitate the action ; he
produces a similar effect, though he may do so by means
of a very different combination of movements. This kind
of imitation is perhaps in many cases to be regarded as
simple ideo-motor action due to the tendency of the idea
to realise itself in action ; but in other cases various
impulses may be operative.

For the sake of completeness a fifth kind of imitation
may be mentioned. It is the imitation by very young
children of movements that are not expressive of feeling
or emotion; it is manifested at an age when the child
cannot be credited with ideas of movement or with deliberate self-conscious imitation. A few instances of this sort

have been reported by reliable observers ; *e.g.*, Preyer [1] stated that his child imitated the protrusion of his lips when in the fourth month of life. These cases have been regarded, by those who have not themselves witnessed similar actions, as chance coincidences, because it is impossible to bring them under any recognised type of imitation. I have, however, carefully verified the occurrence of this sort of imitation in two of my own children ; one of them on several occasions during his fourth month repeatedly put out his tongue when the person whose face he was watching made this movement. For the explanation of any such simple imitation of a particular movement at this early age, we have to assume the existence of a very simple perceptual disposition having this specific motor tendency, and, since we cannot suppose such a disposition to have been acquired at this age, we are compelled to suppose it to be innately organised. Such an innate disposition would be an extremely simple rudimentary instinct. It may be that every child inherits a considerable number of such rudimentary instincts, and that they play a considerable part in facilitating the acquisition of new movements, especially perhaps of speech-movements.

We shall have to consider in later chapters the ways in which these three forms of mental interaction, sympathy, suggestion, and imitation, play their all-important parts in the moulding of the individual by his social environment, and in the life of societies generally.

Play

Another tendency, one that the human mind has in common with many of the animals, demands brief notice, namely, the *tendency to play*. Play also is sometimes ascribed to an instinct ; but no one of the many varieties of playful activity can properly be ascribed to an instinct of play. Nevertheless, play must be reckoned among the native tendencies of the mind of high social value. Children and the young of many species of animal take

[1] *Die Seele des Kindes*, 5te Auflage, Leipzig, 1900, S. 180.

to play spontaneously without any teaching or example. Several theories of play have been put forward, each claiming to sum up the phenomena in one brief formula. The oldest of the modern theories was proposed by the poet Schiller, and was developed by Herbert Spencer. According to this view, play is always the expression of a surplus of nervous energy. The young creature, being tended and fed by its parents, does not expend its energy upon the quest of food, in earning its daily bread, and therefore has a surplus store of energy which overflows along the most open nervous channels, producing purposeless movements of the kind that are most frequent in real life. There is, no doubt, an element of truth in the theory, but it is clearly inadequate to account for the facts, even in the case of the simple play of animals. It does not sufficiently account for the forms the play activities take ; still less is it compatible with the fact that young animals, as well as young children, will often play till they are exhausted. The element of truth is that the creature is most disposed to play when it is so well nourished and rested that it has a surplus of stored energy. But this is true also of work.

Others, looking chiefly at the play of children, have regarded their play as a special instance of the operation of the law of recapitulation ; and they have sought to show that the child retraverses in his play the successive culture periods of human history, owing to the successive development or ripening of native tendencies to the forms of activity supposed to have been characteristic of these periods. This recapitulatory theory of play and the educational practice based on it are founded on the fallacious belief that, as the human race traversed the various culture periods, its native mental constitution acquired very special tendencies, and that each period of culture was, as it were, the expression of a certain well-marked stage in the evolution of the human mind. This view can hardly be accepted, for we have little reason to suppose that human nature has undergone any such profound modifications in the course of the development of civilisation out of barbarism and savagery.

Professor Karl Groos [1] has recently propounded a new theory of play.   He sets out from the consideration of the play of young animals, and he points out the obvious utility to them of play as a preparation for the serious business of life, as a perfecting by practice of the more specialised and difficult kinds of activity on the successful exercise of which their survival in the struggle for existence must depend.   Consider the case of the kitten playing with a ball on the floor   It is clear that, in the course of such playing, the kitten improves its skill in movements of the kind that will be needed for the catching of its prey when it is thrown upon its own resources.   Or take the case of puppies playfully fighting with one another. It seems clear that the practice they get in quick attack and avoidance must make them better fighters than they would become if they never played in this way.

Starting out from considerations of this sort, Professor Groos argues that the occurrence of youthful play among almost all animals that in mature life have to rely upon rapid and varied skilled movements justifies us in believing that the period of immaturity, with its tendency to playful activities, is a special adaptation of the course of individual development, an adaptation that enables the creature to become better fitted to cope with its environment than it could be if it enjoyed no such period of play.   Groos therefore reverses the Schiller-Spencer dictum, and says—It is not that young animals play because they are young and have surplus nervous energy : we must believe rather that the higher animals have this period of youthful immaturity in order that they may play.   The youthful play-tendencies are, then, according to this view, special racial endowments of high biological utility, the products, no doubt, of the operation of natural selection.   If we ask—In what does this special adaptation consist ? the answer is—it consists in the tendency for the various instincts (on the skilled exercise of which adult efficiency depends) to ripen and to come into action in each individual of the species before they are needed for serious use.   We have other and better grounds for

[1] *The Play of Animals* and *The Play of Man.*

believing that the time of ripening of any instinct in the individuals of any species is liable to be shifted forwards or backwards in the age-scale during the course of racial evolution, so that the order of their ripening and of the appearance of the various instinctive activities in the individual does not conform to the law of recapitulation. There is, therefore, nothing improbable in this view that play is determined by the premature ripening of instincts. But it will not fully account for all the facts of animal play, and still less for all forms of children's play. There remains a difficulty of a very interesting kind.

Consider the case of young dogs playfully fighting together. If we simply assume that this is the expression of the prematurely ripened pugnacious instinct, we ought to expect to find the young dogs really fighting and doing their best to hurt one another ; and, since anger is the affective state that normally accompanies the exercise of this instinct, we should expect to observe every symptom of anger as the dogs roll about together. But it is perfectly clear that, although the dogs are capable of anger on other occasions, they make all the movements of combat without anger and in a peculiarly modified manner ; one seizes the other by the throat and pins him to the ground, and so forth ; but all this is done in such a way as not to hurt his opponent ; the teeth are never driven home, and no blood is drawn. That they do no hurt to one another is by no means due to lack of muscular power or of sharp teeth ; nor is there any lack of energy in the movements in general ; in merely chasing one another the utmost exertions are made. This peculiar modification of the combative movements seems to be an essential character of the playful fighting of many young animals, and boys are no exception to the rule. How is it to be accounted for and reconciled with Professor Groos's theory of play ? Mr. F. H. Bradley has made a suggestion in answer to this question.[1] He takes the case of the playful biting of young dogs as typical of play, and points out that, not only in this case but in many others also, a certain restraint of action is manifested in play ; and he

[1] *Mind*, N.S., vol. xv. p. 468.

proposes to regard a certain degree of self-restraint as the psychological characteristic of play. He takes the view that, when the dog bites your hand in play, he knows he must not exert so much force as to hurt you ; " there is restraint, a restraint which later may be formulated as the rule of the game." Mr. Bradley here seems to ascribe to the playfully biting dog a certain deliberate self-restraint. I think that in doing so he greatly over-estimates the complexity of the creature's mental process, and ascribes to it a degree of self-consciousness and a power of intelligent control of conduct of which it is really quite incapable. We might find a parallel to the psychological situation in which Bradley supposes the dog to be, in the case of a boy who, fighting with another in real earnest, is aware that, if he should do the other more than a slight hurt, he will bring punishment upon himself, and who therefore exerts a strong control over his actions and hits his opponent only in places where no great harm can be done To suppose that the mental process of the young dog at all approaches this degree of complexity is, I think, quite impossible. And that this view is untenable is shown also by the fact that young dogs display this playful fighting and its characteristic restraint of move-ment at a very early age, when they can hardly have learnt self-restraint from experience of the ill consequences of biting too hard. It is not that the young dog, when playfully fighting, has the impulse to bite with all his force and that he keeps a strong volitional control over his movements ; we must rather suppose, since the move-ments he makes are in all other respects like those of real combat, that the instinct of which they are the expression is a peculiarly modified form of the combative instinct.

The movements, with their characteristic differences from those of actual combat, must be regarded as instinc-tive, but as due to the excitement of some modified form of the combative instinct, an instinct differentiated from, and having an independent existence alongside, the original instinct. And that the movements are not the expression of the true combative instinct is shown also by the fact that the specific affective state, namely anger, which normally accompanies its excitement, is lacking in playful activity. Professor Groos's theory that play is due to the premature ripening of instincts needs, then, to be modified by the recognition of some special differentiation of the instincts which find expression in playful activity.

It is obvious that Groos's theory is applicable to some of the plays of children, especially the warlike and hunting games of boys and the doll-playing of girls. But there are other forms of childish play which cannot be accounted for in this way and which are not the direct expressions of instincts. The motives of play are various and often complex, and they cannot be characterised in any brief formula; nor can any hard-and-fast line be drawn between work and play. Beside the class of plays to which Professor Groos's formula is applicable we may recognise several principal classes of play motives—such are the desire of increased skill, the pleasure of make-believe, the pleasure in being a cause. But a motive that may co-operate with others in almost all games, and which among ourselves is seldom altogether lacking, is the desire to get the better of others, to emulate, to excel This motive plays an important part, not only in games, but in many of the most serious activities of life, to which it gives an additional zest. For many a politician it is a principal motive, and many a professional and many a commercial man continues his exertions, under the driving power of this motive, long after the immediate practical ends of his professional activity have been achieved; and in the collective life of societies it plays no small part. But, wherever it enters in, it is recognised that it imparts something of a playful character to the activity; a recognition which often finds expression in the phrase " playing the game " applied to activities of the most diverse and serious kinds.

Whence comes this strong desire and impulse to surpass our rivals ? We saw reason for refusing to accept a specific instinct of rivalry or emulation in the animals, for rivalry and emulation imply self-consciousness It is a defensible view that the impulse of rivalry derives from the instinct of self-assertion ; but, though it is probably complicated and reinforced in many cases by the co-operation of this impulse, it can hardly be wholly identified with it. Nor can it be identified with the combative impulse ; for this too seems to persist in the most highly civilised peoples with all its fierce strength and its specific brutal tendency to destroy the opponent. The obscurity of the subject and the importance of this impulse of rivalry in the life of societies tempt me to offer a speculation as to its nature and origin that is suggested by the issue of our discussion of the playful fighting of young animals.

The impulse of rivalry is to get the better of an opponent in some sort of struggle ; but it differs from the combative impulse in that it does not prompt to, and does not find satisfaction in, the destruction of the opponent. Rather, the continued existence of the rival, as such, but as a conquered rival, seems necessary for its full satisfaction ; and a benevolent condescension towards the conquered rival is not incompatible with the activity of the impulse, as it is with that of the combative impulse. Now, these peculiarities of the impulse of rivalry, when stripped of all intellectual complications, seem to be just those of the modified form of the combative impulse that seems to underlie the playful fighting of young animals. May it not be, then, that the impulse of rivalry is essentially this impulse to playful fighting, the impulse of an instinct differentiated from the combative instinct in the first instance in the animal world to secure practice in the movements of combat ? In favour of this view it may be pointed out that in the human race the native strength of the impulse of rivalry seems on the whole to run parallel with, or to be closely correlated with, the strength of the pugnacious instinct. The impulse of rivalry is very strong in the peoples of Europe, especially, perhaps, in the English people ; it constitutes the principal motive to almost all our many games, and it lends its strength to the support of almost every form of activity. It cannot be denied that we are a highly pugnacious people or that our Anglo-Saxon and Danish and Norman ancestors were probably the most terrible fighting-men the world has ever seen. On the other hand, men of the unwarlike races, *e.g.*, the mild Hindoo or the Burman, seem relatively free from the impulse of rivalry. To men of these races such games as football seem utterly absurd and irrational, and, in fact, they are absurd and irrational for all men born without the impulse of rivalry ; whereas men of warlike races, *e.g.*, the Maoris, who, like our ancestors, found for many generations their chief occupation and delight in warfare, take up such games keenly and even learn very quickly to beat us at them.

I think we may even observe in young boys the re-capitulation of the process of differentiation of the impulse of rivalry from the combative instinct   The latter usually comes into play at a very early age, but the former does not usually manifest itself until the age of four or five years. Up to this time the more active playing of boys is apt to be formless and vague, a mere running about and shouting, a form of play sufficiently accounted for by the Schiller-Spencer theory. But then the impulse of rivalry begins to work, and from that time it may dominate the boy's life more and more, in so far as his activities are spontaneous. In this connection it is important to note that the growth of self-consciousness must favour and strengthen the operation of this impulse, whereas it is rather adverse to the display of most of the other instinctive activities in their crude forms.[1]

[1] While living among the hybrid Papuan-Melanesian people of a small group of islands in the Torres Straits, I was much struck by the marked weakness of the impulse of rivalry among them. Though adults and children spent a large proportion of their time in playing, the spirit of rivalry was displayed but feebly in a few of the games and hardly at all in most of their playing. I failed completely to get the boys to take up various English games, and the failure seemed due to the lack of the impulse of rivalry. The same defect or peculiarity seemed to be responsible for the fact that the people were so content with their equality in poverty that, although opportunities for earning high wages in adjacent islands were abundant, few could be induced to avail themselves of them, or to work for more than a few months if they did so. These people are unwarlike, and the men and boys never fight with one another—a striking fact, which certainly is not to be explained by excellence of the social system or refinement of manners ; for but a generation ago these people were notorious for having devoured the crews of several vessels wrecked upon the islands.

A universal tendency of the mind, which is so familiar as to run some risk of being neglected, must be briefly mentioned ; namely, the tendency for every process to be repeated more readily in virtue of its previous occurrence and in proportion to the frequency of its previous repetitions. The formulation of this tendency may be named the law of habit, if the word " habit " is understood in the widest possible sense. In virtue of this tendency the familiar as such is preferred to the less familiar, the habitual and routine mode of action and reaction, in all departments of mental life, to any mode of action necessitating any degree of novel adjustment. And the more familiar and habitual is any mental process or mode of action in a situation of a given type, the more difficult is it to make any change or improvement in it and the more painful is any change of the character of the situation that necessitates an effort of readjustment. This is the great principle by which all acquisitions of the individual mind are preserved and in virtue of which the making of further acquisitions is rendered more difficult, through which the indefinite plasticity of the infant's mind gradually gives place to the elasticity of the mature mind.

Temperament

In order to complete this brief sketch of the more important features of the native mental constitution, a few words must be said about temperament. This is a very difficult subject which most psychologists are glad to leave alone. Yet temperament is the source of many of the most striking mental differences between individuals and peoples.

Under the head of temperamental factors we group a number of natively given constitutional conditions of our mental life that exert a constant influence on our mental processes. This influence may be slight at any one time, but since its effects are cumulative—*i.e.*, since it operates as a constant bias in one direction during mental development and the formation of habits—it is responsible for much in the mental make-up of the adult. Temperament is, as the ancients clearly saw, largely a matter of bodily constitution ; that is to say, that among the temperamental factors the influences on the mental life exerted by the great bodily organs occupy a prominent place. But there are other factors also, and it is impossible to bring them all under one brief formula ; and, since temperament is the resultant of these many relatively independent factors, it is impossible to distinguish any clearly defined classes of temperaments, as the ancients, as well as many modern authors, have attempted to do. Some of the best modern psychologists have been led into absurdities by attempting this impossible task. The truth is that we are only just beginning to gain some slight insight into the conditions of temperament, and progress in this respect must depend chiefly upon the progress of physiology. In one respect only can we make a decided advance upon the ancients—we can realise the great complexity of the problem and can frankly admit our ignorance.

The temperamental factors may conveniently be grouped in two principal classes—on the one hand, the influences exerted on the nervous system and, through it, on mental process by the functioning of the bodily organs ; on the other hand, general functional peculiarities of the nervous tissues. We may best grasp something of the nature of the former class by the observation of cases in which their influence is abnormally great. Of recent years some light has been thrown upon temperament by the discovery of the great influence exerted on mental life by certain organs whose functions had been, and in many respects still are, obscure. The most notable example is perhaps the thyroid body, a small mass of soft cellular tissue in the neck. We know now that defect of the functions of this organ may reduce any one of us to a state of mental apathy bordering on idiocy, and that its excessive activity produces the opposite effect and may throw the mind into an over-excitable condition verging on maniacal excitement. Again, we know that certain diseases tend to produce specific changes of temperament, that phthisis often gives it a bright and hopeful turn, diabetes a dissatisfied and cantankerous turn. It is clear that, in some such cases of profound alteration of temperament by bodily disorder, the effects are produced by means of the chemical products of metabolism, which, being thrown out of the disordered tissues into the blood and reaching the nervous system by way of the blood-stream, chemically modify its processes. It is probable that every organ in the body exerts in this indirect way some influence upon our mental life, and that temperament is in large measure the balance or resultant of all these many contributory chemical influences.

Most of the bodily organs probably co-operate in determining temperament in another way hardly less important. All of them are supplied with afferent nerves, nerves that constantly carry impulses up from the organs to the central nervous system. And all these impulses probably modify in some degree the general working of the nervous system and play some part in determining the "coenæsthesia," the obscure background of consciousness on which the general tone of our mental life chiefly depends. The organs of reproduction afford the most striking example of this kind of temperamental influence. The skeletal system of muscles also probably exerts a great influence of this kind—a well-developed and active muscular system tends to maintain a certain tone of the nervous system that favours an alert and confident habit of mind. Perfect functioning of all the bodily organs not only favours in this way mental activity in general, but tends to an objective habit of mind ; whereas imperfection of organic functions tends to produce an undue prominence in consciousness of the bodily self and, therefore, an introspective and brooding habit of mind.

As regards the part played by the general constitution of the nervous system itself in determining temperament, we are still more ignorant than in regard to the influence of the bodily organs. A few characters of the nervous tissues we can point to with confidence as determining differences of temperament. Such are native differences of excitability, of rapidity of response and transmission of the nervous impulse, and differences in respect to fatigability and rapidity of recuperation. But there are probably other subtle differences of which we know nothing.

Temperament, then, is a complex resultant of many factors each of which is in the main natively determined, and, though they are alterable perhaps by disease and the influence of the physical environment, especially by temperature and food, they are but little capable of being modified by voluntary effort ; and the mental development of individuals is, as it were, constantly biased in this or that direction by peculiarities of temperament, the selective activity of the mind is given this or that trend ; *e.g.*, the child natively endowed with a cheerful temperament will be receptive to bright influences, his thoughts will tend to dwell on the future in pleased anticipation, optimistic ideas will readily find a foothold in his mind, while gloomy, pessimistic ideas will gain no permanent influence over him in spite of being intellectually grasped. And with the child of gloomy temperament all this will be reversed. In this way temperament largely determines our outlook on life, our cast of thought and lines of action.

Temperament must be carefully distinguished from disposition and from character, though these distinctions are not always observed by popular speech and thought. The disposition of a person is the sum of all the innate dispositions or instincts with their specific impulses or tendencies of the kind discussed in Chapter II. Differences of disposition are due to native differences in the strengths of the impulses of the instincts, or to differences in their strength induced by use and disuse in the course of individual development, or more rarely to absence of one or other of the instincts. Thus we properly speak of an irascible, or tender, or timid disposition ; not of irascible, tender, or timid temperament. Character, on the other hand, is the sum of acquired tendencies built up on the native basis of disposition and temperament ; it includes our sentiments and our habits in the widest sense of the term, and is the product of the interaction of disposition and temperament with the physical and social environment under the guidance of intelligence. Thus a man's temperament and disposition are in the main born with him and are but little alterable by any effort he may make, whereas character is made largely by his own efforts.

CHAPTER V

THE NATURE OF THE SENTIMENTS AND THE
CONSTITUTION OF SOME OF THE COMPLEX
EMOTIONS

WE seldom experience the primary emotions discussed in Chapter III. in the pure or unmixed forms in which they are commonly manifested by the animals. Our emotional states commonly arise from the simultaneous excitement of two or more of the instinctive dispositions ; and the majority of the names currently used to denote our various emotions are the names of such mixed, secondary, or complex emotions. That the great variety of our emotional states may be properly regarded as the result of the compounding of a relatively small number of primary or simple emotions is no new discovery. Descartes, for example, recognised only six primary emotions, or passions as he termed them, namely, admiration, love, hatred, desire, joy, and sadness ; and he wrote, " All the others are composed of some out of these six and derived from them." He does not seem to have formulated any principles for the determination of the primaries and the distinction of them from the secondaries.

The compounding of the primary emotions is largely, though not wholly, due to the existence of sentiments, and some of the complex emotional processes can only be generated from sentiments. Before going on to discuss the complex emotions, we must therefore try to understand as clearly as possible the nature of a sentiment.

The word " sentiment " is still used in several different senses. M. Ribot and other French authors use its French equivalent as covering all the feelings and emotions, as the most general name for the affective aspect of mental processes. We owe to Mr. A. F. Shand [1] the recognition of features of our mental constitution of a most important kind that have been strangely overlooked by other psychologists, and the application of the word "sentiments" to denote features of this kind. Mr. Shand points out that our emotions, or, more strictly speaking, our emotional dispositions, tend to become organised in systems about the various objects and classes of objects that excite them. Such an organised system of emotional tendencies is not a fact or mode of experience, but is a feature of the complexly organised structure of the mind that underlies all our mental activity. To such an organised system of emotional tendencies centred about some object Mr. Shand proposes to apply the name "sentiment." This application of the word is in fair accordance with its usage in popular speech, and there can be little doubt that it will rapidly be adopted by psychologists.

The conception of a sentiment, as defined by Mr. Shand, enables us at once to reduce to order many of the facts of the life of impulse and emotion, a province of psychology which hitherto has been chaotic and obscure. That, in spite of the great amount of discussion of the affective life in recent centuries, it should have been reserved for a contemporary writer to make this very important discovery is an astonishing fact, so obvious and so necessary does the conception seem when once it has been grasped. The failure of earlier writers to arrive at the conception must be attributed to the long prevalence of the narrow and paralysing doctrine according to which the task of the psychologist is merely to observe, analyse, and describe the content of his own consciousness.

The typical sentiments are love and hate, and it will suffice for our present purpose if we briefly consider the nature and mode of formation of these two. Now, it is a source of great confusion that, sentiments never having

[1] "Character and the Emotions," *Mind*, N.S., vol. v., and "M. Ribot's Theory of the Passions," *Mind*, N.S., vol. xvi.

been clearly distinguished from the emotions until Mr. Shand performed this great service to psychology, the words "love" and "hate" have been used to denote both emotions and sentiments. Thus the disposition of the primary emotion we have discussed under the name of " tender emotion " is an essential constituent of the system of emotional dispositions that constitutes the sentiment of love ; and the name " love " is often applied both to this emotion and to the sentiment. In a similar way the word " hate " is commonly applied to a complex emotion compounded of anger and fear and disgust, as well as to the sentiment which comprises the dispositions to these emotions as its most essential constituents. But it is clear that one may properly be said to love or to hate a man at the times when he is not at all present to one's thought and when one is experiencing no emotion of any kind. What is meant by saying that a man loves or hates another is that he is liable to experience any one of a number of emotions and feelings on contemplating that other, the nature of the emotion depending upon the situation of the other ; that is to say, common speech recognises that love and hate are, not merely emotions, but enduring tendencies to experience certain emotions whenever the loved or hated object comes to mind ; therefore, in refusing to apply the names "love" and " hate " to any of the emotions and in restricting them to these enduring complex dispositions which are the sentiments, no more violence is done to language than is absolutely necessary for the avoidance of the confusion that has hitherto prevailed. It must be noted that the sentiments of love and hate comprise many of the same emotional dispositions ; but the situations of the object of the sentiment that evoke the same emotions are very different and in the main of opposite character in the two cases. Thus, as Shand points out, when a man has acquired the sentiment of love for a person or other object, he is apt to experience tender emotion in its presence, fear or anxiety when it is in danger, anger when it is threatened, sorrow when it is lost, joy when the object prospers or is restored to him, gratitude towards him who does good to it, and so on; and, when he hates a person, he experiences fear or anger or both on his approach, joy when that other is injured, anger when he receives favours.

It is going too far to say, as Shand does, that with inversion of the circumstances of the object all the emotions called forth by the loved object are repeated in relation to the hated object; for the characteristic and most essential emotion of the sentiment of love is tender emotion, and this is not evoked by any situation of the hated object; its disposition has no place in the sentiment of hate. It is clear, nevertheless, that the objects of these two very different sentiments may arouse many of the same emotions, and that the two sentiments comprise emotional dispositions that are in part identical, or, in other words, that some of the emotional dispositions, or central nuclei of the instincts, are members of sentiments of both kinds. It is, I think, helpful, at least to those who make use of visual imagery, to attempt to picture a sentiment as a nervous disposition and to schematise it crudely by the aid of a diagram. Let us draw a number of circles lying in a row, and let each circle stand for one of the primary emotional dispositions. We are to suppose that the excitement of each one of these is accompanied by the corresponding emotion with its specific impulse. These dispositions must be regarded as natively independent of one another, or unconnected. Let A be the object of a sentiment of hate and B be the object of a sentiment of love; and let α in our diagram stand for the complex neural disposition whose excitement underlies the idea or presentation of A, and let β be the corresponding disposition concerned in the presentation of B. Then we must suppose that α becomes intimately connected with R, F, and P, the central nuclei of the instincts of repulsion, fear, and pugnacity, and less intimately with C and S, those of curiosity and of submission, but not at all with T, the central nucleus of the tender or parental instinct. Whenever, then, α comes into play (*i.e.*, whenever the idea of A rises to consciousness) its excitement tends to spread at once to all these dispositions ; and we must suppose that they are thrown into a condition of sub-excitement which very easily rises to discharging-point in any one of them, or in several together—*e.g.*, in P and R, when the emotional state of the subject becomes one of mingled anger and disgust, and the impulses of these two emotions deter-mine his actions, attitudes, and expressions. Similarly β must be supposed to be connected most intimately with T, the disposition of the tender emotion, and less

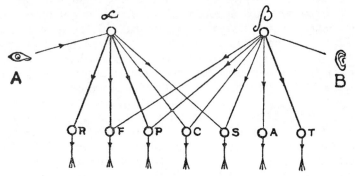

Diagram to illustrate the neural bases of the sentiments of hate and love. A is the object of the sentiment of hate, B that of the sentiment of love ; α and β are the neural dispositions whose excitement accompanies presentations or ideas of A and B respectively ; α is connected with the affective-conative dispositions R, F, P, C, S, and β with T, A, S, C, P, F, with degrees of intimacy indicated by the thicknesses of the connecting lines. The letters of the lower row stand for the names of the instincts, as follows : R=Re-pulsion, F=Fear, P=Pugnacity, C=Curiosity, S=Subjection, A=Self-assertion, T=Parental instinct.

intimately with A, S, C, P, and F, and not at all with R. If this diagram represents the facts, however crudely and inadequately, we may say that the structural basis of the sentiment is a system of nerve-paths by means of which the disposition of the idea of the object of the sentiment is functionally connected with several emotional dispositions. The idea, taken in the usual sense of the word as something that is stored in the mind, may there-fore be said to be the essential nucleus of the sentiment, without which it cannot exist, and through the medium of which several emotional dispositions are connected together to form a functional system. The emotional dispositions comprised within the system of any sentiment are, then, not directly connected together; and, in accordance with the law of forward conduction, the excitement of any one of them will not spread backwards to the cognitive dispositions, but only in the efferent direction, as indicated by the arrows in the diagram. Hence any one such disposition may become an organic constituent of an indefinitely large number of sentiments.

The process by which such a complex psycho-physical disposition or system of dispositions is built up may be supposed to be essentially that process (discussed in Chapter II.) by which an instinctive disposition becomes capable of being directly excited by other objects than its natively given objects, working in conjunction with the law of habit. The oftener the object of the sentiment becomes the object of any one of the emotions comprised in the system of the sentiment, the more readily will it evoke that emotion again, because, in accordance with the law of habit, the connections of the psycho-physical dispositions become more intimate the more frequently they are brought into operation.

After this brief exposition, and this attempt at a physiological interpretation, of Mr. Shand's doctrine of the sentiment, we may pass on to consider some of the complex emotions, and to attempt to exhibit them as fusions of the primary emotions we have distinguished. If we find that most of the complex emotions can be satisfactorily displayed as fusions of some two, or more, of the primary emotions we have distinguished, together with feelings of pleasure and pain, excitement and relaxation, this will be good evidence that the emotions we have designated as the primaries are truly primary, and it will confirm the principle by which we were guided in the choice of these primaries—the principle, namely, that each primary emotion accompanies the excitement of one of the instincts, and is the affective aspect of a simple instinctive mental process.

Since the primary emotions may be combined in a

large number of different ways, and since the primaries that enter into the composition of a secondary emotion may be present in many different degrees of intensity, the whole range of complex emotions presents an indefinitely large number of qualities that shade imperceptibly into one another without sharp dividing lines. The names provided by common speech designate merely a certain limited number of the most prominent of these complexes.

In seeking to analyse the complex emotions we must rely largely on the method recommended by Mr. Shand— we must, that is to say, observe the conative tendencies of the emotions, the nature of the actions to which they impel us. For every emotion, no matter how complex it may be, has its characteristic conjunction of motor tendencies, which together give rise to the characteristic attitudes and expressions of the emotion. How true this is we may realise by considering how successfully a skilful actor can portray even the more complex emotions.

And in attempting to analyse any emotion we must consider it as experienced and displayed at a high pitch of intensity ; for we cannot hope to recognise the elementary qualities and impulses of the primary emotions in complexes of low intensity.

We may roughly divide the complex emotional states into two groups—on the one hand those which do not necessarily imply the existence of any organised sentiment, and on the other hand those which can be experienced only in virtue of the existence of some sentiment within the system of which they may be said to be excited. We will consider first some of the more important emotions of the former class.

Some of the Complex Emotions that do not necessarily imply the Existence of Sentiments

Admiration.—This is certainly a true emotion, and is as certainly not primary. It is distinctly a complex affective state and implies a considerable degree of mental development. We can hardly suppose any of the animals to be capable of admiration in the proper sense of the word, nor is it displayed by very young children. It is not merely a pleasurable perception or contemplation. One may get a certain pleasure from the perception or contemplation of an object without feeling any admiration for it ; *e.g.*, a popular ditty played on a barrel-organ may give one pleasure, though one admires neither the ditty nor the mode of its production, and though one may a little despise oneself on account of the pleasure one feels. Nor is it merely intellectual and pleasurable appreciation of the greatness or excellence of the object. There seem to be two primary emotions essentially involved in the complex state provoked by the contemplation of the admired object, namely, wonder and negative self-feeling or the emotion of submission. Wonder is revealed by the impulse to approach and to continue to contemplate the admired object, for, as we saw, this is the character-istic impulse of the instinct of curiosity ; and wonder is clearly expressed on the face in intense admiration. In children one may observe the element of wonder very clearly expressed and dominant. " Oh, how wonderful ! " or—" Oh, how clever ! " or—" How did you do it ? " are phrases in which a child naturally expresses its admira-tion and by which the element of wonder and the impulse of curiosity are clearly revealed. And as soon as we feel that we completely understand the object we have admired, and can wholly account for it, our wonder ceases and the emotion evoked by it is no longer admiration.

But admiration is more than wonder.[1] We do not simply proceed to examine the admired object as we should one that provokes merely our curiosity or wonder. We approach it slowly, with a certain hesitation ; we are humbled by its presence, and, in the case of a person whom we intensely admire, we become shy, like a child in the presence of an adult stranger ; we have the impulse to shrink together, to be still, and to avoid attracting his attention ; that is to say, the instinct of submission, of self-abasement, is excited, with its corresponding emotion

[1] I would remind the reader that " wonder " is here used in a sense a little different from the usual one (see p. 50).

of negative self-feeling, by the perception that we are in the presence of a superior power, something greater than ourselves. Now, this instinct and this emotion are primarily and essentially social. The primary condition of their excitement is the presence of a person bigger and more powerful than oneself; and, when we admire such an object as a picture or a machine, or other work of art, the emotion still has this social character and personal reference; the creator of the work of art is more or less clearly present to our minds as the object of our emotion, and often we say, " What a wonderful man he is ! "

Is, then, the emotion of admiration capable of being evoked in us only by other persons and their works ? It is obviously true that we admire natural objects, a beautiful flower or landscape, or a shell, or the perfect structure of an animal and its nice adaptation to its mode of life. In these cases no known person is called to mind as the object of our admiration ; but, just because admiration implies and refers to another person, is essentially, in so far as it involves negative self-feeling, an attitude towards a person, it leads us to postulate a person or personal power as the creator of the object that calls it forth. Hence in all ages the admiration of men for natural objects has led them to personify the power, or powers, that have brought those objects into being, either as superhuman beings who have created, and who preside over, particular classes of objects, or as a supreme Creator of all things ; and, if the intellect rejects all such conceptions as anthropomorphic survivals from a ruder age, the admiration of natural objects still leads men to personify, under the name of Nature, the power that has produced them. It is, I think, true that, if this sense of a personal power is not suggested by any object that we contemplate, the emotion we experience is merely wonder, or at least is not admiration. It is because negative self-feeling is an essential element in admiration that the extremely confident, self-satisfied, and thoroughly conceited person is incapable of admiration, and that genuine admiration implies a certain humility and generosity. It may be added that much admiration—all æsthetic admiration, in fact—includes also an element of pleasure, the conditions of which may be very complex.

As an example of the further complication of an emotion, let us consider the nature of our emotion if the object that excites our admiration is also of a threatening or mysterious nature and, therefore, capable of exciting fear—a tremendous force in action such as the Victoria Falls, or a display of the *aurora borealis*, or a magnificent thunderstorm. The impulse of admiration to draw near humbly and to contemplate the object is more or less neutralised by an impulse to withdraw, to run away, the impulse of fear. We are kept suspended in the middle distance, neither approaching very near nor going quite away ; admiration is blended with fear, and we experience the emotion we call **awe**.

Awe is of many shades, ranging from that in which admiration is but slightly tinged with fear to that in which fear is but slightly tinged with admiration. Admiration is, then, a binary compound, awe a tertiary compound And awe may be further blended to form a still more complex emotion. Suppose that the power that excites awe is also one that we have reason to regard as beneficent, one that, while capable of annihilating us in a moment, yet works for our good, sustains and protects us, one that evokes our gratitude. Awe then becomes compounded with gratitude and we experience the highly compound emotion of **reverence**. Reverence is the religious emotion *par excellence* ; few merely human powers are capable of exciting reverence, this blend of wonder, fear, gratitude, and negative self-feeling. Those human beings who inspire reverence, or who are by custom and convention considered to be entitled to inspire it, usually owe their reverend character to their being regarded as the ministers and dispensers of Divine power.

What, then, is **gratitude**, which enters into the emotion of reverence for the Divine power ? Gratitude is itself complex. It is a binary compound of tender emotion and negative self-feeling. To this view it may be objected—If tender emotion is the emotion of the parental instinct whose impulse is to protect, how can this emotion be evoked by the Divine power? The answer to this question is—In the same way as the child's tender emotion towards the parent is evoked, namely, by sympathy. Tender emotion occupies a peculiar position among the primary emotions, in that, being directed towards some other person and its impulse directly making for the good of that other, it is peculiarly apt to evoke by sympathetic reaction, of the kind we studied in Chapter IV., the same emotion in its object; and this sympathetically evoked tender emotion then finds its object most readily in the person to whom it owes its rise. But gratitude is not simply tender emotion sympathetically excited; a child or even an animal may excite our tender emotion in this way; *e.g.*, it may give us something that is utterly useless or embarrassing to us, and by doing so may touch our hearts, as we say; but I do not think that we then feel gratitude, even if the gift involves self-sacrifice on the part of the giver. Mr. Shand maintains that into gratitude there enters some sympathetic sorrow for the person who excites it, on account of the loss or sacrifice sustained by him in giving us that for which we are grateful. It is in this way he would account for the tender element in gratitude; for, according to his view, all tenderness is a blending of joy and sorrow, which are for him primary emotions. But surely we may experience gratitude for a kindness done to us that involves no loss or sacrifice for the giver, but is for him an act of purely pleasurable beneficence. I submit, then, that the other element in gratitude, the element that renders it different from, and more complex than, simple tenderness, is that negative self-feeling which is evoked by the sense of the superior power of another. The act that is to inspire gratitude must make us aware, not only of the kindly feeling, the tender emotion, of the other towards us; it must also make us aware of his power, we must see that he is able to do for us something that we cannot do for ourselves. This element of negative self-feeling, then, is blended with tenderness in true gratitude, and its impulse, the impulse to withdraw from the attention of, or to humble oneself in the presence of, its object, more or less neutralises the impulse of the tender emotion to approach its object ; the attitude typical and symbolical of gratitude is that of kneeling to kiss the hand that gives. This element of negative self-feeling renders gratitude an emotion that is not purely pleasurable to many natures, makes it one that a proud man does not easily experience, and one that does less to develop a sentiment of affection than the giver of good things is apt to expect. And, if the seemingly beneficent act is done, not from pure kindliness or tenderness, but with condescension, if positive self-feeling and a gratified sense of power accompany or enter into the motive of the act, it is apt to evoke negative self-feeling without tenderness, a negative self-feeling painful in quality that may lead to the growth of a sentiment of dislike rather than of love.

Into reverence of the kind we have considered negative self-feeling enters from two sources, as an element of admiration and again as an element of gratitude. But there is a different kind of reverence into which tenderness enters directly, and not merely as an element of gratitude. Let us imagine ourselves standing before a great Gothic cathedral whose delicate and beautiful stonework is crumbling to dust. We shall probably feel admiration for it, and the spectacle of its decay, or of its delicate and perishable nature, awakens directly our tender emotion and protective impulse ; *i.e.*, we experience a tender admiration, a complex emotion for which we have no special name. Now let us imagine ourselves entering the cathedral, passing between vast columns of stone where the dim mysterious light is lost in dark recesses and where reign a stillness and a gloom like that of a great forest ; an element of fear is added to our emotion of tender admiration, and this converts it to reverence (or, if our tender emotion does not persist, to awe). This is a reverence that has less of the personal note, because less of negative self-feeling, than that of which gratitude is a component.[1]

[1] One is tempted to ask, Was it because the external aspect of the Gothic cathedral is apt to fall short of exciting the fear which is essential to reverence, that in so many cases the artists of the Middle Ages covered the exterior with grotesque and horrible figures, like those of Nôtre Dame of Paris ?

The history of religion seems to show us the gradual genesis of this highly complex emotion. Primitive religion seems to have kept separate the superhuman objects of its component emotions, the terrible or awe-inspiring powers on the one hand, the kindly beneficent powers that inspired gratitude on the other. And it was not until religious doctrine had undergone a long evolution that, by a process of syncretism or fusion, it achieved the conception of a Deity whose attributes were capable of evoking all the elements of the complex emotion of reverence.

There is another group of complex emotions of which anger and fear are the most prominent constituents. When an object excites our disgust, and at the same time our anger, the emotion we experience is **scorn**. The two impulses are apt to be very clearly expressed, the shrinking and aversion of disgust, and the impulse of anger to attack, to strike, and to destroy its object. This emotion is most commonly evoked by the actions of other men, by mean cruelty or underhand opposition to our efforts ; it is therefore one from which original moral judgments often spring. It is, I think, very apt to be complicated by positive self-feeling—we feel ourselves magnified by the presence of the moral weakness or littleness of the other, just as on a lower plane the physical weakness or smallness of those about one excites this positive self-feeling, with its tendency to expand the chest, throw up the head, and strut in easy confidence. The name " scorn " is often applied to an affective state of which this emotion is an element ; but, if this element is dominant, the emotion is that we experience when we are said to despise another, and its name is **contempt**, the substantive corresponding to the verb despise ; scorn, then, is a binary compound of anger and disgust, or a tertiary compound if positive self-feeling is added to these ; while contempt is a binary compound of disgust and positive self-feeling, differing from scorn in the absence of the element of anger.

Fear and disgust are very apt to be combined, as on

the near view of a snake or an alligator, and in some persons this binary emotion is provoked by a large number of animals, rats, moths, worms, spiders, and so on, and also by the mere appearance of some men, though more often by their characters.   It is the emotion we call **loathing**, and, in its most intense form, horror. Loathing is apt to be complicated by wonder, which then, in spite of the combined impulses of fear and disgust, keeps us hovering in the neighbourhood of the loathsome object, fascinated, as we say, or in horrible **fascination**.

Again, anger, fear, and disgust may be blended to form a tertiary compound, to which, if to any emotion, the name " hate " can be most properly applied, although it is better to reserve this name for the sentiment of intense dislike or hate, within the system of which this complex emotion is most commonly excited.

Envy is allied to this group of emotions. Without feeling confident as to its analysis, I would suggest that it is a binary compound of negative self-feeling and of anger ; the former emotion being evoked by the superior power or position of the object, the latter by the sense that the envied person is excluding us from the enjoyment of the goods or the position that he has or occupies. I do not think that true envy arises except when this sense of deprivation by, or opposition on the part of, the object is present ; as when, for example, another takes the prize we aimed at, or achieves the position we hoped to occupy, and therefore appears as an obstacle to the realisation of our ends.

Complex Emotions that imply the Existence of Sentiments

We may now consider some of the complex emotional states that we only experience in virtue of having previously acquired some sentiment for the object of the emotion.

Within the sentiment of love several well-defined compounds arise. **Reproach** seems to be a fusion of anger and of tender emotion. " Oh, how could you do it ! " is the natural expression of reproach. The person who is the object of the sentiment of love performs some action which, if performed by an indifferent person, would provoke our anger simply ; but tender emotion, which is habitually evoked by the mere thought of the object of our love, prevents the full development of our anger, fuses with it and softens it to reproach. This is the simplest form, as when a mother chides her little son for cruelty to an animal. A more complex form arises when the sentiment is reciprocated, or supposed to be reciprocated, and its object acts in a way that seems to show indifference to us. In this case the pain of the wound given to our self-regarding sentiment and of the check to our tender emotion is the prominent feature of the affective state and overshadows anger ; perhaps the name " reproach " is most properly given to this more complex state.

The threat of injury or destruction against the object of the sentiment of love excites in us anticipatory pain of its loss and perhaps also some anticipation of the sympathetic pain we should feel if the threat were realised ; and this pain, mingling with tender emotion, and perhaps with a little anger against the source of the threatened harm, gives rise to the state we call **anxiety** or solicitude. In popular language we are said to fear the loss of, or injury to, the object ; but that fear enters into this emotion seems to be very questionable.

Jealousy presents a difficult problem. Animals and very young children are commonly said to exhibit jealousy. A favourite dog will be emotionally moved by the sight of his master fondling a kitten or another dog ; he will sometimes slink away and hide himself and sulk, or he will keep pushing himself forward to be caressed, with sidelong glances at the kitten. Some very young children behave in a similar way, when their mother nurses another child. And in both cases the jealous creature is apt to exhibit anger towards the intruder. These facts do not necessitate the assumption that jealousy is a primary emotion, although, possibly, in order fully to account for them, we should have to admit an instinct of possession or ownership.[1] But even in these cases the existence of a sentiment of affection, however rudimentary, seems to be implied by this conduct. Certainly full-blown jealousy is only developed where some sentiment of love or attachment exists ; and the conditions of its excitement, which constitute the object of the emotion, are complex, being, not a single person and his situation or actions, but the relations between three persons. The presence of a third person who attempts to draw to himself the regard of the object of the sentiment does not of itself excite jealousy, though it may excite anger. Jealousy involves anger of this sort towards the third person, but also some painful check to one's own tender emotion and sentiment. It is, perhaps, possible to imagine a love so wholly disinterested that it would demand no reciprocation of its tender feeling. Such a sentiment would be incapable of jealousy, and, perhaps, a mother's love sometimes approximates to this type, though seldom. The sentiment of love commonly feeds upon, is sustained by, and demands reciprocation, which, being given, excites in turn a positive self-feeling or elation that fuses with the tender emotion, adding greatly to its pleasurable character. And the sentiment is apt to demand for its complete satisfaction the maximum of such reciprocation ; so long as we feel that this maximum is not attained we are uneasy, we lack the complete satisfaction of the self-expansive impulse, the impulse of positive self-feeling. And jealousy arises when the object of the sentiment gives to another, or merely is thought to give to another, any part of the regard thus claimed for the self. It is thus an unstable state of emotion, of which the most constant element is the painfully checked positive self-feeling, and which tends to oscillate between two poles, revenge and reproach, according as one or the other person is more prominently before consciousness. In some cases the tender emotion may be at a minimum or even perhaps lacking, and the sentiment within which this kind of jealousy arises is a purely egoistic sentiment : the object of it is regarded

[1] This we may perhaps identify with the instinct of acquisition mentioned in Chapter III.

merely as a part of one's property, a part of one's larger self, as one of the props on which one's pride is built up ; and the marks of affection, or of subjection, of the object towards oneself are valued merely as contributing to feed one's positive self-feeling and self-regarding sentiment. In this case any expression of regard for a third person on the part of the object of the sentiment provokes a jealousy of which the anger turns mainly upon that object itself.[1]

There is an emotion that is properly called **vengeful emotion** ; it is not merely anger, though anger may be a large element in it. It is of especial interest to the moralist, because it has been one of the principal sources of the institution of public justice, more especially of the branch dealing with personal injuries ; for the pursuit and punishment of murderers by the State, or by officers of the law, has only gradually replaced the system of private vengeance and the blood-feud. One respect in which the impulse of revenge differs from that of simple anger is its long persistence owing to its being developed in connection with a sentiment, generally the self-regarding sentiment. The act that, more certainly than any other, provokes vengeful emotion is the public insult, which, if not immediately resented, lowers one in the eyes of one's fellows. Such an insult calls out one's positive self-feeling, with its impulse to assert oneself and to make good one's value and power in the public eye. If the insult is at once avenged, the emotion is perhaps properly called **resentment**. It is when immediate satisfaction of the impulse of angry self-assertion is impossible that it gives rise to a painful desire ; it is then the insult rankles in one's breast ; and this desire can only be satisfied by an assertion of one's power, by returning an equally great or greater insult or injury to the offender—by " getting even with him." This painful struggle of positive self-feeling, maintaining one's anger

---

[1] Tolstoy's *Kreutzer Sonata* is a study of jealousy of this type arising within a sentiment which was certainly not love, but was a strange blend of hate with an extended self-regarding sentiment It is, I think, obvious that jealousy could not arise within a sentiment of hate, pure and simple.

against the offender, is vengeful emotion or the emotion of revenge.

Though the emotion is most easily evoked, perhaps, by public insult, it may arise also from injury deliberately done to any part of the larger self, any part of that large sphere of objects to which one's self-regarding sentiment extends—e.g., injury or insult to one's family or tribe, or to any larger society with which a man identifies himself; this we see in the case of the blood-feuds, where the killing of one member of a family or tribe excites this emotion in all its other members, who continue to harbour it until they have "got even" with the family of the slayer by killing him or another of its members. On a still greater scale it may be provoked as a collective emotion throughout a nation by defeat in war. In this case the painful conation or desire that arises from the checked impulse of positive self-feeling is apt to predominate greatly over the element of anger. The attitude of the French nation towards Germany for many years after the Franco-Prussian War, and of a large part of the British nation towards the Boers after Majuba, was determined by this emotion excited within the system of that most widely extended form of the self-regarding sentiment which we call the patriotic sentiment.

The view that vengeful emotion is essentially a fusion of anger and wounded self-feeling is not generally accepted. The question has been a good deal discussed in connection with the history of punishment. Dr. Steinmetz, a German authority,[1] takes the view that "revenge is essentially rooted in the feeling of power and authority, its aim is to enhance the 'self-feeling' which has been lowered or degraded by the injury suffered." And he supports this view by showing that primitively revenge is undirected, i.e., seeks satisfaction in any violent assertion of one's power. The best illustration of such undirected revenge is, perhaps, the running *âmok* of the Malay.[2] In these cases the man who has suffered injury or insult

---

[1] *Die Entwickelung der Strafe.*

[2] An excellent account is given by Sir Hugh Clifford in a story called *The Âmok of Dâto Kâya.*

does not deliberately plan out and execute his vengeance on those who have injured him. He broods for a time, no doubt filled with the painful desire arising from his instinct of self-assertion, and then suddenly takes his *kris* and runs through his village, cutting down every living being he encounters, until he himself is slain. This brooding and fierce dejection produced by insult is sometimes very intense among other savages. We know how Achilles sulked in his tent, and cases have been described of savages who have lain prone on the ground for days together and have even died when this emotion and its impulse could find no satisfaction.

Professor Westermarck,[1] on the other hand, maintains against Steinmetz that self-feeling is not an essential element in vengeful emotion. He writes : " Resentment may be described as an aggressive attitude of mind towards a cause of pain. Anger is sudden resentment, in which the hostile reaction against the cause of pain is unrestrained by deliberation. Revenge, on the other hand, is a more deliberate form of non-moral resentment, in which the hostile reaction is more or less restrained by reason and calculation. It is impossible, however, to draw any distinct limit between these two types of resentment, as also to discern where an actual desire to inflict pain comes in." [2]

This view of anger and revenge and of the relations between them is very different to the one proposed in the preceding pages. Westermarck makes resentment the fundamental type of this kind of emotional reaction, and distinguishes two varieties of it, anger and revenge, which, he holds, differ merely in that while anger is sudden and impulsive resentment, revenge is deliberate and controlled resentment. This, I venture to think, is a failure of analysis due to non-recognition of the guiding principle we have followed, the principle that the primary emotions are the affective aspects of the fundamental instinctive mental processes and that all the other emotions are derived from them by fusion or blending. Westermarck

[1] *Origin and Development of the Moral Ideas*, chap. ii.
[2] *Ibid.* p. 22.

seeks to support his view by saying that, if one has written a book and it has been adversely criticised, though our self-feeling receives a painful check we do not seek vengeance on the critic but rather set out to write a better book. Now, it is dangerous to trust to the consideration of the emotions of the most cultivated and intellectual class of men in seeking light on the origin of the emotions, but I think that most authors would avenge themselves on the unjust and damaging critic, if they could find an easy opportunity ; and our literary disputes frequently are but the most refined expression of this emotion.

Our account of these emotions is nearer to that of Steinmetz, but differs from it in recognising that vengeful emotion is essentially a binary compound of anger and positive self-feeling. These two elements may be fused in all proportions, so that revenge ranges from the hot, blind fury of the Malay running *âmok*, or from the emotion of the child furiously striking out at all about him, to the comparatively cold, plotting revenge that can postpone and pursue its satisfaction for years. And the distinction we make between resentment and revenge is that resentment is the fusion of anger and positive self-feeling immediately evoked by an act of aggression and does not necessarily imply the existence of a developed self-regarding sentiment, whereas revenge is the same emotion developed within the system of the self-regarding sentiment—to which circumstance it owes its persistent character—with the addition of painful feeling arising from the continued thwarting of the two impulses.

The vengeful emotion has been regarded by some authors, *e.g.*, by Dr. Mercier,[1] as the root of moral indignation, and Westermarck gives this position to his " resentment." He divides resentments into two great classes, the moral and the non-moral ; the non-moral class consisting of anger and revenge, the moral class of moral indignation and disapproval. This classification seems to involve a cross-division and a confusion, not only because he fails to seize the difference between anger and

[1] *Criminal Responsibility*, Oxford, 1905.

revenge, but also because he has no criterion by which to distinguish his moral from his non-moral resentments. Whether revenge is ever a moral emotion, and whether the disinterested anger against the cruel oppressor that we have called moral indignation (the anger that arises, in the way we have studied in Chapter III., out of the parental instinct exercised on behalf of the defenceless creature) is ever non-moral—these are questions that may be left to the moralists for decision ; but that these two emotions, revenge and moral indignation, are not only intrinsically different, but that they are evoked by very different situations, seems as indisputable as that while one is essentially egoistic the other is essentially altruistic. These two emotions together are the main roots of all justice ; neither alone would have sufficed to engender a system of law and custom that would secure personal rights and liberties, and neither alone would suffice to secure the efficient administration of justice.

Approval and disapproval have been treated of by Westermarck and other writers as emotions. But to describe them as emotions is to perpetuate the chaos of psychological terminology.[1] They are not emotions but judgments, and though, like other judgments, they are often directly determined by emotions, that is not always the case ; for even moral approval and disapproval may be unemotional intellectual judgments made in logical accordance with previously adopted principles.

Shame is an emotion second to none in the extent of its influence upon social behaviour. There are several words closely connected with shame, the loose usage of which is a source of great confusion, e.g., shyness, bashfulness, and modesty ; these are sometimes said to be the names of emotions, sometimes of instincts. But shyness and modesty, like courage, generosity, and meanness, are qualities of character and of conduct arising out of the possession of instincts and sentiments, while shame is a

---

[1] In a recent treatise on ethics, which makes a considerable show of psychological precision, they are described on one page successively as emotions, sentiments, feelings, and judgments.

true secondary emotion, and bashfulness, if not an emotion in the strict sense of the word, is an emotional state.

Shame has given much trouble to psychologists, because it seems to imply and to depend upon self-consciousness, while yet the behaviour of animals and of very young children, whom we can credit only with the merest rudiments of self-consciousness, sometimes seems to express shame. Professor Baldwin [1] has dealt with these emotions in children more successfully perhaps than any other author. He distinguishes two periods in the development of what he calls the bashfulness of the child ; an earlier period, during which what he calls organic bashfulness is evoked by the presence of strangers—this organic bashfulness, which is shown by most children in their first year, he identifies with fear ; a later period in which the child makes efforts to draw attention to himself—this he calls the period of true bashfulness. Baldwin's description of the facts seems to be accurate, but he fails to show the origin of the bashfulness he describes and fails also to show its relation to shame.

The way has been prepared for the solution of these and other difficulties connected with shame by our recognition of positive and negative self-feeling as primary emotions, and by our acceptance of the important distinction between emotions and sentiments that Shand has so clearly pointed out. The earliest reactions of a child towards strangers are, no doubt, symptoms of fear, as Baldwin says. But truly bashful behaviour, which is not usually displayed until the third year, has nothing to do with fear, and is, I submit, symptomatic of a struggle between the two opposed impulses of the instincts of self-display and self-abasement, with their emotions of positive and negative self-feeling—a struggle rather than a fusion, for the impulses and emotions of the two instincts are so directly opposed that fusion is hardly possible. Consider the little boy of three who, in the presence of a stranger, hides quietly behind his mother's skirt with head hung low, averted face, and sidelong glances, until

---

[1] *Social and Ethical Interpretations in Mental Development*, chap. vi. London, 1902.

suddenly he emerges, saying " Can you do this ? " and turns a somersault at the feet of the stranger. In adults the slightly painful agitation that most of us feel when we have to figure before an audience seems to be of the same nature as this childish **bashfulness,** and to be due to a similar struggle between these two impulses and emotions. Our negative self-feeling is evoked by the presence of persons whom we regard as our superiors, or who, by reason of their number and of their forming a collective whole, are able to make on us an impression of power ; but it is not until our positive self-feeling is also excited, until we feel ourselves called upon to make a display of ourselves or our powers, to address the audience, to play a part as an equal among the superior beings, or even merely to walk across the room before the eyes of a crowd, that we experience the slightly painful, slightly pleasurable, but often very intense, emotional agitation which is properly called bashfulness. Whether this state is at all possible in the absence of self-consciousness it is difficult to say. For although either instinct may be excited quite independently of, and prior to the rise of, self-consciousness, it would seem that the idea of the self and some development of the self-regarding sentiment are necessary conditions of the conjunction of the two opposed emotions ; in their absence one of the opposed emotions would simply preclude or drive out the other. In situations that evoke bashfulness the negative self-feeling is, perhaps, as a rule, more directly induced by the presence of the other person or persons, while the positive self-feeling is more dependent on the idea of the self and on the egoistic sentiment.

But the state of bashfulness we have considered is not shame. Shame, in the full sense of the word, is only possible when the self-regarding sentiment has become well developed about the idea of the self, its attributes and powers. Then any exhibition of the self to others as deficient in these powers and attributes, which constitute the self in so far as it is the object of the self-regarding sentiment, provokes shame. The self may appear defective or inferior to others in all other respects, and no shame, though perhaps bashfulness, will be induced. Thus a man whose self, as object of his self-respect, includes courage or athletic prowess, will feel shame if he appears cowardly or bodily incapable; whereas most women, whose selves as objects of their self-regarding sentiments have not the attribute of physical courage or athletic capacity, will run away from a mouse or show themselves incapable of jumping over a fence without the least pang of shame.

Shame, then, is not merely negative self-feeling, nor is it merely negative and positive self-feeling struggling together; it is bashfulness qualified by the pain of baffled positive self-feeling, whose impulse is strong and persistent, owing to the fact that the emotion is excited within the system of the self-regarding sentiment. The conduct that excites our shame is that which lowers us in the eyes of our fellows, so that we feel it to be impossible for our positive self-feeling to attain satisfaction. Shame thus differs from vengeful emotion, which also is provoked by a blow to our self-esteem, in that the blow comes, not from another, but from ourselves; or rather, though it comes from others, it is occasioned by our own conduct, and therefore, though the check to our impulse of self-assertion may provoke our anger, this anger, unlike that of vengeful emotion, is directed against ourselves, and is therefore incapable of finding satisfaction. Hence the pain of the check to our positive self-feeling, which, when it comes from another, may find some relief in the active pursuit of vengeance, can in this case find no relief but is augmented by the pain of baffled anger. Shame, then, seems to be closely allied to vengeful emotion and, especially in brutal natures, is apt to be accompanied by it; but it differs from vengeful emotion in two respects —first, the check to positive self-feeling not only gives rise to a painful and angry desire for self-assertion, but there is no possibility of satisfaction for this desire, of " getting even " with the person from whom the check comes, because that person is oneself; secondly, there is an element of negative self-feeling, with its impulse to withdraw oneself from the notice of others, evoked by the recognition of one's own shortcoming. In revenge in its purest form this element of negative self-feeling has no part ; but, if in the face of insult or injury one has behaved in a cowardly manner, it may complicate the emotional state, which then becomes an imperfect blend of revenge and shame.

Mere bashfulness very readily passes into shame ; for, when in that state, one is acutely aware of one's self in relation to others, and therefore one notices at once any slight defect of one's conduct, and any censure or disapproval based upon it occasions a painful check to positive self-feeling that converts bashfulness to shame The full understanding of shame implies a study of the self-regarding sentiment, which, however, we must postpone to a later page.

We are now in a position to inquire into the nature of sorrow and joy, which we have rejected from our list of primary emotions, because, as was said, they are algedonic or pleasure-pain qualifications of emotional states rather than emotions capable of standing alone.

First, a remark must be made upon one feature of emotions that has been too much neglected. Apart from the pleasure that attends the successful, and the pain that attends the unsuccessful, conation or striving towards an end involved in every emotional state, each primary emotion seems to have a certain intrinsic feeling-tone, just as the sensations that are synthesised in perception have their feeling-tone independently of the success or lack of success of the perceptual conation. And the intrinsic feeling-tone of the emotions seems to follow the same rule as that of sensations, namely, that with increase of intensity of the emotion, pleasant tends to give way to unpleasant feeling-tone ; so that, while at moderate intensities some are pleasant and others unpleasant, at the highest intensity all alike become unpleasant or painful ; and, perhaps, at the lowest intensity all are pleasant. If that is the case, then, like the sensations, the emotions differ greatly from one another in regard to the position of the neutral point of feeling-tone in the scales of their intensities. Thus fear at low intensity does but add a pleasurable zest to any pursuit, as we see especially clearly in children, sportsmen, and adventurous spirits generally; whereas at high intensity it is the most horrible of all experiences. On the other hand, tender emotion is pleasantly toned, save, perhaps, at its highest intensity ; and positive self-feeling is even more highly pleasurable and remains so, probably, even at its highest intensity.

How, then, are we to regard joy and sorrow? Is joy mere pleasure, and are the two words synonymous ? Obviously not ; joy is universally recognised as something more than, and higher than, mere pleasure. Whenever did poet write of pleasure in the lofty strain of the beautiful lines that Coleridge wrote of joy ?

> " O pure of heart, thou needst not ask of me
> What this strong music in the soul may be !
> What, and wherein it doth exist,
> This light, this glory, this fair luminous mist,
> This beautiful and beauty-making power,
> Joy, virtuous lady ! Joy that ne'er was given
> Save to the pure, and in their purest hour.
>
> Joy is the sweet voice, Joy the luminous cloud—
> We in ourselves rejoice !
> And thence flows all that charms or ear or sight,
> All melodies the echoes of that voice,
> All colours a suffusion from that light."

Clearly joy is more than pleasure, however intense. Let us examine what is by common consent the purest type of joy—the joy of a loving mother as she tends her beautiful and healthy child. In this case many factors contribute to produce the joyful emotion : (1) There is æsthetic pleasure in the contemplation of the beauty of the object, a pleasure that any onlooker may share ; (2) sympathetic pleasure reflected by, or induced in, the mother from her smiling child ; (3) tender emotion, in itself pleasantly toned and progressively attaining satisfaction ; (4) positive self-feeling, also intrinsically pleasant and also attaining an ideal satisfaction ; for the mother is proud of her child as an evidence of her

own worth ; (5) each of these two primary emotions
of the mother is developed within the system of a strong
sentiment, the one within the system of her love for her
child, the other within the system of her regard for herself, the two strongest sentiments of her nature, which,
in so far as the child is identified with herself, become
welded together to constitute a master-sentiment or
passion—this renders the emotions more intense and
more enduring ; (6) the fact that the emotions are not
aroused as merely isolated experiences by some casually
presented object, but are developed within strongly
organised and enduring sentiments, gives them a prospective reference ; they project themselves into an
indefinitely prolonged future, and so hope or pleasant
anticipation is added to the complex.

Joy is always, as in this instance, a complex emotional
state, in which one or more of the primary emotions,
developed within the system of a strong sentiment, plays
an essential part. We ought, then, properly to speak,
not of joy, but of joyous emotion. And if, by an illegitimate effort of abstraction, we should seek to separate
joy from the emotions with which it forms an inseparable
whole, we should have to say that it is pleasure, but
pleasure of a high type, pleasure of complex origin,
arising from the harmonious operation of one or more
sentiments that constitute a considerable feature of the
total mental organisation.

Reflection upon **sorrow** yields similar results. Take
the parallel case of the mother sorrowing for the loss
of her child. There is tender emotion, which, though
intrinsically of pleasant feeling-tone, is in this case painful
because its impulse is baffled and cannot attain more
than the most scanty and imperfect satisfaction in little
acts, such as the laying of flowers on the grave ; and this
emotion, being developed within a strong sentiment, is
persistent, and the pain of its ineffectual impulse constantly recurs : again, pride and hope have been dashed
down and few can avoid some negative self-feeling under
such conditions, for a part of the larger self has been
torn away, and some thought of some effort that might

have been made but was not is very apt to increase the intensity of this painful negative self-feeling.

In this case, then, we should properly speak of a sorrowful emotion, which emotion is a painfully toned binary compound of tender emotion and negative self-feeling. And as in this case, so in every other, sorrow implies one or more of the primary emotions excited within a sentiment. Perhaps in every case tender emotion must be an element ; for, take away the tender emotion and only painful negative self-feeling or humiliation remains ; take away that emotion also and nothing remains but some painful depressed feeling that cannot properly be called sorrow, though it might perhaps be called grief. Some such state as this last might be produced by an event that should destroy the sentiment of love at the same time that it removed its object ; *e.g.*, a friend, the object of a strong sentiment, suddenly by some cruel act shows us that he has renounced our friendship and, at the same time, that he is unworthy of it. Under these conditions might be realised a state of intolerable pain, a state almost devoid of impulse or desire, that might be called grief, but not sorrow. But it is hard to imagine even under such conditions a state without some anger, some resentment or disgust, and the corresponding impulse. In so far as grief is properly distinguishable from sorrow, it differs in having less of tender emotion and more of anger, as when the bereaved and grief-stricken father curses God, or the Fates, or the Universe.[1]

In this connection we may consider the difference between pity and sorrow. Pity in its simplest form is tender emotion tinged with sympathetically induced pain. It differs from sorrow, which also is essentially a painful tender emotion, in the sympathetic character of the pain, and in that it does not imply the existence of any sentiment of affection or love, as sorrow does, and is therefore a more transient experience, and one with less tendency to look before and after. There is also, of course, a sorrowful pity, as when one watches the painful and

[1] See further discussion of Joy and Sorrow in the Supplementary Chapter on " The Derived Emotions."

mortal illness of a dear friend. In this case there is
tender emotion and there is sympathetically induced
pain which makes the state one of pity; but there is
also pain arising from the prospect of the loss of the
object of our sentiment of love, which makes the emotion
a sorrowful one. That sorrow does not necessarily include an element of sympathetic pain is clearly shown
by the sorrow of those who have lost a loved one whom
they sincerely believe to have entered on a happier life.
The pain of sorrow is, then, a self-regarding pain, whereas
the pain of pity is not; hence pity is rightly regarded as
the nobler emotion.

Before passing on from this subject, it seems worth
while to inquire, What is happiness? Is happiness
merely pleasure or a sum of pleasures, and if not, what
is it? If only moralists had condescended to ask this
question earnestly and had found the answer to it, how
much of the energy devoted to ethical discussion during
the last century might profitably have been turned into
other channels! The utilitarians constantly assumed
that happiness and pleasure are to be identified, and
used happiness and sum of pleasures as synonymous
terms, generally without pausing to consider, or to seek
to justify, this identification. The principle that the
ultimate test of the relative worth of different kinds of
conduct and character must be the estimation of the
degree in which they contribute to bring about the
greatest happiness of the greatest number, this principle,
which if the phrase " greatest number " is taken as referring to the remoter, as well as to the immediate, future
cannot easily be rejected, was treated as identical with the
maxim that the aim of all conduct should be to increase
the sum of pleasures to the greatest possible extent;
and this maxim, illuminated by Bentham's dictum that
" pushpin is as good as poetry provided the pleasure be
as great," was naturally repulsive to many of the finer
natures; it provoked in them a reaction and drove them
to grope among obscure and mystical ideas for their
ethical foundations, and so has greatly delayed the
general acceptance of the great truth embodied in the

utilitarian doctrines.   J. S. Mill, like the rest, identified happiness with sum of pleasures, and attempted to improve the position by recognising higher and lower qualities of pleasure, and by regarding the higher as indefinitely more desirable than the lower.   This was an effort in the right direction, but so long as happiness is regarded as merely a sum of pleasures, whether higher or lower, and pleasure and pain as the only motives to action, the utilitarian position is untenable.[1]

It is, I think, indisputable that a man may be unhappy while he actually experiences pleasure, and that he might experience one pleasure after another throughout a considerable period without ceasing to be unhappy. Consider the case of a man whose lifelong ambition and hopes have recently been dashed to the ground.   If he were fond of music, he might, when the first shock of disappointment had passed away, attend a concert and derive pleasure from the music, or indulge in other pleasures, and yet be continuously unhappy.   No doubt his unhappiness would make it more difficult to find pleasure and might make his pleasure thin in quality ; but the two modes of experience are, though antagonistic, not absolutely incompatible and mutually exclusive.

In a similar way, a man may be happy while experiencing pain, not merely physical pain, but pain in the proper sense of the word—i.e., painful feeling.   Imagine the case of a man of fine nature who in the past in a moment of weakness has done a mean thing, but who by his efforts has completely repaired the injury done, has set his relations to others on an entirely satisfactory footing, and has become thoroughly happy.   If his mind goes back to that act of meanness, he will have a painful feeling and yet he may continue to be happy without intermission.   Or imagine another, perhaps a clearer, case—that of a person who finds an exalted happiness in seeking to relieve the lot of the sick and distressed. Such a person will often feel sympathetic pain, but, so

[1] Even in so recent and excellent a treatise as Dr. Rashdall's *Theory of Good and Evil* this identification of pleasure with happiness is frequently repeated, verbally at least.

long as he knows he is doing good to others, he is happy and does not cease to be happy in those moments of pitiful emotion. We may even believe that the cause of such sympathetic pain may increase the happiness of him who feels it. Suppose that to a tender-hearted, sympathetic person, who finds his happiness in doing good to others, a friend pours out his troubles in a moment of confidence ; the recipient feels sympathetic pain, but his happiness is at the same time increased because he sees that his friend confides in him and finds relief in doing so. Do not facts of this order show clearly that happiness is no mere sum of pleasures ? What, then, is it ? It may, I think, be indirectly defined by saying that happiness is related to joy in the same way that joy is related to pleasure.[1] Pleasure is a qualification of consciousness of momentary duration or, at most, of a fleeting character, and it arises from some mental process that involves but a mere fragment of one's whole being. Joy arises from the harmonious operation of an organised system or sentiment that constitutes a considerable feature or part of one's whole being ; it has, therefore, potentially at least, a greater persistence and continuity and a deeper resonance ; it is, as it were, more massive than pleasure ; it is more intimately and essentially a part of oneself, so that one cannot stand aside and contemplate it in philosophic or depreciatory detachment, as one may contemplate one's pleasures. Happiness arises from the harmonious operation of all the sentiments of a well-organised and unified personality, one in which the principal sentiments support one another in a succession of actions all of which tend towards the same or closely allied and harmonious ends. Hence the richer, the more highly developed, the more completely unified or integrated is the personality, the more capable is it of sustained happiness in spite of inter-current pains of all sorts. In the child or in the adult of imperfectly developed and unified personality, the pleasure or pain of the moment is apt to fill or dominate the whole of consciousness as a simple wave of feeling, whereas in the

[1] Cp. p. 129.

perfected personality it appears as a mere ripple on the surface of a strong tide that sets steadily in one direction.

If this account of happiness is correct, it follows that to add to the sum of happiness is not merely to add to the sum of pleasures, but is rather to contribute to the development of higher forms of personality—personalities capable, not merely of pleasure, as the animals are, but, of happiness. If this conclusion is sound, it is of no small importance to the social sciences; it goes far to reconcile the doctrine of such moralists as T. H. Green with that of the more enlightened utilitarians; for the one party insists that the proper end of moral effort is the development of personalities, the other that it is the increase of happiness, and these we now see to be identical ends.

In Chapter III. it was said that the definition of emotion there adopted necessitates the exclusion of surprise, as well as of joy and sorrow, from the list of true and primary emotions. This is because surprise is an affective state that implies no corresponding instinct and has no specific conative tendency. It is merely a condition of general excitement which supervenes upon any totally unexpected and violent mental impression; or perhaps it is more accurate to say that it is produced by an impression which is contrary to anticipation, and to which, therefore, we cannot immediately adjust ourselves, which does not evoke at once an appropriate emotional and conative response. It is the momentary state of confused excitement which intervenes between the reception of the impression and the assumption of the appropriate attitude towards it, a moment of conflict and confusion between the habitual anticipatory attitude determined by the course of previous experience and the new attitude provoked by the unusual course of events.

APPENDIX TO CHAPTER V

In the previous editions no attempt was made to deal with the emotion of remorse. The following note is added to make good this serious omission:

Remorse is an emotion which has been commonly regarded by moralists as the most intense of the effects produced by the activity of that peculiar entity " the conscience." It is a complex emotional state implying the existence of a well-developed self-regarding sentiment and, generally, of moral sentiments. It arises upon the recollection of some past action that one deeply regrets; like all regret it is painful owing to the fact that the impulse or desire, which is the root of it and which may be the impulse of any one of several instincts, is directed towards the past rather than towards the future, and is therefore seen to be necessarily and for ever baffled. But it differs from other forms of regret in that the regretted event is one brought about by one's own action. Hence the anger which arises from the baffled desire is directed against oneself, and can find no satisfaction in the utterance of reproaches or curses; for these, being directed against oneself, do but add to the painfulness of the whole complex state; and even the doing of penance (*i.e.*, the infliction of punishment upon oneself), though it yields some satisfaction to the baffled impulse, does not heal the wound to one's self-regard caused by the recognition of the irrevocable failure to realise one's ideal of self. Through this last factor remorse is closely allied with shame, and it might perhaps be adequately defined as shameful and angry regret. See Supplementary Chapter III. for discussion of " regret " as a derived emotion.

CHAPTER VI

THE DEVELOPMENT OF THE SENTIMENTS

WE have seen that a sentiment is an organised system of emotional dispositions centred about the idea of some object. The organisation of the sentiments in the developing mind is determined by the course of experience ; that is to say, the sentiment is a growth in the structure of the mind that is not natively given in the inherited constitution. This is certainly true in the main, though the maternal sentiment might almost seem to be innate ; but we have to remember that in the human mother this sentiment may, and generally does, begin to grow up about the idea of its object, before the child is born.[1]

The growth of the sentiments is of the utmost importance for the character and conduct of individuals and of societies ; it is the organisation of the affective and conative life. In the absence of sentiments our emotional life would be a mere chaos, without order, consistency, or continuity of any kind ; and all our social relations and conduct, being based on the emotions and their impulses, would be correspondingly chaotic, unpredictable, and unstable. It is only through the systematic organisation of the emotional dispositions in sentiments that the volitional control of the immediate promptings

[1] In a recent article criticising M. Ribot's book, *Les Passions* (*Mind*, vol. xvi. p. 502), Mr. Shand has suggested that the sentiment of love is innately organised. I cannot see any sufficient grounds for accepting this suggestion, and I believe that any such assumption will raise more difficulties than it solves. In previous chapters I have suggested that certain of the instincts may have peculiarly intimate innate relations, that, *e.g.*, the instinct of pugnacity is thus specially intimately connected with the maternal instinct and with the sex instinct of the male. But even this seems to me very questionable.

of the emotions is rendered possible. Again, our judgments of value and of merit are rooted in our sentiments; and our moral principles have the same source, for they are formed by our judgments of moral value.

In dealing with the emotions, we named and classed them according to their nature as states of affective consciousness and as tendencies to action; and we may attempt to name and classify the sentiments also according to the nature of the emotional dispositions that enter into the composition of each one. But since, as we have seen, the same emotional dispositions may enter into the composition of very different sentiments, we can carry the naming and classification of them but a little way on this principle, and we have accordingly but very general names for the sentiments. We have the names love, liking, affection, attachment, denoting those sentiments that draw one towards their objects, generally in virtue of the tender emotion with its protective impulse which is their principal constituent; and we have the names hate, dislike, and aversion, for those that lead us to shrink from their objects, those whose attitude or tendency is one of aversion, owing to the fear or disgust that is the dominant element in their composition. The two names love and hate, and the weaker but otherwise synonymous terms liking and dislike, affection and aversion, are very general; each stands for a large class of sentiments of varied, though similar, composition; the character common to the one class being the fundamental tendency to seek the object and to find pleasure in its presence, while that of the other class is the tendency to avoid the object and to be pained by its presence.

We must, I think, recognise a third principal variety of sentiment which is primarily the self-regarding sentiment, and is, perhaps, best called respect. Respect differs from love in that, while tender emotion occupies the principal place in love, it is lacking, or occupies an altogether subordinate position, in the sentiment of respect. The principal constituents of respect are the dispositions of positive and negative self-feeling; and respect is clearly marked off from love by the fact that shame is one of its strongest emotions.

It may be asked—If respect is thus a sentiment that has for its most essential constituents these self-regarding emotions, how can we properly be said to entertain respect for others ? The answer is, I think, that we respect those who respect themselves, that our respect for another is a sympathetic reflection of his self-respect ; for unless a man shows self-respect we never have respect for him, even though we may admire some of his qualities, or like, or even love, him in a certain degree. The generally recognised fact that we may like without respecting, and may respect without liking, shows very clearly the essentially different natures of these two sentiments, love and respect.

The older moralists frequently made use of the expression " self-love," and in doing so generally confounded under this term two different sentiments, self-love and self-respect. Self-love is fortunately a comparatively rare sentiment ; it is the self-regarding sentiment of the thoroughly selfish man, the meaner sort of egoist. Such a man feels a tender emotion for himself, he indulges in self-pity ; he may have little positive self-feeling and may be incapable of shame.[1]

Besides the sentiments of these three main types, love, hate, and respect, which may be called complete or full-grown sentiments, we must recognise the existence of sentiments of all degrees of development from the most rudimentary upward ; these may be regarded as stages in the formation of fully-grown sentiments, although

[1] I shall be told that in restricting in this way the meaning of the term " self-love " I am setting aside a usage consecrated by age and the writings of innumerable moralists. I would anticipate this objection by asking—Why should the psychologist feel any obligation to clog and hamper the development of his science by a regard for the terminology of the pre-scientific ages, while the workers in other scientific fields are permitted to develop their terminology with a single eye to its precision and to the accurate discrimination and classification of the like and the unlike ? The chemist is not held to be under any obligation to class earth, air, fire, and water with his elements, nor does the physicist persist in classing heat and electricity with the fluid substances.

many of them never attain any great degree of complexity or strength. These we have to name according to the principal emotional disposition entering into their composition.

The sentiments may also be classified according to the nature of their objects ; they then fall into three main classes, the concrete particular, the concrete general, and the abstract sentiments—e.g., the sentiment of love for a child, of love for children in general, of love for justice or virtue. Their development in the individual follows this order, the concrete particular sentiments being, of course, the earliest and most easily acquired. The number of sentiments a man may acquire, reckoned according to the number of objects in which they are centred, may, of course, be very large ; but almost every man has a small number of sentiments—perhaps one only—that greatly surpass all the rest in strength and as regards the proportion of his conduct that springs from them.

Each sentiment has a life-history, like every other vital organisation. It is gradually built up, increasing in complexity and strength, and may continue to grow indefinitely, or may enter upon a period of decline, and may decay slowly or rapidly, partially or completely.

When any one of the emotions is strongly or repeatedly excited by a particular object, there is formed the rudiment of a sentiment. Suppose that a child is thrown into the company of some person given to frequent outbursts of violent anger, say, a violent-tempered father who is otherwise indifferent to the child and takes no further notice of him than to threaten, scold, and, perhaps, beat him. At first the child experiences fear at each exhibition of violence ; but repetition of these incidents very soon creates the habit of fear, and in the presence of his father, even in his mildest moods, the child is timorous ; that is to say, the mere presence of the father throws the child's fear-disposition into a condition of sub-excitement, which increases on the slightest occasion until it produces all the subjective and objective manifestations of fear. As a further stage, the mere idea of the father becomes capable of producing the same effects as his presence : this idea has become associated with the emotion ; or, in stricter language, the psycho-physical disposition, whose excitement involves the rise to consciousness of this idea, has become associated or intimately connected with the psycho-physical disposition whose excitement produces the bodily and mental symptoms of fear. Such an association constitutes a rudimentary sentiment that we can only call a sentiment of fear.

In a similar way, a single act of kindness done by A to B may evoke in B the emotion of gratitude ; and if A repeats his kindly acts, conferring benefits on B, the gratitude of B may become habitual, may become an enduring emotional attitude of B towards A—a sentiment of gratitude. Or, in either case, a single act—one evoking very intense fear or gratitude—may suffice to render the association more or less durable, and the attitude of fear, or gratitude, of B towards A more or less permanent.

The same is true of most, perhaps of all, of the emotions of the class that do not presuppose sentiments already formed for the object of the emotion—e.g., of admiration, of anger, of disgust, of pity. We must, then, recognise, as limiting cases on the side of simplicity, sentiments formed by the association of a single emotional disposition with the idea of some object. But it can seldom happen that a sentiment persists in this rudimentary condition for any long period of time. Any such sentiment is liable to die away for lack of stimulus, or, if further relations are maintained with its object, to develop into a more complex organisation. Thus the simple sentiment of fear, created in the way we have imagined, will tend to develop, and will most readily become hate by the incorporation of other emotional dispositions ; anger may be frequently aroused by the harsh punishments and restrictions imposed by the violent-tempered father, perhaps also revenge, disgust, and shame ; and after each occasion on which the father becomes the object of these emotions, they remain more ready to be stirred by him or by the mere thought of him ; they all, in virtue of their repeated excitement by this one object, become associated with the

object more and more intimately, until the mere idea of
him may suffice to throw them all at once into a condition
of sub-excitement, or to arouse all of them in turn or in
conjunction to full activity. So the rudimentary sentiment,
whose only emotional constituent is fear, develops into a
full-blown hatred.

Now let us take parental love as the type of a strong
and highly complex sentiment, and let us consider its
development. By reason of its helplessness, its delicacy,
its distresses, the young child evokes sooner or later the
tender emotion of the parent, if he is at all capable of this
emotion ; and if the parent does not, through laziness
or under the influence of a bad tradition, restrain the
protective impulse, it finds its satisfaction in a series of
tender acts. Each time the emotion and its impulse are
brought into operation by this particular object, they are
rendered more easily excitable in the same way, until the
mere idea of this object is constantly accompanied by some
degree of the emotion, however feeble. This gives the
object a special power of attracting and holding the
attention of the parent, who therefore constantly notices
the child's expressions ; and these evoke by sympathetic
reaction the corresponding feelings and emotions in the
parent. Thus all the tender and attracting emotions are
repeatedly aroused by this one object, either singly or in
combination—pity, wonder, admiration, gratitude, solicitude, as well as sympathetic pain and pleasure, and quick
anger at neglect or injury of the child by others. This,
perhaps, is as far as the sentiment normally develops
while the child is very young. But there comes in the
ordinary course of things a time when the child learns to
reciprocate the parent's sentiment and, by its expressions
of tenderness or gratitude, intensifies the satisfaction of
the parental emotions ; in so doing it welds the father's
sentiment still more strongly than before, and also estab-
lishes the relation presently to be discussed under the
head of active sympathy. But this is not all ; the parent
is apt to identify the child with himself in a peculiarly
intimate way, for he knows that the world in general
regards its qualities and its defects as, in a sense, his

own ; and so his self-regarding sentiment of respect or of pride becomes directly extended to the child ; whatever is admirable about it brings satisfaction to his positive self-feeling ; whatever is defective humbles him, excites his negative self-feeling ; its shame or disgrace is his shame, its triumphs are his triumphs. It is the fusion of these two sentiments, the altruistic and the egoistic, in the parental sentiment that gives it its incomparable hold upon our natures, and makes it a sentiment from which proceed our most intense joys and sorrows. And not only are the various emotions, such as tender emotion and positive self-feeling, excited in complex conjunctions, but it would seem that each emotion excited within the system of any complex sentiment acquires an increased intensity and its impulse an additional energy from its membership in the system, an increment of energy which is greater the larger the number of dispositions comprised within the system.[1] To all this must be added yet another factor—every effort and every sacrifice made on the child's behalf, every pain suffered through it, adds to the strength of the sentiment ; for with each such incident we feel that we put something of ourselves into the object of the sentiment ; and this sense of the accumulation of our efforts and sacrifices gives it an additional value ; we come to regard it as an investment in which we have sunk our capital bit by bit, to lose which would be to lose that which embodies our past efforts. In this way also the child becomes identified with ourselves, so that, as with any other thing, such as a work of art or science, to the shaping of which our best powers have been devoted, approval of it gives us pleasure and disapproval pain, equally with approval or disapproval of ourselves.

Though the parental sentiment in its completest form arises from the fusion of the purely altruistic with the extended self-regarding sentiment, it may be wholly of one or other type. The mother of a child that is mentally

---

[1] For the same reason other sentiments of this type, resulting from fusion of the self-regarding sentiment with the love of an object other than the self (of which patriotism is the most striking example), acquire their power of supplying dominant or extremely powerful motives.

and physically defective can find little occasion for extending to it her self-respect or pride ; it does not minister to her positive self-feeling, but rather, in so far as it is identified with herself, is a cause of shame and pain. Yet the maternal instinct often rises superior to these influences, which would make for hate rather than for love ; the greater needs of the child do but call out more intensely and frequently her tender emotion, and she cherishes it with a sentiment that is almost purely tender.

On the other hand, many a father's sentiment for his children is very little, or not at all, tender, is not properly love, but is a mere extension of his self-regarding sentiment. He is gratified—*i.e.*, his positive self-feeling attains satisfaction—when they are admired or when they achieve success of any kind ; he feels shame when they appear bad-mannered or ill-dressed or stupid ; and he labours to fit them to take a good place in the world, or is ambitious for them, just as he labours for, and is ambitious for, himself ; all, perhaps, without once experiencing the least touch of tender emotion for them.

The sentiment of affection for an equal generally takes its rise, not in simple tender emotion, but in admiration, or gratitude, or pity, and is especially developed by active sympathy. By active sympathy I mean sympathy in the fuller, more usual, sense of the word ; we must carefully distinguish it from the simple, primitive, or passive sympathy discussed in Chapter IV. Active sympathy plays, or may play, a minor part in the genesis of the parental sentiment, but it is of prime importance for the development of the sentiment of affection between equals ; for while the former may be wholly one-sided, the latter can hardly become fully formed and permanent without some degree of reciprocation and of sympathy in this fuller sense.

Active sympathy presents a difficult problem, which we may consider in this connection. It involves a reciprocal relation between at least two persons ; either party to the relation not only is apt to experience the emotions displayed by the other, but he desires also that the other shall share his own emotions ; he actively seeks the sympathy of the other, and, when he has communicated his emotion to the other, he attains a peculiar satisfaction which greatly enhances his pleasure and his joy, or, in the case of painful emotion, diminishes his pain.

This relation of active sympathy is apt to grow up between any two persons who are thrown much together, if they are commonly stirred to similar emotions by similar objects ; and that can only be the case if they have similar sentiments. Two persons may live together for years, and, if their sentiments are very different, if one of them likes and dislikes the things that are for the most part indifferent to the other, there will be no habitual sympathy established between them. There may be a reciprocal sentiment of love without active sympathy, as in some cases of mother and child ; [1] and in such cases there will be reciprocation of tender emotion, and when one party to the relation is in distress the other will pity and succour him. But such a sentiment of love without active sympathy brings little joy and is likely to be troubled by frequent jars, irritations, and regrets. Instances of this kind of relation are common enough ; they show clearly that tender emotion and pity, though often in popular speech and by many psychologists confused with sympathy, do not constitute sympathy ; and they show also that sympathy is not essential to love, that, in short, sympathy (both the simple or passive and the complex active variety) and tender emotion are radically distinct.

If, however, the relation of active sympathy is established between any two persons, some sentiment of affection is pretty sure to grow up in both parties, if they are at all capable of tender emotion ; and, except in the case of parental love, active sympathy is the most sure foundation of love and is an essential feature of any completely satisfying affection.

We have, then, to ask, Why do we seek and find this peculiar satisfaction in the mere fact of another person's sharing our emotion ? In the case of the pleasurable emotions we may see a partial explanation in the fact

[1] *E.g.*, the relation of mother and son in Mr. Wells's *Days of the Comet.*

that the sharing of our emotion by another intensifies our own emotion by way of the fundamental reaction of primitive sympathy,[1] and therefore intensifies our pleasure or our joy.   But the sharing of our emotion intensifies also the painful emotions, anger, revenge, fear, pity, and sorrowful emotion ; yet in these cases also we desire that others shall share our emotion and find a certain satisfaction when they do so.

Some further explanation of active sympathy is therefore required, and in order to find it we must, I think, fall back on the gregarious instinct.   The excitement of this, the pre-eminently social instinct, is accompanied, as we have seen, by no specific emotion of well-marked quality.   In, the simplest cases it operates merely to produce an uneasy restlessness in any member of a herd or other animal society that has become separated from its fellows, impelling him to wander to and fro until he finds and rejoins the herd.   In the present connection it is important that this gregarious impulse seems generally to be called into play in conjunction with some other instinct ;   that is to say, the excitement of any other instinct seems to predispose to the excitement of this one.   This is, perhaps, most obvious in the case of fear.   The gregarious animal may graze in comfort at some distance from his fellows, but at the slightest alarm will run first to join them, before making off in headlong flight.   But it is true also of anger and curiosity, of the migratory instinct, of the food-seeking impulse when sharpened by hunger, and of the mating instinct.   Animals of many species live for the most part more or less scattered, or in family groups only, but come together in vast collections when these special instincts are excited.

It seems, then, that the gregarious instinct supplements, as it were, each of the special instincts, rendering complete satisfaction of their impulses impossible, until each animal is surrounded by others of the same species in a similar state of excitement.   Since man certainly inherits this instinct, we may see in this instinct the principle that we need for the explanation of the develop-

[1] Cp. Chapter IV.

ment of active sympathy from the crude sympathetic reaction or mere sympathetic induction of emotion that we studied in Chapter IV. The blind impulse of the gregarious animal to seek the company of his fellows, whenever one of his other instincts is excited, becomes in us the desire of seeing ourselves surrounded by others who share our emotion ; and it is apt to become directed to seeking the sympathetic response of some one person in whom we are sure of evoking it ; and then, having become habitually directed to that person, it finds a more certain and complete and detailed satisfaction than is possible if it remains unspecialised.

That we are right in thus finding the root of active sympathy in an ancient and deep-seated instinct, and that the impulse of this instinct is distinct from the tender or protective impulse, is shown by the great differences between us in regard to this impulse in spite of similar conditions of life, differences that do not run parallel with our differences in regard to the strength of the tender impulse. There are men who seem almost devoid of active sympathy ; they are content to admire, or to be indignant, or vengeful, or tender, or curious, or grateful, alone, and they derive little or no satisfaction from finding that others are sharing their emotions. Such a man is not necessarily incapable of the tender emotion and the sentiment of love ; he may be tenderly devoted to his family and be capable of the most truly disinterested conduct, but he is by nature a solitary, his gregarious instinct is abnormally weak, and therefore he is content to bury his joys and his sorrows in his own bosom.

On the other hand, the person in whom this impulse is strong can find, when alone, no enjoyment in the things that give him, when in sympathetic company, the keenest delight. He may, for example, be an enthusiastic admirer of natural beauty ; but if, by some strange chance, he takes a walk alone through the most beautiful scenes, his emotional stirrings, which, if shared by others, would be a pure delight, are accompanied by a vague though painful desire, whose nature he may or may not clearly recognise. And the chances are that he occupies himself in making mental notes of the scenes before him and hurries home to give a glowing description of them to some friend who, he knows, will be stirred in some degree to share his emotions. Some persons, in whom this impulse is but little specialised though strong and whose emotions are quick and vivid, are not satisfied until all about them share their emotions ; they are pained and even made angry by the spectacle of any one remaining unmoved by the objects of their own emotions.

Many children manifest very clearly this tendency of active sympathy ; they demand that their every emotion shall be shared at once. " Oh, come and look ! " is their constant cry when out for a walk, and every object that excites their curiosity or admiration is brought at once, or pointed out, to their companion. And if that companion is unsympathetic, or is wearied by their too frequent demands upon his emotional capacities, the urgency of this impulse gives rise to pain and anger and, perhaps, a storm of tears. On the other hand, another child, brought up, perhaps, under identical conditions, but in whom this impulse is relatively weak, will explore a garden, interested and excited for hours together, without once feeling the need for sympathy, without once calling on others to share his emotion.

Active sympathy is, then, egoistic, it is a seeking of one's own satisfaction. There are selfish men in whom this tendency is very strong ; such men wear out their wives, or others about them, by their constant demands for sympathetic emotion, regardless of the strain they put upon their companions, who cannot always be in the mood to sympathise. Such men constantly demand sympathy and give but little. Sympathy, then, whether in the active or the passive form, is not the root of altruism, as Bain and others would have it. Nor is it, as Mr. Sutherland maintains, to be identified with the maternal impulse. But, although it is not in itself an altruistic impulse and is not in any sense the root of altruism, it is a most valuable adjunct to the tender emotion in the formation of altruistic sentiments and in stimulating social co-operation for social ends. The man that has it not at all, or in whom it has become completely specialised (*i.e.*, directed to some one or few persons only), will hardly become a leader and inspirer of others in the reform of social abuses, in the public recognition of merit, in public expression of moral indignation, or in any other of those collective expressions of emotion which do so much to bind societies together, even if they fail of achieving their immediate ends.

It is only when this active sympathy is specialised and is combined in both parties with a reciprocal sentiment of affection, and when each, knowing that the other desires his sympathy and derives from it increase of joy and diminution of pain, desires to procure these results for the other and in turn derives satisfaction from the knowledge that he can and does produce these results—it is only then that sympathy, in the fullest sense of the word, is achieved.

CHAPTER VII

THE GROWTH OF SELF-CONSCIOUSNESS AND OF THE SELF-REGARDING SENTIMENT

IF we would understand the life of societies, we must first learn to understand the way in which individuals become moulded by the society into which they are born and in which they grow up, how by this moulding they become fitted to play their part in it as social beings—how, in short, they become capable of moral conduct. Moral conduct is essentially social conduct, and there could be no serious objection to the use of the two expressions as synonymous; but it is more in conformity with common usage to restrict the term " moral " to the higher forms of social conduct of which man alone is capable.

While the lower forms of social conduct are the direct issue of the prompting of instinct—as when the animal-mother suffers privation, wounds, or death in the defence of her young under the impulse of the maternal instinct —the higher forms of social conduct, which alone are usually regarded as moral, involve the voluntary control and regulation of the instinctive impulses. Now, volition or voluntary control proceeds from the idea of the self and from the sentiment, or organised system of emotions and impulses, centred about that idea. Hence the study of the development of self-consciousness and of the self-regarding sentiment is an important part of the preparation for the understanding of social phenomena. And these two things, the idea of the self and the self-regarding sentiment, develop in such intimate relations with each other that they must be studied together. This development is, as we shall see, essentially a social process, one

which is dependent throughout upon the complex interactions between the individual and the organised society
to which he belongs.

Almost all animals are capable in some degree of
learning to modify their instinctive behaviour in the
light of experience, under the guidance of pleasure and
pain ; and in the young child also this kind of learning
leads to the first steps beyond purely instinctive behaviour.
At first, all efforts and movements of the young infant or
young animal, in so far as they are not mere reflexes, are
directly and wholly due to the instinctive impulses. When
any such movement directly attains its end, the pleasure
of satisfaction confirms the tendency to that particular
kind of action in relation to that kind of object or situation.
If, on the other hand, movements of the kind first made are
not successful, the pain of failure brings them to an end ;
but the impulse persists and some variation of the movements is made, again and again, until success is achieved ;
then the pleasure of satisfaction confirms this last and
successful kind of movement, so that, whenever the same
impulse is again excited, it will work towards its end
by means of this kind of action rather than by means of
any other. Few of the animals rise to higher modes of
learning or acquisition. But in the infant, as his powers of
representation develop, as he becomes capable of free
ideas, the end towards which any instinct impels him
becomes more or less clearly represented in his mind as
an object of desire. The first result of this transformation
of blind appetite or impulse into desire is greater continuity
of effort ; for, when the power of representation of the
object has been attained, the attention is not so readily
drawn off from it by irrelevant sensory impressions of all
sorts.

Then, as the child's intellectual powers develop
further, the train of activity through which the end of
any impulse is attained becomes longer ; a succession of
actions is performed, each of which is only a means
to the end prescribed by the instinctive impulse ; objects
that are in themselves uninteresting are made use of as
means to the end. In all such mediate activities the

original impulse persists as the motive power of the whole sequence In so far as the actions and objects made use of do not bring him nearer to his end, they are discarded ; he turns to others, until he finds those by means of which success is attainable. When, thereafter, a similar situation recurs, this last sequence of actions and objects is the one brought into play.

The principle that the original impulse or conation supplies the motive power to all the activities that are but means to the attainment of the desired end—this principle is of supreme importance for the understanding of the mental life and conduct of men. The train of activity, supported by any one of the instinctive impulses, may become in this way indefinitely prolonged and incessantly renewed ; it may take the predominantly intellectual form of thinking out means for the attainment of the end.

This complication of purely instinctive behaviour in the developing child may be illustrated by a concrete example. Suppose that a hungry young child has by chance found something good to eat in a certain cupboard that has been left open. On the next occasion that he comes hungry within sight of the cupboard, he may at once turn to and help himself to food. So much profiting by experience any of the higher animals may display. Next suppose that the child finds himself hungry while in another part of the house. The idea of the cupboard and of the food in it rises to consciousness, and he goes off to find it and to repeat his successful raid. Again, suppose that on another similar occasion he finds on reaching the cupboard that it is latched and that the latch is out of his reach. He goes and fetches a footstool, but still he cannot reach the latch. Perhaps then the obstruction to his conation excites his anger and leads to a violent assault upon the door ; the assault may be maintained until his baffled anger gives way to despair, his efforts relax, and he weeps. But, if he is an intelligent child, he may turn away from the footstool and drag up a chair and then, reaching the latch, secure the desired food. All this train of varied activity is maintained by the one original hunger-impulse ; the means necessary for the attainment of the end are sought as eagerly as the food, the object capable of directly satisfying the impulse ; the energy of the original hunger-impulse imparts itself to all the mediating actions found necessary for its satisfaction. And, on the recurrence of a similar situation, the child will go at once to seek the necessary chair, neglecting the footstool ; for the pleasure of success has confirmed this tendency, and the pain of failure has destroyed the tendency to seek the ineffectual footstool.

Now imagine a further complication. Suppose that, just as the child is about to seize the food he desires, some harsh elder discovers him and severely punishes him by shutting him up in a dark room where he suffers an agony of fear. On the next recurrence of the situation, the hunger-impulse drives him on as before until, perhaps, he hears in the distance the voice of the person who punished him. This brings to his mind the idea of that person, and this idea re-excites the fear induced by the punishment ; or, more probably, the sound of the voice directly excites the fear-impulse in the way we considered in Chapter II. There then takes place a conflict between the impulse to withdraw and the hunger-impulse ; the former proving stronger and overcoming the latter, he runs away and conceals himself ; presently the fear dies away, the idea of the desired object recurs and restores the original impulse, which then attains its end.

Such a brute conflict of impulses is characteristic of conation on the purely perceptual level of mental life. A rather higher stage is reached when the two impulses persist side by side, and in spite of fear, which keeps him ready to flee at the least noise, the boy steals towards his object, taking every precaution against being seen or heard. In this case the two impulses co-operate in determining each step in the sequence of actions—the one, the desire for food, predominating, the other merely modifying the way in which its end is attained. The state of affective consciousness accompanying the actions that proceed from the co-operation of the two impulses is complex ; it is not simply desire of food, and it is not simply fear, nor is it merely a rapid alternation of these two states, but rather an imperfect fusion of the two for which we have no name.

Behaviour of this kind may imply but a minimum of self-consciousness. It does not necessarily imply that the child has any idea or representation of himself suffering punishment or of the punishment itself. There are, no doubt, even in civilised communities, individuals of low type, brought up under unfavourable circumstances, whose behaviour hardly rises above this level. Whatever power of conceptual thought such a being attains is exercised merely in the immediate service of desire springing directly from some one or other of the primary instinctive impulses ; he may display a certain cunning in the pursuit of his ends and may form certain habits in the service of these impulses, perhaps an habitual caution in the presence of strangers, an habitual brutality towards those of whom he has no fear. He has no sense of responsibility or duty or obligation, no ideal of self; he has but rudimentary sentiments in regard to himself or others, has no character, whether good or bad, in the proper sense of the word, and, therefore, is incapable of true volition. In the case of behaviour on this comparatively low level, it is easy to understand that the instinctive impulses are the primary springs of all activities, and that the pains and pleasures experienced in the course of these activities merely serve to modify the actions motived by these impulses and thereby to shape the habits acquired in the service of them. Such behaviour may be called non-moral ; it can no more be made the subject of moral judgments than the behaviour of animals.

At the other end of the scale of conduct is the man all of whose actions are either the direct issue of volitions or the outcome of habits that are the secondary results of volitions or at least have been deliberately shaped, restrained here, encouraged there, by volitional control. Instead of acting at once upon each impulse, instead of striving to realise each desired end, such a man often resists, if he cannot altogether suppress, his strongest desires, and acts in direct opposition to them ; his conduct does not seem to be the issue of a mere conflict of desires, the stronger one prevailing ; he often seems to act, not in the line of least resistance, but in the line of greatest resistance ; the motives from which he acts may be, as facts of immediate experience, as feelings, emotions, conations, much less intense than the strong feelings, emotions, and desires whose promptings he resists.

How does it become possible for a man thus to act in the line of greatest resistance, to make the feebler prevail over the stronger desire ? It is the capacity for this kind of action that gives the highest moral conduct the appearance of being uncaused, the outcome of a free will, in the sense of a will not proceeding from antecedent conditions in the constitution of the individual. Such conduct raises the problem of the will in its most difficult form.

The child has to pass gradually in the course of its development from that lowest stage of behaviour to this highest stage ; and we must gain some understanding of this genesis of the higher conduct out of the lower, before we can hope to understand the nature of volition and its conditions and effects in the life of societies. The passage is effected by the development of self-consciousness, of the sentiments, and of character. And it is only when we trace the growth of self-consciousness that we can understand how it comes to play its part in determining conduct of the kind that alone renders possible the complex life of highly organised societies. For we find that the idea of the self and the self-regarding sentiment are essentially social products ; that their development is effected by constant interplay between personalities, between the self and society ; that, for this reason, the complex conception of self thus attained implies constant reference to others and to society in general, and is, in fact, not merely a conception of self, but always of one's self in relation to other selves. This social genesis of the idea of self lies at the root of morality, and it was largely because this social origin and character of the idea of self was ignored by so many of the older moralists that they were driven to postulate a special moral faculty, the conscience or moral instinct.

We may roughly distinguish four levels of conduct, successive stages, each of which must be traversed by every individual before he can attain the next higher stage. These are (1) the stage of instinctive behaviour modified only by the influence of the pains and pleasures that are incidentally experienced in the course of instinctive activities ; (2) the stage in which the operation of the instinctive impulses is modified by the influence of rewards and punishments administered more or less systematically by the social environment; (3) the stage in which conduct is controlled in the main by the anticipation of social praise and blame ; (4) the highest stage, in which conduct is regulated by an ideal of conduct that enables a man to act in the way that seems to him right regardless of the praise or blame of his immediate social environment.

The word " self " or " ego " is used in several different senses in philosophical discourse, the clearest and most important of these being the self as logical subject and the empirical self. In considering the genesis of moral conduct and character, we need concern ourselves with the empirical self only. We may have a conception of the self as a substantial or enduring psychical entity or soul whose states are our states of consciousness. Or we may hold that, by the very nature of our thought and language, we are logically compelled to conceive, and to speak of, the self as one pole of the subject-object relation in terms of which alone we are able to describe our cognitive experience, the knowing or being aware of anything. But such conceptions are products of reflection arrived at comparatively late, if at all, in the process of individual mental development, long after the complex conception of the empirical self has been formed through a multitude of experiences of a less reflective character. Those other conceptions of the self are of importance from our present point of view only in so far as they are taken up into, and become part of, the empirical conception of the self. Thus if a man believes that he has, or is, a substantial soul that can continue to enjoy consciousness after the death of the body, that belief is a feature of his total conception of his self which may, and of course often does, profoundly influence his conduct. But it is a feature of the empirical self of a certain number of persons only, and is not a part of the empirical self of others ; nor is it a part essential to moral conduct of the highest order, as we know from many instances. We have briefly to trace the genesis of the idea of the empirical self in so far as it is common to all normally constituted men ; and in doing so we shall follow in the main the description of the process recently worked out by several writers, notably by Professors Baldwin and Royce.

The child's first step in this direction is to learn to distinguish the objects of the external world as things existing independently of himself. How this step is achieved we need not stop to inquire. But we must note that all those features of the child's experience that are not thus extruded or referred to a world of external reality remain to constitute the nucleus of his idea of himself. The parts of his body, especially his limbs, play a very peculiar and important part in this process, because they are presented in consciousness sometimes as things of the outer world, as parts of the not-self, sometimes—when they are the seats of pain, discomfort, heat or cold, or muscular sensations—as parts of the self Thus the conception of the bodily self is in large part dependent on the development of the conception of things as persistent realities of the external world ; and the conception of those things is in turn completed by the projection into it of the idea of the self as a centre of effort, a cause of movement and of resistance to pressure. It is helpful to try to imagine how far the idea of the self could develop in a human being of normal native endowment, if it were possible for him to grow up from birth onward in a purely physical environment, deprived, that is to say, of both human and animal companionship. It would seem that under these conditions he could achieve at best but a very rudimentary and crude idea of the self.

It would be little more than a bodily self, which would be distinguished from other physical objects chiefly by its constant presence and by reason of the special interest that would attach to it as the seat of various pains. There would be a thread of continuity or sameness supplied by the mass of organic sensations arising from the internal organs and constituting what is called the coenæsthesia; and still more intimate and fundamental constituents of the empirical self would be the primary emotions, the conations, pleasures, and pains. The solitary individual's idea of self could hardly surpass this degree of complexity; for the further development of self-consciousness is wholly a social process.

At first the child fails to make a distinction between the two classes of objects that make up his external world, his not-self, namely, persons and inanimate objects. In the first months of life his attention is predominantly drawn to persons, at first merely because they are the objects that most frequently move and emit sounds, later because they bring him relief from hunger and other discomforts. He therefore learns to take interest in these moving objects, he watches them, he is soothed by their presence and distressed by their absence; and very early the mere sound of the mother's voice may still his crying, bringing anticipatory satisfaction of his needs. Very early also the expressions, especially the smile, on the faces of other persons and the cries of other children excite in him as purely instinctive reactions similar expressions, which are doubtless accompanied in some degree by the appropriate feelings and emotions; in this way he learns to understand in terms of his own experience the expressions of others, learns to attribute to them the feelings and emotions he himself experiences. He finds also that things resist his efforts at movement in very various degrees and that they forcibly impress movements on his limbs. So he comes to assume implicitly in his behaviour towards things of the external world the capacities of feeling and effort, of emotion and sympathetic response, that he himself repeatedly experiences. Inanimate objects are at first conceived after the same pattern as persons, and only in the course of some years does he gradually learn to distinguish clearly between persons and things, divesting his idea of inanimate things little by little, but never, perhaps, completely, of the personal attributes, the capacities for feeling and effort, which he recognises in himself. His treatment of inert things as beings possessed of personal attributes shows clearly that his ideas of things in general are bound up with, and coloured by, his rudimentary idea of his self as a being capable of feeling and effort, and that his idea of his self is not at first the idea of a merely bodily self fashioned after ideas of inert objects.

As the differentiation of persons and inert objects proceeds, persons continue to be the more interesting to the young child, for they continue to be the main sources of his pains and pleasures and satisfactions. His attention is constantly directed towards them, and he begins to imitate their behaviour. He finds that they do many things he cannot do, but would like to do ; and often he tends to do as they do simply because their actions arrest his attention and so give direction to the outflow of his abundant motor energies. But much more important than the actions of the people about him are the feelings and emotions that prompt them. The child soon learns that he can play upon these to a certain extent, and so acquires an interest in understanding the attitudes of others towards himself. He widens his experience and his understanding of the emotional attitudes and motives of others by copying them in his imitative play ; he puts himself into some personal relation he has observed, assumes the part of parent or teacher or elder sister, makes some smaller child, a dog, a cat, or a doll, stand for himself, and acts out his part, so realising more fully the meaning of the behaviour of other persons. In this way the content of his idea of his self and of its capacities for action and feeling grows hand in hand with his ideas of other selves ; features of other selves, whether capacities for bodily action or emotional expression, having first been observed without understanding of their inner significance, are translated into personal experience, which is then read back into the other selves, giving richer meaning to their actions and expressions.

And it is not only in play that this imitation of, and consequent fuller realisation of the meaning of, the behaviour of others goes on. It is carried out also in the serious relations of daily life, as when the little girl of five or six years talks to, plays with, comforts, or reproves a younger child in almost exact imitation of her mother.

In this way the child's idea of his self early comes to be the idea, not merely of his body and of certain bodily and mental capacities, but also of a system of relations between his self and other selves. Now, the attitudes of other persons towards him are more or less freely expressed by them in praise, reproof, gratitude, reproach, anger, pleasure or displeasure, and so forth. Hence, as he rapidly acquires insight into the meaning of these attitudes, he constantly sees himself in the reflected light of their ideas and feelings about him, a light that colours all his idea of his self and plays a great part in building up and shaping that idea ; that is to say, he gets his idea of his self in large part by accepting the ideas of himself that he finds expressed by those about him. The process is well illustrated by the case of the unfortunate child who is constantly scolded and told that he is a naughty boy.[1] Under these conditions the normal child very soon accepts these oft-repeated suggestions, learns to regard himself as a naughty boy, and plays the part thus assigned to him. Similarly, if he finds himself constantly regarded as clever, or irresistibly charming, or in any other light, he can hardly fail to regard himself in the same way, and the idea of his self moulded in this way by his social environment affects his conduct accordingly

The child's self-consciousness is, then, nourished and moulded by the reflection of himself that he finds in the minds of his fellows. It is hardly necessary to point out that this is true, not only of the mental but also of

[1] Cf. Kipling's story, *Baa-baa, Black Sheep.*

the bodily self; each of us gets some idea, more or less accurate, of his bodily appearance to others, a process in which civilised folks are greatly aided by the use of the mirror. The vain person is one who is constantly preoccupied with this idea of his bodily or total appearance in the eyes of others, and who never achieves so stable an estimate of himself, his powers, and appearance as to be indifferent to the regards of casual acquaintances.

We are now in a position to consider the transition from the second to the third stage of conduct, from that in which conduct is regulated chiefly by the expectation of rewards and punishments, and in which the subject's attitude in controlling any impulse is expressed by the phrase, I must or must not do this, to that in which the mere expectation of social praise or blame suffices to regulate conduct.

The oppositions and prohibitions that a child encounters in his social relations are not less important for the development of his personality than his sympathetic apprehension of the mental states of others. They serve especially to define and consolidate his ideas of his self and of other selves. When, for example, his desire to perform some particular action meets some personal opposition that his best efforts fail to break down, and especially if such insuperable opposition is consistently and unfailingly forthcoming, he gets both a more vivid idea of the personality of his opponent and a fuller sense of the social import of his own actions. And with his earliest experience of law, in the form of general prohibitions upheld by all members of his social environment, the child makes a further step in each of these directions. It is generally necessary that law shall be enforced at first by physical strength, and that his regard for it shall be encouraged by physical punishment; for the first step towards moral conduct is the control of the immediate impulse, and fear of punishment can secure this control of the immediate impulse by a more remote motive at an earlier age than it can otherwise be effected, fear being the great inhibitor of action. Law takes at

first the form of specific prohibition of some particular
kind of action, and by punishment the child is taught to
hold himself accountable for any action of that kind.   By
the extension of rules in number and generality his sense
of accountability to others is extended, and he is taught to
conceive himself more and more clearly as an agent in
fixed relations to other agents, as a member of a social
system in which he has a defined position ; and the
habit of control, and of reflection before action, is thus
initiated.   In all this a child is in all probability recapitu-
lating the history of social evolution, which, it would
seem, must have begun by the enforcement by the community, or by the strongest member of it, of rules of
conduct upon each member, rules which in primitive
societies were probably prescribed by rigid customs of
unknown origin rather than by the will or caprice of
individuals.

But social conduct founded only upon the fear of
punishment, on the sense of accountability, and on the
habits formed under their influence, is the conduct of a
slave.   It can hardly be called moral, even if laws are
never broken and all prohibitions and injunctions are
observed.   And, though the sense of accountability
founded on fear of punishment may effectively prevent
breaches of the law, it is of but little effect in promoting
positive well-doing.

Why is our conduct so profoundly influenced by
public opinion ?   How do we come to care so much for
the praise and blame, the approval and disapproval, of
our fellow-men ?   This is the principal problem that we
have to solve if we would understand how men are led
to control their impulses in a way that renders possible
the life of complexly organised societies.   For the praise
and blame of our fellows, especially as expressed by the
voice of public opinion, are the principal and most effective
sanctions of moral conduct for the great mass of men ;
without them few of us would rise above the level of mere
law-abidingness, the mere avoidance of acts on which
legal punishment surely follows ; and the strong regard
for social approval and disapproval constitutes an essential

stage of the progress to the higher plane of morality, the plane of obligation to an ideal of conduct.

The strength of the regard men pay to public opinion, the strength of their desire to secure the approval and avoid the disapproval of their fellow-men, goes beyond all rational grounds ; it cannot be wholly explained as due to regard for their own actual welfare or material prosperity, or to the anticipation of the pain or the pleasure that would be felt on hearing men's blame or praise. For, as we know, some men, otherwise rational and sane enough, are prepared to sacrifice ease and enjoyments of every kind—in fact, all the good things of life—if only they may achieve posthumous fame ; that is to say, their conduct is dominated by the desire that men shall admire or praise them long after they themselves shall have become incapable of being affected pleasurably or pain-fully by any expression of the opinions of others. The great strength in so many men of this regard for the opinions of others and the almost universal distribution of it in some degree may, then, fairly be said to present the most important and difficult of the psychological problems that underlie the theory of morals. Some of the moralists have simply ignored this problem, with the result that their moralising is largely vitiated and made unreal. It is perhaps worth while to consider an example of procedure of this kind, provided by a very respectable writer on morals ; the late Dr. T. Fowler [1] wrote : " Human nature, in its normal conditions, is so consti-tuted that the remorse felt, when we look back upon a wrong action, far outweighs any pleasure we may have derived from it, just as the satisfaction with which we look back upon a right action far more than compen-sates for any pain with which it may have been attended." The author went on to say that these pains and pleasures of reflection on our past actions are more intense than any other pains and pleasures, and he proposed to regard them as *the* moral sanction. According to this author's view all moral conduct arises, then, from an enlightened and nicely calculating hedonism ; for he represents the

[1] In *Progressive Morality.*

strongest motives to right conduct as being the desire of this greatest pleasure and the aversion from this greatest pain.

This is a fair example of the procedure of a moralist who has got beyond the old-fashioned popular doctrine of the conscience as a mysterious faculty that tells us what is right and what is wrong and impels us to pursue the right, but who lacks pyschological insight. Of course, if the statement quoted above were true, the moralist would be justified in simply recognising the fact and in leaving it to the psychologist to explain, if he could, how human nature had acquired this remarkable constitution. But the statement is in direct opposition to notorious facts, and in reducing all morality to hedonism it grossly libels human nature. The finest moral acts do not proceed from this desire of the pleasure of self-satisfied retrospection, nor from the aversion from the pain of remorse. When the patriot volunteers for the forlorn hope and goes to certain death, he cannot be seeking the pleasures of retrospective self-approval, and it would be absurd to suppose that he is driven on only by fear of remorse. Strong and fine characters, when forming their decisions pay little or no regard to the prospect of these pleasures and pains of retrospection ; while in the mass of men the pain of remorse for undetected lapses from morality is easily avoided or got rid of, and the pleasure of self-approval for virtues unknown to others is comparatively slight. The most that can be admitted is that in certain morbidly conscientious persons the prospect of these retrospective pleasures and pains may play some part in regulating conduct ; and it may be added that, if we were called upon to advise in the designing of a new type of human nature, we might be tempted to recommend that it should be constituted in this way, if only for the reason that justice would be so admirably served ; for each right or wrong act would then inevitably bring its own internal reward of pleasure or punishment of pain, as the nursery moralists, regardless of truth, have so often asserted that it does. Such a constitution of human nature would then obviate the irreparable injustices of this life which, human nature being what it is, constitute its darkest feature, and for which in every age men have sought to provide a remedy in some system of external rewards and punishments that shall be distributed in this life or another.

We cannot, then, consent to escape the difficulty of this problem by accepting any such false assumption as to the normal constitution of human nature, but must seek its solution in the development of the self-regarding sentiment.

There are two principal varieties of the self-regarding sentiment, which we may distinguish by the names " pride " and " self-respect." No sharp line can be drawn between them, unless we restrict the name " pride " to one extreme type of the sentiment that is but rarely met with ; in popular speech the forms of self-respect that approximate to this type are commonly called pride. Pride, taking the word in the narrow and strict sense, is a simpler sentiment than self-respect, and we may with advantage consider it first.

Imagine the son of a powerful and foolish prince to be endowed with great capacities and to have in great strength the instinct of self-display with its emotion of positive self-feeling. Suppose that he is never checked, or corrected, or criticised, but is allowed to lord it over all his fellow-creatures without restraint. The self regarding sentiment of such a child would almost necessarily take the form of an unshakable pride, a pride constantly gratified by the attitudes of deference, gratitude, and admiration, of his social environment ; the only dispositions that would become organised in this sentiment of pride would be those of positive self-feeling or elation and of anger (for his anger would be invariably excited when any one failed to assume towards him the attitude of subjection or deference). His self-consciousness might be intense and very prominent, but it would remain poor in content ; for he could make little progress in self-knowledge ; he would have little occasion to hear, or to be interested in, the judgments of others upon himself ; and he would seldom be led to reflect upon his own character and conduct. The only influences that could moralise a man so endowed and so brought up would be either religious teaching, which might give him the sense of a power greater than himself to whom he was accountable, or a very strong natural endowment of the tender emotion and its altruistic impulse, or a conjunction of these two influences

A man in whom the self-regarding sentiment had assumed this form would be incapable of being humbled—his pride could only be mortified ; that is to say, any display of his own shortcomings or any demonstration of the superiority of another to himself could cause a painful check to his positive self-feeling and a consequent anger, but could give rise neither to shame nor to humiliation, nor to any affective state, such as admiration, gratitude, or reverence, in which negative self-feeling plays a part. And he would be indifferent to moral praise or blame ; for the disposition of negative self-feeling would have no place in his self-regarding sentiment ; and negative self-feeling, which renders us observant of the attitudes of others towards ourselves and receptive towards their opinions, is one of the essential conditions of the influence of praise and blame upon us.

In many men whose moral training has been grossly defective the self-regarding sentiment approximates to this type of pure pride ; such men may revel in the admiration, flattery, and gratitude of others, but they remain indifferent to moral approval ; they may be painfully affected by scorn or ridicule, and but little by moral censure. And for most of us the admiration and the scorn or ridicule of others remain stronger spurs to our self-feeling than praise or blame, and still more so than mere approval and disapproval.

But the self-regarding sentiment of the man of normally developed moral nature differs from pride in that it comprises the disposition of negative self-feeling as well as that of positive self-feeling ; it is the presence of this disposition within the sentiment that distinguishes self-respect from pride. We have seen that negative self-feeling is normally evoked by the presence of any person who makes upon us an impression of power greater than our own, and that its impulse is to assume an attitude of submission towards that person, an attitude which becomes in the child, as his intellectual powers develop, an attitude of receptivity, of imitativeness and suggestibility. The main condition of the incorporation of this disposition in the self-regarding sentiment is the exercise of authority over the child by his elders. At first this authority necessarily demonstrates its superior power by means of physical force, later by means of rewards and punishments. On each occasion that the exercise of personal authority over the child makes him aware of a superior and inflexible power to which he must submit, his negative self-feeling is evoked ; then his idea of self in relation to that person becomes habitually accompanied and suffused by this emotion in however slight a degree, and he habitually assumes towards that person the attitude of submission. Thus the disposition of this emotion becomes incorporated in the self-regarding sentiment. Thereafter all persons fall for the child into one or other of two classes ; in the one class are those who impress him as beings of superior power, who evoke his negative self-feeling, and towards whom he is submissive and receptive ; in the other class are those whose presence evokes his positive self-feeling and towards whom he is self-assertive and masterful, just because they fail to impress him as beings superior to himself. As his powers develop and his knowledge increases, persons who at first belonged to the former class are transferred to the latter ; he learns, or thinks he learns, the limits of their powers ; he no longer shrinks from a contest with them, and, every time he gains the advantage in any such contest, their power of evoking his negative self-feeling diminishes, until it fails completely. When that stage is reached his attitude towards them is reversed, it becomes self-assertive ; for their presence evokes his positive self-feeling. In this way a child of good capacities, in whom the instinct of self-assertion is strong, works his way up the social ladder. Each of the wider social circles that he successively enters—the circle of his playmates, of his school-fellows, of his college, of his profession—

impresses him at first with a sense of a superior power, not only because each circle comprises individuals older than himself and of greater reputation, but also because each is in some degree an organised whole that disposes of a collective power whose nature and limits are at first unknown to the newly admitted member. But within each such circle he rapidly finds his level, finds out those to whom he must submit and those towards whom he may be self-assertive. Thus, when he enters a great school, the sixth-form boys may seem to him god-like beings whose lightest word is law; and even the boys who have been but a little while in the school will at first impress him and evoke his negative self-feeling by reason of their familiarity with many things strange to him and in virtue of their assured share in the collective power of the whole society. But, when he himself has reached the sixth form, or perhaps is captain of the school, how completely reversed is this attitude of submissive receptivity! When he enters college, the process begins again; the fourth-year men, with their caps and their colours and academic distinctions, are now his gods, and even the dons may dominate his imagination. But at the end of his fourth year, after a successful career in the schools and the playing fields, how changed again is his attitude towards his college society! The dons he regards with kindly tolerance, the freshmen with hardly disguised disdain; and very few remain capable of evoking his negative self-feeling—perhaps a " blue," or a " rugger international," or a don of world-wide reputation; for the rest—he has comprehended them, grasped their limits, labelled them, and dismissed them to the class that ministers to his positive self-feeling. And so he goes out into the great world to repeat the process and to carry it as far as his capacities will enable him to do.[1]

But if once authority, wielding punishment and reward, has awakened negative self-feeling and caused

[1] Professor Baldwin has well described this process, although he does not seem to have recognised the two instincts which, according to the view here taken, are the all-important factors. See *Social and Ethical Interpretations in Mental Development,* part i. chap. i.

its incorporation in the self-regarding sentiment, that emotion may be readily evoked ; and there is always one power [1] that looms up vaguely and largely behind all individuals—the power of society as a whole—which, by reason of its indefinable vastness, is better suited than all others to evoke this emotion and this attitude. The child comes gradually to understand his position as a member of a society indefinitely larger and more powerful than any circle of his acquaintances, a society which with a collective voice and irresistible power distributes rewards and punishments, praise and blame, and formulates its approval and disapproval in universally accepted maxims. This collective voice appeals to the self-regarding sentiment, humbles or elates us, calls out our shame or self-satisfaction, with even greater effect than the personal authorities of early childhood, and gradually supplants them more and more. And, when any individual passes upon us a well-founded judgment of moral approval or disapproval, he wields this power ; and, though he may be personally our inferior, his expressions may influence us profoundly, because we realise that his moral judgment voices the collective judgment of all-powerful society.

The exercise of inflexible authority over the child prevents, then, his self-regarding sentiment taking the form of pride in the strict sense, pride that acknowledges no superior, that knows no shame, and is indifferent to moral approval and disapproval; it gives the sentiment the form of a self-respect that is capable of humility, of the receptive imitative attitude of negative self-feeling ; and, by so doing, it renders the developing individual capable of profiting by example and precept, by advice and exhortation, by moral approval and disapproval.

Does, then, the incorporation of negative self-feeling in the self-regarding sentiment suffice to explain the strength of our regard for public opinion, for the praise and blame of our fellows ? Some further explanation is,

[1] I leave out of account here religious conceptions, which for many, perhaps most, persons play this all-important part in developing the self-regarding sentiment ; not because they are not of great social importance, but because the principles involved are essentially similar to those dealt with in this passage.

I think, required. For we can hardly assume that the two instincts of self-display and self-subjection, which respectively impel us to seek and to avoid the notice of our fellows, impel us also directly to seek approval and avoid disapproval. It might well be contended that positive self-feeling seeks merely to draw the attention of others to the self, no matter what be the nature of the regards attracted ; that it finds its satisfaction simply in the fact of the self being noticed by others. There is much in the behaviour of human beings to justify this view—for example, the large number of men who seek, and who are gratified by, mere notoriety, some of whom will even commit criminal acts in order to secure notoriety ; or again, the large number of people whose dress is clearly designed to attract attention, but which, even by the most disordered imagination, can hardly be supposed to excite admiration or approval ; or again, the curiously great satisfaction most of us find in seeing our names in a newspaper or in print of any kind. We have to ask, Do the many facts of this order imply perversion of instinct, or are they the outcome of its primitive and natural mode of operation ? It is not easy to decide ; but it is at any rate clear that the satisfaction of the impulse is greater when the regards of others are admiring regards, or such as to express in any way the recognition of our superiority in any respect. We shall probably be nearest the truth if we say that the impulse of positive self-feeling primitively finds its satisfaction when the attitude of others towards us is that of negative self-feeling, the normal attitude of men in the presence of one whom they recognise as superior to themselves. But even if this be granted, something more is needed to account for our great regard for praise and approval. Now, the effect upon us of praise and of approval is complex ; they do not, like admiration, simply bring satisfaction to our positive self-feeling ; in so far as praise is accepted as praise, it implies our recognition of the superiority of him who praises and an attitude of submission towards him. It is for this reason that all may admire a great man without impertin-ence, and that he may derive pleasure from their admiration ; whereas it is rightly felt to be an impertinence for any one to praise his superior in any art or department of activity ; and the superior is apt to resent praise coming from such a quarter, rather than to be pleased by it. It is for him to praise if he so chooses. That is to say, since our acceptance of praise involves the recognition of the superiority of him who praises, praise evokes our negative self-feeling ; but since it is an acknowledgment by our superior of our merit, it also elates us ; in other words, it evokes that state of bashfulness in which the impulses and emotions of the two instincts are imperfectly combined, but a bashfulness that is highly pleasant because both impulses are in process of attaining satisfaction. And moral approval, embodying as it does the verdict of society upon us, provokes a like complex satisfaction.

Blame and disapproval also are apt to produce a similarly complex effect. They check the impulse of self-assertion and evoke the impulse of submission ; and the resulting state ranges, according as one or other of these effects predominates, from an angry resentment, in which negative self-feeling is lacking, through shame and bashfulness of many shades, to a state of repentance in which the principal element is negative self-feeling, and which may derive a certain sweetness from the completeness of submission to the power that rebukes us, a sweetness which is due to the satisfaction of the impulse of submission.

The organisation of these two dispositions within the self-regarding sentiment renders us capable of this range of moral emotions ; but still something more is needed to explain the full magnitude of the effects of praise and blame, or of the mere anticipation of them. We may imagine, and, I think, we may also observe, persons in whom the sentiment is strong and whom it renders very sensitive to the opinions of others, yet whose conduct is not effectually controlled by the sentiment; for these persons are content to oscillate between the luxury of the elation induced by praise and the lesser luxury of repentance induced by blame.

In order that blame and disapproval shall exert their

full deterrent effects, it would seem that some other factor or factors must co-operate, that the sentiment must undergo a process of moralisation. We may find one such factor in the influence of punishment during the early days of childhood. Punishment and the fear of punishment are needed by most of us, we said, to initiate the control of the instinctive impulses and the habit of reflection before action. In the normal course of things punishment is gradually replaced by the threat of punishment in the successively milder forms of the frown and angry word, the severe rebuke, blame combined perhaps with reproach, and moral disapproval ; but all of these owe something of their effectiveness to the fact that they retain the nature of, because they continue to produce the effects of, the early punishments ; that is to say, they evoke some degree of fear ; for in virtue of the early punishments the disposition of fear has become incorporated in the self-regarding sentiment, and fear, as we know, is the great inhibitor of action. Fear, then, once incorporated in the sentiment, readily enters into and colours our emotional attitude towards authority in whatever form we meet it, renders us capable of awe and reverence in our personal relations, and is one of the principal conditions of the effectiveness of moral disapproval as a regulator of conduct.[1]

It is possible also that praise and approval owe some part of their power over us to their early association with the grosser forms of reward, which they gradually replace as the moral education of the child progresses.

There is yet another factor that operates in very various degrees in different persons to develop their regard for praise and blame, their sensitiveness towards moral approval and disapproval. It is what we have called active sympathy, that tendency to seek to share our emotions and feelings with others which, as we found, is rooted in primitive or passive sympathy and

[1] It may seem anomalous that fear should enter into the self-regarding sentiment ; but we have to remember that the object of this sentiment is not merely the self, but rather the self in relation to other persons.

in the gregarious instinct. The person in whom this tendency is strong cannot bear to suffer his various affective experiences in isolation ; his joys are no joys, his pains are doubly painful, so long as they are not shared by others ; his anger or his moral indignation, his vengeful emotion, his pity, his elation, his admiration, if they are confined to his own bosom, cannot long endure without giving rise to a painful desire for sympathy Active sympathy impels him, then, not only to seek to bring the feelings and emotions of his fellows into harmony with his own, but also, since that is often impossible, to bring his own into harmony with theirs. Hence he finds no satisfaction in conduct that is displeasing to those about him, but finds it in conduct that pleases them, even though it be such as would otherwise be distasteful, repugnant, or painful to himself. He finds in the praise of his fellows evidence that his emotions are shared by them, and their blame or disapproval makes him experience the pain of isolation. To many children this sense of isolation, of being cut off from the habitual fellowship of feeling and emotion, is, no doubt, the source of the severest pain of punishment ; and moral disapproval, even though not formally expressed, soon begins to give them this painful sense of isolation ; while approval gratifies the impulse of active sympathy and makes them feel at one with their fellows. And, as their social circle widens more and more, so the approval and disapproval of each wider circle give greater zest to their elation and a deeper pain to their shame, and are therefore more eagerly sought after or shunned in virtue of this impulse of active sympathy.

The two principles we have now considered—on the one hand the influence of authority or power, exercised primarily in bringing rewards and punishments, on the other hand the impulse of active sympathy towards harmony of feeling and emotion with our fellows—these two principles may sufficiently account, I think, for the moralisation of the self-regarding sentiment, for that regard for the praise and blame of our fellow-men and for moral approval and disapproval in general, which is so strong in most of us and which plays so large a part in shaping our sentiments, our character, and our conduct. This regard leads on some men to the higher plane of conduct, conduct regulated by an ideal that may render them capable of acting in the way they believe to be right, regardless of the approval or disapproval of the social environment in which their lives are passed.

There are, of course, great differences between men as regards the delicacy with which they apprehend the attitudes of others towards them. These differences are due in part to differences of intellectual power, but in greater part to differences in the degree of development of the self-regarding sentiment. Any man in whom this sentiment is well developed will be constantly observant of the signs of others' feelings in regard to him, and so will develop his powers of perceiving and interpreting the signs of the more delicate shades of feeling that do not commonly find deliberate expression. On the other hand, one whose perceptions are dull and whose self-regarding sentiment is not strong will be moved only by the coarser expressions of general approval and disapproval, by open praise and blame. Of two such men, the one will be said in common speech to have a sensitive conscience, and the other to have a less delicate, or a relatively defective, conscience.

Before going on to consider the higher kind of conduct, we may note some of the ways in which conduct, while remaining upon the plane of regulation by the impulses and emotions evoked by our social circle, may be complicated by altruistic motives. For, just as upon the purely instinctive plane of animal life the parental instinct may impel to behaviour from which we cannot withhold our admiration, so it may do upon this higher or middle plane also, working, of course, in more subtle fashion.

This occurs when the approval and the disapproval of others move us not merely through their appeal to the self-regarding sentiment, but also because we see that the act of approval is pleasing, and the act of disapproval painful, to him who approves or disapproves, and we desire to give him pleasure and to avoid giving him pain. This kind of motive implies the previous growth of a reciprocal sentiment of affection between the parties concerned. Therefore it can never efficiently supply the place of the coarser egoistic motives arising out of the self-regarding sentiment. Nevertheless, within the family circle or other intimate community it constitutes a very effective supplement to the egoistic motives. The conduct of affectionate children is in many cases very largely regulated by this motive from an early age. When they do what they have been taught to believe is right, it is not so much from the motive of securing praise or avoiding blame, as from that of giving pleasure, or avoiding the giving of pain, to those they love.

This is a kind of conduct that has its own peculiar charm, and it tends to the development of a very delicate and sympathetic character, though a narrow one; it cannot lead on to the stronger forms of character and to conduct based on broad moral principles; and it renders the person in whom this kind of motive predominates peculiarly dependent upon the natures of those to whom he is attached. Little girls act from this motive far more commonly, I think, than do boys; the tendency to its predominance seems to be one of the distinguishing features of their sex, as we might expect if it is true that, as we argued in Chapter III., all altruistic conduct has its root and origin in the maternal instinct.

The motive constituted by the co-operation of this altruistic impulse with the egoistic motive of securing praise or avoiding blame, is apt to reach a third degree of complication by the addition of an egoistic motive that is secondary to the altruistic. When a child acts in a way that secures the approval of his mother and pleases her, then, apart from the satisfaction of his tender impulse towards her, the pleasure that he derives from her approval is heightened by his perception of her pleasure in his conduct; and this increase of his own pleasure may have one, or both, of two sources—a simpler and a more complex. It may come by way of that primitive sympathetic reaction in virtue of which another's expression of a feeling or emotion generates the same feeling or

emotion in the observer.[1] There are persons, in whom
this primitive sympathetic tendency is very strong, whose
kindly conduct to those about them proceeds largely from
this motive; they cannot bear to see dull, unhappy
faces about them, for to do so depresses them; they
desire to see those about them bright and joyous, because
that renders themselves bright and joyous. If such a
person is in a position to influence markedly the welfare
of those by whom he is constantly surrounded—if, for
example, he is the head of a family or the master of many
servants who live in close contact with him—his conduct
towards them will be rendered kindly and beneficent up
to a certain point by the desire to secure this sympathetic
pleasure and to avoid sympathetic pain.

The more complex source of the pleasure that constitutes this tertiary motive to kindly conduct is the
sense of being the source of the pleasure the expressions
of which we observe in those round about us. The
impulse of positive self-feeling finds satisfaction in the
recognition by the recipients of our bounty of the fact
that our actions have benefited them, especially if those
recipients exhibit gratitude and deference, or even merely
a lively sense of favours to come. George Meredith's
Egoist is a fine study of conduct founded predominantly on the combination of the desire for reflex sympathetic pleasure with that for this kind of satisfaction of
the impulse of positive self-feeling; and many another
rich man's beneficence derives in the main from this last
source. Such conduct is, of course, thoroughly egoistic,
though it implies a disposition in which the primitive
sympathetic tendency and the altruistic impulse are
present in moderate strength. In many respects such
conduct will closely resemble altruistic conduct; but it
will differ in one very important respect, namely, that
the beneficence arising from the truly altruistic motive,
the impulse of the tender emotion, knows no limits and
may go the length of absolute sacrifice, even of life and
of all that is most valued in life; whereas this pseudo-
altruistic motive will never impel a man to sacrifice

[1] Cf. Chapter IV.

things the pain of the loss of which will counterbalance the pleasure he derives from contemplating the effects of his beneficent actions.

Again, this pseudo-altruistic motive can impel a man to act kindly to those only with whom he is in personal contact—those whose pleasure in, and whose gratitude for, his gifts and kindly attentions he can observe. To a man predominantly swayed by this motive the happiness or misery of all who are outside his circle and are not obtruded upon his attention will be a matter of indifference ; and even within his circle such a man will be unjust, and, like King Lear, will shower benefits upon those who respond most readily with expressions of pleasure and gratitude, and will feel resentment against those who remain unmoved. And his conduct will exert a deleterious influence upon those about him, will encourage flattery and toadying in some ; but it will provoke the scorn of men of sterner fibre, if they are able to understand his motives.

Upon this middle plane of conduct, and alongside the pseudo-altruistic conduct just now considered, must be ranged also the conduct proceeding from certain quasi-altruistic motives which arise from the extension of the self-regarding sentiment and are of the greatest importance for the life of societies.

We have already touched upon this subject in describing the full-blown parental sentiment. The parental sentiment, we said, is apt to be not only a tender sentiment of love for the child, but to be complicated by an extension of the self-regarding sentiment to him and to all that pertains to him, owing to the parent's intellectual identification of the child with himself.

But the child is by no means the only object to which the self-regarding sentiment may be, and very commonly is, extended, especially in men in whom the sympathetic tendency and the gregarious instinct are strong. After the child the family as a whole, both in the past and in the future as well as in the present, is the object to which this extension is most readily effected. A man realises, more especially perhaps in societies less complex than our own, that the family of which he is a part has a capacity for collective suffering and collective prosperity, that it is held collectively responsible and is the collective object of the judgments, emotions, and sentiments of other men ; he recognises that he, being a member of the whole, is in part the object of all these regards. In so far as he does this, all these attitudes of other men appeal to his self-regarding sentiment, evoke within it his anger, his gratitude, his revenge, his positive self-feeling, his shame. Therefore he desires that his family shall prosper and shall stand well in the eyes of men ; and this desire may become a motive hardly less strong than the care for his own welfare and position. The mere community of name of all the members of the family goes a long way to bring about this identification of the self with the family and the consequent extension of the self-regarding sentiment, results which are described by the popular phrase, " Blood is thicker than water."

And this extension should not, and usually does not, stop short at the family ; in primitive societies the tribe and the clan, which are the collective objects of the regards of other tribes and clans, become also the objects of this sentiment ; and among ourselves the growing child is led on in the same way to identify himself with, and to extend his self-regarding sentiment to, his school, his college, his town, his profession as a class or collective unit, and finally to his country or nation as a whole. It should be noted that, in each case, the extension of the sentiment depends upon the existence of the object, the school, the profession, the country, as one object among other similar objects, having to those others relations similar to the relations between persons, and being made by those other collective units and by men in general the object of judgments, emotions, sentiments, and actions, that are capable of evoking our resentment, our elation, our gratitude, and all the specifically personal emotions. So long as any such collective unit has no such " personal " relations, the extension of the self-regarding sentiment to it can hardly take place ; for example, it is not extended to the nation or people that is isolated from all others ;

and the extended sentiment tends to become stronger and more widely distributed the more abundant and intense are the interactions of the nation with others, the more free and vigorous become international rivalry and criticism; that is to say, our patriotic self-knowledge and sentiment, just like individual self-knowledge and senti- ment, are developed by constant interplay with other similar collective selves; they grow in the light of our advancing knowledge of those other selves and in the light of the judgments passed by them upon our collective self and upon one another.

From this kind of extended self-regarding sentiment, then, there may spring motives to conduct that may involve individual self-sacrifice; and, if the sentiment is strong, these motives may be powerful enough to overcome the more narrowly self-regarding motives; but in the main they work in harmony with these, as when the patriot soldier in giving his life in battle brings glory upon himself as well as upon his country.[1]

These quasi-altruistic extensions of the egoistic senti- ment constitute a very important part of the moral equip- ment of the individual; for they lead to the subjection of immediate personal ends in the service of social co- operation undertaken to secure the collective ends that individual action is powerless to achieve. They enrich our emotional life and raise our emotions and conduct to an over-individual plane.

[1] Like the fully developed parental sentiment, the patriotism of many men is a fusion of this quasi-altruistic extension of the self- regarding sentiment with the truly altruistic sentiment of love.

CHAPTER VIII

THE ADVANCE TO THE HIGHER PLANE OF SOCIAL CONDUCT

THE regulation of conduct by regard for the approval and disapproval of our fellow-men in the way discussed in the preceding chapter has certain limitations and drawbacks in spite of its supreme importance for the great mass of mankind.

In the first place the motives involved are fundamentally egoistic, although, as we saw, they may in certain cases be leavened with the altruistic impulse. Secondly, the approval and disapproval of our social circle cease to be effective sanctions of right conduct, as soon as we can be quite sure that our lapse from the standard demanded of us will never be known to those in whose minds we habitually see ourselves reflected and to whose approval and disapproval we attach importance ; or, in other words, the man whose right conduct rests on no higher basis than this sanction will not conform to the accepted code, in spite of opposing desires, when he is in no danger of being " found out." In order to remedy this defect of the sanction of public opinion, many peoples have supplemented it with the doctrine of an all-seeing eye, of a power that can observe all men's deeds, however carefully concealed, and will distribute rewards and punishments either in this life or another, according as these deeds conform to, or transgress, the current code of society. This supplementary sanction has, no doubt, proved very effective at a certain stage of the moral evolution of societies. But it must be recognised that the motives to which this sanction appeals are lower than the motives through which public opinion affects conduct; for it commonly relies upon rewards and punishments of a lower type than public approval and disapproval. Further, since the rewards offered and the punishments threatened are generally extremely remote in time and of uncertain character, and since some uncertainty as to their advent is apt to prevail, they have to be described as of very great magnitude if they are to be effective sanctions of conduct ; and the promise of disproportionately large rewards or punishments is in itself demoralising.

A third limitation of public opinion as the principal sanction of right conduct is that the conduct based upon it is entirely dependent on the nature of the moral tradition and custom of the society in which the individual grows up. Every society has its own code, and regards as absurd or even wicked those features of other codes in which they differ from its own. Illustrations of this fact abound in modern works on morals. Consider the case of the Fijian who regards it as his duty to slay his parents, when they attain a certain age, and gives them a tender and dutiful embrace before despatching them to the grave ; or of certain tribes of Borneo, among whom the taking of a head of man, woman, or child, even by methods involving perfidious treachery, is the surest road to popular esteem [1] ; or, again, the case of men of the same region who feel shame if seen by a stranger without the narrow bands that they commonly wear just below the knee, although no other garment is considered absolutely indispensable.

The sanction of public opinion, then, provides no guarantee against gross defects and absurdities of conduct ; and—what is of more importance—it contains within itself no principle of progress, but tends rather to produce rigid customs whose only changes are apt to be degenerative distortions of elements once valuable.

We have now to consider the ways in which some men

---

[1] I would ask the reader to refrain from taking this remark as applicable to all the peoples of Borneo. Most of these much maligned savages are quite incapable of such conduct, which is peculiar to the Sea Dayaks or Ibans.

advance to a plane of conduct higher than that regulated by the approval and disapproval of their social circle.

As the young child's sphere of social relations widens, he finds that certain of the rules of the family circle are everywhere upheld, that the breaking of them brings universal disapproval. In primitive societies, in which custom is usually extremely rigid and well defined and is unquestioned by any member of the society, this is true of all the current rules of conduct; the breach of any one brings universal disapproval. If the development of the self-regarding sentiment has been initiated in normal fashion by the exercise of authority over the child within the family circle, no boy or man can bear up against universal disapproval, unless he has found some higher source of moral guidance; hence we find that in many primitive or savage societies the rules of conduct, positive and negative, prescribed by custom, are scrupulously observed by all members.

In modern civilised societies, on the other hand, the child is generally subjected in his early years to much more numerous and more strictly enforced rules than the savage child ever knows. But, when he emerges from his home into a wider social sphere, he finds that some only of these rules, such as those against theft and murder, are maintained by the general voice of society, and are embodied in public law; these accordingly he continues to accept and observe. Others of his nursery rules, he finds, are not at all enforced by the opinion and feeling of the social circles in which he moves; while as regards others, again, he discovers that they are maintained by some persons and ignored by others—some of them being accepted in one social circle, others in another. And unless and until the average boy or man has risen to the higher plane of conduct, he will almost inevitably accept the peculiarities of the code of conduct of any circle, so long as he acts as a member of that circle.

The boy's discovery of the diversities of the codes of different members and circles of his society necessarily weakens the influence upon him of the rules in regard to which such diversities obtain; he is led by them to question the sanction of public opinion as applied to these departments of conduct; and, if he conforms to the diverse codes of his various social circles, his habits of moral conduct will not become so firm as they would if he were acquainted with one code only. These diversities of opinion in our complex civilised societies weaken, then, the force with which public opinion bears upon each individual's conduct, and they render the conduct of the mass of civilised men very much less consistent with the standards they profess than is that of most savages and barbarians. This, however, does not imply any innate moral inferiority of the civilised man; and, though it results in many grave social evils of kinds that are hardly known in well-organised savage societies, it brings one great advantage, which more than compensates civilised societies for the uncertainty of conduct and for the appearance of inferior morality on the part of the mass of their members; namely, it gives scope and occasion for the development of higher types of conduct and character than can be found in primitive communities, and hence it renders possible the progress of the moral tradition through the influence of these higher types.

For in primitive societies the precision of the customary code and the exact coincidence of public opinion with the code, allow of no occasion for deliberation upon conduct, no scope for individual moral judgment and choice; they provide no sphere of action for, and no stimulus to the development of, strong character, such as that of the man who can not only resist the promptings of his strongest instinctive impulses, but is capable also of standing up against public opinion and of doing what he judges to be right in defiance of it.

Let the reader try to imagine himself a member of a society whose code prescribes that he shall fall flat on his face whenever he meets his mother-in-law, or that he shall never mention certain of his relatives by name; and let him imagine that these and almost all other details of conduct are prescribed by rules the breach of which is visited with the reprobation of the whole community and often with the severest punishment; he will then understand how little scope is afforded by such a rigid code for the development of character and will.

The exercise of moral judgment is essential to the progress of individuals to the higher plane of conduct, and at this point we must briefly consider the conditions of such judgment. We may take Dr. Fowler's statement of the relation of moral judgment to emotion as representing the traditional and prevalent doctrine. He wrote : " When an action has once been pronounced to be right or wrong, morally good or evil, or has been referred to some well-known class of actions whose ethical character is already determined, the emotion of approval or disapproval is excited and follows as a matter of course "; and again : " No sooner is the intellectual process completed, and the action duly labelled as a lie, or a theft, or a fraud, or an act of cruelty or ingratitude, or the like, than the appropriate ethical emotion is at once excited." [1]   These and similar passages expound the traditional doctrine that the intellectual process of classing, or rightly naming, the conduct on which we pass moral judgment is the primary and essential step in exerting moral judgment, and that any emotion involved in the process is consequent on this intellectual process.   Others, on the other hand, totally reject this doctrine and reverse the order of the process.   Professor Westermarck, for example, maintains that moral judgments are expressions of moral emotions; he writes : " That the moral concepts are ultimately based on emotions either of indignation or approval, is a fact which a certain school of thinkers have in vain attempted to deny." [2]

Here we seem to have two flatly opposed doctrines of moral judgment. According to the one, judgment in every case produces the emotion ; according to the other, the emotion always determines the judgment. We must recognise that both are partially true. We must admit with Westermarck that the doctrine he opposes contains the intellectualist fallacy (against which there has recently been so widespread a reaction),

[1] *Progressive Morality.*
[2] *The Origin and Development of the Moral Ideas.* p. 4.

and that moral judgments are ultimately based on the emotions ; but then we must lay stress on the word " ultimately." For the emotions on which a man's moral judgments are based may be not his own emotions at the time of passing judgment, and not even his own earlier emotions, but the emotions, especially that dis-interested emotion we call moral indignation, of those who in bygone ages have played their parts in the shaping of the moral tradition.

No man, perhaps, ever has learnt to make moral judgments without previously experiencing some emotions of the kind from which the moral tradition ultimately sprang ; but it is at least theoretically possible to do so. For every moral tradition embodies a great number of ready-made judgments formulated in words ; and every well-organised society imposes its moral tradition upon each of its members with tremendous force. The child learns to accept many of these current maxims simply through suggestion, chiefly of the kind we have dis-tinguished as prestige-suggestion ; his parents and teachers repeatedly assert various moral propositions— it is wrong to tell a lie, to steal, to deceive, to be cruel ; it is right to be honest, kind, or generous ; and the voice of society, with its irresistible prestige, re-enforces these assertions. The child accepts these and many other similar propositions, and will apply them to the conduct of himself and others, before he can understand the ground of them, and before actions of the kind to which they are applicable have evoked in him any emotion that could determine the appropriate moral judgment. For example, a child will accept on suggestion, and will appropriately apply, the proposition that it is wrong to put your elbows on the table ; and, if he has acquired in some degree the sentiment for law or rule, he may pass the judgment, " You are very naughty to put your elbows on the table," with some indignation, just as he might reprove another for stealing or cruelty. It would be absurd to maintain that his condemnation of the elbows is an original moral judgment arising out of moral indignation. We must, in short, distinguish between original moral judgment and imitative moral judgments. As regards the latter, the traditional doctrine is true— the act of classing precedes and determines the moral emotion ; as regards original moral judgments, Wester- marck is in the right—they proceed directly from emotions.

The acceptance by the normal child of the major part of the current maxims is inevitable, if they are authoritatively asserted to him ; and his regard for them and conformity to them are secured by that process of development of the self-regarding sentiment by the agency of rewards and punishments, praise and blame, which we studied in the foregoing chapter. As regards these imitative judgments, we may go even farther than Dr. Fowler and the intellectualists, and may say that they may be made, not only without antecedent emotion, but also without any consequent moral emotion, that they may be purely intellectual, though this is seldom the case. That is to say, we accept certain maxims of conduct, either purely by suggestion or in part also in virtue of original judgments springing from our emotions and sentiments ; thereafter the accepted maxims or principles may give rise to moral judgment by way of a purely intellectual process,[1] the recognition of the agree- ment or disagreement of conduct with those principles, a process that may be expressed in syllogistic form—all lies are wrong ; that is a lie, therefore that is wrong And action also may follow in virtue of another previously accepted principle ; *e.g.*, I ought to punish your wrong conduct, therefore I punish you. Of course, such purely intellectual judgments, unsupported by emotion directly evoked by the conduct judged of, will not lead to efforts, on behalf of the right and against the wrong, so energetic as the efforts that may follow upon emotional judgments.

It is through original moral judgments of approval and disapproval that a man rises to the higher plane of conduct ; therefore it is in them that we are chiefly interested in the present connection.

[1] That is, a process as purely intellectual as any mental process can be ; the motive power of the process is not the impulse of some emotion directly evoked by the action judged.

Judgments of approval and disapproval are of two great classes, the æsthetic and the moral, which are differentiated from a common stock, but never completely differentiated by most men. We continue to use the same verbal expressions for judgments of both kinds ; ought, should, must, good, bad, wrong, and right are terms we use equally in moral and in æsthetic judgment. Such judgments are commonly said to spring from emotions of approval and disapproval, and, though there is much looseness and vagueness in current accounts of these alleged emotions, they are described, or referred to, by many authors as the specifically moral emotions. This is only one more illustration of the chaotic condition in which the psychology of the emotions still remains.

We have already seen that judgments of approval and disapproval may be purely intellectual processes, determined by previously accepted principles, and that such judgments may or may not be followed by appropriate emotions having as their objects the actions on which judgment has been passed. The question remains, Are there any specific emotions from which original moral judgments spring and which might be described as emotions of approval and disapproval ? The answer, I think, must be—Certainly not, there is no specific emotion of approval or of disapproval. For it is impossible to point to any such emotions distinct from those we have already recognised, and either form of judgment may spring from any one of several of those primary emotions or of the complex emotions. Judgment of approval may be prompted by admiration, gratitude, positive self-feeling, or by any one of the emotions when induced by way of the primitive sympathetic reaction ; judgment of disapproval springs most frequently from anger, either in its primary uncomplicated form,[1] or as an element in one of its secondary combinations, such as

[1] For example, some young children pass the original moral judgment, " You are naughty," upon any person who interferes with their play or work, who obstructs in any way the operation of any impulse and so evokes their anger.

shame, reproach, scorn, but also from fear and disgust. And they may, perhaps, be prompted by feelings of pleasure and pain respectively without emotion, though judgments having this source are properly æsthetic rather than moral judgments. In the young child these original moral judgments spring from the unorganised emotions; but in the adult they are more commonly prompted by emotions excited within some sentiment by actions affecting the object of the sentiment.

It is notorious that the sentiments determine our moral judgments. A man's concrete sentiments are apt to lead him to judgments that are valid only for himself, that have little objective or supra-individual validity; or, as is commonly said, they pervert his judgment. Thus it is notoriously difficult to pass moral judgments of general or objective validity upon the acts of those we love or hate. In the one case the emotions that determine approval are apt to play too great a part—for the principal emotions of the sentiment of love are of this order; in the other case those which determine disapproval. The abstract sentiments, on the other hand, such sentiments as the love of justice, truth, courage, self-sacrifice, hatred of selfishness, of deception, of slothfulness—these alone enable us to pass moral judgments of general validity. These sentiments for abstract objects, the various qualities of conduct and of character, are the specifically moral sentiments. It is, then, through the development of such abstract sentiments that the individual's moral development and the refinement of his moral judgment, both of his own acts and those of others, is effected, and that his moral principles are formed. And it is as regards this development of the abstract moral sentiments that the individual is most open to the influence of his social environment.

No man could acquire by means of his own unaided reflections and unguided emotions any considerable array of moral sentiments; still less could he acquire in that way any consistent and lofty system of them. In the first place, the intellectual process of discriminating and naming the abstract qualities of character and conduct is quite beyond the unaided power of the individual; in this process he finds indispensable aid in the language that he absorbs from his fellows. But he is helped not by language only; every civilised society has a more or less highly developed moral tradition, consisting of a system of traditional abstract sentiments. This moral tradition has been slowly formed and improved by the influence of the great and good men, the moral leaders of the race, through many generations; it has been handed on from generation to generation in a living form in the sentiments of the *élite*, the superior individuals of each generation, and has been embodied in literature, and, in partial fashion, in a variety of institutions, such as the Church. And every great and organised department of human activity, each profession and calling of a civilised society, has its own specialised form of the moral tradition, which in some respects may sink below, in other respects may rise above, the moral level of the unspecialised or general tradition.

The moral tradition of any society lives, in its fullest completest form, only in the strong moral sentiments of a comparatively few individuals, those who are expressively called "the salt of the earth." The great majority of men participate in it only in a very partial manner and in very diverse degrees, as regards both the strength of their moral sentiments and the nature and number of such sentiments as they in any degree acquire. And it is only by the absorption of the moral tradition that any man can acquire a respectable array of moral sentiments; even the great moral reformer begins by absorbing the moral tradition, before he can go on to add to it, or to reform it, in some respect. This is the truth expressed by T. H. Green when he wrote: " No individual can make a conscience for himself. He always needs a society to make it for him." [1]

If an individual is to acquire abstract moral sentiments, he must not grow up in a society that is completely bound by the laws of rigid and uniform custom. Rigid custom is the cement of society in the ages preceding the forma-

[1] *Prolegomena to Ethics*, p. 351.

tion of a moral tradition, and the breaking of the rigid bonds of custom, bonds which were probably essential for the preservation of primitive societies, was the prime condition of the growth of the moral tradition of the progressive nations. In the same way, it is a prime condition of the moral progress of individuals ; the individual also must not be bound in absolute obedience to any system of rules of conduct prescribed by custom or in any other manner. For in either case he has no occasion for reflection upon conduct, no scope for the free exercise of moral judgment and choice, no opportunity of acquiring by absorption the traditional system of moral sentiments.

Suppose that, as is the case in many savage societies, the conduct of each of us in every social relation were prescribed by a rigid custom ; suppose, as was suggested above, that you must never speak to, or look at, your mother-in-law ; that, if you meet her out of doors, you must fall flat on your face until she has passed by ; and that infringement of this customary law is invariably punished by death or other severe penalty. Suppose also that all the rest of your social behaviour were defined with similar precision and rigidity. Or imagine the case of a member of one of the mediæval religious communities whose only duty, to which he was trained from earliest youth, was unquestioning obedience to his superior. It is easy to understand that under such conditions we should hardly be led to reflect on conduct, to acquire the moral sentiments, or to make moral judgments of any kind ; for our own conduct, we should merely have to ascertain what behaviour custom prescribes for each situation and to observe its prescription ; and, as regards the conduct of other men also, there would be no scope for moral judgment but only for the ascertainment of fact. Did he, or did he not, neglect this observance ? If he did, he must be punished ; if not, he is to go free. That is to say, under such a system there is scope only for the merely legal attitude, but none for that of moral judgment.

But the child growing up in the midst of a complex

and cultured society, coming in contact with various social circles in which diversities of code and opinion obtain, and reading history and romance, becomes acquainted with a great variety of opinions, of moral codes, and of character and modes of conduct; while language leads him to the formation of a certain number of abstract conceptions of qualities of conduct and character, however vague and fluctuating. If, under these conditions, the child were left entirely without moral guidance, he would acquire some abstract moral sentiments, whose nature would be determined by the strongest emotional dispositions of his native disposition and by the chance circumstances of his life; he would acquire some sentiment of liking for all those qualities and types of conduct and character which brought him the most frequent and intense satisfactions, both ideal and actual, and some sentiment of hate or dislike for those which most often thwarted his efforts and brought him pain. That is to say, he would build up certain abstract sentiments by means of a series of original moral judgments coming from his emotions and his concrete sentiments.

But when the child is thus brought into contact with a variety of characters, codes, and opinions, he normally comes also under strong influences that mould his growing abstract sentiments. The moral sentiments that are most fully embodied in the moral tradition of his time and country are impressed upon him on all hands by precept and example—*e.g.*, love of common honesty and of courage, dislike of meanness and of cruelty; while of other moral sentiments belonging to the more refined part of the moral tradition, he finds some entertained by some persons, others by other persons. Among all these persons some will impress their abstract sentiments upon him more than others; and, in the main, those that so impress him will be those whose power, or achievements, or position, evoke his admiration. Of all the affective attitudes of one man towards another, admiration is that which renders him most susceptible to the other's influence; and it is easy to see why this should be so, if our analysis of admiration was correct. We said [1] that admiration is compounded of wonder and negative self-feeling. The impulse of wonder, then, keeps his attention directed upon the admired person ; the impulse of negative self-feeling throws him into the submissive, receptive, suggestible attitude towards the object of his admiration. Hence the child accepts by suggestion the moral propositions of the persons he admires, he imitates their actions and sympathetically shares their moral emotions ; and so his developing abstract sentiments are moulded in accordance with those of the admired persons. If these persons deliberately aim at moulding his sentiments, the extent of their influence in this direction is only limited by his intellectual capacity for forming abstract conceptions of the various qualities of conduct and character.

The child, then, builds up his abstract sentiments by means of a series of emotional judgments, judgments of approval and disapproval, which are original in the sense that they spring from his emotions and concrete sentiments ; but they are not independently formed judgments, but rather emotional judgments made under the very powerful directing influence of personal suggestion and sympathy. In modern societies this influence is exerted, not only through personal contact, but on a very great scale by literature ; for, in so far as we learn to grasp in some degree the personality of an author and to admire him, the expressions of his abstract sentiments exert this personal influence upon us, more especially, of course, upon the young mind whose sentiments are not fully formed and crystallised. This, of course, is the principal reason that literature read as such, as the expressions of great personalities that evoke our admiration, is so superior, as food for the growing mind, to the productions of the daily and weekly press ; for, no matter how well written these may be, nor how admirable the moral sentiments expressed or implied, they fail to exert the great influence of an admired personality. Even if the author of acknowledged eminence is not intrinsically

[1] See p. 110.

superior to one less generally recognised, he will exert a greater moulding influence upon the abstract sentiments of his readers, simply because their knowledge that so many others admire, and have admired, this author, increases by mass-suggestion and sympathy their admiration for him, and so increases also their receptivity towards him and all his opinions and expressions.

In all this absorption of the more refined parts of the moral tradition, the native disposition of the individual will make itself felt more or less. If the training of the moral sentiments is most carefully and skilfully supervised from the first years of life, the native disposition will make itself felt, not so much in the nature of the abstract objects for which sentiments of liking and disliking are acquired, but rather in the strength of the various sentiments and the force of the emotions awakened within them. But if, as is more usually the case, a certain liberty of choice is allowed to the young mind, its native disposition exerts a greater selective influence, and, by determining the choice of admired models, may lead to a vastly greater development of some of the moral sentiments than of others. And, no matter how strong the moulding influences may be, they must fail to develop any strong sentiment for an abstract object, if that sentiment involves or implies an emotional capacity or instinct that is natively defective; if, for example, a man's native disposition comprises only a weak instinct of curiosity, he will hardly acquire a strong sentiment for the life of learning and research; if it is defective in the instinct of self-assertion and its emotion of positive self-feeling, he will hardly acquire a strong sentiment for self-perfection; if it is defective in the protective instinct and its tender emotion, he will hardly acquire a strong sentiment for altruism and self-sacrifice.

When the abstract sentiments have been acquired, they determine our emotional responses to the conduct and character of ourselves and others; the intellectual process of classing an act under its proper heading, the apperception of it as an act of justice, of self-sacrifice, or of cruelty, is apt to call out at once the appropriate emotion in some degree, and secures our approval or disapproval, in accordance with the nature of the sentiment we have acquired for that quality or class of action. The objects of our sentiments of love and hate necessarily become objects of desire and aversion. Thus, if we have acquired the sentiment of love of justice and we are credibly informed that any person is in serious danger of suffering injustice, the desire of justice, arising within the abstract sentiment, impels us to efforts to secure justice.[1] The strength of the motive, the intensity of the desire or aversion awakened within the system of the sentiment, depends in such cases upon the strength of the sentiment. In most men the desires and aversions arising from the abstract sentiments are apt to be much inferior in strength to those excited within the concrete sentiments ; hence, as motives of these two classes are frequently opposed in tendency, the mere possession of moral sentiments does not always suffice to determine a man to action in accordance with them. A sentiment of love for an individual may, and often does, give rise to a desire that conflicts with the desire for justice arising from the sentiment for justice ; and the self-regarding sentiment with its strong emotions is especially apt to conflict with the moral sentiments. Hence it is possible for a man to have the most beautiful moral sentiments and yet to act in ways that are not altogether admirable.

Even the purely altruistic sentiments, the love of beneficence or of mankind in general, will not necessarily suffice to enable a man to reach the highest plane of conduct—not even if they are strong. The habit of self-criticism is required, and this implies, and arises from, a strong self-regarding sentiment. The special moral sentiments must be brought into connection with, and organised within, the system of a more compre-

---

[1] The effective operation of this sentiment on a great scale has recently been illustrated in several cases in which the most disinterested efforts of private individuals have corrected the effects of miscarriages of legal procedure—e.g., the cases of Mr. Beck and Mr. Edalji. Some years ago the unjust condemnation of Major Dreyfus produced in France a still more striking and famous display of disinterested effort on behalf of the principle of justice.

hensive sentiment—what may be called the master sentiment among all the moral sentiments, namely, the sentiment for a perfected or completely moral life. If a man
acquires this sentiment, he will aim at the realisation of
such a life for all men as far as possible ; but, since he
has more control over his own life than over the lives of
others, he will naturally aim at the perfection of his own
life in the first place   In this sentiment, then, the altruistic
and egoistic emotions and sentiments may find some sort
of reconciliation ; that is to say, they may become
synthesised in the larger sentiment of love for an ideal
of conduct, the realisation of which involves a due proportion of self-regarding and of altruistic action ; and
the desire for the realisation of this ideal may become
the master-motive to which all the abstract sentiments
lend whatever force they have.

It is worth noting in passing that in many persons
æsthetic appreciation of the beauty of fine character
and conduct may play a large part in the genesis of
the ideal of conduct and of the sentiment of love for this
ideal.   Not all admiration is æsthetic admiration, but
if the object that we admire on account of its strength
or excellence of any kind presents a complex of harmoniously organised and centralised relations and activities,
the mere contemplation of it pleases us, in so far as we
are capable of grasping the harmony of its complex
features ; that is to say, it affords us an æsthetic satisfaction, and therefore has a certain value for us and becomes
an object of desire.   A fine character, or a life finely lived,
has these æsthetic properties, and therefore our admiration
of it will be an æsthetic admiration, in so far as we appreciate its harmony and unity ; we are then disposed to
desire all the more strongly that our own character shall
be of this nature, shall appear to the world, or all that
part of it whose opinion we most value, as having æsthetic
properties that lend it a certain dignity and nobility ;
our self-regarding sentiment seeks this additional satisfaction, we desire and strive to realise this æsthetic
ideal.

The desire resulting in this way from æsthetic apprecia-

tion blends in very various proportions with the purely
moral desire for the realisation of the ideal of conduct ;
and in some persons of the type of Marius the Epicurean
this desire may be the principal factor in the regulation of
conduct.

CHAPTER IX

VOLITION

WE have now sketched the way in which an individual may acquire an ideal of conduct and the way in which his primary instinctive dispositions, becoming organised within the complex moral sentiments, may impel him to strive to realise such an ideal. We have seen that both of these achievements, the acquisition of the ideal and of the sentiment for the ideal, are rendered possible only by the absorption of the more refined parts of the moral tradition, under the influence of some of the personalities in whom it is most strongly embodied. These persons, we said, exert this influence upon us in virtue principally of the admiration that they evoke in us. This admiration, which renders us receptive to their opinions and examples, and responsive to their emotions, may be, of course, and often is, blended with fear, yielding the tertiary compound emotion which we call awe; and this may be further complicated by an infusion of tender emotion, which renders the complex emotion one of reverence; when the influence of the persons who excite these complex emotions becomes the more powerful in proportion to the additional strength of the complex impulses evoked by them.

It was, I think, in the main because the older moralists neglected to take sufficiently into account the moral tradition and the way in which it becomes impressed upon us, and because they treated of the individual in artificial abstraction from the social relations through which his moral sentiments are formed, that they were led to maintain the hypothesis of some special faculty, the conscience, or the moral sense or instinct, or the moral consciousness,[1] in seeking to account for moral conduct.

But, though we may have accounted for the desire to realise an ideal of conduct, we have still to account for the fact that in some men this motive acquires predominance over all others and actually regulates their conduct in almost all relations and situations. For some men acquire the ideal and the sentiment, but fail wholly or in part to realise the ideal. We have to recognise that the desire that springs from the completed moral sentiment is usually of a thin and feeble sort in comparison with the fiercer, coarser desires that spring directly from our instincts and from our concrete sentiments. It is therefore no matter for surprise that, in so many cases, the acquirement of an ideal of conduct and of the sentiment for it does not suffice to secure its realisation. How, then, are we to account for the fact that the conduct of the good man is in the main regulated according to the promptings of these weaker desires, and against the stronger more urgent prompting of the more primitive desires ? It is this appearance of the overcoming of the stronger by the weaker impulse or motive, in so many cases of right action following upon a conflict of motives and the exercise of moral effort, that leads Pro-

[1] This hypothesis is no longer maintained by any considerable body of instructed opinion. A traditional doctrine of a different type, equally inconsistent with the view expounded in this book, is that of the Rationalist school of Ethics. The essential feature of their teaching is that they treat " moral approbation as essentially an act of judgment, as the works of Reason, as coming from the intellectual side of our mental nature." This is the position maintained in its most moderate and reasonable form by Dr. Rashdall in his *Theory of Good and Evil*, and in his later book, *Is Conscience an Emotion ?* (Boston, 1914). In the latter book he has undertaken to defend this position against the criticism of it implied in the account of our moral nature contained in these pages. I have replied to his arguments in an article published in the *Hibbert Journal* for January 1921. Here I can only point out that my account does not imply that Conscience is an emotion, and that it does not, of course, deny that Reason plays a part in all our moral judgments, though it does deny that Reason alone, without the aid of moral experience, of the moral tradition, and of moral character, is capable of leading us to true moral judgments. Cf. p. 326.

fessor James to define moral action as " action in the line of the greatest resistance." [1]

It is in these cases of moral conflict that volition, or effort of the will in the fullest sense of the word, comes in to determine the victory to the side of the weaker impulse. Professor James puts the matter schematically in this way :

I (ideal impulse) in itself weaker than P (the native propensity).

I+E (effort of will) stronger than P.

Professor James, like many others, finds here an ultimate and irresolvable problem in face of which we can only say—*The will* exerts itself on the side of the weaker motive and enables it to triumph over its stronger antagonists—while leaving the word " will " simply as the name for this possibility of an influx of energy that works on the side of the weaker motive, an influx of energy of whose source, causes, or antecedents we can say nothing. That is to say, Professor James, failing to carry the analysis of volition beyond the point of determining what the effects of volition are, adopts the doctrine of indeterminism. I do not propose to go at length into the world-old dispute between libertarians and determinists. But the acceptance of the libertarian doctrine in its more extreme form would be incompatible with any hope that a science of society, in any proper sense of the word " science," may be achieved ; for in face of each of the most important problems of such a science, we should have to content ourselves with the admission of impotence.[2]

---

[1] *Principles of Psychology*, vol. ii. p. 549.

[2] This we may see most clearly in the case of the problem of the evolution of the moral tradition. If, as we have said, the moral tradition has been slowly evolved by the influence of the precept and example of the great moral leaders, and if, as the libertarians maintain, all the moral victories of such leaders, in virtue of which they attain their ascendancy over their fellow-men and their power of moulding the moral tradition, have this mysterious and utterly incomprehensible source, then the growth of the moral tradition may be described but cannot be explained, and we have no—or but very little—ground to suppose that what we can learn of its growth in the past will justify any assumptions or forecasts as to its growth in the future. And this must remain true no matter how small be the quantity of " will energy " postulated by the libertarians to account for the turning of the scale in the conflict of motives.

Some attempt must therefore be made to show that the effort of volition is not the mysterious and utterly incomprehensible process the extreme libertarians would have it to be; but that it is to be accounted for by the same principles as other modes of human activity; that it involves no new principles of activity and energy, but only a more subtle and complex interplay of those impulses which actuate all animal behaviour and in which the ultimate mystery of mind and life resides.

The dispute has been conducted upon two different grounds, the moral and the psychological. On the former ground it has been urged, again and again, that if we do not recognise freedom of the will, do not recognise some degree of independence of antecedent conditions in the making of moral choice, we cannot recognise any moral responsibility, and that, therefore, to deny the freedom of the will is to undermine all morality and to deprive our systems of rewards and punishments, of praise and blame, of all logical justification. This argument implies a false conception of responsibility and of the proper nature and purpose of rewards and punishments, although it has been urged by many persons who might have been expected to avoid this confusion of popular thought.

Responsibility means accountability—to be responsible for a wrong action means to be rightly liable to punishment. If to punish means simply to inflict pain from the motive of resentment or revenge, then it may fairly be said that it is illogical for the determinist to hold any one liable to punishment, *i.e.*, responsible, that he ought rather to say : " Poor fellow, you could not help it ; therefore I, recognising that you are merely a piece of mechanism, will not vent my resentment upon you ; you are not responsible." But the infliction of pain from the motive of revenge or resentment is entirely a-moral or immoral. Punishment is only justifiable, is only moral punishment, when inflicted as a deterrent from further wrong-doing, and as an influence capable of moulding character. That is to say, men are only morally responsible, or rightly liable to punishment, if the punishment may fairly be expected to deter them from further wrong-doing, or to modify their natures for the better.[1] It is for this reason that, while we rightly punish children and animals, we do not punish madmen. These last are not rightly liable to punishment, they are not held responsible, because it has been found that punishment will not exert on them its normal deterrent and improving effects.[2] The attitude of the judge, or father, who has to punish, is then : " I punish you in order that you may be deterred from repetition of your bad conduct. I know that you could not help it, but, if you are not punished, you will, on the next occasion of temptation, still be unable to avoid misconduct; whereas, if I now punish you, you will in all probability be deterred ; and the punishment may initiate or strengthen in you the habit of control of your impulses, and, by inducing in you a greater regard for authority, it may set the growth of your self-regarding sentiment upon the right lines." In other words, according to the determinist view, if a man is morally punishable, *i.e.*, responsible, it is because his wrong action was the outcome of his own nature, was determined by conditions of which the most important lie in his mental constitution, and because it may reasonably be hoped that punishment may modify his nature for the better.

If the opposed view is true, if a man's voluntary actions are not in the main determined by conditions comprised within the system of his mental constitution, the only ground for punishing him must be the emotion of resentment or revenge. For, if the issues of our moral conflicts are decided, not by the conditions of our own natures, but by some new beginning, some causal factor having no antecedents, or by some mysterious influence

---

[1] I purposely avoid touching upon the more difficult moral problem, How far is punishment of one man justified by its deterrent or reforming effects upon others ?

[2] In so far as punishment will produce these effects upon madmen they have a moral right to be punished. The medical profession generally ignores this truth in its perennial conflict with the lawyers. It is for them to determine which of the mental diseases render the patient's conduct incapable of being controlled by punishment or by the threat of it, and which leave him still susceptible to the deterrent and reforming influence of punishment.

coming upon us from an unknown source, a prompting from God or devil—or from any other source the libertarian likes to assign it outside our own natures—then clearly we deserve neither praise nor blame, neither reward nor punishment ; and it is useless to attempt to modify the issue of such conflicts by modifying our natures by means of these influences.[1] That is to say, if the extreme libertarian doctrine is true, there can be no moral punishment of a wrong-doer, but only vengeful harming of him, and therefore there can be no moral responsibility. The argument from moral responsibility is therefore altogether on the side of the determinist. It is the advocates of free will who would undermine moral responsibility.

But there is another argument for free will based on moral needs, which is not to be set aside so easily. If, as the determinist asserts, each of my actions is completely determined by antecedent conditions and processes that are partly within my own nature, partly in my environment, why should I make any moral effort ? My conduct will be what it will be, the issue of conditions that existed and determined it in every detail long before I was born ; therefore it would be foolish of me to take pains to choose the better course and to make efforts to realise it. This is the real crux of this dispute. This is the legitimate inference from determinism. This is its moral difficulty, which has seldom been squarely faced by its advocates, and never overcome by them. To say, as so many of them say, that we are free to act in accordance with our own natures, that the conditions of our actions are within us, and that this is all the freedom that any reasonable man can desire—to say this does not remove, or in any degree lessen, this moral difficulty. Such reflections may, no

---

[1] The only possible answer of the libertarians to this argument seems to be : Yes, but if this outside influence is " a very little one," we may, by means of punishment, give the good influences a better chance of determining a favourable issue of our moral conflicts. This seems to be the line recent defenders of free will are inclined to take. They are, nevertheless, bound to admit that, since the magnitude of these outside influences is unknown, the recognition of them must weaken the case for punishment, and must diminish to an unknown and quite incalculable extent our moral responsibility.

doubt, be satisfactory enough to those who believe that their own natures are above serious reproach, but not to those who can point to undesirable ancestry and unmistakable flaws in their native dispositions. Nothing is more difficult than to give any helpful answer to one who adopts this line of justification for moral slackness ; we can only hold him responsible and punish him. One may suspect that the determinists, most of whom try to put aside this difficulty by some scornful reference to Oriental fatalism, are in general really afraid of it, and have entered into a conspiracy resolutely to ignore, since they cannot dispel, this dark shadow on human life.

But psychology must not allow its investigations and theories to be biased by moral needs ; and it must not easily accept, as evidence in favour of free will, the difficulty of finding in our mental constitution the source of that influx of energy which seems to play the decisive rôle in volition.[1]

[1] The most successful defence of indeterminism yet made is that of Dr. Schiller (*Studies in Humanism*). His position is not quite the same as Professor James's. He suggests that there may arise conjunctions of conditions whose issue is indeterminate in the sense that opposing forces are exactly balanced in an unstable equilibrium, which we might compare to that of a billiard ball balanced on a knife-edge. A strictly minimal force might then determine the issue in either direction, and so produce very important consequences ; *e.g.*, if the knife-edge were on the water-parting of the Rocky Mountains, the ball might reach the Atlantic or the Pacific Ocean, according to the direction of this minimal force. Dr. Schiller points out truly enough that, for anything we know, such situations may occur in both the physical and moral spheres ; for, if their issue is thus determined by some such minimal force that is not determined by antecedent conditions, the calculation of the strength of the opposing forces, with sufficient accuracy to enable us to discover the presence of this unconditioned factor, is beyond our power, and we shall probably never be able to make this calculation for the physical, and certainly never for the moral, world. If this unconditioned factor is assumed to be in every case of strictly minimal strength, the admission of its reality will not seriously undermine the principles of moral responsibility ; but it will, as pointed out above, introduce an incalculable element among the factors which the student of society has to try to take into account, and therefore will make difficult if not impossible the attempt to construct a science of history and of society. Whether it would lighten in any degree the moral difficulty of determinism discussed above is a more difficult and subtle problem ; I cannot at present see that it can have any such result, save in the following way : it would allow us to believe in " a power, not ourselves, that makes for

The psychological problem we have to face is, then, this : Can we give any psychological account of the conditions of the effort of will, which, being thrown on the side of the weaker, more ideal, motive, may cause it to prevail over the coarser, more primitive, and stronger motive ?

We have recognised that all impulses, all desires and aversions, all motives—in short, all conations—fall into two classes : (1) those that arise from the excitement of some innate disposition or instinct ; (2) those that arise on the excitement of dispositions acquired during the life of the individual by differentiation from the innate dispositions, under the guidance of pleasure and of pain. We may, then, restate our problem in more general terms, as follows : Is volition only a specially complex case of conation, implying some conjunction of conations of these two origins rendered possible by the systematic organisation of the innate and acquired dispositions ?　Or does it involve some motive power, some source of energy, some power of striving, of an altogether different order ?　Clearly we must attempt to account for it in terms of the former alternative, and we may only adopt the latter if the attempt gives no promise of success. It may fairly be claimed, I think, that we can vaguely understand the way in which all volition may be accounted for as a special case of conation, differing from other conations, not in kind, but only in complexity. We may see this most clearly if we form a scale of conations ranging from the simplest type to the most complex and obscure type, namely, moral choice achieved by an effort which, in the struggle of higher and lower motives, brings victory to the side of the higher but weaker motive. If types of conation can be arranged in such a scale, each type differing from its neighbours only very slightly, that

righteousness," and such a belief might encourage and stimulate us to make efforts towards the realisation of the purpose of that power. Since, then, a decision of this question cannot be attained on empirical grounds, it remains open to us to postulate indeterminism ; and if such postulation makes for the predominance of right conduct, it is difficult to find any good reason for refusing to follow James and Schiller when they ask us to commit ourselves to it.

will afford a strong presumption of continuity of the scale ;
for if volition involves some peculiar factor, not operative
in other conations, we ought to be able to draw a sharp
line between the volitional and the non-volitional conations.
That such a scale can be made is, I think, indisputable ;
and an attempt to illustrate it will be made on a later page.

But, though we cannot draw any sharp line between
volitions and conations of other types, it is convenient
and justifiable to reserve the name " volition," or act of
will, for a particular class of conations, and we must
first try to determine what are the marks of the conations
of this class.

Some authors do not recognise this distinction, but
describe all conations, every form of mental activity,
as issuing from the will. For Schopenhauer, for example,
the blind appetitions displayed by lowly organisms were
acts of will, equally with our greatest moral efforts ; for
Professor Bain there was no such distinction, because he
regarded all activities as alike prompted simply by pleasure
or pain, as efforts to secure pleasure or to escape from
pain. And it was for many years a common practice to
class all bodily movements as either unconscious reflex
actions or voluntary actions. But of late years increase of
insight into the simpler modes of action and the better
comprehension of the large part they play in our lives,
have led to the general recognition of the propriety of
the distinction of volitional and non-volitional conations.
Herbert Spencer and others, confining their attention to
the conations expressed in bodily movements, have
regarded as volitional all movements that are immediately preceded by the idea of the movement.[1] But this
precedence of the idea of movement is merely the mark of
ideo-motor action, and many such movements take place
in an automatic or machine-like fashion that is very
different from unmistakable volition.

Others adopt as the criterion of volitional action its
antecedence by the idea or representation of the end to

[1] This view seems to be maintained still by Professor Höffding
in a recent article in the *Revue Philosophique* (1907), " Sur la Nature
de laVolonté."

be achieved by it. But this is common to all action prompted by desire, to all conation that is not mere blind appetition. And a man may struggle against the prompting of a desire whose end is clearly represented. We commonly and properly say in such cases that the man's will, or the man himself, struggles against the desire and masters it, or is mastered by it. Clearly, then, volition is something other, and more, than simple desire, and more than desire issuing in action. Nor can we be content to regard as volitional every action issuing from a conflict of desires ; for such conflicts take place on a plane of mental development lower than that at which volition proper becomes possible.

Professor Stout,[1] criticising Mr. Shand's conclusion that a volition is a unique differentiation of conation, a special form of conation that is incapable of being analysed or described,[2] puts the problem in this way : " How does a volition differ from a desire ? " And the answer he proposes is that a " volition is a desire qualified and defined by the judgment that, so far as in us lies, we shall bring about the attainment of the desired end." That volition involves such a judgment is true, I think, of the special class of volitions we call resolutions, but not of all volitions ; and, even if it were true of all, it certainly would not adequately describe the difference between desire and volition. We have seen that in the typical case of volition, that of hard moral choice, the effort of will somehow supports or reinforces the weaker motive, and enables it to get the better of the stronger motive. Now, a mere judgment has no such motive power ; rather, the judgment, " I shall do this and not that " is merely the mode in which the accomplished volition is explicitly expressed when the circumstances demanding the one, or the other, mode of action lie still in the future; the judgment is an effect of, rather than the essence of, the volitional process.

The essential mark of volition—that which distinguishes it from simple desire, or simple conflict of desires —is that the personality as a whole, or the central feature

[1] *Mind*, N.S., vol. v. [2] *Ibid.* vol. iv.

or nucleus of the personality, the man himself, or all that which is regarded by himself and others as the most essential part of himself, is thrown upon the side of the weaker motive ; whereas a mere desire may be felt to be something that, in comparison with this most intimate nucleus of the personality, is foreign to the self, a force that we do not acknowledge as our own, and which we, or the intimate self, may look upon with horror and detestation.

Before following up this clue and attempting to trace the source of this energy with which the idea of the self seems to support one of the conflicting motives, we must ask, What is the immediate effect of volition ? According to a widely accepted view we can only will a movement of some part of the body. This view is explicitly maintained by Bain, and has received the endorsement of Professor Stout. Yet it is, I think, quite indefensible. We may, and often do, effectively will the continuance of a sensation or an idea in consciousness ; by an effort of will one can maintain at the focus of consciousness a presentation or idea, which, but for the volition, would be driven out of the focus by other ideas or sense-impressions. Those who accept the view that we can will only a movement, or a motor adjustment of some kind, usually try to explain away these cases of voluntary direction of attention to sense-impressions or objects of any kind, by saying that in these cases the immediate effect of volition is merely some appropriate muscular adjustment of a sense-organ, which adjustment aids indirectly in maintaining the idea or sense-impression at the focus of consciousness. Thus Dr. Stout writes : " The volition to attend is strictly analogous to the volition to move the arm, or perform any other bodily action. It follows from this that our voluntary command of attention must depend on our voluntary command of the motor processes of fixation." [1] But, though the statement of the former of these two sentences is unimpeachable, the conclusion drawn in the second has no logical connection with it. It would seem that this doctrine owes its prevalence to the fact that the sequence

[1] *Analytic Psychology*, vol. i. p. 243.

of movement upon volition to move is an immediately observable and undeniable fact, one so familiar that we are apt to overlook the inexplicable and mysterious nature of the sequence, and to accept it as a matter of course ; just as most of us accept as a matter of course the equally mysterious, inexplicable, and familiar sequence of sensation upon stimulation of a sense-organ.

There are two sufficient grounds for rejecting this doctrine. First, desire notoriously tends to maintain the idea of its object or end at the focus of consciousness ; our thought keeps flying back to dwell on that which we strongly desire, in spite of our best efforts to banish the idea of it from our minds.

This power of desire to maintain the desired object at the focus of consciousness, to keep our attention directed to such an object, is, like the persistent bodily striving that characterises all conation and marks off such action most clearly from mechanical process, the immediate expression of psychical work, and involves, as was said above, the central mystery of life and mind and of their relation to matter. No one contends that desire maintains the presentation of its end indirectly only by way of motor adjustments ; such maintenance is rather an essential and immediate effect of every impulse that rises above the level of blind appetition and becomes conscious of its end. Why, then, should we deny to volition, which is desire and more than desire, a power that desire unmistakably possesses ? Secondly, that volitional effort can directly maintain a presentation at the focus of consciousness may easily be shown by appropriate experiment.[1]

We must, then, reverse the position ; instead of saying that volitional direction of attention is an indirect effect of volitional innervation of some muscular apparatus, we must recognise that volitional innervation of muscles is but a special case of volition, and that the essential and

[1] Experiments that seem to establish this point were described by the author in the fourth of the series of papers entitled " Physiological Factors of the Attention-Process," *Mind*, N.S., vol. xv. Some of these experiments have since been repeated and confirmed by MM. Et. Maigre and H. Piéron (*Revue de Psychiatrie et de Psychologie Expérimental*, Avril, 1907).

immediate effect of all volition is the maintenance of a presentation at the focus of consciousness. For, when we will a movement, we do but reinforce the idea of that movement so that it tends more strongly to issue in movement. We may therefore follow Professor James when he asserts that " the essential achievement of the will is to attend to a difficult object and hold it fast before the mind," and, again, that " effort of attention is thus the essential phenomenon of will." In the special case in which the object to which we direct our attention by a volitional effort is a bodily movement, the movement follows immediately upon the idea in virtue of that mysterious connection between them of which we know almost nothing beyond the fact that it obtains.

Effort of attention is, then, the essential form of all volition. And this formulation of the volitional process, the holding of an idea at the focus of consciousness by an effort of attention, covers every instance of volition. Let us consider a few of the principal types of volitional effect. In deliberation we have the ideas of two different lines of action rising alternately to the focus of consciousness, either one being checked or inhibited by the other before it can determine action ; in the act of volitional choice we give permanence and dominance to the one idea, and in so doing we exclude the other more or less completely from consciousness. Again, in making a resolution to follow a certain line of conduct, we form as clear an idea as possible of that line of conduct, and we hold the idea steadily before the mind by an effort of attention. It is true that we may formulate our resolution in the form of a judgment—I am going to do this ; but that is something additional, not an essential part of the volitional process. Once more, in volitional recollection of some fact we have forgotten, *e.g.*, the name of a man of whom we are thinking, our volition merely holds the idea of this man before consciousness, so that it has the opportunity to develop its various aspects, its associative setting, the place and time and company in which we have seen the man ; all of which, of course, increases the chance that his name will be reproduced or recollected.

We have now to go on to the more serious part of the problem of volition, and to ask, Can we give any account of the process that results in this holding of a presentation at the focus of consciousness to the exclusion of rival presentations ? The thoroughgoing libertarian should reply : " No, this act of will, this holding of the attention, is not conditioned by the mind or character, it has no antecedents in the mental processes of the subject who is said to will, therefore we may not hope to give any psychological account of its antecedents or conditions, if it has any." Professor James does not go quite so far as this ; having correctly defined the essential effect of volition, he claims to be able to trace one step backwards the process of which it is the issue. He tells us that the holding fast of the one idea at the focus of consciousness is effected by suppressing or inhibiting all rival ideas that tend to exclude it ; the favoured idea then persists in virtue of its own energy and works its appropriate effects, whether in the production of bodily movement or in the determination of the further course of mental process.

Professor Wundt teaches a very similar doctrine. For him volition is one aspect of apperception, and apperception is essentially the inhibition of all presentations save the one that rises to the focus of consciousness. According to these two great authorities, then, volition is essentially a negative function, an inhibiting of irrelevant presentations. But neither of them explains how the inhibition is effected, whence comes the inhibiting force, or what are the conditions of its operation. Presumably, according to Professor James, this is where every attempt to trace the volitional process from its effects backwards comes against a dead wall of mystery, because the inhibiting stroke issues from some region inaccessible to our intellects, or simply happens without antecedents.

But this doctrine of the primarily inhibitive character of the volitional process is, I think, a false scent ; and it is not to be expected that we can successfully trace back the process, if we make this false start. What gives it a certain plausibility is the fact that volitional attention, like all attention, involves inhibition of all presentations other than the one held at the focus of consciousness; but this inhibition is a secondary or collateral result of the essential process, which is primarily a reinforcement of the one idea, the idea of the end that we will. Throughout the nervous system, with the exception possibly of those most primitive parts directly concerned in the control of the visceral organs, inhibition always has this character, appears always as the negative aspect, or complementary result, of a positive process of innervation. There is no good evidence of inhibiting impulses sent out to the muscles of the voluntary system; and we control involuntary tendencies either by innervating antagonistic muscles, or by directing our attention elsewhere by an effort of will; that is to say, by concentrating the energy of the mind and nervous system in one direction we withdraw it from, or prevent its flowing in, any other direction. We may see this most clearly when we attempt to exert volitional control over the deep-seated sensation-reflexes, such as the tendency to sneeze or the tendency to flinch under a sudden pain or threat. Most of us learn to suppress a sneeze by volitionally accentuating the energy of the respiratory movements—we make regular, rapid and forced inspirations and expirations; and in order to avoid flinching or winking we strongly innervate some group of muscles, perhaps almost the whole muscular system, but most habitually and most strongly the muscles of the jaw, brow, and hands. And all the other instances of inhibitions that play so large a part in our mental and nervous life appear to be of this type, the supplementary or negative aspects of positive excitations.[1] We must not, then, reverse the order, as Wundt and James do, in the case of volition, and make inhibition the primary and essential aspect of the process. We must conclude that volition essentially involves a positive increase of the energy with which an idea maintains itself in conscious-

[1] For a fuller discussion of this question and a theory of the inhibitory process see a paper by the author, " The Nature of Inhibitory Processes within the Nervous System," in *Brain*, vol. xxvi., and his review of Professor Sherrington's " Integrative Action of the Nervous System," in *Brain*, vol. xxx.

ness and plays its part in determining bodily and mental processes.

So we come back from our brief discussion of the views of other writers to the position that in the typical case of volition, when in the conflict of two motives the will is thrown on the side of one of them and we make a volitional decision, we in some way add to the energy with which the idea of the one desired end maintains itself in opposition to its rival.

This conclusion constitutes an important step towards the answer to the question with which we set out—Is volition merely a specially complex conjunction of the conative tendencies of the two kinds that we have recognised from the outset ? For it shows us that the essential operation of volition is the same as that of desire, namely, the holding the idea of the end at the focus of consciousness so that it works strongly towards the realisation of its end, prevailing over rival ideas and tendencies.

We are now in a position to follow up the clue that we left on one side some little way back. We recognised that in the typical case of volition a man's self, in some peculiarly intimate sense of the word " self," is thrown upon the side of the motive that is made to prevail.

That the empirical self, the idea of his self that each man entertains, plays an essential part in volition has been widely recognised. The recognition seems to be implied by the obscure dictum, approved by Mr. Bradley and several other writers, that in volition we identify the self with the end of the action. It was expressed by Dr. Stout when he wrote that the judgment, " I am going to do this," is the essential feature of volition by which it is distinguished from desire ; and it is more clearly expressed in his latest volume,[1] where he writes, " What is distinctive of voluntary decision is the intervention of self-consciousness as a co-operating factor." But he does not, I think, make quite clear how self-consciousness plays this rôle.[2]

[1] *The Groundwork of Psychology.*
[2] Some authors wax scornful when they examine the statement that the self is the all-important factor in volition. But the view they

No mere idea has a motive power that can for a moment withstand the force of strong desire, except only the pathologically fixed ideas of action, and the quasi-pathological ideas of action introduced to the mind by hypnotic suggestion.[1] And the idea of the self is no exception to this rule. The idea of the self, or self-consciousness, is able to play its great rôle in volition only in virtue of the self-regarding sentiment, the system of emotional and conative dispositions that is organised about the idea of the self and is always brought into play to some extent when the idea of the self rises to the focus of consciousness. *The conations, the desires and aversions, arising within this self-regarding sentiment are the motive forces which, adding themselves to the weaker ideal motive in the case of moral effort, enable it to win the mastery over some stronger, coarser desire of our primitive animal nature and to banish from consciousness the idea of the end of this desire.*

In the absence of a strong self-regarding sentiment, the idea of the self, no matter how rich and how accurate its content, can play but a feeble part in the regulation of conduct, and can exert little or no influence in moral choice. We may see this clearly if we imagine the case of a man who combines full and accurate self-knowledge with almost complete lack of self-respect and pride. The case is hardly realised, because, as we have seen, advance in self-knowledge depends upon the existence of the self-regarding sentiment. But it is approximately realised by men who, having attained self-knowledge, afterwards, through a series of moral misfortunes, lose

scornfully reject is that which makes the abstract *ego*, the logical subject of all our experiences, or the transcendental self, the source of the power of the will. If self is meant to be taken in either of these two senses in this connection, the scorn of these writers is perhaps justifiable when they stigmatise it as a mere metaphysical abstraction. It is for this reason better to say always the idea of self (rather than simply the self) is an essential factor in volition.

[1] Ideas of this latter kind have not the irresistible force often attributed to them. Dr. Bramwell has argued very strongly that if they are opposed to the organised tendencies of the subject they will in no case realise themselves in action (*Hypnotism, its History, Theory, and Practice*). In my opinion his view is in the main correct, though, no doubt, he has a little overdriven it.

their self-respect more or less completely. In such a man accurate self-knowledge would simply enable him to foresee more accurately than others what things would bring him the greatest satisfactions and pains, and to foretell his own conduct under given conditions. He might become a very paragon of prudence, but hardly of virtue. Such a man might have acquired and might retain admirable moral sentiments ; he might even have formed an ideal of conduct and character, and might entertain for this ideal a sentiment that led him to desire its realisation both for himself and others. But, if he had lost his self-respect, if his self-regarding sentiment had decayed, his conduct might be that of a villain in spite of his accurate self-knowledge and his moral sentiments. On each occasion on which a desire, springing from a moral sentiment, came into conflict with one of the coarser and stronger desires, it would be worsted ; for there would be no support for it forthcoming from the sentiment of self-respect. Something like this is, I take it, the condition of the man who becomes an habitual drunkard after acquiring admirable moral sentiments. He may still desire the realisation of all that is good and moral, and may have a lofty ideal of conduct ; but, if he has become known to all the world as a sot and has become aware of the fact, he can no longer find in his self-regarding sentiment a support for his better, more ideal, motives. Whereas, so long as his drinking is secret and is preceded on each occasion by a struggle in which his self-respect takes part with his moral sentiments against the desire for drink, there is still room for hope that he may reform his habits.

We may, then, define volition as *the supporting or reinforcing of a desire or conation by the co-operation of an impulse excited within the system of the self-regarding sentiment.*

Since, as we have seen, the growth of the self-regarding sentiment is a gradual process, there can be no sharp line drawn between complex conations that are volitional and those that are not. Between, on the one hand, the simple desire conscious of its end but not complicated by

self-consciousness, and, on the other hand, the moral effort
that gives the victory to the ideal motive—which is volition
in the fullest sense—there is a large range of complex
conations in which the self-regarding emotions and
conations play parts of all degrees of importance and
refinement. It is instructive and important for our
purpose to devise cases illustrating the principal stages in
the transition from simple conflict of impulses to volition
in the fullest sense.

Let us take, as illustrating the stages in this scale:

1. The case of a child who desires food that is in
a dark room and who is impelled in opposite directions
by this desire and by his fear of the dark place. If either
impulse overcomes the other and action follows, that is
not a case of volition.

2. Suppose that the child has been punished on some
previous occasion because his fear has overcome him, and
suppose that the memory of this punishment and his
aversion to it enable his desire for food to overcome his
fear. Is that a case of volition? In the simplest conceivable case of behaviour of this sort, such as might be
exhibited by a young child or a dog, I should say no.

3. But, if the child has attained some degree of self-
consciousness and says, " I don't want to be punished, so
I will go and get it," we might perhaps call this volition
of the lowest grade.

4. As illustrations of stages successively higher in the
scale, suppose the child to say, " I must go and get it,
for mother will scold me if I don't " ; or again—

5. " I will do it because, if I don't, the other boys
will call me a coward."

6. Or let him say, " I will do it, for one ought to
be able to put aside this absurd fear, and I should be
ashamed if any one knew that I was afraid of going in
there."

In all these cases, except the first, the influence of the
social environment is clearly the factor that leads to
the mastery of the one impulse by the other. And the
last two cases, which clearly imply the existence of the
sentiment of self-respect and the co-operation of an impulse

awakened within it, would generally be admitted to be cases of volition.

7. But now consider a case in which, although social disapproval is ranged on the side of the restraining impulse, the effort of will, being thrown on the side of the motive for action, enables it to overcome the restraining impulse. Suppose that our imaginary agent is a man of great attainments whose life and work are publicly recognised as of great value to the community; and suppose that he suddenly finds himself before a burning house in which a child remains in imminent danger. To save the child seems impossible, and, though the man's protective impulse strongly prompts him to make the attempt, he is restrained by a very real fear. We may suppose that the impulse of fear is more than strong enough to overcome the rival impulse, if these two were left to fight it out alone; and we may suppose that the influence of his friends and of society in general is thrown upon the side of his fear—his companion tells him that it would be wicked to sacrifice his valuable life in this hopeless attempt, and he knows that this will be the general opinion of his fellows and that he will be regarded by many as a vainglorious fool. Nevertheless, our hero feels that to make the attempt is the higher line of conduct, he deliberates a few moments, and then, choosing to act, throws himself into the forlorn hope with all his energy. Here is a case of undeniable volition, of hard choice, and of action in the line of greatest resistance. The appeal of social approval and disapproval to the self-regarding sentiment seems to be all against the decision actually taken, yet the will seems to triumph over that as well as over the restraining impulse of fear.

Is it, then, impossible to bring this case under our definition of volition? Must we fall back on indeterminism and say: Here was an action that was performed by sheer volition against all the motives arising from the man's mental constitution; all the factors of which we can give any psychological account were against action, yet the will triumphed over them? I do not think we need draw this conclusion; for the principles of explanation we have hitherto relied upon will not fail us altogether in this case.

We may imagine two rather different ways in which such volition can be accounted for.

1. The man may be moved to his decision by the belief that his conduct would be approved by persons whose approval he values more highly, whose approval appeals more strongly to his self-regarding sentiment, than the approval of all his friends and contemporaries. He may think of such men as Chinese Gordon and others for whom he may have a profound admiration or reverence ; or he may believe in a purely ideal personality ; and, though he may believe that these persons will never know of his action, yet his assurance that, if they knew, they would approve, awakens a motive within his self-regarding sentiment that overrides all others and determines his hard choice ; just as on a lower plane, in the type of volition illustrated by our sixth case, one says, " I will overcome this fear, for what would my companions say if they knew I was afraid."

2. On the other hand, our hero may decide from principle. He may long ago have decided after reflection that courageous self-sacrifice for the good of others is a principle superior to all other considerations. Whether his opinion is right may be for others a fair matter of dispute, but not for him ; he has made up his mind after mature and cool deliberation ; and now a case arises calling for the application of his principle, and he acts in accordance with it and against what might seem overwhelmingly strong motives. Such action is the type of resolution, of resolute adherence to decisions once formed ; and it is the highest type of resolute action, because in this case the decision was not formed in face of the special circumstances calling for its application, but was of a general nature.

How, then, does the possession of this principle supply the motive power that overcomes the other strong motives ? The bare verbal formula, " I will always prefer self-sacrifice to self-seeking," has no motive power, or but a minimum. In the first place, this preference for self-sacrifice is a moral sentiment acquired in the main by selective absorption from the higher moral tradition in the way we noticed in the preceding chapter ; and this moral sentiment has been incorporated in the sentiment for the ideal of conduct that our hero has set up for himself. His self-regarding sentiment demands that he shall live up to this ideal ; he feels shame when he does not, elation and satisfaction when he does ; that is to say, the impulse of self-assertion organised within his sentiment of self-respect gives rise to a strong desire to realise his ideal under all circumstances.

But, in order that his adopted principle may powerfully affect his conduct, something more is needed. He must have a strong *sentiment for self-control.* Of all the abstract moral sentiments, this is the master-sentiment for volition and especially for resolution. It is a special development of the self-regarding sentiment. For the man in whom this sentiment has become strong the desire of realising his ideal of self-control is a master-motive that enables him to apply his adopted principles of action, the results of his deliberate decisions, in spite of the opposition of all other motives. The operation of this sentiment, more than anything else, gives a man the appearance of independence of the appeal of the voice of society, and of all other persons, to his self-regarding sentiment. It enables him to substitute himself, as it were, for his social environment.

These two interpretations of this particular case seem to me to illustrate the two principal types of higher volition natural to men of different dispositions. The former case, in which the determining motive is the desire of the approval of the ideal spectator, illustrates, perhaps, the more usual source of the moral volition of the man in whom active sympathy is strongly developed. In principle it presents no difficulty, if we have sufficiently accounted for the influence of approval and disapproval in general. It implies merely a greater refinement of discrimination between those whose approval we value or are indifferent to than is exercised by the average man.

The other type is characteristic of the less social, less

sympathetic, man.   In this case it is less easy to trace
the energy of volition back to the self-regarding sentiment.
For we found that this sentiment has for its object, not
the self merely, but the self in its relations to others, the
emotional and conative dispositions of the sentiment being
excited by the regards and attitudes of others towards the
self.   And it is now suggested that a man may achieve
a hard moral choice in opposition to social approval or
disapproval by substituting himself, more or less completely, for his fellow-men as the spectator whose regards
evoke the impulses of his self-regarding sentiment and in
whose approval they find their satisfaction.   It is doubtful
whether this substitution is ever completely achieved ;
for, as we have seen, the idea of the self, the consciousness
of self, is in its very origin and essential nature a consciousness of the self in its social relations ; and probably some
vague social reference always persists.   But, in any case,
it is clear, I think, that this kind of volition, which seems
almost to render a man independent of his social environment, can only be attained to by the development of the
self-regarding sentiment under social influences.   Most of
us make some progress towards this substitution.   At
first our self-regarding sentiment is sensitive to the regards
of every one and of all social circles ; and then, as we
find that different persons and circles regard the same
conduct and our same self very differently, we learn to
set these off against one another more or less, we learn
to despise the opinions and regards of the mass of men
and to gain confidence in our own personal and moral
judgments ; thus our own estimate of ourselves, which
in early life is apt to fluctuate with every passing regard
of our fellows, becomes stable and relatively independent.
    Most of us, perhaps, may be said to achieve a stage
in this process at which our self-regarding sentiment
and emotions have for their object the self in relation
to the select group of persons who are of similar ways
of thinking with ourselves, those who share our moral
sentiments and from whom we have in the main absorbed
them ; and, when we make a moral effort, it is with some
more or less vague reference to this select circle.   All this

applies to the self, not only in its strictly moral aspects, but in all others also ; and one of the great advantages of being fully grown up is that we cease to suffer so acutely and so frequently the elations and the humiliations which in early life we are so liable to experience in face of every attitude of approval or disapproval, whether expressed or merely implied.

There are two doctrines from which we must carefully distinguish this of the self-approbative impulse :

1. There is Adam Smith's fiction of the well-informed and impartial spectator, the man within the breast, whose approval we seek ; this may be regarded as a first approximation to the truth.

2. There is the hedonistic doctrine, which we rejected in an earlier chapter, to the effect that in making a moral effort we are always seeking the pleasure of self-satisfaction or seeking to avoid the pain of remorse. The kind of volition we are considering may, and, I think, usually does, involve no anticipation of these pleasures and pains. The pleasure or pain may result, but the desire of, or aversion from, it is not necessarily or commonly an important part of the motive ; what we desire, or are averse from, is not the pleasure of approval or the pain of disapproval, but the approval or disapproval themselves ; and, whether the approval is our own or another's, the source of the additional motive power, which in the moral effort of volition is thrown upon the side of the weaker, more ideal, impulse, is ultimately to be found in that *instinct of self-display or self-assertion* whose affective aspect is the emotion of positive self-feeling. That this is true we may see clearly in such a simple case of volition as that of a boy overcoming by effort of the will, owing to the presence of spectators, an impulse of fear that restrains him from some desired object. He makes his effort and overcomes his fear-impulse, because, as we say, he knows his companions are looking at him ; the impulse of self-display is evoked on the side of the weaker motive. And the same is true of those more refined efforts of the ill in which the operation of this impulse is so deeply obscured that it has not hitherto been recognised.

Moral advance and the development of volition consist, then, not in the coming into play of factors of a new order, whether called the will or the moral instinct or conscience, but in the development of the self-regarding sentiment and in the improvement or refinement of the " gallery " before which we display ourselves, the social circle that is capable of evoking in us this impulse of self-display ; and this refinement may be continued until the " gallery " becomes an ideal spectator or group of spectators or, in the last resort, one's own critical self standing as the representative of such spectators.

To this statement the objection may be raised that it seems to make what we commonly call a prig of every man who makes any moral effort. It may be said that the ordinarily good man simply does what seems to be right as judged by its social effects, regardless of the figure he cuts in his own or others' eyes ; that that is the only truly moral conduct ; and that to care about, and to be moved by the thought of, the figure one will cut is the mark of a prig. But any one who raises this objection and maintains that the outward-looking attitude is the only truly moral one, proves the truth of the position maintained above by his resentment and by his implied admission that the attitude of the agent is of so much importance for the estimation of the moral worth of conduct ; for he shows that he desires that he himself and other good men should be regarded as acting in the outward-looking attitude and not in that inward-looking one which he characterises as priggish. There are two important differences between the truly moral man and the prig. The prig finds in the desire for an admirable and praise-worthy attitude his only, or at least his predominant, motive to right doing ; whereas the moral agent desires the right for its own sake in virtue of his moral sentiments, and habitually acts from this motive ; and it is only when a moral conflict arises with the necessity for moral choice and effort, that the self and the self-regarding impulse play the decisive rôle. Again, the truly moral man has an ideal of conduct so high that he can hardly attain to it, and, realising this, he is moved by the desire not to fall short of it and not to incur the disapproval of his ideal spectators; whereas the prig's ideal is so easily within his reach that he constantly attains it and achieves the pleasure of self-approval—"he puts in his thumb and pulls out a plum, and says—What a good boy am I."

Our study of volition is not complete without some consideration of the relation of will to what is called character. Character has been defined as "that from which the will proceeds"; and will might equally well be defined as "that which proceeds from character." What, then, is character? At the outset we said that character is something built up in the course of life, and that it must therefore be distinguished from disposition and from temperament, which are in the main natively given. There can be no doubt, I think, that the sentiments constitute a large part of what is properly called character. But do they constitute the whole of character? Or is there some other acquired feature of the adult mental constitution that is an essential feature of character in the strict sense of the word? That there is, beside the sentiments, some such additional feature involved in character, seems to be proved by the existence of persons who have many strong sentiments and who yet cannot be said to have strong character. They are the sentimentalists.

One essential condition of strong character seems to be the organisation of the sentiments in some harmonious system of hierarchy. The most usual or readiest way in which such systematisation of the sentiments can be brought about, is the predominance of some one sentiment that in all circumstances is capable of supplying a dominant motive, that directs all conduct towards the realisation of one end to which all other ends are subordinated. The dominant sentiment may be a concrete or an abstract sentiment; it may be the love of money, of home, of country, of justice. When any such sentiment acquires decided predominance over all others, we call it a ruling passion; whenever other motives conflict with the motives arising within the system of a ruling passion, they go to the wall, they are powerless to oppose it.

Take the case of a man whose ruling passion is the

love of home, say, of a beautiful ancestral home that is dilapidated and encumbered with debts when it first becomes his own. He sets out to restore its ancient glories, perhaps entering upon the task with reluctance. As time goes on his sentiment gains strength, he acquires the habit of working for this one end, of valuing all things according to the degree in which they contribute towards it. All other motives become not only relatively, but absolutely, weaker for lack of exercise ; that is to say, they are never allowed to determine action and so tend to atrophy from disuse. The man loses his other sentiments, or interests, as we say ; he gives up sport, art, horses, and what not, and may become indifferent to the opinions of his fellow-men, may be content to appear miserly and to commit mean actions in the service of his ruling passion.

Can such a man be said to have acquired a strong character ? In contrast with the man whose sentiments are but little systematised, he may seem to have strong character. This other man will be drawn this way and that. If he is of sympathetic nature, he will be liable to be dominated first by one, then by another, sentiment, according to the nature of the social influences that bear upon him, the opinions and sentiments of each social circle he enters. He will make no sustained effort in any direction, except under the spur of necessity. And the man of specifically weak character, or lacking in character, is the man whose sentiments not only have not been organised in any system, but have not been consolidated and confirmed by habitual action in accordance with their prompting, because the man has constantly allowed himself to be moved by the entirely unorganised and fleeting impulses evoked sporadically by each situation as it arises Habitual action on the motives supplied by the systematised sentiments is, then, an essential factor in character, over and above the possession of the sentiments.

Does, then, the possession of a master-sentiment of ruling passion of any kind, such as the passion for a home that we considered just now, or one for money or for any other concrete or abstract object, in itself constitute character, when confirmed, as a ruling passion always is, by habitual action from the motives it supplies ? It does not constitute strong character in the full sense of the words. It seems to give the man a strong will in relation to all that affects the object of his master-sentiment ; but he has not strong will and character in the full sense, but rather what might be called specialised character. In relation to all objects and situations that are not in any way connected with his ruling passion, or if the object of it is irrevocably taken from him, such a man may display deplorable weakness or lack of will and character. In fact, he cannot properly be said to have a strong will or to exert volition ; his ruling passion supplies him with motives so strong that, in all situations in which its object is concerned, conflict of motives and deliberation can hardly occur and volition is not needed ; while in all other situations he is incapable of volition.

There is only one sentiment which by becoming the master-sentiment can generate strong character in the fullest sense, and that is the self-regarding sentiment. There is a lower imperfect form of the sentiment, ambition or the love of fame, the ambition to become publicly recognised as a man of this or that kind of ability or power. When this sentiment becomes a ruling passion it may cover almost the whole of conduct, may supply a dominant motive for almost every situation, a motive which, arising within the self-regarding sentiment, determines volition in the strict sense in which we have defined it. But it is not properly a moral sentiment, and, though it may generate character, the character formed through its agency is not moral character.

For the generation of moral character in the fullest sense, the strong, self-regarding sentiment must be combined with one for some ideal of conduct, and it must have risen above dependence on the regards of the mass of men ; and the motives supplied by this master-sentiment in the service of the ideal must attain an habitual predominance. There are men, so well described by Professor James, who have the sentiment and the ideal of the right kind, but in whom, nevertheless, the fleeting, unorganised desires repeatedly prove too strong for the will to overcome them. They lack the second essential factor in character, the habit of self-control, the habitual dominance of the self-regarding sentiment; perhaps because the native disposition that is the main root of self-respect is innately lacking in strength; perhaps because they have never learnt to recognise the awful power of habit, and have been content to say, " This time I will not trouble to resist this desire, to suppress this impulse; I know that I can do so if I really exert my will." Every time this happens, the power of volition is weakened relatively to that of the unorganised desires; every time the self-regarding sentiment masters an impulse of some other source, it is rendered, according to the law of habit, more competent to do so again—the will is strengthened as we say. And, when the habitual dominance of this master-sentiment has been established, perhaps after many conflicts, it becomes capable of determining the issue of every conflict so certainly and easily that conflicts can hardly arise; it supplies a determining motive for every possible situation, namely, the desire that I, the self, shall do the right. So this motive, in the individual for whom it has repeatedly won the day in all conflicts of motives, acquires the irresistible strength of a fixed consolidated habit; and, in accordance with the law of habit, as it becomes more and more fixed and invariable, it operates more and more automatically, *i.e.*, with diminishing intensity of its conscious aspect, with less intensity of the emotion and desire from which the habit was generated, and with less explicit reference to the persons in whose eyes the self seeks approval.

In this way the self comes to rule supreme over conduct, the individual is raised above moral conflict; he attains character in the fullest sense and a completely generalised will, and exhibits to the world that finest flower of moral growth, serenity. His struggles are no longer moral conflicts, but are intellectual efforts to discover what is most worth doing, what is most right for him to do.

It is important to note, especially in view of the analogy

to be drawn between the individual will and the national, or other form of collective or general, will, that the development of self-consciousness and of the self-regarding sentiment renders the behaviour of the individual progressively less dependent upon his environment; that it involves a continuous advance from action of the type of immediate response to the impressions made on the sense-organs and an approximation towards complete self-determination, towards conduct that is the issue of conditions wholly comprised within the constitution of the mind. Like the evolution of mind in the race, this advance involves also a progress from predominantly mechanical to predominantly teleological determination, a continuous increase of the part played by final causes relatively to that of purely mechanical causes in the determination of the behaviour of the individual. No doubt the vague movements of the infant are teleological or purposive in the lowliest sense of the word; but actions do not become the expressions of conscious purpose until the individual attains the capacity of representing the end towards which he feels himself impelled. At the intermediate level of development of the personality, the ends or final causes of his actions are immediate, various, and often inharmonious with one another; with the development of a unified personality (*i.e.*, of clear self-consciousness, a consistent ideal of conduct and a strong sentiment for the self and for that ideal), these are more and more superseded and controlled by a single all-powerful final cause, the ideal of the self.

The foregoing account of volition differs from those of other writers in the stress laid upon the systematic organisation of the conative dispositions in the moral and self-regarding sentiments; and its principal claim to originality is the attempt made to exhibit the continuity of the development of the highest types of human will and character from the primary instinctive dispositions that we have in common with the animals. Especial importance, as an essential factor in volition, has been attached to the impulse of self-assertion or self-display and its concomitant emotion of positive self-feeling. It may seem paradoxical and repugnant to our sense of the nobility of moral conduct, that it should be exhibited as dependent on an impulse that we share with the animals and which in them plays a part that is of secondary importance and utterly a-moral.   It should, however, be remembered that the humble nature of the remote origins of anything we justly admire or revere in nowise detracts from its intrinsic worth or dignity, and that the ascertainment of those origins need not, and should not, diminish by one jot our admiration or reverence.

SECTION II

THE OPERATION OF THE PRIMARY TEN-DENCIES OF THE HUMAN MIND IN THE LIFE OF SOCIETIES

CHAPTER X

THE REPRODUCTIVE AND THE PARENTAL INSTINCTS

IN the first section of the book certain primary or fundamental tendencies of the human mind were distinguished and described, and it was asserted that these are the prime movers, the great motive powers, of human life and society, and that therefore a true understanding of the nature and operation of these tendencies must form the essential basis of all social psychology, and in fact of the social sciences in general. I propose to devote this section to the illustration of the truth of this position, and to consider very briefly some of the principal ways in which each of these primary tendencies plays its part in shaping the social life of man and in determining the forms of institutions and of social organisation.

The processes to be dealt with are so complex, the operations of the different factors are so intricately combined, their effects are so variously interwoven and fused in the forms of social organisations and institutions, that it would be presumptuous to attempt to prove the truth of most of the views advanced. I would therefore repeat and especially emphasise in regard to this section the remark made in the introduction to this volume to the effect that, in spite of the dogmatic form adopted for the sake of brevity and clearness of exposition, my aim is to be suggestive rather than dogmatic, to stimulate thought and promote discussion rather than to lay down conclusions for the acceptance of the reader.

The reproductive instinct is in a sense antisocial rather than social. Nevertheless, its importance for society needs no demonstration ; for it is clear that, if it could be abolished in any people, that people would very soon disappear from the face of the earth. In all animal species the strength of this instinct is maintained at a very high level by natural selection ; for the production by each generation of offspring more numerous than themselves—in some cases many thousand times more numerous—has been an essential condition of the survival of the species, of the better adaptation of species to their environment, and of the evolution of new species. In the human species also it is one of the strongest of the instincts ; so strong is it that the control and regulation of its impulse is one of the most difficult problems for the individual and for society. In every age and country its operation is to some extent regulated by rigid social customs, or by laws, which are commonly enforced by the severest penalties.

In many animal species the reproductive instinct secures the perpetuation of the species without the co-operation of any parental instinct, whilst some animals, e.g., the working bee, have a parental but no reproductive instinct ; but all human beings, with rare exceptions, possess both these instincts ; and there is probably some degree of correlation between the strengths of the two instincts—that is to say, in the individuals in whom one of them is strong the other will also be strong in the majority of cases, and vice versa. The social operations and effects of these two instincts are in certain respects so intimately interwoven and blended that they cannot be clearly distinguished. This intimate association of the two instincts, which is undoubtedly of great social advantage, makes it necessary to discuss them conjointly.

The work of Malthus on Population was the first to

attract general attention to the social operation of these instincts. Malthus pointed out that, if these instincts were given free play in any society of fairly secure organisation, the rate of increase of the population would be exceedingly rapid, and that the actual rate of increase in all civilised societies being much lower than the maximal rate, implies that the instincts are commonly controlled in some degree. The population of most European countries has increased during the historic period at a very slow rate, except during part of the ninteeenth century, when the invention of so many forms of machinery almost suddenly multiplied man's power of producing the necessaries of life. That of some European countries has passed through periods of great diminution ; thus it is estimated that Spain enjoyed, towards the close of the Roman occupation, a population of twenty millions, and that this sank as low as six millions in the eighteenth century.[1] Even when we remember the ravages made by plague, famine, and war, and the large number of persons that throughout the Middle Ages was condemned to celibacy through the influence of the Church, this slow rate of increase, or actual decrease, of population remains something of a mystery.[2] But it is clear that in the present age prudent control of these instincts plays a great part in keeping down the birth-rate. The population of France is almost (or, but for immigration, quite) stationary, and it is notorious that this is due very largely to prudent control. And statistics, showing that the numbers of marriages and births in various countries vary with the cost of the prime necessaries of life and with the prosperity of trade and agriculture, prove that such control plays its part in most of the civilised countries.

The parental instinct is the foundation of the family, and, with few exceptions, all who have given serious attention to the question are agreed that the stability of the family is the prime condition of a healthy state of

---

[1] See Buckle's *History of Civilisation in Europe.*

[2] Professor Pollard attributes it in part to voluntary control induced by the system of land tenure, as in modern France. *Factors in Modern History,* p. 135.

society and of the stability of every community.[1] Although
a contrary opinion has been maintained by certain writers,
it is in the highest degree probable that the family was
the earliest form of human society.[2] We have no certain
record of any tribe or community of human beings in
which the family in one form or another does not exist.
It is reduced perhaps to its lowest terms among some of the
negrito peoples, where the co-operation of the father with
the mother in the care of the offspring—which is the
essential feature of the family—continues only until the
child is weaned and can walk.[3]

It is probable that these two instincts in conjunction, the reproductive and the parental instincts, directly
impel human beings to a greater sum of activity, effort,
and toil, than all the other motives of human action taken
together.

The parental instinct especially impels to actions that
involve self-sacrifice, in the forms of suppression of the
narrower egoistic tendencies and of heavy and unremit-
ting toil on behalf of the offspring. Since these sacrifices
and exertions on behalf of the children are a necessary
condition of the continued existence and the flourishing
of any society, whether small or large, we find that among
all peoples, save the very lowest in the scale of culture,
the institution of marriage and the duties of parenthood
are surrounded by the most solemn social sanctions,
which are embodied in traditional public opinion and in
custom, in formal laws, and in the rites and doctrines of
religion. These sanctions are in the main the more
solemnly and rigidly maintained by any society, the higher

---

[1] For an excellent discussion of the importance of the family see
Mrs. Bosanquet's *The Family*, and the works of the school of Le Play,
especially *La Constitution Essentielle de l'Humanité*.

[2] Professor Keane asserts this to be the issue of the lively discussion
that has been waged on this topic. See his *Ethnology*.

[3] It is, I think, true without exception that the family is found
in every animal species, of which the males, as well as the females,
are endowed with the parental instinct and co-operate in the care of
the young; that is to say, the coexistence of the reproductive and
parental instincts in the members of both sexes suffices to determine
the family, the parental impulse being commonly directed to the adult
partner, as well as to the offspring.

the degree of civilisation attained by it and the freer and more nearly universal the play of the intellectual faculties among the members of that society. This correlation is accounted for by the following considerations. The use of reason and intelligent foresight modifies profoundly the operation of all the instincts, and is especially apt to modify and work against the play of the reproductive and parental instincts. Among the higher animals these instincts suffice to secure the perpetuation of the species by their blind workings. And we may suppose that the same was true of primitive human societies.[1] But, with the increase of the power and of the habit of regulating instinctive action by intelligent foresight, the egoistic impulses must have tended to suppress the working of the parental instinct ; hence the need for the support of the instinct by strong social sanctions ; hence also the almost universal distribution of such sanctions. For those societies in which no such sanctions became organised must have died out ; while only those in which, as intelligence became more powerful, these sanctions became more formidable have in the long-run survived and reached any considerable level of civilisation. There has been, we may say, a never-ceasing race between the development of individual intelligence and the increasing power of these social sanctions ; and wherever the former has got ahead of the latter, there social disaster and destruction have ensued.

At the present time many savage tribes and barbarous communities are illustrating these principles ; they are rapidly dying out, owing to the failure of the social sanctions to give sufficient support to the parental instinct against developing intelligence. It is largely for this reason that contact with civilisation proves so fatal to so many savage peoples ; for such contact stimulates their intelligence, while it breaks the power of their customs and social sanctions generally and fails to replace

---

[1] It has been asserted by Messrs. Spencer and Gillen (*The Northern Tribes of Central Australia*) that some of the Australian tribes are utterly ignorant of the relation of the reproductive act to childbirth, but doubt has been thrown on this statement.

them by any equally efficient.[1] A weakening of the social sanctions of the parental and reproductive instincts by developing intelligence has played a great part also in the destruction of some of the most brilliant and powerful societies of the past, notably those of ancient Greece and Rome.[2]

Among peoples of the lower cultures the failure of the social sanctions to maintain the predominance of the reproductive and parental instincts over the egoistic tendencies supported by intelligence, shows itself mainly in the form of infanticide ; in the highly civilised nations it takes the forms of pre-natal infanticide, of great irregularity of the relations between the sexes, of failure of respect for marriage, of aberrations of the reproductive instinct (which so readily arise wherever the social sanctions become weakened), and, lastly, of voluntary celibacy and restriction of the family.[3]

Mr. Benjamin Kidd [4] has argued that the prime social function of any system of supernatural or religious sanctions is the regulation and the support of the parental instinct against the effects of developing intelligence. This statement contains a large element of truth, though it is perhaps an overstatement of the case. However that may be, it is clear that one of the most momentous problems facing the most highly civilised peoples of the present time is whether they will be able to maintain their

---

[1] The well-meant efforts of missionaries may sometimes play a considerable part in this process ; e.g., it has been observed that the abolition of polygamy, in communities in which females are more numerous than the males, has led to such gross irregularities in the sexual relations as to diminish greatly the rate of reproduction.

[2] See the frequent references to the prevalence of voluntary childlessness in Professor Dill's two volumes, *Roman Society in the Last Century of the Empire*, and *Roman Society from Nero to Marcus Aurelius*, also M. de Lapouge's *Les Selections Sociales*, in which the share of these influences in the destruction of ancient Greece is discussed in some detail. Dr. W. Schallmayer argues to similar effect of the decline of both Greece and Rome (*Vererbung u. Auslese im Lebenslauf d. Völker*).

[3] One of the most remarkable illustrations of the tendencies discussed in this paragraph was afforded by the flourishing among the natives of the Sandwich Islands of an association, the members of which bound themselves on frankly hedonistic grounds to avoid parenthood.

[4] *Social Evolution.*

places against their rivals in the international struggle, in spite of the secularisation of social sanctions and of the institution of marriage, and in spite of the rapid spread of the habit of independent thought and action among the people. For all these are influences that weaken those social supports of the parental instinct which seem to have been necessary for the continued welfare of the societies of every age.

Up to this point of our discussion we have assumed that the strength of these two instincts remains unchanged from generation to generation, and that any changes of their operation in societies are due to changes of customs and social sanctions. But this assumption may be questioned. It may be that the instincts themselves are growing weaker. And this is the assumption commonly made by writers in the newspapers who call attention from time to time to the fall of the birth-rate, which has continued at an increasing rate in nearly all civilised countries during the last thirty or forty years. They commonly attribute it to a decay or progressive weakening of the maternal instinct, under some mysterious influence of civilisation. But there is no good evidence that any such decay is occurring ; while, on the other hand, a number of considerations justify us in asserting with some confidence that the fall of the birth-rate, which seems inevitably to accompany the attainment of a high level of civilisation, is not due to any such decay of the parental instinct, but rather is to be attributed to social changes of the kinds noted above. In the first place, this instinct, like all other human and animal qualities, is subject to individual variations which, in our present state of ignorance, we call spontaneous ; and it is probable that in every society there have been persons in whom it was decidedly less strong than in the average human being. Now, in respect to this instinct, as well as the instinct of reproduction, natural selection operates in the most certain and direct fashion ; for there can be no doubt that persons in whom either, or both, of these instincts are weak will on the average have fewer children than those in whom the instincts are strong. This particular variation is thus constantly eliminated, and the strength of the instinct is thereby maintained from generation to generation. This deduction is strongly supported by the fact that in our own country one-quarter of the people of each generation become the parents of about one-half of the population of the succeeding generation.[1] There can be no doubt that, among this quarter of the population, the parental, and probably also the reproductive, instinct is on the average stronger than in the remaining three-quarters who produce the other half of the next generation.[2]

This view receives further strong support from the fact that it is among the most cultured and leisured classes of any community that the falling birth-rate first and most strongly manifests itself. This seems to have been the case in Greece and Rome, and it has been statistically established for this country as well as for several others ; [3] while in the United States of America the difference in this respect between the cultured descendants of the earlier colonists in the Eastern States and the less civilised hordes of later immigrants seems to be generally admitted and to be recognised as a matter for serious regret. And it is of course among the cultured classes that the supernatural and social sanctions are most weakened by the habit of independent thought and action. Again, it is in Australia where the supernatural and other sanctions are relatively weak and the average level of education and intelligence is high, that the fall of the birth-rate is exhibited very markedly by all classes of the community. On the other hand, the Jews are a people that has been at a fairly high level of civilisation more continuously and for a longer total period than any other outside Asia ; yet they remain prolific, for the super-natural and social sanctions that maintain the family

---

[1] See Professor Karl Pearson's *Chances of Death*.

[2] There are certainly among the celibates of our population a certain number of persons who know of sexual desire only by hearsay and who regard it as a strange madness from which they are fortunately free. Cf. Professor Forel's *Sexuelle Frage*.

[3] See especially David Heron (Drapers' Company Research Memoir), *On the Relation of Fertility to Social Status*, 1906.

have retained an undiminished strength ; a fact which may be ascribed to the peculiar position of Jewish communities : they live mingled with others, yet distinct from them, a position which results in the constant shedding or loss from the community of those members who find its religious teachings or social institutions unsuited to their temperament and disposition.

We may find similar evidence in the history of other peoples of long-continued civilisation—evidence, that is, that where religious and other sanctions give adequate support to the family instincts no serious diminution of fertility occurs. It is for this reason that ancestor-worship is so eminently favourable to national stability. The cult of the ancestor and of the family, with the *patria potestas*, the immense authority given by law and custom to the head of the family, counted for much in the strength and stability of ancient Rome. In fact, the high civilisations of ancient Greece and Rome rested on a firm basis of this kind until their decline began.[1]

The cult of the ancestor has played a similar part in Japan. For there, as in the early days of Greece and of Rome, the welfare of the dead man is dependent on the daily ministrations of his living descendants, and they in turn, according to the still-prevailing belief, owe their successes and prosperity to the active benevolence of the spirits of their ancestors.[2] Hence the interests of each generation are intimately bound up with those of the generations that have gone before and of those that shall come after. Hence, in order to secure his own happiness as well as that of his ancestors and descendants, a man's first care and duty is to bring up a family that will carry on the ancestral cult. It is probable that China also owes her immense stability and latent power in large measure to similar causes.

Hitherto we have considered the social importance of the parental instinct only in its relation to the family.

---

[1] See especially *La Cité Antique*, by Fustel de Coulanges.

[2] See the books of the late Lafcadio Hearn, especially *Japan : An Interpretation*. His account was borne out by the recent newspaper-accounts of the solemn national thanksgiving to ancestors after the successes of the late war.

But, if our account of this instinct in Chapter III. was correct, it is the source, not only of parental tenderness, but of all tender emotions and truly benevolent impulses, is the great spring of moral indignation, and enters in some degree into every sentiment that can properly be called love. We shall then attribute to it in these derived or secondary applications a wider or narrower field of influence in shaping social actions and institutions, according as we incline to see much or little of true benevolence at work in the world. That the impulse of this instinct is one of the great social forces seems to me an indisputable fact. Especially is this true in many of the countries in which the Christian and the Buddhist religions prevail. Some writers would seem to regard the charity and benevolence displayed in such societies as wholly due to the mild teaching of these religions. But no teaching and no system of social or religious sanctions could induce benevolence in any people if their minds were wholly lacking in this instinct. Such influences can only favour or repress in some degree the habitual and customary manifestations of the innate tendencies; and the fact that these religions have gained so wide acceptance shows that they appeal to some universal element of the human mind; while the specially strong appeal of Christianity to the feminine mind,[1] the Catholic cult of the Mother and Infant, and the unmistakably feminine cast of the whole system as compared with Mohammedan and other religions, shows that we are right in identifying this element with the parental, the primarily maternal, instinct.

This instinct, save in its primary application in the form of the mother's protection of her child, is not, like the reproductive instinct, one of overwhelming force; hence the extent of its secondary manifestations is profoundly influenced by custom and training. To this fact must be ascribed in the main the very great differences between communities of different times and races in respect to the force with which the instinct operates outside the family. The savage who is a tender father

[1] According to Mr. Fielding Hall, the same is true of Buddhism; see *The Soul of a People*, and *A People at School*.

may behave in an utterly brutal manner to all human beings other than the members of his tribe. But such brutal behaviour is sanctioned by the public opinion of the tribe, prescribed by custom and example, and provoked by tribal feuds. That races differ in respect to the strength of this instinct is probable ; but that any are entirely devoid of it, it is difficult to believe—if only because such a race would fail to rear its progeny, and therefore could not survive. Everywhere one may see traces of its influence. In the ancient classical societies it seems to have played a very restricted part ; but, even in the worst days of Rome's brutal degradation, many a man was kindly to his slaves, and the practice of manumission was at times so prevalent as to excite some uneasiness. On the other hand, it is not necessary to suppose that the great extension of benevolent action, which is undoubtedly one of the most notable features of the present age of our civilisation, denotes any increase in the innate strength of this instinct. How this great extension has been brought about in modern times is a most interesting problem, the discussion of which does not fall within the scope of this book. But we may note some of its most important social effects.

Among the most obvious of these effects are the humanitarian regulations of civilised warfare, and the devotion of vast amounts of human energy, of money and material resources of all kinds, by our modern civilised communities to the relief of the poor and suffering, to the hospitals, and to the many organisations for the distribution of charity and the prevention of cruelty. A social change of more importance from the point of view of world-history is the abolition of slavery and serfdom throughout the regions of Western civilisation. This great change, which marks an epoch in the history of civilisation, is undoubtedly attributable to the increased influence of this instinct in modern times. It is no doubt true that the main question at issue in the American war of North and South was the maintenance of the federal union of the States. And there is some truth in the cynical dictum that the abolition of slavery comes when slavery ceases to be economically advantageous—the specially advantageous conditions being an unlimited area of highly fertile soil creating a demand for an abundance of unskilled labour. But in the liberation of the slaves of the British West Indies, which cost the English people twenty millions of hard cash, disinterested benevolence certainly played a great and essential part; and the same is true of the liberation of the serfs of Russia in 1861.[1]

But of still more wide-reaching importance is the admission to political power of the masses of the people, which in this and several other countries has been carried very nearly as far as legislation can carry it. This no doubt has been due to the rise of a demand for such admission on the part of the masses; but, as Mr. B. Kidd [2] has forcibly argued, this demand was itself largely created by the teachings of leaders moved by the benevolent impulse, and it would have failed to obtain satisfaction if the power-holding classes had been devoid of this impulse, and if very many of their members had not been moved by it to accede to this demand and to aid in the accomplishment of this great political change.

[1] See Sir D. Mackenzie Wallace's *Russia,* chap. xxix.
[2] *Principles of Western Civilisation.*

CHAPTER XI

THE INSTINCT OF PUGNACITY

THE instinct of pugnacity has played a part second to none in the evolution of social organisation, and in the present age it operates more powerfully than any other in producing demonstrations of collective emotion and action on a great scale. The races of men certainly differ greatly in respect to the innate strength of this instinct; but there is no reason to think that it has grown weaker among ourselves under centuries of civilisation; rather, it is probable, as we shall see presently, that it is stronger in the European peoples than it was in primitive man. But its modes of expression have changed with the growth of civilisation; as the development of law and custom discourages and renders unnecessary the bodily combat of individuals, this gives place to the collective combat of communities and to the more refined forms of combat within communities. It is observable that, when a pugnacious people is forcibly brought under a system of civilised legality, its members are apt to display an extreme and, to our minds, absurd degree of litigiousness.

The replacement of individual by collective pugnacity is most clearly illustrated by barbarous peoples living in small, strongly organised communities. Within such communities individual combat and even expressions of personal anger may be almost completely suppressed, while the pugnacious instinct finds its vent in perpetual warfare between communities, whose relations remain subject to no law. As a rule no material benefit is gained, and often none is sought, in these tribal wars, which often result in the weakening and even the extermination of whole villages or tribes.   Central Borneo is one of the few regions in which this state of things still persists.   The people are very intelligent and sociable and kindly to one another within each village community ; but, except in those regions in which European influence has asserted itself, the neighbouring villages and tribes live in a state of chronic warfare ;   all are kept in constant fear of attack, whole villages are often exterminated, and the population is in this way kept down very far below the limit at which any pressure on the means of subsistence could arise.   This perpetual warfare, like the squabbles of a roomful of quarrelsome children, seems to be almost wholly and directly due to the uncomplicated operation of the instinct of pugnacity.   No material benefits are sought ; a few heads, and sometimes a slave or two, are the only trophies gained ; and, if one asks of an intelligent chief why he keeps up this senseless practice of going on the warpath, the best reason he can give is that unless he does so his neighbours will not respect him and his people, and will fall upon them and exterminate them.   How shall we begin to understand the prevalence of such a state of affairs, if we regard man as a rational creature guided only by intelligent self-interest, and if we neglect to take account of his instincts ?   And it is not among barbarous or savage peoples only that the instinct of pugnacity works in this way.   The history of Christendom is largely the history of devastating wars from which few individuals or societies have reaped any immediate benefit, and in the causation of which the instinct of pugnacity of the rulers, or of the masses of the peoples, has played a leading part. In our own age the same instinct makes of Europe an armed camp occupied by twelve million soldiers, the support of which is a heavy burden on all the peoples ; and we see how, more instantly than ever before, a whole nation may be moved by the combative instinct—a slight to the British flag, or an insulting remark in some foreign newspaper, sends a wave of angry emotion sweeping across the country, accompanied by all the characteristics of crude collective mentation, and two nations are ready to rush into a war that cannot fail to be disastrous to both of them. The most serious task of modern statesmanship is, perhaps, to discount and to control these outbursts of collective pugnacity. At the present time custom is only just beginning to exert some control over this international pugnacity, and we are still very far from the time when international law, following in the wake of custom, will render the pugnacity of nations as needless as that of the individuals of highly civilised states, and physical combats between them as relatively infrequent.

It might seem at first sight that this instinct, which leads men and societies so often to enter blindly upon deadly contests that in many cases are destructive to both parties, could only be a survival from man's brutal ancestry, and that an early and a principal feature of social evolution would have been the eradication of this instinct from the human mind. But a little reflection will show us that its operation, far from being wholly injurious, has been one of the essential factors in the evolution of the higher forms of social organisation, and, in fact, of those specifically social qualities of man, the high development of which is an essential condition of the higher social life.

It was said above that the earliest form of human society was in all probability the family, and, indeed, it is probable that in this respect primitive man did but continue the social life of his prehuman ancestors. But what form the primitive family had, and in what way more complex forms of society were developed from it, are obscure and much-disputed questions. Hence any attempt to show how the human instincts played their parts in the process must be purely speculative. Nevertheless it is a legitimate and fascinating subject for speculation, and we may attempt to form some notion of the socialising influence of the instinct of pugnacity among primitive men by adopting provisionally one of the most ingenious of the speculative accounts of the process. Such is the account offered by Messrs. Atkinson and Andrew Lang,[1] which may be briefly sketched as follows. The primitive society was a polygamous family, consisting

[1] *The Primal Law.*

of a patriarch, his wives and children. The young males, as they became full-grown, were driven out of the community by the patriarch, who was jealous of all possible rivals to his marital privileges. They formed semi-independent bands hanging, perhaps, on the skirts of the family circle, from which they were jealously excluded. From time to time the young males would be brought by their sex-impulse into deadly strife with the patriarch, and, when one of them succeeded in overcoming him, this one would take his place and rule in his stead. A social system of this sort obtains among some of the animals, and it seems to be just such a system as the fierce sexual jealousy of man and his polygamous capacities and tendencies would produce in the absence of any modifying law or moral tradition. This prohibition enforced by the jealousy of the patriarch is the *primal law*, the first example of a general prohibition laid upon the natural impulse of a class of human beings and upheld by superior force for the regulation of social relations.

We have seen in Chapter V. that jealousy is an emotion dependent upon the existence of a sentiment. Whether we have to recognise among the constituent dispositions of the sentiment an instinct of acquisition or possession, is a difficult question to which we found it impossible to give a decided answer. But, however that may be, it is clear that the principal constituent of the emotion of male jealousy, especially of the crude kind excited within the crude sentiment of attachment or ownership which the primitive patriarch entertained for his family, is anger ; in the human, as well as many other species, the anger excited in connection with the sexual instinct is of the most furious and destructive intensity. If, then, we accept this hypothesis of the " primal law," we must believe that the observance of this law was enforced by the instinct of pugnacity.

Now an instinct that led to furious and mortal combat between the males of any group might well determine the evolution of great strength and ferocity and of various weapons and defensive modifications of structure, as sexual characters, in the way that Darwin supposed it to have done in many animal species.[1] But it is not at first sight obvious how it should operate as a great socialising force. If we would understand how it may have done so, we must bear in mind the fact, so strongly insisted on by Walter Bagehot in his brilliant essay, *Physics and Politics*,[2] that the first and most momentous step of primitive men towards civilisation must have been the evolution of rigid customs, the enforced observance of which disciplined men to the habit of control of the immediate impulses. Bagehot rightly maintained that the achievement of this first step of the moral ladder must have been a most difficult one ; he wrote : " Law, rigid, definite, concise law, was the primary want of early mankind ; that which they needed above anything else, that which was requisite before they could gain anything else," *i.e.*, before they could gain the advantages of social co-operation. Again, he wrote : " In early times the quantity of government is much more important than its quality. What is wanted is a comprehensive rule binding men together, making them do the same things, telling them what to expect of each other, fashioning them alike, and keeping them so. What the rule is does not matter so much. A good rule is better than a bad one, but a bad one is better than none." When Bagehot goes on to tell us how law established law-abidingness, or the capacity of self-control, in human nature, his account ceases to be satisfactory ; for he wrote when biologists still believed with Lamarck and Darwin and Spencer in the inheritance of acquired characters. That such inheritance is possible we may no longer assume, though very many writers on social topics still make the assumption, as Bagehot did, and still use it as the easy key to all problems of social evolution. For Bagehot simply assumed that the habit of self-control and of obedience to law and custom, forcibly induced in the members of succeeding generations, became an innate quality by transmission and accumulation from generation to generation. While, then, we may accept Bagehot's dictum that it is difficult to exaggerate the difference between civilised and primitive men (*i.e.*, really

[1] *The Descent of Man.*   [2] International Scientific Series.

primitive men, not the savages of the present time) in respect to their innate law-abidingness, and while we may accept also his view that the strict enforcement of law played a great part in producing this evolution, we cannot accept his view of the mode of operation of law in producing this all-important change.

But the hypothesis of the " primal law " enables us to conceive the first step of the process in a manner consistent with modern biological principles. For offence against the " primal law " meant death to the offender, unless he proved himself more than a match for the patriarch. Hence the ruthless pugnacity of the patriarch must have constantly weeded out the more reckless of his male progeny, those least capable of restraining their sexual impulse under the threat of his anger. Fear, the great inhibitor, must have played a great part in inducing observance of the " primal law " ; and it might be suggested that the principal effect of the enforcement of this law must have been to increase by selection the power of this restraining instinct. But those males who failed to engage in combat would never succeed in transmitting their too timorous natures to a later generation ; for by combat alone could the headship of a family be obtained. Hence this ruthless selection among the young males must have led to the development of prudence, rather than to the mere strengthening of the instinct of fear.

Now prudent control of an impulse implies a much higher type of mental organisation, a much greater degree of mental integration, than is implied by the mere inhibition of an impulse through fear. No doubt the instinct of fear plays a part in such prudent control, but it implies also a considerable degree of development of self-consciousness and of the self-regarding sentiment and a capacity for deliberation and the weighing of motives in the light of self-consciousness. If an individual has such capacities, a moderate strength of the fear-impulse will suffice to restrain the sex-impulse more effectively than a very strong fear-impulse operating in a less-developed mind. The operation of the " primal law " will, therefore, have tended to secure that the successful

rival of the patriarch should have strong instincts of sex
and of pugnacity, and a but moderately strong fear-
instinct, combined with the more developed mental
organisation that permits of deliberation and of control
of the stronger impulses through the organised co-operation of the weaker impulses. That is to say, it was a
condition which secured for the family community a
succession of patriarchs, each of whom was superior to his
rivals, not merely in power of combat, but also and chiefly
in power of far-sighted control of his impulses. Each such
patriarch, becoming the father of the succeeding generation, will then have transmitted to it in some degree his
exceptional power of self-control. In this way the " primal
law," enforced by the fiercest passions of primitive man,
may have prepared human nature for the observance of
laws less brutally and ruthlessly enforced, may, in short,
have played a great part in developing in humanity that
power of self-control and law-abidingness which was the
essential condition of the progress of social organisation.

If we consider human societies at a later stage of
their development, we shall see that the pugnacious
instinct has played a similar part there also. And in
this case we are not compelled to rely only on speculative
hypotheses, but can find inductive support for our inference
in a comparative study of existing savage peoples.

When in any region social organisation had progressed
so far that the mortal combat of individuals was replaced
by the mortal combat of tribes, villages, or groups of any
kind, success in combat and survival and propagation
must have been favoured by, and have depended upon,
not only the vigour and ferocity of individual fighters,
but also, and to an even greater degree, upon the capacity
of individuals for united action, upon good comradeship,
upon personal trustworthiness, and upon the capacity of
individuals to subordinate their impulsive tendencies and
egoistic promptings to the ends of the group and to the
commands of the accepted leader. Hence, wherever such
mortal conflict of groups prevailed for many generations,
it must have developed in the surviving groups just those
social and moral qualities of individuals which are the

essential conditions of all effective co-operation and of the higher forms of social organisation. For success in war implies definite organisation, the recognition of a leader, and faithful observance of his commands ; and the obedience given to the war-chief implies a far higher level of morality than is implied by the mere observance of the " primal law " or of any other personal prohibition under the threat of punishment. A leader whose followers were bound to him by fear of punishment only would have no chance of success against a band of which the members were bound together and to their chief by a true conscientiousness arising from a more developed self-consciousness, from the identification of the self with the society, and from a sensitive regard on the part of each member for the opinion of his fellows.

Such conflict of groups could not fail to operate effectively in developing the moral nature of man ; those communities in which this higher morality was developed would triumph over and exterminate those which had not attained it in equal degree. And the more the pugnacious instinct impelled primitive societies to warfare, the more rapidly and effectively must the fundamental social attributes of men have been developed in the societies which survived the ordeal.

It is not easy to analyse these moral qualities and to say exactly what elements of the mental constitution were involved in this evolution. In part the advance must have consisted in a further improvement of the kind we have supposed to be effected by the operation of the "primal law," namely, a richer self-consciousness, and increased capacity for control of the stronger primary impulses by the co-operation of impulses springing from dispositions organised about the idea of the self. It may also have involved a relative increase of strength of the more specifically social tendencies, namely, the gregarious instinct, the instincts of self-assertion and subjection, and the primitive sympathetic tendency ; the increase of strength of these tendencies in the members of any social group would render them capable of being more strongly swayed by regard for the opinions and feelings of their fellows, and so would strengthen the influence of the public opinion of the group upon each member of it.

These results of group-selection produced by the mortal conflicts of small societies, and ultimately due to the strength of the pugnacious instinct, are very clearly illustrated by the tribes of Borneo. As one travels up any one of the large rivers, one meets with tribes that are successively more warlike. In the coast regions are peaceful communities which never fight, save in self-defence, and then with but poor success ; while in the central regions, where the rivers take their rise, are a number of extremely warlike tribes, whose raids have been a constant source of terror to the communities settled in the lower reaches of the rivers. And between these tribes at the centre and those in the coast regions are others that serve as a buffer between them, being decidedly more bellicose than the latter but less so than the former. It might be supposed that the peaceful coastwise people would be found to be superior in moral qualities to their more warlike neighbours ; but the contrary is the case. In almost all respects the advantage lies with the warlike tribes. Their houses are better built, larger, and cleaner ; their domestic morality is superior ; they are physically stronger, are braver, and physically and mentally more active, and in general are more trustworthy. But, above all, their social organisation is firmer and more efficient, because their respect for and obedience to their chiefs, and their loyalty to their community, are much greater ; each man identifies himself with the whole community, and accepts and loyally performs the social duties laid upon him. And the moderately warlike tribes occupying the intermediate regions stand midway between them and the people of the coast as regards these moral qualities.[1]

[1] These statements are based not merely on my own observations during a sojourn of six months among these tribes, but also on the authority of my friend, Dr. Charles Hose, who for more than twenty years has exercised a very remarkable influence over many of the tribes of Sarawak, and has done very much to establish the beneficent rule of the Rajah, H.H. Sir Charles Brooke, over the wilder tribes of the outlying districts.

Yet all these tribes are of closely allied racial stocks, and the superior moral qualities of the central tribes would seem to be the direct result of the very severe group-selection to which their innate pugnacity has subjected them for many generations. And the greater strength of their pugnacious instinct, which displays itself unmistakably in their more martial bearing and more fiery temper, is probably due ultimately to the 'more bracing climate of the central regions, which, by favouring a greater bodily activity, has led to more frequent conflicts and a stricter weeding out of the more inoffensive and less energetic individuals and groups.

Such tribal conflict, which in this remote region has continued up to the present time, has probably played in past ages a great part in preparing the civilised peoples of Europe for the complex social life that they have developed. Mr. Kidd has insisted forcibly upon this view, pointing out that the tribes of the central and northern regions of Europe, which have played so great a part in the later history of civilisation, were subjected for long ages to a process of military group-selection which was probably of extreme severity, and which rendered them, at the time they first appear in history, the most pugnacious and terrible warriors that the world has ever seen.[1] This process must have developed not only the individual fighting qualities, but also the qualities that make for conscientious conduct and stable and efficient social organisation. These effects were clearly marked in the barbarians who overran the Roman Empire. The Germanic tribes were perhaps more pugnacious and possessed of the military virtues in a higher degree than any other people that has existed before or since. They were the most terrible enemies, as Julius Cæsar found ; they could never be subdued because they fought, not merely to gain any specific ends, but because they loved fighting, *i.e.*, because they were innately pugnacious. Their religion

---

[1] *Principles of Western Civilisation*, p. 156 : " The ruling fact which stands clearly out in regarding this movement of peoples as a whole, is that it must have represented a process of military selection, probably the most sustained, prolonged, and culminating in character that the race has ever undergone."

and the character of their gods reflected their devotion
to war ; centuries of Christianity have failed to eradicate
this quality, and the smallest differences of opinion and
belief continue to furnish the pretexts for fresh combats.
Mr. Kidd argues strongly that it is the social qualities
developed by this process of military group-selection
which, more than anything else, have enabled these peoples
to build up a new civilisation on the ruins of the Roman
Empire, and to carry on the progress of social organisation
and of civilisation to the point it has now reached.

These important social effects of the pugnacious
instinct seem to be forcibly illustrated by a comparison
of the peoples of Europe with those of India and of China,
two areas comparable with it in extent, in density of
settled population, and in age of civilisation. In neither
of these areas has there been a similar perennial conflict
of societies. In both of them, the mass of the people
has been subjected for long ages to the rule of dominant
castes which have established themselves in successive
invasions from the central plateau of Asia, that great
breeding-ground of warlike nomadic hordes. The result
in both cases is the same. The bulk of the people are
deficient in the pugnacious instinct ; they are patient
and long-suffering, have no taste for war, and, in China
especially, they despise the military virtues. At the
same time they seem to be deficient in those social qualities
which may be summed up under the one word "conscientiousness," and which are the cement of societies
and essential factors of their progressive integration.
Accordingly, in the societies formed by these peoples,
the parts hang but loosely together—they are but partially
integrated and loosely organised. Among these peoples
Buddhism, the religion of peace, found a congenial home,
and its precepts have governed the practice of great
masses of men in a very real manner, which contrasts
strongly with the formal acceptance and practical neglect
of the peaceful precepts of their religion that has always
characterised the Christian peoples of Western Europe.

In this connection it is interesting to compare the
Japanese with the Chinese people. Whether the strain

of Malayan blood in the Japanese has endowed them from the first with a stronger instinct of pugnacity than their cousins the Chinese, it is impossible to say. But it is certain that the people, in spite of the fact that they have long recognised in their Emperor a common spiritual head of the empire, have been until very recently divided into numerous clans that have been almost constantly at war with one another, society being organised on a military system not unlike that of feudal Europe. Hence the profession of the soldier has continued to be held in the highest honour, and the fighting qualities, as well as the specifically social qualities of the people, have been brought to a very high level.

In Japan also Buddhism has long been firmly established ; but, as with Christianity in Europe, its preaching of peace has never been practically accepted by the mass of the people ; the old ancestor-worship has continued to flourish side by side with it, and now, on the accentuation of the warlike spirit induced by contact with the outside world, seems to be pushing the religion of peace into the background.

In addition to this important rôle in the evolution of the moral qualities, the pugnacious instinct has exerted a more direct and hardly less important influence in the life of societies.

We have seen how this instinct is operative in the emotion of revenge and in moral indignation. These two emotions have played leading parts in the growth and maintenance of every system of criminal law and every code of punishment ; for, however widely authors may differ as to the spirit in which punishment should be administered, there can be no doubt that it was originally retributive, and that it still retains something of this character even in the most highly civilised societies. The administration of criminal law is then the organised and regulated expression of the anger of society, modified and softened in various degrees by the desire that punishment may reform the wrong-doer and deter others from similar actions.

Though with the progress of civilisation the public

administration of justice has encroached more and more on the sphere of operation of the anger of individuals as a power restraining offences of all kinds, yet, in the matter of offences against the person, individual anger remains as a latent threat whose influence is by no means negligible in the regulation of manners, as we see most clearly in those countries in which the practice of duelling is not yet obsolete. And in the nursery and the school righteous anger will always have a great and proper part to play in the training of the individual for his life in society.

It was suggested in Chapter IV. that emulation is rooted in an instinct which was evolved in the human mind by a process of differentiation from the instinct of pugnacity. However that may be, it seems clear that this impulse is distinct from both the combative and the self-assertive impulses; and just as, according to our supposition, the emulative impulse has acquired in the course of the evolution of the human mind an increasing importance, so in the life of societies it tends gradually to take the place of the instinct of pugnacity, as a force making for the development of social life and organisation.

It is among the peoples of Western Europe, who, as we have seen, have been moulded by a prolonged and severe process of military selection, that the emulative impulse is most active. With us it supplies the zest and determines the forms of almost all our games and recreations; and Professor James is guilty of picturesque exaggeration only, when he says " nine-tenths of the work of our world is done by it." Our educational system is founded upon it; it is the social force underlying an immense amount of strenuous exertion; to it we owe in a great measure even our science, our literature, and our art; for it is a strong, perhaps an essential, element of ambition, that last infirmity of noble minds, in which it operates through, and under the direction of, a highly developed social self-consciousness.

The emulative impulse tends to assert itself in an ever-widening sphere of social life, encroaching more and more upon the sphere of the combative impulse, and supplanting it more and more as a prime mover of both individuals and societies. This tendency brings with it a very important change in the conditions of social evolution. While the combative impulse leads to the destruction of the individuals and societies that are least capable of self-defence, the emulative impulse does not directly lead to the extermination of individuals or societies. It is, rather, compatible with a tender solicitude for their continued existence ; the millionaire, who, prompted by this impulse, has succeeded in appropriating a proportion of the wealth of the community vastly in excess of his deserts, may spend a part of it on free libraries, hospitals, or soup-kitchens. In fact, the natural tendency of the emulative impulse is to preserve, rather than to destroy, defeated competitors ; for their regards bring a fuller satisfaction to the impulse, and the exploitation of their labour by the successful rival is the natural issue of competition. Therefore, as emulation replaces pugnacity within any society, it tends to put a stop to natural selection of individuals within that society ; so that the evolution of human nature becomes increasingly dependent on group-selection. And if international emulation should completely supplant international pugnacity, group-selection also will be rendered very much less effective. To this stage the most highly civilised communities are tending, in accordance with the law that the collective mind follows in the steps of evolution of the individual mind at a great interval of time. There are unmistakable signs that the pugnacity of nations is being supplanted by emulation, that warfare is being replaced by industrial and intellectual rivalry ; that wars between civilised nations, which are replacing the mortal conflicts between individuals and between societies dominated by the spirit of pugnacity, are tending to become mere incidents of their commercial and industrial rivalry, being undertaken to secure markets or sources of supply of raw material which shall bring industrial or commercial advantage to their possessor.

The tendency of emulation to replace pugnacity is,

then, a tendency to bring to an end what has been an important, probably the most important, factor of progressive evolution of human nature, namely, the selection of the fit and the extermination of the less fit (among both individuals and societies) resulting from their conflicts with one another.[1]

[1] The attempt now being made to found a science and an art of Eugenics owes its importance largely to this tendency.

CHAPTER XII

THE GREGARIOUS INSTINCT

IT was pointed out in Chapter III. that the gregarious instinct plays a great part in determining the forms of our recreations ; and in Chapter VI. it was shown how, in co-operation with the primitive sympathetic tendency, it leads men to seek to share their emotions with the largest possible number of their fellows. Besides determining the forms of recreations, this instinct plays a much more serious part in the life of civilised societies. It is sometimes assumed that the monstrous and disastrous growth of London and of other large towns is the result of some obscure economic necessity. But, as a matter of fact, London and many other large towns have for a long time past far exceeded the proportions that conduce to economic efficiency and healthy social life, just as the vast herds of bison, or other animals, referred to in Chapter III., greatly exceed the size necessary for mutual defence. We are often told that the dulness of the country drives the people to the towns. But that statement inverts the truth. It is the crowd in the towns, the vast human herd, that exerts a baneful attraction on those outside it. People have lived in the country for hundreds of generations without finding it dull. It is only the existence of the crowded towns that creates by contrast the dulness of the country. As in the case of the animals, the larger the aggregation the greater is its power of attraction ; hence, in spite of high rents, high rates, dirt, disease, congestion of traffic, ugliness, squalor, and sooty air, the large towns continue to grow at an increasing rate, while the small towns diminish and the country villages are threatened with extinction.

That this herding in the towns is not due to any economic necessities of our industrial organisation, is shown by the fact that it takes place to an equally great and regrettable extent in countries where the industrial conditions are very different. In Australia, where everything favours an agricultural or pastoral mode of life, half the population of a continent is crowded into a few towns on the coast. In China, where industry persists almost entirely in the form of handicrafts and where economic conditions are extremely different from our own, we find towns like Canton containing three million inhabitants crowded together even more densely than in London and under conditions no less repulsive.

In England we must attribute this tendency chiefly to the fact that the spread of elementary education and the freer intercourse between the people of the different parts of the country have broken down the bonds of custom which formerly kept each man to the place and calling of his forefathers ; for custom, the great conservative force of society, the great controller of the individual impulses, being weakened, the deep-seated instincts, especially the gregarious instinct, have found their opportunity to determine the choices of men. Other causes have, of course, co-operated and have facilitated the aggregations of population ; but without the instinctive basis they would probably have produced only slight effects of this kind.

The administrative authorities have shown of late years a disposition to encourage in every possible way this gregarious tendency. On the slightest occasion they organise some show which shall draw huge crowds to gape, until now a new street cannot be opened without the expenditure of thousands of pounds in tawdry decorations, and a foreign prince cannot drive to a railway station without drawing many thousands of people from their work to spend the day in worse than useless idleness, confirming their already over-developed gregarious instincts. There can be no doubt that the excessive indulgence of this impulse is one of the greatest demoralising factors of the present time in this country, just as it was in Rome in the days of her declining power and glory.

In this connection we may briefly consider the views of Professor Giddings[1] on "the consciousness of kind," which he would have us regard as the basic principle of social organisation. He writes, "In its widest extension the consciousness of kind marks off the animate from the inanimate. Within the wide class of the animals it marks off species and races. Within racial lines the consciousness of kind underlies the more definite ethnical and political groupings, it is the basis of class distinctions, of innumerable forms of alliance, of rules of intercourse, and of peculiarities of policy. Our conduct towards those whom we feel to be most like ourselves is instinctively and rationally different from our conduct towards others, whom we believe to be less like ourselves. Again, it is the consciousness of kind, and nothing else, which distinguishes social conduct, as such, from purely economic, purely political, or purely religious conduct ; for in actual life it constantly interferes with the theoretically perfect operation of the economic, political, or religious motive. The working man joins a strike of which he does not approve rather than cut himself off from his fellows. For a similar reason the manufacturer who questions the value of protection to his own industry yet pays his contribution to the protectionist campaign fund. The Southern gentleman, who believed in the cause of the Union, none the less threw in his fortunes with the Confederacy, if he felt himself to be one of the Southern people and a stranger to the people of the North. The liberalising of creeds is accomplished by the efforts of men who are no longer able to accept the traditional dogma, but who desire to maintain associations which it would be painful to sever. In a word, it is about the consciousness of kind that all other motives organise themselves in the evolution of social choice, social volition, or social policy."

All that attraction of like to like, which Giddings here attributes to the " consciousness of kind " is, I think

[1] *Principles of Sociology*, p. 18 (my quotation is abridged).

to be regarded as the work of the gregarious impulse, operating at a high level of mental life in conjunction with other impulses. That " consciousness of kind," the recognition of degrees of likeness of others to one's self, underlies all such cases as Professor Giddings mentions, and is presupposed by all social life, is true only if we use the words in a very loose sense. If we would state more accurately the facts vaguely implied by this phrase, we must say that the gregarious impulse of any animal receives satisfaction only through the presence of animals similar to itself, and the closer the similarity the greater is the satisfaction. The impulse of this instinct will bring and keep together in one herd animals of different species, as when we see horses and bullocks grazing together, or birds of several species in one flock; but it brings and keeps together much more powerfully animals of one species. Just so, in any human being the instinct operates most powerfully in relation to, and receives the highest degree of satisfaction from the presence of, the human beings who most closely resemble that individual, those who behave in like manner and respond to the same situations with similar emotions. An explicit " consciousness of kind " in any literal sense of the words implies a relatively high level of mental development and a developed self-consciousness, and this is by no means necessary to the operation of the gregarious instinct. And such " consciousness of kind " can of itself do nothing, it is not a social force, is not a motive, can of itself generate no impulse or desire. It is merely one of the most highly developed of the cognitive processes through which the gregarious instinct may be brought into play. If this instinct were lacking to men, the most accurate recognition of personal likenesses and differences would fail to produce the effects attributed to " consciousness of kind."

It is because we are not equally attracted by all social aggregations, but find the greatest satisfaction of the gregarious impulse in the society of those most like ourselves, that a segregation of like elements occurs in all communities. Among uncivilised people we usually find communities of the same tribe, and tribes closely allied by blood, occupying contiguous areas ; and the effects of this tendency persist in the civilised countries of the present day in the form of local differences of physical and mental characters of the populations of the various counties or other large areas.

The same tendency is illustrated by the formation in the United States of America of large, locally circumscribed communities of various European extractions : and in our large towns it manifests itself in the segregation of people of similar race and occupation and social status, a process which results in striking differences between the various districts or quarters of the town, and striking uniformities within the limits of any one such quarter. In this tendency we may find also an explanation of the curious fact that the traders dealing in each kind of object are commonly found closely grouped in one street or in neighbouring streets—the coach-builders in Long Acre, the newsvendors in Fleet Street, the doctors in Harley Street, the shipping offices in Leadenhall Street, and so on. This segregation of like trades, which might seem to be a curious economic anomaly under our competitive system, is not peculiar to European towns. It forced itself upon my attention in the streets of Canton, where it obtains in a striking degree, and also in several Indian towns.

We may briefly sum up the social operation of the gregarious instinct by saying that, in early times when population was scanty, it must have played an important part in social evolution by keeping men together and thereby occasioning the need for social laws and institutions ; as well as by providing the conditions of aggregation in which alone the higher evolution of the social attributes was possible ; but that in highly civilised societies its functions are less inportant, because the density of population ensures a sufficient aggregation of the people ; and that, facilities for aggregation being so greatly increased among modern nations, its direct operation is apt to produce anomalous and even injurious social results.

CHAPTER XIII

THE INSTINCTS THROUGH WHICH RELIGIOUS CONCEPTIONS AFFECT SOCIAL LIFE

MANY authors have written of the religious instinct or instincts, though few have made any serious attempt to make clear the meaning they attach to these phrases. Those who use these phrases usually seem to imply that this assumed religious instinct of man is one that is his peculiar endowment and has no relation to the instincts of the animals. But I do not know that this is now seriously maintained by any psychologist. The emotions that play a principal part in religious life are admiration, awe, and reverence. In Chapter V. we have analysed these emotions and found that admiration is a fusion of wonder and negative self-feeling ; that awe is a fusion of admiration with fear ; and that reverence is awe blended with tender emotion.[1]

Religion has powerfully influenced social development in so many ways, and the primary emotions and impulses through which the religious conceptions have exerted this influence have co-operated so intimately, that they must be considered together when we attempt to illustrate their rôle in social life.

Something has already been said of the rôle of fear in the chapter treating of pugnacity. Whether or no the hypothesis of the " primal law " be well founded, fear

[1] Thus Professor M. Jastrow writes : " The certainty that the religious instinct is, so far as the evidence goes, innate in man, suffices as a starting-point for a satisfactory classification." The same author tells us that " the definite assumption of a religious instinct in man forms part of almost every definition of religion proposed since the appearance of Schleiermacher's discourses " (*The Study of Religion*, pp. 101 and 153).

must have played in primitive societies some such part as was assigned to it in discussing that doctrine. That is to say, fear of physical punishment inflicted by the anger of his fellows must have been the great agent of discipline of primitive man ; through such fear he must first have learnt to control and regulate his impulses in conformity with the needs of social life.[1]

But, at an early stage of social development, awe must have supplemented and in part supplanted simple fear in this rôle. For, as with the development of language man became capable of a fuller life of ideas, the instinct of curiosity, which in the animals merely serves to rivet their attention upon unfamiliar objects, must have been frequently excited by the display of forces that in creatures of a lower level of development excite fear only. This instinct must then have kept his thoughts at work upon these objects of his wonder, and especially upon those which excited not only wonder but fear. These must have become the objects of man's awful contemplation, and he began to evolve theories to account for them, theories of which, no doubt, he felt the need as guides to action in the presence of these forces.

We may assume that primitive man lacked almost completely the conception of mechanical causation. For the modern savage mechanical causation is the explanation of but a small part of the natural processes which interest him through affecting his welfare for good or ill. For those of us who have grown up familiar with the modern doctrine of the prevalence of mechanical causation throughout the material world, it is difficult to realise how enormous is the distortion of the facts of immediate experience wrought by that doctrine, by how great an effort of abstraction it has been reached. The savage is familiar with the sequence of movement upon impact, but such sequences are far from invariable in his experience, and constitute but a very small proportion of the events which interest him. The fall of bodies to the ground, the flowing of water, the blowing of the wind, the motions of the heavenly bodies, the growth and movements of animals and plants, thunder, lightning, rain, fire, and the emission and reflection of light and heat— these are prominent among the things that interest him, and in none of them is there any obvious indication of mechanical operation. The one kind of causation with which the uncultured man is thoroughly familiar is his own volitional action, issuing from feeling, emotion, and desire; and this naturally and inevitably becomes for him the type on which he models his theories of the causation of terrible events. Here we touch the fringe of an immense subject, the evolution of religious conceptions, which we cannot pursue. It must suffice to say that Professor Tylor's doctrine of animism, as set forth in his great work on *Primitive Culture*, is probably the best account we yet have of the early steps of this evolution. Let us note merely that in all probability primitive man, like ourselves, was apt to accept without wonder, without pondering and reasoning upon them, the beneficent processes of nature, the gentle rain, the light and warmth of the sun, the flowing of the river, the healthy growth of animal and vegetable life; but that his wonder was especially aroused by those things and events which excited also his fear, by disease and death, pestilence and famine, storm and flood, lightning and thunder, and the powerful beasts of prey. For, while the beneficent processes are regular, gentle, and familiar, these others are apt to come suddenly, irregularly, and apparently capriciously, and are therefore unfamiliar and startling, as well as hurtful and irresistible. On such objects and events, then, man's wondering thoughts were concentrated, about them his imagination chiefly played. Hence it followed that the powers which his imagination created for the explanation of these events were conceived by him more or less vaguely as terrible powers ready at every moment to bring disaster upon him and his community. Therefore he walked in fear and trembling, and was deeply concerned to learn how to avoid giving offence to these mysterious and fearful powers. And, as soon as these powers began to be conceived by man as personal powers, they must have evoked in him the attitude and impulse of subjection and the emotion of negative self-feeling, which are rooted in the instinct of subjection. Or perhaps it would be truer to say that, as man began to form conceptions of these forces of nature, they evoked in him the impulse and emotion of this instinct, threw him into the submissive attitude characteristic of this instinct, which is essentially a personal attitude, one implying a personal relation ; and that primitive man, finding himself in this attitude before these powers, was thus led to personify them, to attribute to them the personal attributes of strength and anger, which are the normal and primitive excitants of this instinct. Hence his emotion took the complex form of awe (a tertiary compound of fear, wonder, and negative self-feeling [1]) ; that is, he not only feared, and wondered at, these powers, but humbled himself before them, and sought to gain and to obey the slightest indications of their wills.[2]

It is obvious that conceptions of this sort, once achieved and accepted by all members of a community with un-

---

[1] Cf. p. 113.

[2] Certain of these forces of nature were less terrible than others, e.g., rain, and the growth of plants and animals, and man made the bold experiment of attempting to control them, proceeding by a purely empirical method and guided by the slightest indications to belief in the success of his experiments ; such seemingly successful procedures then became conventional and recognised modes of influencing these powers. In so far as man seemed to find himself able to control and coerce any of these forces, his attitude and emotion in presence of them would be those of the instinct of self-assertion, even though he might continue to be filled with fear and wonder. This complex emotional state seems to be the characteristically superstitious one, and the attitude and practices are those of magic. I suggest that the fundamental distinction between religious and magical practices is not, as is sometimes said, that religion conceives the powers it envisages as personal powers, while magic conceives them as impersonal ; but rather that the religious attitude is always that of submission, the magical attitude that of self-assertion ; and that the forces which both magical and religious practices are concerned to influence may be conceived in either case as personal or impersonal powers. Hence the savage, who at one time bows down before his fetish in supplication, and at another seeks to compel its assistance by threats or spells, adopts towards the one object alternately the religious and the magical attitude. The same fundamental difference of attitude and emotion distinguishes religion from science, into which magic becomes trans- formed as civilisation progresses.

questioning belief, must have been very powerful agencies of social discipline. The cause of every calamity, befalling either the individual or the community, would be sought in some offence given to the beings thus vaguely conceived ; and primitive man would be apt to regard as the source of offence any action at all unusual, at all out of the ordinary, whether of individuals or of the community. Hence the conceptions of these awe-inspiring beings would lead to increased severity of social discipline in two ways : firstly, by causing society to enforce its customary laws more rigidly than was the rule so long as breaches of the law were regarded as merely natural offences against members of the community ; for the breaking of custom by any individual was now believed to bring grave risks to the whole community, which therefore was collectively concerned to prevent and to punish any such breach : secondly, by producing a very great increase in the number and kinds of customary prohibitions and enforced observances ; for *post hoc ergo propter hoc* is the logic of uncultured man, and every unusual act followed by success or disaster must have tended to become a customary observance or the subject of a social prohibition.

Thus these conceptions of supernal powers, the products of man's creative imagination working through, and under the driving power of, the instincts of fear, curiosity, and subjection, became the great generators and supporters of custom. The importance of the social operation of these instincts was, then, very great ; for the first requisite of society, the prime condition of the social life of man, was, in the words of Bagehot, a hard crust or cake of custom. In the struggle for existence only those societies survived which were able to evolve such a hard crust of custom, binding men together, assimilating their actions to the accepted standards, compelling control of the purely egoistic impulses, and exterminating the individuals incapable of such control.

We see the same result among all savage communities still existing on the earth, and among all the peoples of whom we have any record at the dawn of civilisation.

Their actions, whether individual or collective, are hampered, controlled, or enforced at every step by custom. In Borneo, for example, an expedition prepared by months of labour will turn homeward and give up its objects if bad omens are observed—if a particular bird calls on one side or the other, or flies across the river in some particular fashion ; or a newly married and devoted couple will separate if on the wedding day the cry of a deer is heard near the house.

There is no end to the curious and absurd customs, generally supported by supernatural sanctions, by which the actions of savages and barbarians are commonly surrounded and hemmed in. We have to remember that, in the case of existing savage communities, the growth and multiplication of customs may have been proceeding through all the ages during which the few progressive peoples have been evolving their civilisation. But enough is now known of the primitive age of ancient Greece and Rome to show that the great civilisations of these states took their rise among peoples bound hand and foot by religious custom and law as rigidly as any savages,[1] and to show also that the dominant religious emotion was fear.[2]

[1] The system of omens of the Romans was not only similar in general outline to that of some existing communities, but closely resembled in many of its details that observed at the present day by tribes of Central Borneo—a remarkable illustration of the uniformity of the human mind. (See paper by the author, in conjunction with Dr. C. Hose, on "The Relations of Men and Animals in Sarawak," *Journal of the Anthropological Institute*, 1901.)

[2] Fustel de Coulanges has drawn a vivid picture of the dominance of this religion of fear in ancient Greece and Rome ; he writes : " Ainsi, en temps de paix et en temps de guerre, la religion intervenait dans tous les actes. Elle était partout présente, elle enveloppait l'homme. L'âme, le corps, la vie privée, la vie publique, les repas, les fêtes, les assemblées, les tribunaux, les combats, tout était sous l'empire de cette religion de la cité. Elle réglait toutes les actions de l'homme, disposait de tous les instants de sa vie, fixait toutes ses habitudes. Elle gouvernait l'être humain avec une autorité si absolue qu'il ne restait rien qui fût en dehors d'elle. . . . Cette religion était un ensemble, mal lié de petites croyances, de petites pratiques, de rites minutieux. Il n'en fallait pas chercher le sens ; il n'y avait pas à réfléchir, à se rendre compte. . . . La religion était un lien matériel, une chaine qui tenait l'homme esclave. L'homme se l'était faite, et il était gouverné par elle. Il en avait peur et n'osait ni raisonner, ni discuter, ni regarder

We may assume with confidence that the formation of a mass of customary observance and prohibition was a principal feature of the evolution of all human societies that have risen above the lowest level and have survived through any considerable period of time ; not only because the existence of such a crust of custom is observable in all savage and barbarous communities, but also because in its earlier stage the process must have so strengthened the societies in which it took place that rival societies in which it failed could not have stood up against them in the struggle for existence. And this essential step of social evolution was, as we have seen, in the main produced by the co-operation of the instincts of fear, curiosity, and subjection.

The difficult thing to understand is how any societies ever managed to break their cake of custom, to become progressive and yet to survive. As a matter of fact, very few have become progressive, and fewer still have long survived the taking of this step. The great majority have remained in the bonds of custom. And these customs have grown ever more rigid and more remote in form from primitive customs, and often more unreasonable and absurd ; in many cases they have assumed forms so grotesque that it is difficult to suggest their psychological origin and history ; and in many cases their multiplicity and rigidity have increased, until they have far exceeded the socially advantageous limits.

In many regions the fearful element in religion pre-

en face. . . . Ni les dieux n'aimaient l'homme, ni l'homme n'aimait ses dieux. Il croyait à leur existence, mais il aurait parfois voulu qu'ils n'existassent pas. Même ses dieux domestiques ou nationaux, il les redoutait, il craignait d'être trahi par eux. Encourir la haine de ces êtres invisibles était sa grande inquietude. Il était occupé toute sa vie à les apaiser. . . . En effet, cette religion si compliquée était une source de terreurs pour les anciens ; comme la foi et la pureté des intentions étaient peu de chose, et que toute la religion consistait dans la pratique minutieuse d'innombrables prescriptions, on devait toujours craindre d'avoir commis quelque négligence, quelque omission ou quelque erreur, et l'on n'était jamais sûr de n'être pas sous le coup de la colère ou de la rancune de quelque dieu." As to the rites : " L'altération la plus légère troublait et bouleversait la religion de la patrie, et transformait les dieux protecteurs en autant d'ennemis cruels " (La Cité antique, pp. 186–196).

dominated more and more, the gods increasingly assumed a cruel and bloodthirsty character, until, as in the case of the Aztecs of ancient Mexico, the religious ritual by which they were appeased involved the sacrifice of herds of victims, and their altars were constantly wet with human blood.

These elements and forces of primitive religion have lived on, continuing to play their parts, while religion rose to a higher plane on which tender emotion, in the form of gratitude, mingled more and more with awe, blended with it, and converted it to reverence.

This change in the nature of religious emotion among those peoples that have survived and progressed was a natural consequence of their success in the struggle of groups for survival. For the surviving communities are those whose gods have, in the main, not only spared them, not only abstained from bringing plague and famine and military disaster upon them in too severe measure, but have actively supported them and enabled them to overcome their enemies. Communities that are continuously successful in battle naturally tend to conceive the divine power as a god of battles who smites the enemy hip and thigh and delivers them into the hands of his chosen people to be their slaves and to add to their wealth and power. Thus the early Romans, as they emerged triumphant from successive wars with the neighbouring cities and grew in power and wealth, naturally and inevitably acquired some confidence in the beneficence of their gods ; they began to fear them less and to feel some gratitude towards them.

The utterly cruel gods could continue to survive only among communities not subjected to any severe struggle with other groups, as, for example, among the comparatively isolated Aztecs of Mexico.

Nevertheless, in almost all religions, fear of divine punishment has continued to play its all-important part in securing observance of social custom and law, and in leading communities to enforce their customs with severe penalties. The divine power remains for long ages a very jealous god (or gods), whose anger against a whole people may be stirred by the offences of individuals. This feature, namely, communal responsibility before the gods, to which in primitive societies the supernatural sanctions owe their tremendous power as agents of social discipline, was clearly present even in the religion of Athens at the time of its highest culture; and even in our own age and country the belief still survives and finds occasional expression (or did so very recently) in the observance of days of national humiliation.

But, as societies became larger and more complex, this principle necessarily weakened. Man's sense of justice rebelled against the ascription of so much injustice to the gods, whom he was learning to regard with gratitude and reverence as well as awe. Man is never long content to worship gods of moral character greatly inferior to his own. Hence the onus of responsibility for breaches of law and custom tends to be shifted back to the offending individual. And then, since it was obvious in every age that the wicked man often flourishes during this life, it became necessary to assume that the vengeance of the supernatural powers falls upon him in the life beyond the grave. Hence we find that, while societies are small and compact, communal responsibility for individual wrong-doing is the rule, and the idea of punishment after death is hardly entertained; but that, with the growth in size and complexity of a society and with the improvement of its moral ideas, belief in communal responsibility declines, and belief in punishment of wrong-doing after death arises to take its place as the effective sanction of custom and law. The most notable example of this process is, of course, afforded by the hell-fire which has played so great a part in the sterner forms of Christianity. And the long persistence of fear and awe in religion is well illustrated by the phrase widely current among the generation recently passed away, " an upright, god-fearing man," a phrase which expresses the tendency to identify uprightness with god-fearingness, or, rather, to recognise fear as the source and regulator of social conduct. It is a nice question : To what extent is the lapse from orthodox observances, so remarkable and widespread among the more highly civilised peoples at the present time, due to the general softening of religious teaching, to the lapse of the doctrine of divine retribution to a very secondary position, and to the discredit into which the flames of hell have fallen ? [1]

It has been contended by some authors that religion and morality were primitively distinct, and that the intimate connection commonly obtaining between them in civilised societies arose comparatively late in the course of social development. This contention, which is opposed to the view of religious development sketched in the foregoing pages, is true only if we attach an unduly narrow meaning to the words " religion " and " morality." Although many of the modes of conduct prescribed by primitive and savage custom and enforced by supernatural sanctions are not such as we regard as moral, and are in many cases even detrimental to the simple societies in which such customs obtain, and so cannot be justified by any utilitarian principle, yet we must class the observance of such custom as moral conduct. For the essence of moral conduct is the performance of social duty, the duty prescribed by society, as opposed to the mere following of the promptings of egoistic impulses. If we define moral conduct in this broad sense, and this is the only satisfactory definition of it [2]—then, no matter how grotesque and, from our point of view, how immoral the prescribed codes of conduct of other societies may appear to be, we must admit conformity to the code to be moral conduct ; and we must admit that religion from its first crude beginnings was bound up with morality in some such way as we have briefly sketched ; that the two things, religion and morality, were not at first separate and later fused together ; but that they were always intimately related,

---

[1] On the great rôle of fear in the more primitive forms of religion, and the decline of its influence in recent times, see an article by Professor J. H. Leuba, " Fear, Awe, and the Sublime in Religion," in the *American Journal of Religious Psychology*, vol. ii.

[2] There is, of course, the higher kind of morality of the man who, while accepting in the main the prescribed social code, attempts by his example and precept to improve it in certain respects.

and have reciprocally acted and reacted upon one another throughout the course of their evolution. We must recognise also that a firm and harmonious relation between them has been in every age a main condition of the stability of societies.

The hypothetical sketch of the early development of morality, the most essential condition of all development of social life, contained in the foregoing pages may be summarised as follows : Moral conduct consists in the regulation and control of the immediate promptings of impulse in conformity with some prescribed code of conduct. The first stage was the control of impulse through fear of individual retribution. Advance from this level took place through three principal changes : (1) the general recognition and customary observance of individual rights which ‘before had been claimed only by individuals and enforced only by their superior strength ; (2) an increase in the number of kinds of action regulated by customary law ; (3) an increase of the effectiveness of the sanctions of these laws ; the principal change in this connection being the introduction of supernatural powers (*i.e.*, powers which we regard as supernatural) as the guardians or patrons of custom, resulting (*a*) in the stern enforcement of customs by the whole community, which feels itself collectively responsible to these powers, and (*b*) in the supplementing of the fear of human retribution by the fear of divine retribution ; (4) a change in the innate dispositions of men, consisting in a development of those features of the mind which render possible a prudent and more complete control of the primary impulses, a change effected in the earlier stages chiefly by individual selection, in later stages chiefly by military group-selection.

In the production of this evolution of morality the instincts of pugnacity (probably largely under the form of male jealousy) and of fear were the all-important factors as regards the first stages ; while in later stages these great socialising forces were supplemented by the impulses of curiosity or wonder, of subjection, and, at a still later stage, by the tender protective impulse evoked principally in the form of gratitude towards the protecting deities.

A few more words must be said about the rôle of curiosity as a force in the life of societies. For although it has no doubt played, largely under the forms of wonder and admiration, a leading part in the evolution of religion, and in so far has been one of the conservative forces of society, it has played also a no less important part of a very different tendency. The instinct of curiosity is at the base of many of man's most splendid achievements, for rooted in it are his speculative and scientific tendencies. It has been justly maintained by J. S. Mill, by T. H Buckle, and others, that the free and effective operation of these tendencies in any society is not only the gauge of that society's position in the scale of civilisation, but also the principal condition of the progress of a people in all that constitutes civilisation. No attempt can be made here to support this view. But it may be pointed out that its truth is brought home to the mind by cursorily reviewing the periods of the greatest achievements of speculative reason. Such a review will show that these periods coincide approximately with the periods of the most rapid progress of social evolution; each such period of the life of a people being commonly followed by one of social stagnation, during which the leading minds remain content to brood over the wisdom of the ancient sages, Confucius, Aristotle, or Galen, regarding their achievements as unapproachable, authoritative, and supreme.

It is the insatiable curiosity of the modern European and American mind that, more than anything else, distinguishes it from all others and is the source of the immensely increased power over nature and over man that we now possess. Contrast our sceptical, insatiable, North-Pole-hunting disposition with that of most Eastern peoples.[1]

[1] This contrast cannot be better illustrated than by quoting a part of a letter from a Turkish official to an English seeker after statistical information : " The thing you ask of me is both difficult and useless. Although I have passed all my days in this place, I have neither counted the houses nor inquired into the number of the inhabitants ; and as to

If we attempt briefly to characterise the achievements that we owe to the speculative tendencies rooted in the instinct of curiosity, we find that they may for the most part be summed up under the head of improvements in our conception of causation. Mr. Stuart Glennie has formulated, as the fundamental law of intellectual development, the law of the advance from a quantitatively undetermined to a quantitatively determined conception of the reciprocal action or interaction of all things ; that is to say, he maintains that the main cause of human progress is the advance from very imperfect and misleading views of causation to more accurate views ; and in place of Comte's three stages of thought—the theological, the metaphysical, and the positive—he would distinguish the magical, the supernatural, and the scientific stages of this advance in man's notion of causation.

There is truth in this formulation ; but we must recognise that the stages do not succeed one another in clearly distinguishable periods of time, but rather that the three modes of thought coexist among every people that has progressed beyond savagery, and will probably always coexist : we must recognise that progress consists in, and results from, the increasing dominance of the second, and especially of the third, over the first, rather than in any complete substitution of one for another.

The magical mode of thought and practice is the immediate expression of man's need and desire to control the forces of his environment, while yet he knows nothing

what one person loads on his mules and the other stows away in the bottom of his ship that is no business of mine. But, above all, as to the previous history of this city, God only knows the amount of dirt and confusion that the infidels may have eaten before the coming of the sword of Islam. It were unprofitable for us to inquire into it. O my soul ! O my lamb ! seek not after the things which concern thee not. Thou camest with us and we welcomed thee—go in peace. . . . Listen, O my son ! There is no wisdom equal unto the belief in God ! He created the world and shall we liken ourselves unto Him in seeking to penetrate into the mysteries of His creation ? Shall we say, Behold this star spinneth round that star, and this other star with a tail goeth and cometh in so many years ! Let it go ! He from whose hand it came will guide and direct it." The letter is quoted in full by Professor James (from whom I copy) from Sir A. Layard's *Nineveh and Babylon*.

of their nature.   At this stage man conceives all things
to be capable of reciprocal action, but as to the modes of
their interaction he has but the vaguest and most in-
accurate notions.   Hence, in attempting to control these
forces, he adopts whatever procedure suggests itself in
virtue of the natural associative conjunctions of his ideas ;
as when he attempts to cause rain by sprinkling water on
the ground with certain traditional formalities, to raise
wind by whistling or by imitating the sound of it with the
bull-roarer, to bring disease or death by maltreating an
effigy of his enemy, to cure pain and disease by drawing
it out of the body in the form of a material object or
imaginary entity.

Though belief in the efficacy of such practices has
maintained itself with wonderful persistency through
long ages, yet the lack of success that so often attends
them forbids man to remain for ever satisfied with them,
or to feel that he has a power of control over nature adequate to his needs.   Hence his imaginative faculty,
operating under the impulse of curiosity or wonder,
evolves great supernatural powers which he regards with
awe and submission.   Society recognises these powers,
and a traditional cult of them grows up, and the system
of supernatural explanation of natural events enters upon
its long period of dominance.   All the unprogressive
societies of the earth remain (as so well depicted in the
passage quoted in the footnote of p. 271) in this stage in
which theories of causation are predominantly supernatural and personal.

But in most societies there have been, throughout the
period of dominance of supernatural explanations, a
certain number of men whose curiosity was not satisfied
by the current systems.   They have maintained the
magical attitude, and, impelled by curiosity, have sought
to increase their direct influence upon natural forces by
achieving a better understanding of them.   These are the
wizards, the medicine-men, the alchemists and astrologers,
the independent thinkers, who at almost all times and
places have been reprobated and persecuted by the official
representatives of the supernatural cults.   In most of the

societies that have survived in the struggle for existence, the impulse of curiosity has not been strong enough to make head against these repressive measures. For the strength of the social sanctions, derived from the belief in the supernatural powers and from the awe and reverence excited by the ideas of these powers, was a main condition of the strength and stability of society ; and no society has been able to survive in any severe and prolonged conflict of societies, without some effective system of such sanctions. Hence we find a survival of the primitive predominance of the magical conception of causation only among peoples such as the natives of Australia, which, owing to their peculiar geographical conditions, have never been subjected to any severe process of group-selection. While all societies that have made any considerable progress in civilisation have been enabled to do so only in virtue of the stability they derived from their system of supernatural sanctions.

Hence the age-long, inevitable, and radical antagonism between the conservative spirit of religion and the progressive spirit of inquiry. The progress of mankind has only been rendered possible by their coexistence and conjoint operation. In the main, those societies which, in virtue of the strength and social efficiency of their system of supernatural beliefs and sanctions, have been most stable and capable of enduring, have been least tolerant of the spirit of inquiry, and therefore least progressive; on the other hand, the flourishing of scepticism has been too often the forerunner of social decay, as in ancient Greece and Rome. Continued progress has been rendered possible only by the fact that the gains achieved by the spirit of inquiry have survived the dissolution of the societies in which they have been achieved (and to which that spirit has proved fatal) through becoming imitatively taken up into the culture of societies in which the conservative spirit continued to predominate.

At the present time it may seem that in one small quarter of the world, namely, Western Europe, society has achieved an organisation so intrinsically stable that it may with impunity tolerate the flourishing of the spirit of inquiry and give free rein to the impulse of curiosity. But to assume that this is the case would be rash.   The issue remains doubtful.   The spirit of inquiry has broken all its bonds and soared gloriously, until now the conception of natural causation predominates in every field ; and, if the notion of supernatural powers still persists in the minds of men, it is in the form of the conception of a Divine Creator who maintains the laws that He has made, but does not constantly interfere with their operation. This change of belief, this withdrawal of supernatural power from immediate intervention in the life of mankind, inevitably and greatly diminishes the social efficiency of the supernatural sanctions.   Whether our societies will prove capable of long surviving this process is the most momentous of the problems confronting Western Civilisation.   The answer to it is a secret hidden in the bosom of the future.   If they shall survive the change, it can only be because the impulse of curiosity, carrying forward the work that it has so splendidly begun, will rapidly increase man's understanding of, and control over, his own nature and the conditions of healthy and vigorous social life.[1]

Of the instinct of self-display little need be said in this section.   Not because it is not of the first importance for social life, but because what was said of it in Section I. suffices to show the view I take of its importance and how it becomes incorporated in the self-regarding sentiment and plays a part in all true volition.   Here I would only add that in my view it plays a similarly essential part in all true collective volition, being incorporated in the sentiment for the family tribe, or nation, or other social aggregate that exerts such volition.   But the discussion and illustration of the nature of collective mental processes falls outside the plan of this volume.

Of the social functions of the instinct of submission something has been said in Section I. and in the foregoing pages of this Section.   But one of its most important social operations is the determination of the imitative,

---

[1] See the conclusion of Earl Balfour's lecture on "Decadence," Cambridge, 1908.

suggestible attitude of men and of societies towards one another ; and of this something will be said in the last chapter.[1]

[1] For a fuller discussion of the religious tendencies of primitive man, the reader may be referred to Mr. R. R. Marett's *Threshold of Religion* (London, 1909). In that work Mr. Marett traces back the evolution of religion to a preanimistic stage, which he proposes to denote by the word " animatism." It will be seen that my own brief sketch is in substantial agreement with his view.

CHAPTER XIV

THE INSTINCTS OF ACQUISITION AND CONSTRUCTION

T**HE** two instincts last mentioned in Chapter III., namely, those of acquisitiveness or cupidity and of construction, are not directly social in their operation, but indirectly they exert important effects in the life of societies, of which a few words may be said.

The importance of the instinct of acquisition, from our present point of view, is due to the fact that it must have greatly favoured, if it was not an essential condition of, that accumulation of material wealth which was necessary for the progress of civilisation beyond its earliest stages.

There are still in existence people who support themselves only by hunting and the collection of wild fruits, having no houses or fixed places of abode, nor any possessions beyond what they carry in their hands from place to place.[1] Among them this instinct would seem to be deficient ; or, perhaps, it is that it never is able to determine the formation of a corresponding habit owing to their wandering mode of life. Among pastoral nomads the working of the instinct is manifested in the vast herds sometimes accumulated by a single patriarchal family.[2] But it was only when agriculture began to be extensively practised that the instinct could produce its greatest social effects. For grain of all sorts lends itself especially well to hoarding as a form of wealth. It is

---

[1] One of the most interesting of such peoples are the Punans of Borneo, a remarkably pleasing, gentle-mannered, handsome, and fair-skinned race of forest-dwellers.

[2] See *Comment la Route crée le Type social*, by M. Ed. Demolins.

compact and valuable in proportion to its bulk, can be
kept for long periods without serious deterioration, and is
easily stored, divided, and transported.   Most of the
civilisations that have achieved any considerable development have been based on the accumulation of stores of
grain.   Besides being a very important form of capital,
it was one of the earliest and most important objects of
trade, and trade must always have exerted a socialising
influence.

Although in highly civilised societies the motives
that lead to the accumulation of capital become very
complex, yet acquisitiveness, the desire for mere possession of goods, remains probably the most fundamental
of them, blending and co-operating with all other motives ;
this impulse, more than all others, is capable of obtaining
continuous or continually renewed gratifications ;   for
while, in the course of satisfaction of most other desires,
the point of satiety is soon reached, the demands of this
one grow greater without limit, so that it knows no satiety.
How few men are content with the possession of what they
need for the satisfaction of all other desires than this
desire for possession for its own sake !   It is this excess of
activity beyond that required for the satisfaction of all
other material needs, that results in the accumulation
of the capital which is a necessary condition of the development of civilisation.   It might be plausibly maintained that the phenomena with which economic science
is concerned are in the main the outcome of the operation
of this instinct, rather than of the enlightened self-interest
of the classical economists.

The possession and acquisition of land affords satisfaction to this desire in a very full degree, land being
a so permanent and indestructible form of property.
And this instinct has played its part, not only in the
building up of large private estates—the tendency to the
indefinite growth of which everywhere manifests itself—
but also in the causation of the many wars that have been
waged for the possession of territories.   Wars of this
type are characteristic of autocracies ;   for the desire to
possess is more effective in promoting action when the

thing to be acquired is to become the possession of a single individual, than if it is to be shared by all the members of a democratic community. Accordingly, one of the most striking effects of the democratisation of States is the passing away of wars of this worst type.

The principal social effects of the instinct of construction are produced by the necessity for co-operation in works of construction that surpass the powers of individuals, especially architectural works. Among all peoples, this tendency to co-operation in large architectural constructions, huge totem poles, monoliths, temples, or massive tombs like the Pyramids of Egypt, shows itself as soon as they attain a settled mode of life ; and these works tend to confirm them in the settled mode of life, and to strengthen the social bonds

CHAPTER XV

IMITATION, PLAY, AND HABIT

IN Chapter IV. we discussed the three fundamental forms of mental interaction — suggestion, sympathy, and imitation. In each case, we said, the process of interaction results in the assimilation of the mental state of the recipient or patient to that of the agent. In each case we need a pair of words to denote the parts of the agent and of the patient respectively. "Suggest" denotes the part of the agent in assimilating the cognitive state of the patient to his own ; but we have no word for the part played by the patient in the process, unless we adopt the ugly expression—"to be suggestioned." "Imitate" and "sympathise" denote the part of the patient in the process of assimilation of his actions and of his affective state to those of the agent ; but we have no words denoting the part of the agent in these processes. Since these three processes co-operate intimately in social life, we may avoid the difficulty arising from this lack of terms by following M. Tarde,[1] who extends the meaning of the word "imitation" to cover all three processes as viewed from the side of the patient. If we do that, we still need a correlative word to denote all three processes viewed from the side of the agent. I propose to use the words "impress" and "impression" in this sense.[2] We may also follow M. Tarde in using "contra-imitation" to denote the process of contra-suggestion viewed from the side of the patient.

Impression and imitation are, then, processes of

---

[1] *Les Lois de l'Imitation*, Paris, 1904, and *Les Lois sociales*, Paris, 1902.
[2] Following in this respect Professor Giddings.

fundamental importance for social life. M. Tarde writes : " Nous dirons donc . . . qu'une société est un groupe de gens qui présentent entre eux beaucoup de similitudes produites par imitation ou par contre-imitation " ;[1] and in thus making imitation the very essence of social life he hardly exaggerates its importance. In Section I. we have considered some of the ways in which imitation moulds the growing individual and assimilates him to the type of the society into which he is born. In this Section we must consider the results of imitation from the point of view of the society as a whole rather than from that of the development of the individual.

Imitation is the prime condition of all collective mental life. I propose to reserve for another volume the detailed study of collective mental processes. Here I would dismiss the subject by merely pointing out that when men think, feel, and act as members of a group of any kind—whether a mere mob, a committee, a political or religious association, a city, a nation, or any other social aggregate—their collective actions show that the mental processes of each man have been profoundly modified in virtue of the fact that he thought, felt, and acted as one of a group and in reciprocal mental action with the other members of the group and with the group as a whole. In the simpler forms of social grouping, imitation (taken in the wide sense defined above) is the principal condition of this profound alteration of the individual's mental processes. And, even in the most developed forms of social aggregation, it plays a funda-mental part (although greatly complicated by other factors) in rendering possible the existence and operation of the collective mind, its collective deliberation, emotion, character, and volition.

Without entering further into the discussion of the conditions, nature, and operations of the collective mind, we may note some of the principal points of interest presented by imitation as a social factor.

In the development of individual human beings, imitation, as we have seen, is the great agency through

[1] *Les Lois de l'Imitation*, p. xii.

which the child is led on from the life of mere animal impulse to the life of self-control, deliberation, and true volition. And it has played a similar part in the development of the human race and of human society.

The mental constitution of man differs from that of the highest animals chiefly in that man has an indefinitely greater power of learning, of profiting by experience, of acquiring new modes of reaction and adjustment to an immense variety of situations. This superiority of man would seem to be due in the main to his possession of a very large brain, containing a mass of plastic nervous tissue which exceeds in bulk the sum of the innately organised parts and makes up the principal part of the substance of the cerebral hemispheres. This great brain, and the immense capacity for mental adaptation and acquisition implied by it, must have been evolved hand in hand with the development of man's social life and with that of language, the great agent and promoter of social life. For to an individual living apart from any human society the greater part of this brain and of this capacity for acquisition would be useless and would lie dormant for lack of any store of knowledge, belief, and custom to be acquired or assimilated. Whereas animal species have advanced from lower to higher levels of mental life by the improvement of the innate mental constitution of the species, man, since he became man, has progressed in the main by means of the increase in volume and improvement in quality of the sum of knowledge, belief, and custom, which constitutes the tradition of any society. And it is to the superiority of the moral and intellectual tradition of his society that the superiority of civilised man over existing savages and over his savage forefathers is chiefly, if not wholly, due. This increase and improvement of tradition has been effected by countless steps, each relatively small and unimportant, initiated by the few original minds of the successive generations and incorporated in the social tradition through the acceptance or imitation of them by the mass of men. All that constitutes culture and civilisation, all, or nearly all, that distinguishes the highly cultured European intellectually and morally from the men of the Stone Age of Europe, is then summed up in the word "tradition," and all tradition exists only in virtue of imitation; for it is only by imitation that each generation takes up and makes its own the tradition of the preceding generation; and it is only by imitation that any improvement, conceived by any mind endowed with that rarest of all things, a spark of originality, can become embodied within the tradition of his society.

Imitation is, then, not only the great conservative force of society, it is also essential to all social progress. We may briefly glance at its social operations, under these two heads:[1]

Imitation as a Conservative Agency

The similarities obtaining between the individuals of any one country, any one county, social class, school, university, profession, or community of any kind, and distinguishing them from the members of any other similar community, are in the main due to the more intimate intercourse with one another of the members of the one community, to their consequent imitation of one another, and to their acceptance by imitation of the same tradition. Under this head fall similarities of language, of religious, political, and moral convictions, habits of dressing, eating, dwelling, and of recreation, all those routine activities which make up by far the greater part of the lives of men.[2]

There is widely current a vague belief that the national

[1] The following summary account of the social operations of imitation is in large part extracted from M. Tarde's well-known treatise, *Les Lois de l'Imitation*.

[2] The last century has seen a great change in respect to the force with which his immediate social environment bears upon the individual; but, that the form of each man's religious belief is determined for him by the tradition of his society, was strictly true almost without exception in all earlier ages, and still remains true as regards the mass of men. There has been a similar weakening as regards the influence of political tradition, but still it is roughly true that "every little boy and girl that's born into this world alive is either a little Liberal or else a little Conservative," and for the most part continues so throughout life.

characteristics of the people of any country are in the main innate characters. But there can be no serious question that this popular assumption is erroneous and that national characteristics, at any rate all those that distinguish the peoples of the European countries, are in the main the expressions of different traditions. There are innate differences of mental constitution between the races and sub-races of men and between the peoples of the European countries ; and these innate peculiarities are very important, because they exert through long periods of time a constant bias or moulding influence upon the growth of national cultures and traditions. But, relatively to the national peculiarities acquired by each individual in virtue of his participation in the traditions of his country, the innate peculiarities are slight and are almost completely obscured in each individual by these superimposed acquired characters. If the reader is inclined to doubt the truth of these statements, let him make an effort of imagination and suppose that throughout a period of half a century every child born to English parents was at once exchanged (by the power of a magician's wand) for an infant of the French, or other European, nation. Soon after the close of this period the English nation would be composed of individuals of French extraction, and the French nation of individuals of English extraction. It is, I think, clear that, in spite of this complete exchange of innate characters between the two nations, there would be but little immediate change of national characteristics. The French people would still speak French, and the English would speak English, with all the local diversities to which we are accustomed and without perceptible change of pronunciation. The religion of the French would still be predominantly Roman Catholic, and the English people would still present the same diversity of Protestant creeds. The course of political institutions would have suffered no profound change, the customs and habits of the two peoples would exhibit only such changes as might be attributed to the lapse of time, though an acute observer might notice an appreciable approximation of the two peoples towards one another in all these respects. The inhabitant of France would still be a Frenchman and the inhabitant of England an Englishman to all outward seeming, save that the physical appearance of the two peoples would be transposed. And we may go even further and assert that the same would hold good if a similar exchange of infants were effected between the English and any other less closely allied nation, say the Turks or the Japanese.

The dominance of the traditional characters, acquired by each generation through imitation, over innate characters holds good not only in respect to the characters mentioned above, but also, though perhaps in a smaller degree, in respect to those modes of activity which are regarded as essentially the expressions of individuality, namely, the various forms of art-production, of science, of literature, of conversation. The immensely increased intercourse of peoples characteristic of the present age has already done much to obscure these national differences and peculiarities, but we have only to go back to earlier ages to see that the force of imitation is in these fields of human activity, as well as in all others, immensely greater than the force of individuality or of innate peculiarities. For, the further back we go in time and in cultural level, the more strictly and locally peculiar does each kind of cultural element appear. So persistent are such traditional peculiarities that archæologists and anthropologists confidently trace the distribution and affinities of extinct peoples and races throughout great periods of time and large areas by noting peculiarities of modes of sepulture, of carving, of building, of the shape, size, or ornamentation of pottery, of weapons, or of any other durable manufactured article, or even slight peculiarities in the mode of laying stones together to form a building of any kind.

It is a general law of imitation that modes of doing persist more obstinately than modes of thinking and feeling. Hence the many remarkable instances of survival of former stages of culture generally take the form of practices whose meanings and original purposes have been long forgotten or completely transformed. One of

the most interesting examples of such vestigial remnants
of an earlier culture is the survival of the forms of marriage
by capture among the peasantry of various European
countries up to, or nearly up to, the present time ; and,
in fact, the practice of throwing rice and old shoes after
the departing bridegroom, which is still observed among
us, is probably the last surviving remnant of the forms
of marriage by capture. In some parts of Europe there
survives a vestige of another form of marriage, namely,
marriage by purchase—the bridegroom gives to the parents
of his bride a few grains of corn ; and it is the more
striking that the old practice persists in the shape of this
formal act, where the actual spirit of the transaction has
been transformed into its opposite, and the bride is expected to bring to her husband, or to buy him with, a
substantial dowry. In a similar way nearly all our old-
fashioned village festivals are survivals of the practices,
the pagan rites and ceremonies, by means of which our
ancestors propitiated and honoured the various powers or
divinities whom they conceived to preside over the processes of nature that most nearly affected their welfare.
The May-day festival, for example, is probably a survival
from the rites by means of which some god or goddess
of vegetation was worshipped and propitiated ; and many
other instances might be cited.[1]   At the present time the
transformation of such religious rites into mere holiday
festivals may be observed in actual and rapid progress
in various odd corners of the world.[2]

This tendency of practices to survive by continued
imitation, long after their original significance has been
forgotten, has had far more important effects than that of
preserving vestiges as curiosities for the anthropologists.
There can be no doubt that practices so surviving the
memory of their significance have in many cases been
interpreted and been given a new meaning by the generations that found themselves performing them in blind

[1] Cf. especially Professor J. G. Frazer's *Golden Bough*.
[2] The process was going on rapidly in the islands of the Torres
Straits at the time I spent some months there ten years ago. The
natives had been converted to Christianity (nominally, at least) some
twenty years before the date of my visit.

obedience to tradition ; although, from the nature of the case, it can seldom be possible to attain more than a speculative probability in regard to such transformations and developments. As an example of processes of this kind, we may note Robertson Smith's speculation to the effect that the ever-burning altar fire, which became among so many peoples a symbol and a condition of the life and prosperity of a people or a city, was a re-interpreted survival of the fire which originally was used to consume the parts of the sacrificial victim too holy to be otherwise disposed of.[1] And of many of the symbolical rites of the higher religions it has been shown that they may with some plausibility be regarded as re-interpreted survivals of older rituals.

Dr. A. Beck [2] goes further, and argues forcibly that all, or most, myths and dogmas, and, in fact, all religious conceptions of the lower cultures, were arrived at by this process of re-interpretation of survivals of practices once of practical utility.

Among some peoples the conservative power of imitation is, of course, displayed much more strongly than among others. The force of custom is generally supreme among peoples at a low level of culture. Among them the sufficient justification and supreme sanction of all action is custom. And, even after a people has made considerable progress in the scale of civilisation, it is always liable to become fixed and stationary once more under the supremacy of tradition ; then no innovation, no invention made within the nation, no ideas coming from outside it, can obtain a foothold or find general acceptance within it, because no individual and no other people has in the eyes of that people a prestige that can rival the prestige of its own past and of the great men of its own past history. A society, arrived at a fair level of civilisation and sufficiently strongly organised to resist violent attacks from without, may persist through long ages almost unchanged, as we see in the case of the Chinese people. Then, with every generation that passes

[1] *Religion of the Semites.*
[2] *Die Nachahmung,* Leipzig, 1903.

away, the prestige of the past becomes greater, because it becomes more deeply shrouded in the mists and the mystery of age ; and so the cake of custom becomes ever harder and more unbreakable.

Imitation as an Agent of Progress

If imitation, maintaining customs and traditions of every kind, is the great conservative agency in the life of societies, it plays also a great and essential part in bringing about the progress of civilisation. Its operation as a factor in progress is of two principal kinds : (1) The spread by imitation throughout a people of ideas and practices generated within it from time to time by its exceptionally gifted members ; (2) the spread by imitation of ideas and practices from one people to another. There are certain features or laws of the spreading by imitation that are common to these two forms of the process.

The spread of any culture element, a belief, an art, a convention, a sentiment, a habit or attitude of mind of any kind, tends to proceed in geometrical progression, because each individual or body of individuals that imitates the new idea and embodies it in practice becomes an additional centre of radiation of that idea to all individuals and groups that come in contact with it ; and also because, with each step of the spread of the idea over a wider area and to larger numbers of persons, the power of mass-suggestion grows in virtue of mere numbers.

The rapidity of the spreading of a culture-element by imitation among any people depends in great measure upon two conditions : first, the density of population ; secondly, the degree of development of means of communication and the degree of use made of these means. These propositions are so obviously true that we need not dwell upon them. We have only to look around us to see how, in our own country at the present time, the rapid development of the means of communication during the latter part of the nineteenth century has so facilitated spread by imitation among our dense population as to bring about a very high degree of uniformity in many respects. Local dialects are rapidly passing away, and local peculiarities of dress and social convention have already been almost obliterated, while local sports, such as golf, have spread in a few years throughout the country. The rate of spreading of trivial passing fashions is marvellous—a new way of shaking hands, the fashion of dropping the " g " and saying " Good mornin'," the shape and size of ladies' hats or a style of wearing the hair, such games as ping-pong and diabolo—all these and a hundred other fashions suddenly and mysteriously appear and, having in a few months ravaged the whole country like deadly pestilences, disappear as suddenly as they came. In almost all such cases imitation and contra-imitation work strongly together ; each victim is moved not only by the prestige of those whom he imitates, but also by the desire to be different from the mass who have not yet adopted the fashion. And it is owing to this strong element of contra-imitation that these trivial fashions are usually so fleeting ; for, as soon as the fashion has spread to a certain proportion of the total population, the operation of contra-imitation is reversed and begins to make for the abolition of the fashion and its supplanting by some other—the mistress cannot possibly continue to wear the new shape of hat, however becoming to her, because her maids and her humbler neighbours have begun to imitate it.

These trivial fashions generally pass away completely. But all new ideas that spread by imitation must first become fashions, before they can become embodied in tradition as customs ; and the easy catching-on and rapid spread of new fashions are sure indications that the culture of a people is mobile and plastic, that it is ready and likely to embody new features in its customs, beliefs, and institutions, and so to undergo change ; though such change is not necessarily or always progress towards a better state of civilisation or of social organisation.

Imitation modifies a people's civilisation in one of two ways—by substitution or by accumulation ; that is to say, the new culture-element, spreading by imitation

among a people, either conflicts with, drives out, and
supplants some older traditional element, or constitutes
an extension, complication, and enrichment of the existing tradition.   Thus a language or a religious system
may be imitated by one people from another, and may
completely supplant the indigenous language or religion.
But more commonly it becomes worked up with the
indigenous language, or religion, enriching it and rendering it more complex and more adequate to the needs of
the people ; as when, for example, the Norman-French
language was largely imitated by the English people,
and so became in large part incorporated in the English
language ; or as when the religion of Buddha was adopted
by the Japanese people, partially fusing with, rather than
supplanting, their national Shinto religion of ancestor-
worship.

An idea or practice that has once begun to be imitated
by a people tends to spread to the maximum extent
possible under the given conditions of society ; and then
the custom or institution in which it has become embodied
tends to persist indefinitely with this maximum degree of
intensity and diffusion ; and it only recedes or disappears
under the influence of some newly introduced antagonistic
rival.   In illustration of this law we may cite tea-drinking,
tobacco-smoking, or lawn tennis.   It is when imitation
of any idea has reached this saturation point or degree of
maximum diffusion, that the statistician shows numerically
the constancy of the occurrence of its external manifestations, and cites his figures to prove that the actions of
man are as completely determined and as predictable
as the motions of the heavenly bodies.

The imitation of peoples follows the fundamental
law of all imitation—the law, namely, that the source
from which the impression comes is one enjoying prestige,
is an individual or collective personality that is stronger,
more complex, or more highly developed, and therefore
to some extent mysterious, not completely ejective, to
the imitators.   Whether the ideas of an individual shall
be accepted by his fellow-countrymen depends not so
much upon the nature of those ideas as upon the degree

of prestige which that individual has or can secure. The founders of new religions have always secured prestige, partly by their personal force and character, partly by acquiring a reputation for supernatural powers by means of falling occasionally into trance or ecstasy, or by the working of miracles, or in virtue of a reputed miraculous origin, or by all of these together. A great general, having secured prestige by his military exploits, may then, like the first Napoleon, impress his ideas of social organisation upon a whole people. A statesman, having secured prestige by his eloquence and parliamentary skill, can then set the tone of political life, and, under the two-party system, can make approximately one-half of the people of his country accept his ideas almost without question. Of this, two very striking illustrations have recently been afforded by English political changes—the acceptance of Gladstone's " Home Rule " idea and of Mr. Chamberlain's idea of Protection. If the latter idea should become generally accepted, it will be a most striking instance of social imitation on a great scale Ten years ago the dogma of Free Trade was universally accepted in this country, save by a few sceptics, who for lack of prestige could get no hearing ; yet now half, or nearly half, the country clamours for Protection. And this great change is almost entirely due to the influence of one self-reliant man of established prestige.

But originality is a very rare quality, and still more rarely is it combined with the moral and physical and social advantages necessary for the acquisition of high prestige ; hence, if the progress of each nation took place only by the acceptance of the ideas of its own great men, progress would have been very much slower than it actually has been.

The imitation of one people by another has been a principal condition of the progress of civilisation in all its stages, but more especially in its later stages. The people that is imitated by another is always one of more highly evolved civilisation or of greater skill and power in the use of the particular idea or institution that is imitated. The most striking example of this process afforded by history is the imitation of the Romans by the peoples of Western Europe whom they conquered, and, at a later period, by the peoples by whom they were conquered. The immense prestige of the Romans enabled them to continue to impress their language, their religion, their laws, their architecture, and all the principal features of their material civilisation upon these peoples, even when their military power had declined. On the other hand, although the Romans conquered the Grecian world, they were not imitated by it ; but rather themselves became the imitators in respect to most of the higher elements of culture ; for the prestige of Greece in respect to all forms of art and literature was greater than that of Rome.

The imitation of Western Europe by Japan is, of course, the most striking instance of modern times. And this case is unique in that the imitation is in the main self-conscious and deliberate, whereas in all former ages national imitation has been largely of lower forms. For in national as in individual imitation we have to recognise very different modes of imitation, ranging from the immediate unreflecting acceptance of a mode of thought or action to its adoption by an organised national effort of collective volition after careful deliberation.

Perhaps the great influence of national imitation on the progress of civilisation is illustrated most clearly by the study of national arts, especially of architecture. The distinctive forms of art of each nation can, almost without exception, be traced back to two or more ancestral sources, from the blending and adaptation of which the new national art has resulted. The work of archæologists largely consists in tracing these streams of influence and the results of their blendings.

The farther back we go towards periods of simpler civilisation, the more striking becomes the evidence of diffusion of ideas by imitation. For, in the simpler civilisations of past ages, ideas were fewer and, therefore, of greater individual importance. We find, for example, evidence of the almost world-wide diffusion of certain myths—of which a notable example has been worked out in detail by Mr. Hartland in his *Legend of Perseus*.

And this wide diffusion of myths constitutes, perhaps, the most striking illustration of imitation on a great scale, because in this case the operation of imitation is not complicated by any material, or other definite social, advantages or disadvantages resulting from or accompanying it on the part of the imitated or of the imitating people.

The same is, perhaps, less strictly true of such customs as peculiar modes of sepulture, *e.g.*, burning or mound-burial. But the process of imitation has achieved its most important results in the case of the great discoveries that have increased man's power over nature and constituted essential steps in the evolution of civilisation—agriculture, the domestication of animals, the use of the arch and dome in building, of the bow and of gunpowder in warfare, of the wheel in locomotion, the art of printing, of glass-making, the application of steam as a substitute for other forms of power; each of these has been discovered in some one or two places only, has been first applied among some one or two peoples only, and has been diffused by imitation throughout the world.

Our present civilisation—so rich and complex in language, in laws, in science and art, in literature, in institutions and material resources—is, then, the outcome, not of the original discoveries and ideas of men of our own race, or of any one people, but of the peoples of the whole world. No one of the leading European nations has created its own civilisation, but each one has rather appropriated the various elements of its culture from all the peoples of the earth, adapting them and combining them to meet its special needs, and itself contributing a small though important part to the whole.

There is one rule or law which, as M. Tarde has pointed out, holds good of international collective imitation, but not of individual imitation. It is that, as Tarde expresses it, such imitation proceeds from within outwards ; that is to say, the ideas and sentiments of a people are first imitated by another, and, not until they have become widely spread and established, are the forms in which they are externalised, or expressed and embodied, imitated also. Thus, in the greater instances of national imitation, for example, the imitation of British parliamentary institutions by other nations, there occurs first a period during which the ideas and sentiments underlying them are imitated ; and it is not until this assimilation of ideas has passed beyond the stage of fashion and they have become a part of the national tradition, that effective imitation of the institutions themselves is possible. If such institutions are imposed upon a people by authority before this stage of assimilation has been reached, the institutions will be liable to break down hopelessly. Hence the failure of parliamentary government in various South African republics, and in Russia, and its inevitable failure in the Philippine Islands if introduced there by the authority of the American people. It is in accordance with this law that among civilised peoples the study of foreign literature, in which the ideas of other peoples are conveyed most clearly and in the most diffusible form, usually prepares the way for imitation of institutions, arts, laws, and customs. Thus the Renaissance of Western Europe was prepared for by the study of Hellenic literature, and the spread of British political institutions was preceded by the study of the writings of our political philosophers, from Hobbes and Locke to Adam Smith, Bentham, and Mill.

Within any nation imitation tends always to spread from upper to lower classes, rather than in the reverse direction. This is due to the fundamental law of imitation, namely, that prestige is the principal condition that enables one person or group to impress others. And in international imitation this spreading from above downwards through the social strata is especially clearly manifested ; for it is usually by the upper classes, or by sections of them, that imitations of foreign ideas and customs are originally made, the further spread of the foreign elements then proceeding by class-imitation. In this way aristocracies of many nations have performed valuable services for which they have not usually been given due credit. In all earlier ages royal courts have served as centres for the reception and diffusion of foreign ideas. Owing to the greater freedom of communication between courts than between other parts of nations, foreign ideas were more readily introduced and assimilated by the members of a court, and from them were transmitted to the rest of the nation ; whereby its life was enriched and its civilisation advanced. In this way, for example, the court of Frederick the Great introduced French culture to a relatively backward Prussia.

In recent times royal courts and hereditary aristocracies have been to a great extent superseded in these functions by the great capitals, which are in a sense their offspring. Thus Paris has succeeded to the French court as the centre of assimilation and diffusion of foreign ideas, and its immense prestige enables it to impress its ideas upon the whole of France. The aristocracy of intellect, which in former ages was usually an appanage of the courts and now is generally gathered in the capitals, plays an important part both in introducing foreign ideas and in securing to court or capital the prestige which renders possible the diffusion of those ideas.

Besides thus serving as the means of introducing and diffusing foreign ideas, hereditary aristocracies and courts are enabled, in virtue of their prestige and quite independently of any merits of their members, to secure another important advantage to nations, namely, by setting a common standard, which is accepted for imitation by all classes of the people, they make for homogeneity of the ideas and sentiments of the people ; and this is a great condition of national strength. It is, then, perhaps, no mere coincidence that the progressive nations have been the nations whose social organisation comprises an hereditary aristocracy and a hierarchy of classes; whereas the unprogressive nations, those which though strongly organised have ceased to progress, are those which have had no native aristocracy, or have been organised on the caste system—a system which precludes class-imitation. This impossibility of class-imitation under a strict caste system is, no doubt, one of the principal conditions of the stagnation of the Brahmanic civilisation of India. And the backwardness of Russia may be ascribed in large measure to the same condition ; for there the conquering northmen, the Varegs, established a military and bureaucratic aristocracy which has remained relatively ineffective in civilising the masses of Slav peasantry, owing to the lack of any middle classes by whom the aristocrats might have been imitated. The stationary state of the civilisation of China, and the great difference as regards the rapidity of permeation by European ideas between the Chinese and the Japanese (who are closely allied by blood), must be ascribed in great measure to the absence of an hereditary native aristocracy among the Chinese. For in Japan a native aristocracy of great prestige has in recent years imitated the ideas of Western civilisation and, by impressing these foreign-gathered ideas and institutions upon the mass of the people, has produced and is still producing a very rapid advance of Japanese civilisation in many important respects. Whereas in China there exists no native aristocracy—for the Manchu nobles are regarded as barbarian usurpers and have not the prestige, even if they had the will, to play the same rôle as the aristocratic class of Japan ; and the governing class, which consists of men of letters chosen by examination from among all classes of the people, has no hereditary class-prestige, and therefore has but little power of impressing upon the people the ideas which it has acquired from Western civilisation.

In England the influence of the hereditary aristocracy in securing homogeneity of national thought, sentiment, and custom, has been very great. An Englishman notoriously loves a lord and imitates him ; and, though this national snobbishness lends itself to ridicule and has its bad aspects, especially perhaps in that it has done much to abolish the picturesque local and class differences of speech and manners and dress, it has yet aided greatly in making the English people the most mentally homogeneous nation in the world, and so in bringing it farther than any other along the path of evolution of a national self-consciousness and a truly national will.

Contra-imitation demands a few words of separate notice. It plays a considerable part, as Tarde has pointed out, in rendering societies homogeneous. Some small societies or associations of cranks and faddists owe their existence chiefly to its operation.   In national societies also it is operative, especially strongly perhaps in the English nation.   Most Englishmen would scorn to kiss and embrace one another or to gesticulate freely, if only because Frenchmen do these things ; they would not wear their hair either long or very closely cropped, because Germans do so ; they would not have a conscript army or universal military training, because nearly every other European nation has them.   The Chinese people shows how contra-imitation may operate as a considerable con- servative power in a people among whom it is strongly developed.   It prevents or greatly retards their assimila- tion by imitation of foreign ideas, and at the same time it confirms them in the maintenance of those practices, such as the wearing of the queue, by means of which they make themselves visibly distinguished from all other peoples.

Play

It is hardly necessary to say anything of the socialising influence of the play tendency.   It is obvious that even its cruder manifestations, athletic contests and games of all sorts, not only exert among us an important influence in moulding individuals, preparing them for social life, for co-operation, for submission, and for leadership, for the postponement of individual to collective ends, but also are playing no inconsiderable part in shaping the destinies of the British Empire, by encouraging a friendly inter- course and rivalry between its widely scattered parts, and by keeping the various parts present to the consciousness of each other part.   Wherever games have been customary, they must have exerted similar socialising influences in some degree.   The modern Olympic games (in this respect resembling those of ancient Greece), and the many inter- national sporting contests of the present time, are doing something to bring nations into more sympathetic rela- tions, and may yet do much more in this direction.

The play impulse is usually regarded as one of the principal roots of artistic production.   In so far as this is the case, it has its share in the socialising influences of art, which are so great and so obvious that it is hardly necessary to mention them. The works of art produced within a nation direct the attention of individuals towards certain aspects of life and nature, and teach them all to experience the same emotions in face of these aspects. In this way they tend to the increase of mutual understanding and sympathy, and they further that homo-geneity of mind which is an essential condition of the development of the collective mental life of a people.

In a similar way art tends to soften and socialise the relations between nations. When of two nations each has learnt to appreciate and admire the art-products of the other, the gulf between them is bridged over and a firm foundation for mutual sympathy and regard is laid. As a prominent instance, consider how greatly the art of the Japanese has facilitated their entrance into the exclusive circle of civilised and progressive peoples. Or again, consider how great an influence towards European solidarity is exerted by the common admiration of the nations of Europe for the sculpture of ancient Greece, for the music of modern Germany, the Gothic architecture of France and England, the paintings of Italy.

Habit

Of the great general tendencies common to the minds of all men of all ages, the last of our list in Section I. was the tendency for all mental processes to become facilitated by repetition, the tendency to the formation of habits of thought and action which become more and more fixed in the individual as he grows older ; and the consequent preference, increasing greatly in each individual with advancing age, for the familiar and the dislike of all that is novel in more than a very moderate degree.

It was said above that imitation is the great con-servative tendency of society, because it leads each genera-tion to adopt with but little change the mass of customs and traditions of the preceding generation. But imitation is conservative in virtue only of the co-operation of the tendency we are now considering. For this tendency sets narrow limits to that other tendency of imitation—the tendency to produce social changes by the introduction into any class or people of the ways of thought and action of other classes or peoples. It is this tendency which secures that each generation imitates chiefly its predecessor rather than any foreign models ; for the native, and local, and class ways of thought, feeling, and action are the models first presented to the child ; under their influence the earliest habits are formed, and a strong bias is determined ; so that, by the time the individual comes under the influence of foreign models, he is already moulded to the pattern of his nation, his class, his locality, and is but little capable of radical change ; that is to say, in virtue of habits formed on the pattern of his class and nation, he is already refractory to the influence of foreign models, save in a small degree. In short, the formation of habits by the individuals of each generation is an essential condition of the perpetuation of custom, and custom is the principal condition of all social organisation.

One point is worthy of special notice in this connection. The prevalence of certain conditions of life, of certain types of culture and modes of occupation, within a society are favourable to the influence of the elder members of the society, while other conditions are unfavourable to their influence. Thus, the mode of life of pastoral peoples, especially of pastoral nomads, is eminently favourable to the influence and authority of the elder men ; their long experience renders their judgments highly valuable in all that concerns the welfare of the herds, and their bodily infirmity does not diminish this value. On the other hand, among tribes of people much given to warfare the physical vigour and the bold initiative of youth are high qualifications for leadership ; hence the influence of the elders is relatively less. Accordingly, we find that societies of the former kind are in general extremely stable and conservative. They develop a patriarchal system, and under the conservative influence of their patriarchs they remain unchanged for long ages.

There are pastoral nomads still existing under a social organisation which has remained unchanged since the dawn of history and, not improbably, from a much more remote period. On the other hand, the warlike peoples are much more liable to change. We have already seen that they have been the most progressive peoples ; and their progress has been due in part, no doubt, to the effects of military group-selection and to the moralising influences of war, but in part also to their less conservative character which they owe to the diminished influence of the older, and therefore more conservative, individuals.

The tendency to the formation of habits, which pervades every function of the mind, exerts in yet another way an immense influence on private life, and, perhaps, an even greater influence on the collective life of societies ; I refer to the tendency to convert means into ends. It is hardly too much to say that in very many persons, not given to reflection on and analysis of motives, the ends of their actions seldom come clearly and explicitly to consciousness. Their actions are largely determined by the blind instinctive impulses on the one hand, and on the other, by simple acquiescence in, and imitation of, the kinds of activity they see going on about them. Of many women especially is this true. Many a woman who spends half her energies in making things clean and tidy and setting her house in order either never explicitly recognises the end of this activity, namely, domestic comfort, convenience, and happiness, or else, losing sight of this end and transforming the means into an end, sacrifices in a considerable degree the true end to the perfection of the means. With men nothing is commoner than that the earning of money, at first undertaken purely as means to an end, becomes an end in itself. So with all of us, the perfection of powers, whether of the body or of the mind, the acquisition of learning, of a good literary style, or of any other accomplishment, is very apt to become an end in itself, to which the true end may be in large measure sacrificed ; and some moralists even expressly commend the transformation of such means into ends.

In the collective thought and action of societies this tendency appears even more strongly than in private conduct, and for this reason—while a man may question the usefulness of any particular mode of activity that is practised by a few of his fellows only, he is less likely to raise any such question in regard to any practice that he finds faithfully observed by all his fellows. The fact that all his fellows observe the practice is sufficient to put it beyond criticism and to lead him to regard it as an end in itself. And this is one of the principal bases of custom. The ends or purposes of many customs are lost in the mists of antiquity. In some cases, perhaps, the end has never been clearly defined in any one man's mind. The custom may have arisen as a compromise or fusion between diverse customs, or through some purely instinctive mode of reaction, or through perverted imitation of some foreign model. But, however and for whatever purpose instituted, a custom once established, the practice of it always becomes in some degree an end in itself, and men are prepared to maintain it, often at great cost of effort or discomfort, long after it serves any useful end. Hence the fact that meaningless formalities and rites continue to surround almost all ancient institutions.

Besides thus playing its part as one of the conservative forces, this tendency leads also to many mistaken social efforts and institutions, or to the undue emphasis of social truths. Thus, such things as liberty and equality are seen by a Rousseau to be means to human happiness ; he preaches liberty and equality ; his ideas are accepted by the masses, and liberty and equality become for them ends in themselves, and all social well-being is for a time sacrificed to them. In a similar way Free Trade was preached by Cobden as a means to an end. The idea was widely accepted, and for great numbers of men the means has become an end. So also by setting up as ends liberty and equality, which are but means to human welfare and happiness, the people of the United States of America have brought upon themselves the insoluble negro problem ; and the British people, in virtue of the same tendency, is in danger of creating a similar problem in South Africa.

Our brief review of the social operations of the primary tendencies of the human mind is finished. Enough perhaps has been said to convince the reader that the life of societies is not merely the sum of the activities of individuals moved by enlightened self-interest, or by intelligent desire for pleasure and aversion from pain ; and to show him that the springs of all the complex activities that make up the life of societies must be sought in the instincts and in the other primary tendencies that are common to all men and are deeply rooted in the remote ancestry of the race.

THEORIES OF ACTION

MY principal aim in writing this volume was to improve the psychological foundations of the social sciences by deepening our understanding of the principles of human conduct. In the three and a half years which have elapsed since the appearance of its first edition, I have discerned here and there in subsequent publications what seem to be traces of its influence. But none of the writers who have criticised or otherwise referred to the book seems to have noticed that it propounds a theory of action which is applicable to every form of animal and human effort, from the animalcule's pursuit of food or prey to the highest forms of moral volition. I therefore add this appendix to the present edition with a threefold purpose. First, I desire to draw attention to this theory of action by throwing it into stronger relief ; secondly, I desire to present it in the form of a distinct challenge both to my colleagues the psychologists, and especially to writers on moral philosophy, to whose hands the positive theory of conduct has been too largely confided by the psychologists ; thirdly, I desire to help young students of psychology and ethics to understand the relation of the theory of action expounded in this book to other theories of action widely current at the present time. The execution of this threefold design involves a somewhat technical and controversial discussion hardly suited for the general reader ; I have therefore preferred to present it in the form of an appendix, rather than to insert it in the body of the text.

I will first state dogmatically and explicitly the theory of action which is implied throughout this volume, and will then justify it by showing the inadequacy of the other theories of action that have been most widely accepted.

Human conduct, which in its various spheres is the topic with which all the social sciences are concerned, is a species of a wider genus, namely, behaviour. Conduct is the behaviour of self-conscious and rational beings ; it is the highest type of behaviour ; and, if we desire to understand conduct, we must first achieve some adequate conception of behaviour in general and must then discover in what ways conduct, the highest type, differs from all the lower types of behaviour.

We sometimes speak of the behaviour of inert or inorganic things, such things as tools, or weapons, or even the weather. But in such cases we usually recognise more or less clearly that we are using the word playfully—we playfully regard the object as alive—and the ground of our doing so is generally that it seems to set itself in opposition to our will, and to strive to frustrate or hinder the accomplishment of our purpose. It is generally recognised that the word " behaviour " implies certain peculiarities which are only found in the movements of living things. These peculiarities are the marks of life ; wherever we observe them, we confidently infer life. We form our notion of behaviour by the observation of the movements of living things ; and, in order to explicate this notion, we must discover by what marks behaviour is distinguished from all merely physical or mechanical movements. If in imagination we construct a scale of types of behaviour ranging from the simplest to the most complex,[1] we find that at all levels of complexity behaviour presents four peculiar marks.

1. The creature does not merely move in a certain direction, like an inert mass impelled by external force ; its movements are quite incapable of being described in the language with which we describe mechanical movements ; we can only describe them by saying that the creature strives persistently towards an end. For its

[1] For such a scale of instances of behaviour I would refer the reader to my volume in the Home University Library, *Psychology, the Study of Behaviour*.

movements do not cease when it meets with obstacles, or when it is subjected to forces which tend to deflect it : such obstacles and such opposition rather provoke still more forcible striving, and this striving only terminates upon the attainment of its natural end ; which end is generally some change in its relation to surrounding objects, a change that subserves the life of the individual creature or of its species.

2. The striving of the creature is not merely a persistent pushing in a given direction ; though the striving persists when obstacles are encountered, the kind and direction of movement are varied again and again so long as the obstacle is not overcome. Behaviour is a persistent trial or striving towards an end, with, if necessary, variation of the means employed for its attainment.

3. In behaviour the whole organism is involved. Every action that we recognise as an instance of behaviour is not merely a partial reaction, such as the reflex movement of a limb, which seems to be of a mechanical or quasi-mechanical character ; rather, in every case of behaviour, the energy of the whole organism seems to be concentrated upon the task of achieving the end : all its parts and organs are subordinated to and co-ordinated with the organs primarily involved in the activity.

4. The fourth mark of behaviour is equally characteristic and probably equally universal with the other three, though it is less easily observed ; it is, namely, that, although, on the recurrence of a situation which has previously evoked behaviour, the creature may behave again in a very similar manner, yet the activity is not repeated in just the same fashion as on the previous occasion (as is the case with mechanical processes, except in so far as the machine has been in some degree worn out on the former occasion) ; there is as a rule some evidence of increased efficiency of action, of better adaptation of the means adopted to the end sought—the process of gaining the end is shortened, or in some other way exhibits increased efficiency in subserving the life of the individual or of the species.

When we survey the whole world of material things

accessible to our perception, these seem, as a matter of
immediate observation and apart from all theories of
the relation of mind to matter, to fall into two great
classes, namely (1) a class consisting of those things
whose changes seem to be purely physical happenings,
explicable by mechanical principles; (2) a class of things
whose changes exhibit the marks of behaviour and seem
to be incapable of mechanical explanation, but rather to
be always directed, however vaguely, towards an end—
that is to say, are teleological or purposive; and this
class constitutes the realm of life.

The four peculiarities which, as we have seen, characterise behaviour are purely objective or outward marks
presented to the observation of the onlooker. But to
say that behaviour is purposive is to imply that it has
also an inner side or aspect which is analogous to, and
of the same order as, our immediate experience of our
own purposive activities. We are accustomed to accept
as the type of purposive action our own most decidedly
volitional efforts, in which we deliberately choose, and
self-consciously strive, to bring about some state of affairs
that we clearly foresee and desire. And it has been the
practice of many writers, accepting such volitional effort
as the type of purposive activity, to refuse to admit to
the same category any actions that do not seem to be
prompted and guided by clear foresight of the end desired
and willed. When purposive activity is conceived in
this very restricted way, and is set over against mechanical
processes, as process of a radically different type, there
remains the difficulty of assigning the place and affinities
of the lower forms of behaviour.

One way of solving the difficulty thus created is
that adopted by Descartes, namely, to assign all the
lower forms of behaviour to the mechanical category.
But this is profoundly unsatisfactory for two reasons:
(1) As we have seen, behaviour everywhere presents the
outward marks which are common to the lower forms
of behaviour and to human conduct, and which set
it so widely apart from mechanical processes; (2) this
way of dealing with the difficulty creates a still greater

difficulty, namely, it sets up an absolute breach between men and animals, ignoring all the unmistakable indications of community of nature and evolutional continuity between the higher and the lower forms of life.

The creation of this second difficulty has naturally resulted in the attempt to solve it by forcing the truly purposive type of process into the mechanical category ; that is, by regarding as wholly illusory the consciousness of striving towards an end which every man has when he acts with deliberate purpose ; by assuming that we are deceived when we believe ourselves to be real agents striving more or less effectively to determine the course of events and to shape them to our will and purpose. The demonstration that this view is untenable requires a very long and intricate argument, which cannot be presented here even in briefest outline.[1] It must suffice to say, that the acceptance of this view would be subversive of all moral philosophy, would deprive ethical principles and ethical discussion of all meaning and value ; for if our consciousness of striving to achieve ends, to realise ideals, to live up to standards of conduct, if all this is illusory, then, to seek to determine what we ought to do and to be, or to set up standards or norms or ideals, is wholly futile ; such endeavours can at best only serve to make us more acutely aware of our impotence in face of such ideals.

We can only avoid this difficulty and this impasse by recognising that the commonly entertained notion of purposive activity is too narrow, and that it must be widened to include the lower forms of behaviour as well as the higher forms which constitute human conduct.

The only serious objection that can be raised to this widening of the notion of purposive activity is the contention that the word " purpose " essentially implies on the part of the agent consciousness of the goal that he seeks to attain, of the end he pursues ; it may be said

[1] To the presentation of this argument I have devoted a separate volume (*Body and Mind, a History and Defence of Animism*, London, 1911), to which I would refer any reader who desires to form an opinion on this difficult question.

that it is only in so far as the agent may reasonably be regarded as clearly conscious of the goal he seeks that we can claim to understand in any sense or degree how the end determines the course of the activity, how, in short, the action is teleologically determined. And it may be said, with truth, that we are not warranted in believing that the lower animals are capable of conceiving, or of being in any way clearly conscious of, the ends of their actions ; and therefore, it may be said, it is illegitimate to regard the lower forms of behaviour as purposive or to claim that our immediate experience of purposive activity in any way enables us to understand them

This objection may be removed by the following considerations. Mental process seems to be always a process of striving or conation initiated and guided by a process or act of knowing, of apprehension ; and this knowing or cognition is always a becoming aware of something, or of some state of affairs, as given or present, together with an anticipation of some change. That is to say, mental life does not consist in a succession of different states of the subject, called states of consciousness or ideas or what not ; but it consists always in an activity of a subject in respect of an object apprehended, an activity which constantly changes or modifies the relation between subject and object. Now this change which is to be effected, and which is the goal or end of action, is anticipated with very different degrees of clearness and adequacy at different levels of mental life. In many of our own voluntary actions the end is anticipated or foreseen in the most general manner only ; to take a trivial but instructive instance : you cough in order to clear your throat ; or, experiencing a slight irritation in your throat, you put out your hand, take up a glass of water, and drink, in order to allay it. How very sketchy and ill-defined may be your thought of the end of your action ! And even in the execution of our most carefully-thought-out, our most purposeful, actions, our anticipatory thought or representation of the end to be achieved falls far short of its actual fulness of concrete detail. The anticipation of the end of action is, then, always more or less incomplete; its adequacy is a matter of degree. Therefore we ought not to assume that a clear and full anticipation or idea of the end is an essential condition of purposive action; and we have no warrant for setting up the instances in which anticipation is least incomplete as alone conforming to the purposive type, and for setting apart all instances in which anticipation is less full and definite as of a radically different nature.

It is important also to note that the representation or idea of the end is not truly the cause or determining condition of the purposive activity. The merely cognitive process of representing or conceiving the end or the course of action does not of itself suffice to evoke the action; we can imagine many possible actions or ends of actions, without carrying them out or feeling any inclination to pursue them; in fact it often happens that the more clearly we envisage the end and course of a possible action, the more strongly averse to it do we become. The truth is that the anticipatory representation of the end of action merely serves to guide the course of action in detail; the essential condition of action is that a conative tendency, a latent disposition to action, shall be evoked. Where the anticipatory representation of the end is vague and sketchy and general, there the action will be general, vague, imperfectly directed in detail; where it is more detailed and full, there action is more specialised, more nicely adjusted to the achievement of its end.

From our own experience we are familiar with actions in which anticipation of the end varies from that of the most clear and detailed nature through all degrees of incompleteness down to the most vague and shadowy, a mere anticipation of change of some undefined kind. We are therefore able to form some notion of the inner or subjective side of the action of animals, even of those lowest in the scale of organisation. Putting aside a limited number of animal actions which owe their definiteness and precision to guidance at every point by new impressions falling from moment to moment upon the sense-organs (as in the most striking instances of purely

instinctive action), we see that, as we go down the scale
of life, actions become less precisely guided in detail,
and present more and more the character of random or
but vaguely directed efforts; in this corresponding to
what we may legitimately suppose to be the increasing
vagueness of the anticipatory representations by which
they are guided. The theoretical lower limit of this
series would be what has been well called (by Dr. Stout)
anoëtic sentience; a mere feeling or sentience involving
no objective reference and giving rise only to movement
or effort that is completely undirected. This lower limit
is approached in our own experience when we stir uneasily
or writhe or throw ourselves wildly about, under the
stimulus of some vaguely localised internal pain. But
we do not ourselves experience the limiting case, and
it is questionable whether we can properly suppose it
to be realised in the simplest instances of animal behaviour; it seems probable that the actions of even the
lowliest animals imply a vague awareness of something,
together with some vague forward reference, some vague
anticipation of a change in this something.

Knowing, then, is always for the sake of action; the
function of cognition is to initiate action and to guide
it in detail. But the activity implies the evoking, the
coming into play, of a latent tendency to action, a conative disposition; every such tendency or conative disposition is either of a very general or of a more specialised
or specific character; and each such conative tendency,
when awakened or brought into play, maintains itself
until its proper or specific end is attained, and sustains
also the course of bodily and mental activity required
for the attainment of that end. When, then, any creature
strives towards an end or goal, it is because it possesses
as an ultimate feature of its constitution what we can
only call a disposition or latent tendency to strive towards
that end, a conative disposition which is actualised or
brought into operation by the perception (or other mode
of cognition) of some object. Each organism is endowed,
according to its species, with a certain number and variety
of such conative dispositions as a part of its hereditary

equipment for the battle of life; and in the course of its life these may undergo certain modifications and differentiations.

To attempt to give any further account of the nature of these conative dispositions would be to enter upon a province of metaphysical speculation, and is a task not demanded of psychology. I will only say in this connection that we may perhaps describe all living things as expressions or embodiments of what we may vaguely name, with Schopenhauer, Will, or, with Bergson, the vital impulsion (*l'élan vital*), or, more simply, life; and each specifically directed conative tendency we may regard as a differentiation of this fundamental will-to-live, conditioned by a conative disposition. At the standpoint of empirical science, we must accept these conative dispositions as ultimate facts, not capable of being analysed or of being explained by being shown to be instances of any wider more fundamental notion. To adopt this view is to assert that the facts of behaviour, the empirical data of psychology, must be explained in terms of fundamental conceptions proper to it as an independent science. The physicist works, and explains his facts, in terms of the conception of mechanical process, not necessarily concerning himself with the metaphysical problem that underlies this conception; for example, he accepts as an ultimate fact the tendency of a moving mass to continue to move in a straight line without change of velocity. In a similar manner the psychologist may work, and explain his facts, in terms of the conception of purposive or appetitive process. The physicist studies mechanical processes of all kinds in order to arrive at the most general laws of mechanical process; and his explanation of any one fact of observation consists in exhibiting it as an instance of the operation of such general laws; that is, in showing that it conforms to the type, that it may be analytically regarded as a conjunction of simple mechanical processes obeying the most general laws of mechanism. Just in the same way the psychologist has to study appetitive processes of all kinds and of all degrees of complexity, in order to ascertain the most general laws of appetitive process. And his explanation of any process of the kind with which he is concerned must consist in exhibiting it as an instance of the operation of such general laws of appetition, in showing how it may be analytically regarded as a conjunction of appetitions according to the general laws of appetition that he has established. According to this view, then, the acts of human beings, all our volitions, our efforts, our resolutions, choices, and decisions, have to be explained in terms of the laws of appetition. When, and not until, we can exhibit any particular instance of conduct or of behaviour as the expression of conative tendencies which are ultimate constituents of the organism, we can claim to have explained it.

Owing to the great development of physical science in modern times and to the immense success that has attended its attempts to explain physical facts in terms of the laws of mechanism, there obtains very widely at the present time the opinion that we understand mechanical process in some more intimate sense than we can understand appetitive process; and that, therefore, it is the business of all science to explain its facts in terms of the laws of mechanism, and that appetitive processes can only be rendered intelligible if they can be reduced to the mechanical type. But this is a delusion. Of the two types of process, we certainly understand the appetitive more intimately than the mechanical; for we directly experience appetition, we have an inside acquaintance with it, as well as acquaintance of the purely external kind which is the only kind of acquaintance that we have with mechanical process. And when metaphysicians attempt to go behind the distinction of mechanical and appetitive processes (which for science is fundamental) and attempt to show that processes of the two types are really of like nature, the most plausible view seems to be that which regards mechanical process as reducible to the appetitive type or regards it as, perhaps, representing a degradation of process of the appetitive type. This, at least, is the view which has been and is maintained by some of the most distinguished metaphysicians and which

seems to involve less serious difficulties than the acceptance of the converse view.[1]

I have now stated explicitly the theory of action which
is implied by the doctrines of instinct, of sentiment, and
of volition, expounded in this volume ; and it remains to
justify it by showing the inadequacy of other theories of
action.

The theory of action most widely accepted by psychologists at the present time is, perhaps, the theory which
regards all organisms as merely machines and all behaviour
as mechanically determined. I put this aside for the
reasons already stated.

Of other theories, the one which has exercised the
greatest influence in modern speculation is the theory
of psychological hedonism ; this is the theory of action
which was unfortunately adopted by the founders of
Utilitarianism as the psychological foundation of all
their social and ethical doctrines.[2] It asserts that the
motive of all action is the desire to obtain increase of
pleasure or diminution of pain. It claims to be an
empirical induction from the undeniable fact that men do
seek pleasure and do try to avoid pain. But its strange
power to hold the allegiance of those who have once
accepted it is to be explained by the fact that it seems to
afford a rational explanation of all conduct, to show a
sufficient cause for all action. Whenever an action can
be regarded as an effort in pursuit of pleasure or in avoidance of pain, we seem to have an explanation which is
ultimate and intelligible. We feel no need to inquire :
Why should any one prefer pleasure to pain, or seek to
gain pleasure and to avoid pain ? No other theory of
the ground of action seems at first sight so self-evident
and satisfying.

It is, no doubt, possible to show the fallacious nature

[1] The most thorough and convincing defence of this view is to
be found in Professor James Ward's recently published volume of
Gifford Lectures, *The Realm of Ends*, London, 1911.

[2] The critics of Utilitarianism have concentrated their attack upon
this false psychological doctrine ; but the student of Ethics should not
be misled into supposing that the Utilitarian principle, as the criterion
of the good or the right, stands or falls with psychological hedonism.

of the doctrine by careful examination of our own motives
and unbiased consideration of the conduct of other men.
For such consideration shows that, when we desire any
object or end, as, for example, food, what we normally
desire is the object or end itself, not the pleasure that
may attend the attainment of the end. But the complexity of the human mind is so great, its springs of
action so obscure, that, in almost every instance of human
behaviour, it is possible for the psychological hedonist
to make out a plausible interpretation in terms of his
theory. Two facts play into his hands : first, the fact
that the attainment of any desired object or goal brings
satisfaction or pleasure ; for the desired object or goal
can then be ambiguously described as a pleasure, and the
agent can be said to have been moved by desire for this
pleasure : secondly, the fact that, even though a man be
really moved by the desire of pleasure, he may choose to
sacrifice the pleasure of the immediate future (or even
to suffer pain) in order to secure a greater pleasure at a
later time. And the hedonist, when he cannot plausibly
interpret an action—such as one involving the sacrifice of
life in the cause of duty—in terms of his theory in any other
way, can always assert that the agent was moved by his
aversion to the pain of remorse which he foresees to be
the consequence of neglect of duty.

For these reasons the easiest and surest refutation of
the hedonist theory of action is provided by the consideration of animal behaviour. For we may observe
numberless instances of action, of persistent striving
towards ends, on the part of lowly animals which cannot
be credited with the power of anticipating or desiring
the pleasure that may accrue from success.

A second theory of action, which claims to be of
general validity, ascribes all conation, all mental and
bodily striving, not to desire of future pleasure or aversion
from future pain, but to the influence of present pleasure
or pain ; that is to say, feeling (in the sense of pleasure
or pain) is regarded as an essential link between cognition
and conation ; it is maintained that cognition only moves
us to action in so far as it evokes in us pleasurable or

painful feeling. This may conveniently be designated the pleasure-pain theory of action. It is widely accepted at the present time ; it is more subtle and less easily refuted than the theory of psychological hedonism, which is no longer seriously to be reckoned with. The difficulty of refuting this doctrine arises from the fact that mental process has almost invariably some feeling-tone, is coloured, however faintly, with pleasure or with pain ; so that it is possible to attribute with some plausibility almost every instance of activity to the feeling which accompanies and qualifies it. This theory rightly recognises that what we normally desire and strive after is some object or end which is not pleasure itself, though its attainment may be accompanied by pleasurable feeling ; that, for example, when we are hungry we normally desire food rather than the pleasure of eating. But it asserts that the moving power of the desire, that which prompts us to action, is the feeling, the pleasure or pain, which we experience at the moment of desire and of action ; that, when we desire food, that which prompts us to strive after it is neither the pleasure which we anticipate from eating nor the pain which we anticipate from fasting, but the pleasure which arises from the thought of eating or the pain which immediately qualifies the sensation of hunger.

The last sentence indicates the line of criticism by which this theory may be shown to be untenable. We must ask—Is the hungry man prompted to seek food by the pleasure of the thought of eating or by the pain of hunger ? Some of the pleasure-pain theorists incline to the one view, some to the other, and some [1] boldly solve the difficulty by accepting both, asserting that desire always involves both pain and pleasure. These last assert, for example, that the desire of food is pleasant in so far as it is or involves the thought of eating, and that it is at the same time painful in so far it is a state of unsatisfied appetite or craving. The assumption that consciousness may be at any one moment both pleasurably and painfully toned is one of very doubtful validity ; but

[1] Professor J. H. Muirhead, for example, in his *Elements of Ethics*.

it is a further and perhaps more serious objection to this view, that the pleasure and the pain which are assumed to coexist should be assumed also to prompt to the same kind of action. And if the pleasure and the pain are assumed to alternate in consciousness, rather than to coexist, the same difficulty remains. As a matter of fact, every kind of desire or striving may be pleasurable or painful—pleasurable in so far as it progresses towards its goal, painful in so far as it is thwarted ; and yet the desire and the striving may persist while the feeling tone alternates from the extreme of pleasure to extreme of pain. Thus the desire of the lover persists, whether he be raised to the height of bliss by the expectation of success, or cast down to depths of torment by a rebuff.

If we consider the animals, we shall again be led to the true view. It is now generally admitted that we cannot attribute to the lower animals " ideas," or any power of clearly representing, or thinking of, things not present to the senses ; therefore we cannot attribute their actions to the pleasure of the idea of attaining the end pursued ; yet such animals strive under the spur of hunger, as we say, and of other appetites. Therefore, in the lower realms of life all action must be attributed by the pleasure-pain theory to present pain. But the pain of hunger seems to be in our own case the pain of unsatisfied craving ; that is, the pain is conditioned by the craving, and presupposes it—if there were no craving, there would be no pain. But the craving is essentially a conation, a tendency to action, however vaguely directed. Hunger, then, is not a pain which excites to action ; but it is fundamentally a tendency to action, which, when it cannot achieve its proper end, is painful ; it is, in short, an appetition arising from a specific conative disposition. And it seems in the highest degree probable that this is true of the hunger of animals and of all the pains to which the pleasure-pain theory finds itself compelled to attribute their activities.

The assumption, necessarily made by the pleasure-pain theory, namely, that all the actions of animals (save possibly some of those of the highest animals) are prompted by pain, is, then, unsatisfactory, and seems to invert the true relation of feeling to conation. That human desires and actions are not exclusively or in any large measure due to present pain is obvious ; the pleasure-pain theory, therefore, attributes them in the main to the pleasure which accompanies the thought of the desired end or goal. The necessity of assuming that the actions of animals and those of men are predominantly prompted by the opposite principles (pain and pleasure respectively) should give pause to the pleasure-pain theory. But, if we waive this objection and inquire after the source or condition of the pleasure which is supposed to accompany the thought of the end of action and to prompt to action, we shall find that here too the theory inverts the true relation of feeling to conation. Desire, or the thought of the desired end, is pleasant in so far as an appetite or conation obtains some degree of ideal satisfaction through the belief in the possibility of presently achieving the act, or in so far as the activities prompted by the desire successfully achieve the steps which are the means to the end. Thus hunger, even acute hunger, is pleasant if we know that the bell will presently summon us to a well-spread table, or if we are in the act of obtaining the food we desire ; yet, if the hungry man knows that it is impossible for him to obtain food, if, for example, he is a castaway in an empty boat, the thought of food is a torment to him, though he cannot cease to desire it, or prevent himself from dwelling upon the thought of it.

Both the pleasure and the pain of hunger seem, then, to be conditioned by the craving, the conative tendency, the specifically directed impulse or appetition. And this seems to be true not only of the desire for food, but of many other desires. When, for example, we desire the applause of our fellows, when we are consumed with what is called disinterested curiosity, when we desire to avenge ourselves or vent our wrath on one who has insulted us, when we desire to relieve distress, when we are impelled by sexual desire ; in all these cases the state of desiring is painful in so far as efforts are unavailing or attainment appears impossible, and pleasurable in so far as we are able to anticipate success or take effective steps towards the desired end. And in each case the strength of desire, of the conative tendency, seems to be quite, or almost quite, independent of the quality and of the intensity of its hedonic tone; while, on the other hand, the hedonic tone seems to be manifestly conditioned by the conative tendency, its quality by the success or failure of the striving, its intensity by the strength of the tendency. When, then, the pleasure-pain theorist tells us that feeling determines conation, we must ask what determines the feeling; and, if he replies that cognition of some object is the immediate condition of feeling, we point to these numerous instances in which the feeling-tone of the thought of the object varies from pleasure to pain, its quality and strength being obviously determined, not directly by cognition, but by the conation it evokes.

But if, for the purpose of the argument, we accept the thesis that the pleasure of the idea of the end, the pleasure that we experience in contemplating the end of action, is the spur that prompts and sustains action, and inquire why is the thought of the desired end pleasant, we find that two different answers are returned. Some of the pleasure-pain theorists tell us that the thought of the desired end or of the achievement of the end is pleasant because this end is in congruity with our nature.[1] Now this can only mean that the end of action which on being contemplated appears pleasant is one to which we naturally tend, that is, is one towards which we feel impelled in virtue of a conative disposition directed to such an end. To give this answer is then implicitly to give up the pleasure-pain theory and to admit the truth of the view maintained in these pages.

The other answer to this question as to the source or ground of the pleasure we feel in contemplating the end of action, is to assert that all feelings are primarily the pleasures and pains of sense, that certain sensations are intrinsically pleasant and others intrinsically unpleasant, and that all other pleasures and pains are derived from these by association. According to this doctrine, which

[1] *E.g.*, Professor Muirhead, *op. cit.*

has been most fully elaborated by G. H. Schneider,[1] the sight of food is pleasant, because the pleasure of its taste has become associated with the visual impression according to the principle of contiguity ; and the pleasure thus associated with the visual perception or representation of food is the condition of the desire for food, and prompts and sustains our efforts to obtain it. This answer may seem plausible when applied to explain desires whose satisfaction normally involves sense-pleasures ; though even in their case it is open to several very serious objections. First, the notion of the association of pleasure with ideas of objects according to the principle of contiguity is of very questionable validity. Secondly, the fact that the feeling-tone of desire for an object may vary, as we have seen, from the extreme of pain to the extreme of pleasure is irreconcilable with this view ; for it shows that there is no fixed association of pleasure with the idea of the desired object, but that the feeling-tone of the thought of the object is a function of the way we think about it, being pleasant when we think of it as attainable, unpleasant when we think of it as unattainable. Further, this answer has no plausibility when applied to the many desires the satisfaction of which involves no sense-pleasure, such as the desires for applause, for revenge, for knowledge.

And we may attack the doctrine at the root by questioning its fundamental assumption, namely, that certain sensations are intrinsically pleasurable and others intrinsically painful. This assumption seems most plausible in the case of what are called physical pains, but even in this connection its validity may be seriously questioned. It may be maintained that what we call a painful sensation is essentially a sense-impression which evokes aversion, a conative tendency to escape or withdraw from the situation, a tendency which usually manifests itself clearly enough, as when the hand is snatched away from a hot surface or a pricking point ; and that painful feeling only arises in so far as this conation fails to attain its end. It seems to be just for this reason that such sensations as toothache and other strong sensations from inflamed

[1] *Der Menschliche Wille*, Berlin, 1882.

organs are so intensely painful. The various organs are endowed with their capacities for evoking these strong sensations, in order that they may be withdrawn from the influence of the excessive stimuli—the sensitivity of the teeth, for example, serves primarily to prevent our biting strongly on hard substances on which they might be broken. But when, as in toothache, tendencies which such strong sense-impressions excite fail to terminate the impression, and we vainly throw ourselves about, rock to and fro, or writhe in a thousand ways, the situation is intensely painful. Our power of voluntarily supporting sense-impressions that normally are painful points in the same direction. When for any reason we voluntarily submit to strong sense-impressions (as when we have a tooth filled by the dentist, making up our minds to submit to the necessary pain), we suppress by a strong effort of will partially or wholly the tendency to escape the strong sense-impression ; and, in so far as we are successful in this, it loses its painful character. In this way also, I think, we must understand such extreme examples of fortitude as the calm behaviour of the Indian brave or the Christian martyr under torture ; the training and beliefs of such persons render them capable of voluntarily submitting to the torture and of suppressing by strong volition the tendency to struggle to escape evoked by the strong sense-impressions ; and, in so far as they succeed in this, the experience ceases to be painful—the stake and the rack are robbed of their terrors. For the same reason hunger voluntarily submitted to (as when we fast for the sake of our health) is but a matter of small discomfort, though we are told that it is very painful when suffered involuntarily.

It may be maintained with equal plausibility that the pleasures of sense are also conditioned by conation. If we consider the case of the pleasures of the palate, we see that the pleasant tastes are those which stimulate us to maintain the processes of mastication and deglutition. According to the pleasure-pain theory, these activities are induced and maintained by the pleasure which the taste excites. But how can this view be maintained in face of the fact that the same taste qualities cease to be pleasing so soon as they cease to evoke these activities ? Thus, one who likes sweet things finds the taste of sugar pleasant so long as it subserves its normal function of exciting the processes of ingestion ; but as soon as repletion ensues, the tendency to mastication and deglutition can no longer be excited by the sweet taste (for this requires the co-operation of certain visceral conditions which are abolished by repletion), and the mastication of the sugar then ceases to be pleasant, and may even become decidedly unpleasant, if for any reason we persist in it.

It appears, then, that even in those instances most favourable to the pleasure-pain theory, the facts are difficult to reconcile with it, and are more consistently in harmony with the opposite view, namely, that pleasure and pain are always conditioned by the success and failure of conation, respectively. And the superiority of the latter view will be established if we can point to instances in which activity is unmistakably independent of pleasure and pain ; for by such instances, the pleasure-pain theorist would be compelled to admit that his theory of action holds good of some activities only, and that others require a different theory for their explanation, namely, the theory which makes feeling dependent on conation and which seems quite adequate to the explanation of the types of activity most favourable to the pleasure-pain theory. Such instances we may find at the two extremes of human behaviour ; namely, in the actions implying the highest moral effort and in merely habitual actions. Whether or no we accept as true the story of the voluntary return of Regulus to captivity and death, we all recognise that it represents a possible type of conduct. Now, while psychological hedonism has to explain such conduct by supposing that Regulus was more averse to the pains of remorse than to those of bodily torture and death, the pleasure-pain theory is driven to suppose that the contemplation of the heroic line of action yielded Regulus a high degree of pleasure, and that this pleasure impelled him to pursue this line of action even though he anticipated from it a painful death; or the alternative explanation might be suggested, that he found his absence from Carthage so painful that he was impelled by this pain to return thither. Surely, whether from the ethical or the psychological standpoint, this form of the hedonic theory, when applied to such instances of hard choice, appears hardly less fantastic than psychological hedonism! Surely it is obvious that men do often carry through a line of action which is to them painful in every phase, in the contemplation of it, in deciding upon it, and in its execution and achievement! Consider the more familiar instance of the father who feels himself impelled to inflict severe punishment upon a beloved child, such as the withholding from it the enjoyment of something to which they had both looked forward, hoping to enjoy it together. At every stage the father hates the necessity laid upon him, and knows that he himself is sacrificing a keen pleasure and undertaking a painful task. It would be absurd to say that the father's conduct is sustained by the pleasure of the thought of the improved conduct or character of his son which the punishment may bring about. Even if at times he may find consolation in this thought, it can be but momentarily; and such pleasure will be in the main wholly submerged and neutralised by his sympathetic pain and by the violence he does to the immediate promptings of parental love.

Instances of purely habitual and quasi-mechanical actions are not less decisive. We sometimes find ourselves performing some trivial familiar action, without having intended or resolved to do it, but merely because we happen to be in a situation in which this action is habitually performed; as when one winds up one's watch on changing one's waistcoat. Such "absent-minded" actions involve a minimum of attention, but are nevertheless conations; they are the expressions of habits, and seem to be independent of pleasure and pain, whether anticipated or experienced at the moment. Such an action is immediately induced by the sense-impressions of the moment; they bring into play the specialised conative disposition which is the habit. Such actions, better perhaps than any others, enable us to understand in some degree the way in which many of the actions of the animals are performed.

We may pass on to consider other theories of action , and we may notice first the only remaining theory which makes any claim to be applicable to human behaviour of all types and levels. This is the intellectualist theory of action which attributes action immediately to " ideas," ignoring the obvious fact that the development and organisation of character, or of the conative side of the mind, is largely distinct from and independent of the development and organisation of knowledge, the cognitive side of the mind. Prominent among older exponents of this theory was Herbart, and, among contemporaries, Professor Bosanquet and (if I have not wholly failed to understand his writings) Mr. F. H. Bradley.

According to this theory, the mind consists of a more or less highly organised system of ideas ; and every idea is both an intellectual entity and a tendency to action. The type of all the higher forms of action is the so-called ideo-motor action, the action which is supposed to result directly from the presence in consciousness of the idea of that action. Volition is merely a somewhat complicated instance of such ideo-motor action.

Now, it may be seriously questioned whether any action really conforms to the alleged ideo-motor type. Actions proceeding from so-called fixed ideas have usually been regarded as examples *par excellence* of ideo-motor action. But the modern developments of psycho-pathology are making it clear that in all such cases the fixed idea is fixed, and is capable of determining action, just because it is functionally associated with some strong conative tendency. But, putting aside this objection and accepting for the purpose of the discussion the notion of ideo-motor action, I urge that it would be manifestly absurd to say that action which is carried out with painful effort against inner and outer difficulties of all sorts, is simple ideo-motor action. We have to ask—What gives the one idea of action the power to prevail over other ideas of action equally vividly conceived ? Bradley's answer to this question is that the self identifies itself with the end the idea of which prevails.[1] Bosanquet answers that it is attention to the one idea. Both answers are true if the "self" and "attention" are understood in the true sense ; that is, if the self is understood as the vast organisation of conative dispositions which is the character, and if attention is understood as conation revealing itself in cognition. But for Bosanquet attention is merely apperception in the Herbartian sense, the fusion of an idea with a mass of congruous ideas ; and since conation is not recognised, the congruity implied is logical congruity. Whatever idea of action, then, is congruous with other ideas of action is apperceived or attended to, and therefore predominates over other ideas ; and this is volition. Bosanquet adds that "in cases of deliberative action at a high level of consciousness, the self or personality participates, *i.e.*, one of the ideas which are striving for predominance reinforces itself by the whole mass of our positive personality." [2] But he explains that the whole self or personality is merely a mass of ideas with their accompaniments of feeling, " a fabric of ideas accompanied with their affections of pleasure and pain, and having a tendency to assert themselves in so far as they become partly discrepant from reality." [3] And in Bradley's view also the self seems to be merely a " fabric of ideas." In this intellectualist theory of action, then, conation, or will, which, as has been maintained throughout this volume, is the very foundation of all life and mind, is simply ignored ; and my criticism of it must consist in pointing to all that has been said of instinct, sentiment, and volition in this book. Unless all this is the purely fanciful construction of a diseased brain, this intellectualist doctrine is radically false. I will only point out in addition that, when we turn to the lower forms of life, the impotence of this theory is at once clear ; for, since at that level we cannot postulate " ideas," all action has to be interpreted as purely mechanical reflex action ; and we are then faced with the problem of evolving intellect and will from

[1] Series of papers in *Mind*, N.S., vols. ix.–xiii.
[2] *Psychology of the Moral Self*, p. 77.   [3] *Op. cit.* p. 91.

unconscious mechanism, a task to which, as is generally recognised, the ingenuity of Herbert Spencer himself proved inadequate.[1]

All other theories of human conduct may be classed together in virtue of the fact that they place moral conduct in a separate category, apart from all other forms of behaviour, and attribute it to some special faculty peculiar to human beings, which they call "conscience," or "the moral sense," or "reason," or the "rational will," or "the sense of duty"—a faculty which seems to be conceived as having been implanted in the human mind by a special act of the Creator, rather than as being the product of the slow processes of evolution. Most of those who attribute moral conduct to any such special faculty recognise that human nature comprises also certain lower principles of action, which they call animal propensities, instincts, or passions; and these are regarded as regettable survivals of our animal ancestry, unworthy of the attention of a moral philosopher.

All these doctrines are open to two very serious objections: (1) that they are incompatible with the principle of the continuity of evolution; (2) that they are forms of the "faculty doctrine" whose fallacies have so often been exposed. But a few words must be said about the more important of them. When authors tell us that "reason" is the principle of moral action, it is necessary to point out that the function of reason is merely to deduce new propositions from propositions already accepted. Suppose a hungry man to be in the presence of a substance which he does not recognise as food; by the aid of reason he may discover that it is edible and nutritious, and he will then eat it or desire to eat it; but, if he is not hungry, reason will not create the desire or impel him to eat. And in the moral sphere the function of reason is the same. Reason aids us in determining what is good, and in deducing from our knowledge of the good conclusions as to what actions are right. But, unless a man already hungers for righteousness,

---

[1] See for further criticism of the ideo-motor theory my article, "Motives in the Light of Recent Discussion," in *Mind*, N.S., vol. xxix.

already desires to do whatever is right, to be whatever is virtuous, unless, that is, he possesses the moral sentiments and moral character, reason cannot impel him to do right or to desire it. To create desire is a task beyond its competence ; it can only direct pre-existing tendencies towards their appropriate objects. It is therefore a grave error on the part of some authors [1] to say that reason may create a desire for a moral quality ; or to say (as Sidgwick said) that in rational beings as such the cognition or judgment that this is right or ought to be done " gives an impulse or motive to action." For this is not true of rational beings as such—in Satan, we may suppose, no such impulse would be awakened by this issue of the reasoning process. It is true only of moral or moralised beings as such, beings who already desire to be virtuous and to do the right. It is only by arbitrarily and implicitly defining the " rational being " as one who desires to do right, that the doctrine is made to seem plausible. Nor is this doctrine, that moral conduct proceeds from the reason, appreciably improved when " the rational will " is put in the place of " reason." This may seem to avoid the intellectualist fallacy of assigning intellectual processes as the springs of action. But, unless some further account of the will is given, this doctrine is in no way superior to the doctrine of " conscience " ; for the " rational will " remains a mere word by which we denote the fact that we do make deliberate moral choices and decisions, and that such choice is not merely the issue of a brute conflict of opposed desires.

Though the intuitionist doctrines which attribute moral judgment, moral choice and effort, to a special faculty have been variously stated, and though the supposed faculty has received a variety of names, they are essentially similar and need not be separately considered. We may consider that form which derives from Kant and attributes our moral judgments and

---

[1] *E.g.*, Dr. Rashdall, who writes : " It is true that the action cannot be done unless there is an impulse to do what is right or reasonable on our part, but such a desire may be created by the Reason which recognises the rightness " (*Theory of Good and Evil*, vol. i. p. 106).

conduct to "the sense of duty." It is no longer seriously contended that all the actions of any moral being spring from the "moral faculty." It is admitted that upon most of the ordinary occasions of life our actions spring from other principles or sources. But it is maintained that, in deliberation which issues in moral decision, this issue is determined by the co-operation of "the sense of duty." The "sense of duty" is in fact the last refuge of intuitionism, of those moralists who insist upon making of man's moral nature a mystery, separate from the larger mystery of mind, and implying laws of an order radically different from those which govern behaviour in general. Canon Rashdall writes: "In claiming for the idea of duty not merely existence but authority, we have implied that the recognition that something is our duty supplies us with what we recognise upon reflection as a sufficient motive for doing it. . . . The recognition of the thing as right is capable of producing an impulse to the doing of it." [1] And he speaks of the "sense of duty" as being "the one all-sufficient motive present to the consciousness" at moments of moral crisis.[2]

This doctrine, if true, obviates the need for all psychological investigation or reflection on the part of the moral philosopher; except in so far as he desires to expose the errors of his predecessors, by showing how they proceed from a false and unnecessarily complicated psychology, such as that of Kant or that of the founders of Utilitarianism. For the whole of the positive psychology required by him is contained in a nutshell, in the sentence : "Reason proclaims my duty, and my sense of duty impels me to do it." But some of the modern exponents of intuitionism, unfortunately for the consistency of their doctrine, are not content to leave their "sense of duty" an utterly mysterious faculty of which nothing more can be said. Sidgwick asserted that the notion of "ought" or duty is too elementary to admit of formal definition ; and in the same spirit Dr. Rashdall tells us that the idea that something ought to be done "is an unanalysable

[1] *Theory of Good and Evil*, vol. i. p. 104.
[2] *Op. cit.* vol. i. p. 121.

idea which is involved in all ethical judgments." But he ventures further and tells us that " Duty means precisely devotion to the various kinds of good in proportion to their relative value and importance " ;[1] and again : " At bottom the sense of duty is the due appreciation of the proportionate objective value of ends."[2] From this it appears that, by the admission of a prominent exponent of the intuitionist doctrine, " the sense of duty " is not an ultimate element of the moral consciousness, is not an unanalysable idea and at the same time an impulse to action ; rather it appears as the highly abstract name for all that immensely complex part of the mental organisation which is the moral character, and which comprises the system of the moral sentiments and the developed self-regarding sentiment. For it is the possession of developed moral character, and this alone, that enables us to judge rightly of the relative values of moral goods and impels us to pursue the best; and, as I have tried to show in this book, and as indeed is now generally admitted, this complex organisation which is moral character is only acquired by any individual by a slow process of growth continued through many years under the constant pressure of the social environment and of the moral tradition. Our " sense of duty " is, in short, at the lower moral level our sense of what is demanded of us by our fellows ; and, at the higher moral level, it is our sense of what we demand of ourselves in virtue of the ideal of character that we have formed. How and why we respond to these demands made upon us by our fellows and by ourselves, and how we come to make these demands, I have tried to show by means of a general theory of action, a theory of the moral sentiments and a theory of volition.

Before dismissing the theory of " a moral faculty," I must add that in one respect the intuitionist doctrine is true ; namely, it is true that, when we have acquired moral sentiments, we do frequently both pass moral judgments and make moral efforts without any weighing of the consequences of action. But to admit or to establish this is neither to justify the doctrine of " a moral faculty,"

[1] *Op. cit.* vol. i. p. 125.　　[2] *Op. cit.* vol. i. p. 128.

nor to deny that our moral judgments frequently need correction by reference to the consequences of action upon human welfare, the only true and ultimate criterion of moral value.

We may admit also the possibility that, though the moral sentiments are in the main built up anew in each individual in the way roughly sketched in the pages of this volume, some predisposition to their formation may be inherited, and that, in so far as this is the case, the capacity of moral judgment, which is rooted in them, may be said to be innate and, in that sense, *a priori*.

It only remains to show that the theory of action here set forth is implied in the doctrines of some eminent philosophers (although it has not been explicitly stated by them), and most clearly perhaps by T. H. Green and Professor Stout. These authors recognise the actions of animals as true conations or expressions of will, in the wider sense of the word " will." They recognise that human nature is capable of, or liable to, similar modes of primitive conation ; and that desire is a comparatively complex mode of conation of which, perhaps, in the proper sense, men only are capable. But they do not claim that volition or moral conduct is nothing more than the issue of a conflict of desires. They rightly tell us that these simpler modes of conation, blind impulses, cravings, and desires, are something that each man experiences as, in a sense, forces acting upon him, impelling him towards this or that line of action ; and that he knows that his true self can either oppose such tendencies, or can accept them ; and that only when the self thus intervenes to accept or resist desire or impulse do we perform a volitional act. And by the self they do not mean an abstract entity of which no account can be given. Green tells us that by the true self he means the character of the man ; he uses also the term " conscience " to convey the same notion ; and by conscience he means something which has a history in the life of the individual, something that is slowly built up in the course of moral training and under the influence of the social environment ; conscience or moral character is, in short, in Green's view, an organised system of habits of will.

Stout also tells us that volition is distinguished from mere conflict of desires by the decisive intervention of self-consciousness ; and that this self, which in moral conflict self-consciously throws itself upon the side of one desire and against others, is a unified system of interests. Now an interest is, for Stout, a conative tendency with the accompanying potentialities of feeling ; and the self, therefore, is a unified system of conative tendencies.

These authors, then, have put forward in very general terms the theory of action which I am defending. They recognise will as a fundamental faculty co-ordinate with cognition ; they recognise that in all organisms (animals and men alike), this faculty of striving is directed either vaguely or with more or less of precision towards certain kinds of action which tend to secure specific ends ; that when these conative tendencies are brought into play in relative isolation, sporadic impulse, desire, or action is the result ; and they recognise that moral volition and moral conduct depend upon the systematic organisation of such tendencies ; that, in short, moral volition expresses character or is character in action. Their doctrines, then, imply the thesis here maintained ; namely, that in order to explain or understand any action, we have to exhibit it as the expression of some single conative disposition, or of a conflict of, or of some conjunction of, such tendencies, according to the plan of organisation of the character ; and that, when we thus show it to be an instance of conation or appetition conforming to the most general laws of appetition, we do all that as men of science we can be called upon to do.

SUPPLEMENTARY CHAPTER II

THE SEX INSTINCT

IN previous editions of this book the sex instinct was dismissed with a few words only,[1] partly because of the difficulty of treating of it satisfactorily in a book designed to appeal to the general reader, partly because it had been discussed at great length by several able writers, and because it seemed that in respect to this one department of human conduct the main thesis of my book was already generally accepted—the thesis, namely, that human activities, both mental and bodily, are only to be explained or understood by tracing them back to a number of innate dispositions, tendencies to feel and act in certain more or less specific ways, in certain situations ; tendencies which manifest themselves in each normal individual of the species independently of previous experience of such situations, and which, like the similar innate tendencies of the animals, may properly be called instinctive.

But I have found that to obtain general acceptance of this theory of human action is not so easy a task as I had supposed it to be. And, since the consideration of sexual experience and conduct affords the clearest illustrations and the most obvious support of the theory, I feel that it would be foolish to neglect to make good this serious omission.

The addition of this supplementary chapter seems to be called for also by the widespread interest in, and lively controversies over, questions of mental pathology which have sprung up in recent years and in which the question of the rôle of sex has figured very prominently.

[1] Under the name " Instinct of Reproduction," which, as I now see is apt to mislead (p. 70).

Throughout the greater part, and more especially throughout the higher part, of the animal kingdom, the members of each species are of two kinds, male and female, and reproduction is sexual—that is to say, reproduction depends upon the fusion of a living cell formed in the body of a male (the sperm cell) with one formed in the body of a female (the egg) to form the germ which evolves into the new individual. This fusion, together with the processes by which the two cells are brought together, is the process of fertilisation. In plants, among many species of which sexual reproduction is also the rule, fertilisation is left as it were to chance ; the plant does nothing more than produce a quantity of male or female germ cells, or both (pollen and ovules), and set these in such positions that external forces of nature (generally insects or the wind) bring together cells of the two kinds. But in the animal kingdom it is the rule that a great economy of germ cells is effected by the operation of the sex instinct, an instinct which impels individuals of opposite sex to approach one another at the time when their germ cells are ready to take part in the process of fertilisation. In many species of fish we see the operation of the sex instinct at its simplest ; the male merely swims close to a female and ejects a cloud of sperm cells into the water, at the same time as the female extrudes into the water a number of eggs ; and the final approximation and fusion of the egg and sperm cells is effected by the active approach of the latter to the former and by a process of penetration of the egg by the sperm, when contact has been effected. This active approach of the sperm cell to the egg and its penetration of it remain very obscure. We are not concerned with it here, further than to note that it strikes the keynote of male and of female sexuality throughout the animal scale—namely, the active seeking of the female by the male and the relatively passive or merely attractive rôle of the female. Apart from this final act of the germ cells, the process of fertilisation consists essentially in the two stages of the operation of the sex instinct : first, the near approach of two individuals of opposite sex ; secondly, the discharge of the reproductive cells in such a way that they come into near neighbourhood of one another.

The sex instinct is Nature's provision for the effecting of these first two stages of the process of fertilisation, the process which initiates the development of each new individual. Like other instincts it is a complex, innately organised, psycho-physical disposition, consisting of three parts, each subserving one of the three phases that we distinguish in every complete mental or psychophysical process, namely, the cognitive, the affective, and the conative ; three parts which, from the point of view of nervous function and structure, we may call the afferent or sensory, the central, and the efferent or motor.[1]

It is important to note that, even at the simple level of sex activity displayed by the fishes, the operation of the instinct implies or presupposes a differentiation of the two sexes in respect of external or perceptible characters which serve as recognition marks of sex. For, in the absence of such perceptible differences between the sexes (commonly called secondary sex characters), it would be impossible for the male to distinguish the female of his species from his fellow males, and hence impossible to achieve that first stage of the process of fertilisation, the approach of the male to the female. Accordingly we find that in all bisexual animal species the two sexes are differentiated by the possession of such recognition marks of sex—marks which may be perceptible by any one of the senses, but which in the higher animals most commonly appeal to the eye, though not infrequently to the other great organs of perception at a distance, namely, the ear and the nose.

It is still more important to note that this first stage

---

[1] I adhere to the description of the structure of an instinct offered in Chapter II. ; but I recognise that this summary statement of the relation of the affective and conative parts of the disposition is very inadequate. The relation between them is more obscure and in some sense more intimate than that between them and the cognitive part For purposes of exposition it would usually suffice to treat of the affective and conative parts of the disposition as forming a functional unit.

of the fertilisation process, the approach of the male to the female, presupposes (on the part of the male at least) an innate capacity to recognise the female, *i.e.*, to distinguish the female from the male, to perceive her as different by reason of her recognition marks of sex. For though it may seem plausible to suppose that, in the more intelligent and social species, the male learns through experience to distinguish the female, this cannot be maintained of the less intelligent species, and is clearly inadmissible of the many species in which the male, on first encountering the adult female, is attracted by her in a way in which he is not attracted by males. The innate capacity or disposition to recognise the other sex by aid of the recognition marks of sex is, then, an essential feature or part of the complex innate disposition which is the sex instinct. Without this perceptual side the instinct would be wellnigh useless to the animals ; it would achieve the first essential step of the process of fertilisation, but very wastefully and uncertainly. The sex instinct, then, illustrates very clearly a much-neglected fact of instinct on which I have insisted in the earlier chapters of this volume, the fact, namely, that an instinct is not only an innate disposition to act and to feel in a more or less specific manner, but is also an innate disposition to perceive or perceptually discriminate those things towards which such reactions are demanded by the welfare of the species.

In many species it is not sufficient that the cognitive side of the instinct should enable the perceptual discrimination of one sex from the other. A further differentiation of it is required. For the second stage of the process of fertilisation, the extrusion of the germ cells at the required place and time, is also accomplished instinctively. In the simplest cases the mere proximity of two individuals of opposite sex seems to suffice to produce or excite this further reaction ; as when the male fish or frog merely pours out his germ cells into the water in which the female is laying her eggs. But in many species the second stage of the process involves a more complex action or train of actions, that is to say, as in so

many other cases, the motor issue of the excitement of
the instinct is not a single reaction or a single or repeated
movement of one kind, but a chain or series of reactions,
each step of which brings about a new situation that
evokes the next step.

In mammals the second stage of the process of fertilisation is complicated by the necessity of bringing the sperm
cells into the near neighbourhood of the egg, while the
egg still remains within the womb of the female ; this
being the only place in which the fertilised egg finds the
conditions necessary to the earlier stages of its development. In order that the sperm cells may be brought
into such a position that they may of their own feeble
powers of locomotion reach the egg in the womb, the
male is provided with the organ of intromission, the penis,
and the female with the vagina or sheath, the antechamber
to the womb. And to the same end the sex instinct is
modified and complicated in such a way that the second
stage of the process of fertilisation, the emission of the
sperm cells by the male, is no longer excited by the mere
proximity to, or by mere contact with, the female. It is
necessary that the organ of the male shall enter the antechamber of the womb, and that emission of the sperm
cells shall not take place until this is accomplished. In
order that the second stage of fertilisation shall be completed in this manner, the sex instinct of the male requires
to be complicated on its perceptive as well as on its executive side. The male accordingly is endowed, not only
with the capacity of recognising the female, but also with
the capacity of singling out the entrance to the womb.
And on its executive side the male's instinct is complicated
in such a way that he is impelled to embrace the female
and to introduce his organ to the vagina, and thereupon
to execute movements which, by stimulating the highly
sensitive skin of the organ, excite the emission of the
sperm cells   The sex instinct of the mammalian female
requires less modification than that of the male ; for, her
rôle being passive and receptive rather than active and
aggressive, she does not need to be innately endowed
with the capacity of singling out the male organ and of

actively seeking to effect its introduction to her body (a point of some importance for the understanding of the difference between male and female sexuality). Nevertheless, in some species the instinct seems to impel her to respond to the movements of the male with appropriate corresponding behaviour. The activities of the male reach their natural end with the emission of the sperm cells ; and in the female the embrace culminates in a peculiar activity of the internal sex organs which facilitates the approach of the sperm cells to the egg in the womb, and which, like the act of emission in the male, constitutes the climax and termination of the sexual act (the orgasm). In both sexes the activity of the sex instinct is supported by a powerful impulse and accompanied by an emotional excitement, which, when the process of fertilisation runs its normal course, waxes throughout, attains its climax at the moment of orgasm, and then suddenly subsides. And the whole activity seems normally to be highly pleasurable, in accordance with the general law that the natural and unimpeded progress of any instinctive activity towards its natural end is pleasurably toned.

This brief and general description of the nature and operation of the sex instinct in mammals holds good for the human species ; and, although the operation of the instinct is often (especially among persons of culture and refinement) very much complicated and obscured by the influence of the will, and of personal sentiments and ideals, it nevertheless is often displayed in relatively uncomplicated and direct fashion. Indeed, a principal source of the difficulties and dramas of civilised life is to be found in the fact that, owing to the great strength of the impulse of this instinct, men, and even women, who have attained a high level of character and culture, are liable to be swept away by a flood of sexual passion, and, the restraints normally maintained by their higher sentiments being temporarily broken through, to be impelled to yield to the prompting of the instinct in a manner almost as simple and direct as the mating of the animals.

As in most species of the higher animals, the sex

instinct in man does not attain its full development until the period of youth, the period of growth and acquisition, is wellnigh completed. The questions of the age at which the instinct normally comes into operation in man, and of the course of its development, are still in dispute ; and in respect to them opinions still differ very widely. These very important topics will be discussed in a final section of this chapter. At present we may confine our attention to some special features and problems of the fully developed instinct in man.

It is maintained by some high authorities on the psychology of sex [1] that the activities which I have described in the foregoing paragraphs as constituting the first and second stages of the process of fertilisation are respectively the expressions of two impulses which they denote by the term impulses of " contrectation " and of " detumescence." But it would be a mistake to attribute these two stages of the sexual act to separate instincts. In the animal world we may observe numerous instances of " chain instincts,"—instincts, that is to say, each of which manifests itself in a chain of activities ; each step of such a chain prepares the way for a further step, the new situation created by each step modifying in detail the direction and operation of the impulse, while yet the impulse towards the one biological end seems to dominate and to supply the conative energy of the whole process. As examples of such chain instincts we may cite those which impel most of the constructive efforts of animals (the nest-building of birds, the web-weaving of spiders), and such actions as those by which a squirrel buries a nut in the ground, or a bird first lays eggs in some chosen spot and then broods over them. Just as in these instances the first step of the instinctive process creates a situation which excites the second step, so the first stage in the process of fertilisation in man prepares in a double manner the situation which excites the activities of the second stage. The perception of a suitable individual of the opposite sex evokes the impulse of approach, and

---

[1] Especially A. Moll (*Untersuchungen ü. d. Libido Sexualis.* Berlin. 1897) and Havelock Ellis (*The Psychology of Sex.* Philadelphia, 1911).

at the same time tends to bring about that state of tumescence or turgescence of the sex organs which (in the male at least) is a necessary preliminary to the second stage of the process. But, though the bodily activities of the two stages are different, the quality of the emotional conative excitement that accompanies the activities is recognisably the same throughout both stages.

This emotional conative excitement, when it occurs uncomplicated by other emotions and tendencies, is properly called " lust." It is unfortunate that this word has lost its respectability owing to the opporbrium heaped upon lust by Christian moralists. But, for the purposes of psychology, it is a necessary and useful word. We must frankly recognise that, in spite of all the hard things that have been said about lust, it is an essential element in the emotional conative attitude of human lovers towards one another ; and that, no matter how much the attitude and the feeling of refined lovers may be modified and complicated by other tendencies, lust nevertheless strikes the ground tone and supplies the chief part of the mental and bodily energy which is put forth so recklessly and copiously in the service of sex love.

But, while it is necessary to recognise that lust enters into and colours the emotions evoked in the lover by the presence or the thought of the beloved one, we must avoid the mistake (not infrequently made) of assuming that the mere direction of the sex impulse towards a particular person in itself constitutes sexual love. Such habitual direction of the sex impulse towards one person is certainly an essential condition or feature of sex love ; but an habitual lusting for a particular person would be a crude sentiment not worthy of the name of love. Sex love is a complex sentiment, and in its constitution the protective impulse and tender emotion of the parental instinct are normally combined with the emotional conative disposition of the sex instinct, restraining, softening, and ennobling the purely egoistic and some-what brutal tendency of lust.

The presence of the maternal element in the attitude of a woman towards her lover has been recognised by countless writers of romance. And that the tender protective element commonly enters into the sentiment of the man for the beloved woman is equally obvious. That sex love should thus combine the most purely altruistic with the most ruthlessly egoistic tendency of human nature, seems sufficiently accounted for in the case of the woman by the great strength of the maternal impulse and the ease with which it is aroused in her in all personal relations ; and in the man it is perhaps sufficiently accounted for by the fact that woman, especially at the age at which she is most strongly attractive to man, resembles in many respects, both mental and physical, the child, the normal object of the parental or protective impulse.

It is, then, a mistake to attribute to the sex instinct, all the manifestations of sex love ; for this sentiment is commonly highly complex, and involves not only the emotional-conative dispositions of the sexual and parental instincts, but those of other instincts also, notably those of the instincts of self-display and self-abasement. The importance of distinguishing between the sex instinct and the sentiment of sex love, and of recognising the complex constitution of the latter, is well illustrated by the controversies raised among the mental pathologists by the doctrines of Professor Sigmund Freud. Freud proposes to extend very greatly the sphere commonly attributed to sexuality in human life, assigning a sexual root to mental and nervous disorders of almost every kind, as well as to all dreams and to other processes of normal mental life that have no obvious connection with sex. It seems to me that this immense extension of the sphere of sexuality (which has excited acute opposition to Freud's doctrines and obscures for many the important and valuable truths contained in them) is in large part an error due to the neglect of the distinction insisted upon in the foregoing paragraph. For Freud and his disciples, taking the sentiment of sex love as the type of all love, regard as manifestations of sexuality all modes of behaviour and of feeling that are of the same kind as those that occur as phases in the life-history of this sentiment. They are thus led to regard as sexual, or as containing a sexual element, the love of parents for their children and of children for their parents, as well as every other variety of love and every manifestation of tender emotion. Expressions of other emotional and conative tendencies that commonly enter into the composition of the sentiment of sex love have been in a similar way and for the same reason regarded by writers of this school as indicative of the presence of the sexual tone in relations in which they are displayed, or spoken of as components of the normal sexuality of man and woman.[1] If we carefully observe this distinction, we shall find no reason to regard the sex instinct as comprising any tendencies other than those which are directly concerned in effecting the first and second stages of the process of fertilisation.

If we adopt this relatively restricted view of the scope of the sex instinct in man, it still appears as one of considerable complexity on its executive side; and on its perceptual side it is certainly more complex than has commonly been assumed. In earlier chapters of this book I have urged, in opposition to a widely held view, that the structure of an instinct generally involves one or more perceptual dispositions which render the possessor of the instinct capable of attentively singling out and discriminatively perceiving objects or situations of the kind that demand the instinctive reaction. The sex instinct is no exception to this rule. We have seen that in the animals the presence of the recognition marks of sex implies that the sex instinct renders them capable of distinguishing the members of the opposite sex from those of their own, and that this truth is especially obvious in the case of those animals which react sexually on the first occasion of encountering a member of the other sex.

---

[1] For example, the cruelty sometimes displayed or invited in the course of sexual relations (the extremer forms of which are known as " Sadism " and " Masochism ") has been regarded as a component of normal sexuality. But, as I have argued elsewhere (*Proc. of Royal Soc. of Med.*, Sect. of Psychiatry, 1914), these manifestations seem referable to the instincts of self-display and self-abasement operating with abnormal intensity under the special conditions of the sexual relation.

In man, since the sexual instinct does not normally ripen or become excitable until the individual has greatly developed both his perceptual capacities and his power of self-direction, no such direct evidence of the innate perceptual organisation of the instinct can be cited ; but there is no reason to believe that in this respect the sex instinct of the human species has undergone any considerable degree of degeneration or involution. And we have indirect evidence supporting the view here maintained. In the first place, the great emotional effect and æsthetic value of the human form, especially of the female form for man, can hardly be accounted for without this assumption. But of greater evidential value is the fact that the boy or youth who knows nothing of the facts of sex may, and often does, experience the strong and for him altogether mysterious attraction and emotional influence of the female form, and may find that his imagination is strongly occupied by ideas of it, even against his will. If we reject the view I am urging, we are compelled to regard the direction of the sex impulse towards the opposite sex as determined by experience of sexual pleasure obtained through contact with the other sex ; or as resulting from the acquired knowledge that the other sex is the natural object of the impulse and that only through a member of that sex can the sexual impulse, craving, or desire, obtain full satisfaction. Attempts have been made to explain the fact in both these ways. The former way is a special application of the pleasure-pain theory of action, the fallacy of which has been exposed in the foregoing chapter. Both kinds of attempt break down in face of the fact that the sex attraction is sometimes felt and displayed prior to all experience of sexual pleasure and to all knowledge of the facts of sex.[1]

It is true that perverted example, or early acquaint-

---

[1] The best-known attempt of this sort is that of Professor Freud, who would explain the direction of the sex impulse of man towards woman by the assumption that the male infant derives sexual pleasure from the act of sucking at his mother's breast. It is, I submit, a sufficient refutation of this view to ask—How, then, does the sex instinct of woman become directed towards man ? How explain the fact that homosecxuality is not the rule in women ?

ance with perverse modes of obtaining sex pleasure, may and too often does pervert the direction of the sex impulse, in the ways denoted by the terms " sexual inversion " and " sexual fetishism " ; but the fact that the normal direction of the sex impulse so often asserts itself in spite of early acquired experience and knowledge of these unfortunate kinds is strong evidence that the impulse is innately directed to the opposite sex.[1] And such innate direction necessarily implies that the instinct is innately organised on its afferent side for the perceptual discrimination of the opposite sex by aid of the secondary sex characters.

Consideration of the sex instinct thus affords very strong support to the view of the nature of instinct adopted and maintained throughout this volume, the view, namely, that an instinct is an innately organised disposition, not only to act and feel in a certain manner, but also to perceive the object upon which the action and the feeling are directed. Psychologists are very slow to accept this view, although much of the behaviour of animals, especially of the higher insects, implies it in the most obvious and unmistakable fashion. Their reluctance seems to be due to the fact that " innate ideas " are out of fashion, and that to admit innate dispositions to perceive objects of special kinds is perilously near to admitting " innate ideas " ; for it is but a small step from an innate perceptual disposition to an innate disposition to represent, or think of, an object apart from its presentation to the senses. In my view there are good grounds for believing that dispositions of both kinds are inheritable and innate ; and in any case we ought to be guided in this question by impartial consideration of the facts, rather than by the prevailing philosophical fashions.[2]

[1] It is the opinion of several of the most experienced and judicious students of these problems that in some cases of sexual inversion or homosexuality the direction of the sex impulse towards the same sex is innately determined ; and some of the published cases are difficult, if not impossible, to reconcile with the opposite view. Such cases obviously lend strong support to the view that the normal direction of the sex impulse is innately determined.

[2] Since the publication of the first edition of this book, Professor Stout seems to have adopted this view of instinct (*Manual of Psychology*,

The principal thesis of this book is that each instinct is a great source or spring of the psycho-physical energy [1] that supports our bodily and mental activities. This principle is illustrated very vividly by the sex instinct.

It is generally recognised that in men and animals alike the sex impulse is apt to manifest itself in very vigorous and sustained efforts towards its natural end ; and that in ourselves it may determine very strong desire, in the control of which all the organised forces of the developed personality, all our moral sentiments and ideals, and all the restraining influences of religion, law, custom, and convention too often are confronted with a task beyond their strength.

It is generally recognised also how the energy of this impulse may quicken and animate the whole organism, and how it sustains and invigorates all activities which are entered upon as steps or means towards the attainment of the end of the instinct. In this connection the sex instinct is especially interesting in two respects. First, it illustrates better than any other the fact that the instinct may work strongly within us, impelling us to actions that bring us nearer to the end of the instinct, while yet that end remains undefined in consciousness. Thus a youth, though totally inexperienced in and ignorant of sexual relations, nevertheless may feel very strongly attracted to a member of the other sex, impelled to seek her neighbourhood, to follow her, and to find enormous emotional value and significance in the slightest contact. In such a person the sex impulse may be nothing more than a vague restlessness, a blind craving for some object or impression or experience that he cannot define to himself ; yet under favouring conditions the impulse may carry him on irresistibly to the accomplishment of

3rd edition), and Professor Lloyd Morgan has recently made some sligh advance towards it (" Are Meanings Inherited ? " *Mind*, vol. xxiii.).

[1] I have attempted to develop this notion and to render it more intelligible in physiological terms in a paper entitled " The Sources and Direction of Psycho-physical Energy," read on the occasion of the opening of the Phipps Psychiatrical Institute at Baltimore, and published in the *American Journal of Insanity*, vol. lxix. 1913.

the actions which constitute both the first and second stages of the process of fertilisation.

Secondly, the social consequences of the sexual act are so serious that great hindrances are opposed to its completion, both by the constitution of human nature (especially female nature) and by the customs and conventions, the traditions and ideals which a moralised society imposes upon its developing members. Yet the conditions that tend to excite the instinct are very frequently realised in normal social intercourse. Hence it follows that in most members of a civilised society (especially in the younger celibate members) the instinct is frequently excited in some degree, but only comparatively rarely (in some cases never) permitted to accomplish its end. The impulse of this instinct, therefore, in addition to subserving the primary function of reproduction of the species, plays a large part (in co-operation with other tendencies) in determining the forms and maintaining the activities of social intercourse. In the games of children and young people, in their dances and social gatherings, the mingling of the sexes gives a zest to the enjoyment and adds to the vigour of both bodily and mental activity, through the appeal to the sex instinct ; even though the gathering be of the most decorous and no single participant be capable of defining the end of the instinct or be aware of the source of his special animation. And in such games as kiss-in-the-ring, in the sophisticated dances of modern society, in flirtations of all degrees, and in the more or less self-conscious efforts of deliberate courtship, the operation of the sex impulse is obvious enough.

Dance and song and the writing of love letters, which figure so largely in the arts of courtship, connect the large fields of social activity in which the influence of the sex impulse is very obvious with an equally extensive and perhaps even more important province of human activity in which the influence of the sex instinct is more obscure but undoubtedly present, namely, the production and enjoyment of works of art.

The dance and song and literary composition which

are used more or less deliberately in courtship may clearly be brought under the general principle that the conative energy of the instinct maintains all activities that appear to be means towards the attainment of the instinctive end. In this respect they are comparable to the efforts of the young man to secure an economic position which will enable him to marry the girl of his choice; efforts which, as we know, are often very energetic and long sustained.

But this principle will hardly explain the part of the sex impulse in those æsthetic activities whose clearly envisaged and sufficient end seems to be the completed work of art. Perhaps we may partially explain the influence of the sex instinct in such works by invoking the principle that the means to an end tend, when that end is long pursued, to become desired as ends in themselves; and where the end of an instinct is not explicitly defined in consciousness, as is so frequently the case with the sex instinct, this conversion of means into ends is no doubt especially apt to occur.

But the connection between the sex instinct and artistic production is probably more direct in many instances. The stirring of the sex impulse may suffuse the body with energy and the mind with a vague emotion and a longing for something indefinable; and this surplus energy, not being consciously directed to any end, and being denied the opportunity and the conditions which would lead on the impulse to define itself in action and in thought, vents itself in spontaneous and self-sufficing, *i.e.* purely lyrical, activities, such as mere gambollings, dance, or song. If this be admitted, it remains a very difficult problem to explain how and why these modes of expending the sex energy assume the forms which we regard as specifically artistic. This is perhaps the most fundamental problem of æsthetics. No doubt much is due to example and tradition; but I do not think that the full answer can be given, unless we recognise far more fully than is usual with psychologists the innate organisation of the perceptual side of the sex instinct. If we consider the facts on the comparatively simple plane of animal life, we find, I think, the key to the understanding of the relation of sex to art. Who can doubt that the female nightingale is thrilled by the music of the male as by no other sound ; that the evolutions of the male pigeon are pleasing to the hen bird ; and that in both cases this is true because the sex instinct is so organised as to be excited by these impressions ? That the stimulation of the sex instinct in men and women yields a pleasurable excitement even when there is no anticipation of further indulgence of it, is sufficiently shown by the extent to which the lower forms of art, literature, and public entertainment rely upon a titillation of the sex impulse in making their appeal to the public. When the plastic and pictorial arts represent beautiful human forms, they make appeal to the same element ; but in their higher expressions they present these objects in such a way as to evoke also wonder and admiration, a respectful or even reverential attitude which prevents the dominance of the sex impulse over the train of thought, and, arresting its bodily manifestations, diverts its energy to other channels. This diverted energy then serves to reinforce the intellectual activity required for the apprehension of the various subtle harmonies of line and light and colour; that is to say, the energy liberated by the appeal to the sex instinct is utilised in enhancing the activity of purely æsthetic apprehension.

But, even though this account be in the main correct, it seems probable that we still have not exhausted the indirect influences of the sex instinct. It is widely held, and though it is difficult to adduce any convincing or crucial evidence, the view appears well founded, that the energy of the sex impulse, if it is not expended wholly in its own channels of expression, may function as a reinforcer of purely intellectual activities in situations that make no appeal to the instinct. If this be true, we can hardly hope to find any psychological explanation of the facts, though physiology may render them in some degree intelligible.

Such indirect utilisation of the sex instinct as a great fund of energy available for other than purely sexual activities is the process which Freud has proposed to call

" sublimation " ; and we may conveniently adopt this term and recognise the general truth of the notion, without committing ourselves to the acceptance of all, or indeed of any other, of the Freudian doctrines.

The regulation of the sex instinct always has been and must ever continue to be a difficult problem for the human race. And the difficulty of the problem increases, rather than diminishes, with every forward step of civilisation and every increase of the control of far-sighted intelligence over the more immediate promptings of human nature. For the intellect of man, being superimposed upon this strong animal tendency, whose exercise, because of its great strength, is attended by such intense pleasure or gratification, leads him to seek to obtain the greatest possible amount of this pleasure, and at the same time to seek, with ever more success as intellect and knowledge increase, to frustrate the end for the sake of which this strong instinct was evolved. This is a fundamental disharmony of human nature which not only endangers the happiness of individuals of all times and places, but also threatens every advancing civilisation with stagnation and decay. Nature cannot solve the problem for us by altering the innate constitution of the human race ; for to weaken either factor of this discord would be fatal to humanity ; the weakening of the instinct would mean the extinction of the race ; the weakening of the intellect would mean the loss of human attributes and of all that renders human life of more value than the animals'.

The system of sexual morality represents the cumulative effort of society to control and counteract this inevitable result of Nature's supreme achievement, the superposition of man's higher moral and intellectual capacities upon a basis of animal instincts ; it is the attempt to solve this problem which Nature has left unsolved, to harmonise the life of intellect and the development of self-conscious moral personality with the needs of the race and the promptings of the instinct which at lower levels of evolution effectively serves life's most fundamental law, namely, propagation and increase. And so we find that in societies of all levels of culture the operation of this most powerful instinct is more or less successfully regulated by an array of laws and conventions, supported by the strongest sanctions of custom and public opinion, of religion and of superstition. And, apart from its primary operations, the great strength of the sex impulse gives it, as we have seen, a wide range of secondary functions of great importance for the higher life of mankind. The problem before every civilisation that aspires to attain and maintain a high level of culture is, therefore, not merely so to regulate the sex instinct as to prevent its exerting an influence injurious to the interests of the higher culture, while it performs its all-important primary function ; but also to direct it in such a fashion that its immense energy shall be brought as freely as possible into the service of the higher culture. Hence the importance of a knowledge of the nature and working of the instinct and of its normal course of development.

Among those who have recognised the existence of the sex instinct in man, it has been usual to regard it as lying latent in the child up to the age of puberty, and as then rapidly maturing, and attaining its full strength in the course of a year or two.

But in recent years a very different view of the course of sexual development has been vigorously propagated by the school of medical psychologists of which Professor Freud is the leader and inspirer. It is not yet possible to form a decided opinion upon the doctrines of this school. I incline strongly to the view that they have extended to normal individuals generalisations which are true only of a certain number of persons of somewhat abnormal constitution, from among whom their patients have been drawn. But, since it is possible that their views are in the main true of the normal constitution, and since, even if as I suggest they are true only of a minority, this minority may be numerous, it seems necessary to give here some brief outline of them.

Freud's doctrine [1] differs from generally received views in maintaining that the sexual life of the individual begins its development at or even before birth. Freud

[1] *Three Contributions to the Sexual Theory.* New York, 1910.

asserts that the child's sexuality, although awake from earliest infancy, is not at first an impulse definitely directed towards any object, but consists rather in a capacity for finding pleasure in a variety of modes of sensory stimulation and bodily movement. Without going so far as to maintain (with some authors) that all pleasure is sexual, he regards the pleasure found in these stimulations and movements as essentially sexual.[1] The thumb-sucking of infants is regarded as the type of such infantile sexual processes. Freud sees in this habit a blind seeking of sexual gratification; he regards it as the source of a number of peculiar hysterical troubles of later life, and believes that it always involves the risk of the development of such troubles. He describes the mucous membrane of the lips, therefore, as an "erogenous zone," *i.e.*, a sensory area stimulation of which may give rise to sexual excitement. And he believes that every infant possesses, in addition to the primary erogenous zone (which consists of the external sex organs themselves), a number of such zones, any one of which may become unduly prominent, if in any way it is unduly stimulated, thus bringing about a perversion of the sex impulse; for normal development can only take place if all these zones become duly subordinated to the primary one. Accordingly, he describes the normal infant as "polymorphous perverse," and believes that accidents of development leading to perversion very frequently occur.

This initial stage of objectless sexual excitement or "auto-erotism" is said normally to persist throughout the period of infancy proper; until, about the age of seven years, there begin to operate certain tendencies which repress or keep in check the crude sex impulses, namely, shame, loathing, and disgust. Under favourable conditions of environment and training, the sex tendencies remain more or less completely repressed throughout the period of childhood proper. At puberty they increase in strength; but, if the repressing forces are now

[1] It is not made clear, nor is it easy to understand, what meaning we are to attach to this statement; for Freud lays down no criterion and no definition of sexuality.

reinforced by moral training and æsthetic ideals, they manifest themselves only in sublimated forms ; that is to say, the energy of the sex impulse is diverted from the channels of direct sexual expression and is " long-circuited " into channels in which it supports and intensifies intellectualised and refined modes of concern with the natural object of the impulse, namely, persons of the opposite sex. The processes of repression and sublimation are regarded as somewhat precarious, and as liable at every stage to suffer interferences which will lead to crude and direct manifestations of a normal or perverted kind. It is said, for example, that the sex impulse of the boy normally and properly becomes directed towards the opposite sex by the pleasure that he obtains from the tender ministrations of his mother ; but that there is great danger in encouraging the boy's affection towards his mother and in her lavishing caresses upon him, because such treatment is apt to result in his sex impulse becoming too strongly fixed upon this its first object, a result which may afterwards lead to troubles of various kinds. The impulse, thus directed, becomes, it is said, repressed, driven into subconsciousness, where it works in a subterraneous fashion, and expresses itself in indirect and symbolical ways in the youth's thoughts, feelings, and conduct. It is said, for example, that the youth grows jealous of his father ; but that this jealousy, being repressed, may show itself only in an exaggerated deference towards him. If this state of affairs continues, no great harm is done, save that the youth is rendered incapable of falling in love in a normal manner with a girl of his own age. But in some cases, it is said, this state of things issues in the most awful domestic tragedies of which *Hamlet* and *Œdipus Rex* are the type. This school of psycho-pathology describes such a repressed but subconsciously operating tendency as a " complex " ; it speaks of a repressed sexual attraction to the mother with a consequent repressed jealousy of the father, as of the type of the " Œdipus complex " ; and it claims to have traced the influence of complexes of this type in the forms of many myths, legends, and works of literature.

In attempting to form an opinion on this Freudian doctrine of infantile sexuality, it is important to remember that, even if we find ourselves compelled to reject it for the normal majority, it may be at least partially true of a minority. For, in regard to the most fundamental point at issue, namely, the age at which sexuality is to be attributed to the child, general biological considerations prepare us to find that individuals differ widely in this respect. It may well be that in an unknown proportion of human beings the sex instinct begins to be excitable at a very early age, while in others, probably the great majority, this occurs at a much later stage of development ; and it is not improbable that the neurotic patients, on the study of whom the Freudian doctrine is chiefly based, belong to the minority, and that it is just this peculiarity of constitution that renders them liable to their disorders. In considering the question of infantile sexuality, we must therefore attach but little weight to the evidence of it drawn from the study of psycho-neurotic patients, and must rather weigh the positive indications for and against it provided by healthy persons.

I have already indicated the fallacy of one piece of reasoning advanced in support of the Freudian view, namely, the acceptance of all manifestations of personal love or affection as evidence of sexuality ; for this, as was said, is due to the confusion of the sexual instinct with the sentiment of love. Only one other piece of evidence on this side seems deserving of serious consideration ; the fact, namely, that a considerable number of infants acquire the habit of playing with their sex organs in a manner which implies that such stimulation is pleasurable. If this were the rule with the majority of infants the argument would be very weighty. But that is by no means true. And we must remember that the infants who acquire this habit may belong to the minority of abnormal innate constitution whose existence we have admitted to be probable. It is very possible also that, by undue stimulation of the sex organs of a normal infant (an act of which unscrupulous persons are sometimes guilty), the sex instinct may be forced to a precocious and partial development. In these two ways we may account for the auto-erotism which seems to be manifested by some infants, without regarding it as a normal stage in the development of the sex instinct. It may be added that most of the other arguments adduced by Freud in support of his doctrine of infantile sexuality (such as, *e.g.*, the prevalence of thumb-sucking) may be dismissed on the ground that the doctrine of erogenous zones, with which they are bound up, is in itself very obscure, seems incapable of being rendered clear and self-consistent, and betrays a conception of the nature of the sex instinct which is vague, chaotic, and elusive, uncontrolled by consideration of the facts of animal instinct and inconsistent with these facts. In support of this last point of this indictment, it may suffice to point out that the Freudian conception of the nature and development of sexuality is radically incompatible with the view that the sex impulse is directed towards the opposite sex by the innate organisation of the instinct—a view which is certainly true of many of the animals and which in its application to the human species is, as we have seen, very strongly based.

On the other side, two strong arguments may be adduced. First, a large number of autobiographical accounts of sexual development have been published.[1] Examination of these reveals the fact that, in a very large proportion of cases, the first stirrings and promptings of sex feeling that can be remembered by the subject were experienced in or about the eighth year of life. Freud maintains that infantile sex experiences are not remembered by the adult because the memory of them is actively repressed. But he entirely fails to explain why those which he supposes to occur before the eighth year should be forgotten, while those which occur between that age and puberty are remembered. It is also very important to note in this connection that a certain number of these autobiographers can distinctly remember having been made in infancy (*i.e.*, before the eighth year) the victims of unscrupulous persons who have deliberately attempted,

[1] Notably by Havelock Ellis in his *Psychology of Sex*, and by A. Moll in his *Untersuchungen der Libido Sexualis*.

but without success, to excite them sexually ; while their accounts show that similar attempts made a few years later have been or, if repeated, would undoubtedly have been successful.

Secondly, the observation of the behaviour of children gives strong support to this view. It is at about the age of eight years that the behaviour of children commonly begins to exhibit indications of their attraction towards and a new interest and feeling towards members of the other sex. Before this age some children display warm personal affection ; but such displays commonly involve nothing that implies the operation of the sex instinct. And one feature of them constitutes indirect but weighty evidence of the absence of the sex element, namely, the complete absence of any reserve or bashfulness in their relations with the objects of their affection, although in other circumstances bashfulness may be strongly displayed. On the other hand, as soon as the sex instinct begins to be operative (*i.e.*, from about the eighth year onwards) bashfulness is apt to dominate the attitude of the child in his relations to persons of the other sex (especially, perhaps, in relations of the boy to girls whose attraction for him is strong). This change of attitude and expression [1] takes place, then, at about the age to which adult reminiscence agrees in attributing the first promptings of the sex impulse ; and it can, I submit, only be explained by the assumption that a new and powerful factor normally comes into operation about this age, a factor which can be assigned to no other source than the sex instinct, and which, if we identify it with the sex impulse, affords adequate explanation of the facts.

The manifestations of the sex instinct are intimately related with and modified by modes of behaviour which are popularly attributed to a vaguely conceived function or faculty termed modesty. But the attribution of them to " modesty " is by no means an explanation of them. " Modesty " and " modest " are terms properly used to

---

[1] It is clearly brought out in " A Preliminary Study of the Emotion of Love between the Sexes," by Sanford Bell (*American Journal of Psychology*, 1902).

denote the quality of character or of conduct characterised by such behaviour. Some authors assume that the tendency to such behaviour is a component of the sex instinct ; but, since this quality is displayed in a variety of situations that make no appeal to the sex instinct, that way of accounting for it is hardly justifiable.

It seems clear that modesty is closely allied to bash-fulness. We may confine our attention to the modesty displayed in sex relations, and it is convenient to denote this form of modesty by the special term " pudor." We may, I think, regard pudor, together with all other forms of modesty and of humility, and the element of shrinking in bashfulness, as all alike expressions under different circumstances and at different levels of intellectualisa-tion, of one fundamental tendency, namely, the shrinking impulse of the instinct of self-abasement.

The behaviour of the females of many animal species, as well as the human, in the presence of the male is apt to be coy ; this coyness of the female is essentially a refusal and avoidance of the sexual approaches of the male in spite of the excitement of her sex instinct. If, as Darwin and Wallace and other biologists have main-tained, sexual selection has been an important factor of evolution, female coyness has had a great biological rôle to play. For, by necessitating the active pursuit and the courtship of the female by the male, female coyness gives scope for the operation of sexual selection ; the male better endowed with strength or skill to overcome his rivals, or with beauty of voice or form or colour to excite more strongly the attention of the female, is given scope for the exercise or display of these advantages and oppor-tunities to profit by them which he would hardly enjoy to the same extent, if the females of his species yielded at once to the advances of every male. The probability that female coyness plays this important rôle in evolution affords some ground for the view that it is the expression of a special instinct whose function it is to give scope for sexual selection. But the principle of economy of hypo-thesis forbids us to make this assumption, if the facts can be otherwise explained. And it is, I think, possible to regard coyness as but the manifestation of pudor under the special circumstances of the approach and pursuit of the ardent male. In fact, it would, perhaps, be more correct to describe coyness as essentially bashfulness displayed by the female under these circumstances. For bashfulness, as we have seen (Chapter V.), seems to be essentially the expression of a conflict between the opposed instincts of self-display and self-abasement. And, in the coy behaviour of the female pursued by the male, her movements of retreat and avoidance, which are attributable to the latter instinct, are commonly varied at moments by movements of self-display ; the dominance of one or other tendency being determined from moment to moment by the increase or diminution of the male's aggressiveness.

That the impulses of self-display and self-abasement should habitually complicate the operation of the sex impulse is an inevitable consequence of the nature of the three instincts from which they respectively spring. For the sex impulse necessarily intensifies self-consciousness, at the same time that it impels the individual to seek the presence of his or her fellows and to become attentive to their regards ; that is to say, it brings members of the two sexes into just such relations to one another as are best fitted to lead to the excitement of the instincts of self-display and self-abasement. And, in order to account for the greater prominence of pudor and of coyness in the female than in the male, we have only to assume that the impulse of the instinct of self-abasement is in general stronger in woman than in man, an assumption which is borne out by many other peculiarities of feminine behaviour and feeling. In both the pudor and the coyness of the adult woman, the direct operation of this impulse is commonly complicated by other more intellectualised tendencies, notably by the desire to avoid transgressing the conventions of her society and the shrinking from the possibility of inducing disgust in the male. For we must recognise that disgust is primarily and specially excited by the secreta and excrementa of the body. And Nature, with an utter disregard for the dignity and high potentialities of the sexual functions, has placed our organs of reproduction in the closest anatomical and even physio-logical association with the body's principal channels of excretion.

The intimate connection of the operation of these two impulses with that of the sex instinct is clearly illus-trated by the fashions of dress of almost every country and every age, and especially clearly perhaps by contemporary fashions in women's dress. It is a disputed question whether clothing was primarily used for the concealment or for the display of the body. The former view has been commonly accepted ; but of late several authors have argued that the primitive function of clothing was to adorn and to draw attention to the sex characters of the body. But there is, I think, little room for doubt that clothing has from the first served both purposes ; as it certainly does at the present time. In many subtle ways woman's dress manages, without transgressing the limits set by convention, to draw attention to and to accentuate her secondary sex characters ; and that it serves at the same time to conceal the body is also obvious. And many masculine fashions of dress serve the same two opposed purposes.

The foregoing remarks on pudor, coyness, and bash-fulness in sex relations bear out the view that their almost sudden onset or increase at about the eighth or ninth year is due to the awakening of the sex instinct. These considerations justify us in accepting as well founded the view that in the normal child the sex instinct first begins to make itself felt about the eighth year, though it is possible that even in normally constituted children it may be precociously awakened in some degree by improper influences. The most positive evidence that the instinct is commonly functional in the period of childhood proper is afforded by the frequency of cases in which children, through lack of control, bad example, and only too fre-quently the malpractices of older persons upon them, are led to exercise or to attempt to exercise the bodily activities of sex, not only under the form of self-abuse, but also as more or less successful efforts at connection with one another.

During this period (from the eighth year to puberty) the sex impulse is commonly weak and but very vaguely directed; though it is, I think, an overstatement to say (with Dessoir and Moll) that the instinct is at this age quite undifferentiated or not at all directed to the opposite rather than towards the same sex. During this period the maturation and extrusion of the germ cells does not normally occur in either sex, even if sexual connection takes place. This is only one of many facts which indicate that the excitation of the bodily manifestations of sex is highly undesirable at this age. During this period the inexperience, the ignorance, the curiosity, the natural suggestibility and plasticity of the child, and the weak differentiation or direction of its sex impulse towards the opposite sex, while stimulation of it is nevertheless capable of yielding a pleasurable excitement; all these combine to render the child peculiarly susceptible to perversion of the instinct. It follows that initiation into perverted practices of any kind is peculiarly dangerous at this age; and there can be little doubt that many cases of homosexuality or inversion, and of " fetishism " (the fixation of the sex impulse upon unnatural objects) are determined by unfortunate experiences at this age. That the sex instinct so frequently turns towards its proper object and undergoes a normal development at puberty, in spite of influences which tend to its perversion during childhood, is strong evidence that its direction towards the opposite sex is determined by its innate constitution.

Reflection upon these special conditions and dangers of the child in respect of its sexual development must force us to the conclusion that the strong condemnation of pederasty which is common to most of the higher civilisations is entirely justifiable. There is among us a considerable number of persons who would defend the practice of sexual love between persons of the same sex; asserting that this is purely a private concern of individual taste and feeling; and that the present state of the law and of public opinion in this country inflicts grievous hardship upon a number of persons whose sex impulse is innately directed to their own sex. The answer to all such pleas must be that, while we may pity the misfortune of such persons, they must, like others born with mental and bodily malformations still harder to bear, learn to adapt themselves as best they may to the social institutions formed for the regulation of the lives of normally constituted men and women, and must, if necessary, suffer in silence. If sexual inversion were always and only a purely innate peculiarity, there would be much to be said on the side of those who plead for individual freedom in this matter. But, so far from this being the case, it seems to be clearly proved that the example and influence of sexual perverts may and actually does determine the perversion of many individuals who, if shielded from such influences, would develop in a normal manner. This being so, it follows that the social approval of homosexuality or of pederasty (even in its milder and less ignoble forms) tends to set up a vicious circle, the operation of which misdirects the sex impulse of increasing numbers of the successive generations, and therefore (as in ancient Greece) tends to the decay of the normal relations between the sexes and to the destruction of the society which has taken this false step.

The peculiar condition of the sex instinct in the child, with its liability to perversion, provides a weighty argument against the two strict segregation of the sexes at this age. For there can be little doubt that, although excitation of sexual feeling and activity to crude and direct expressions is very undesirable at this age, the awakening of the instinct in such a way that its impulse remains subdued and severely restricted in expression, while directed towards the opposite sex, is a safeguard against perversion ; and it is probable that even at this age the energy of its impulse may be " sublimated " in the service of intellectual, moral, and æsthetic development.

The foregoing paragraph may not be interpreted without reserve as a justification of " co-education of the sexes " ; but it does support the view that the normal family, containing several boys and girls and maintaining friendly relations with other similar families, provides the best environment for the child. The repression and sublimation of the sex impulse during childhood and youth is an essential condition for the development and maintenance in any society of a high level of culture. And of such repression and sublimation, respect of the boy for woman is the principal condition. It is here that the influence of good mothers and pure sisters is of so much importance. If woman were by nature nothing more for man than an object capable of stimulating his " erogenous zones " more effectively than objects of any other class, she would be merely the chief of many " fetish objects," and an unrestrained and excessive indulgence of the sexual appetite would be the inevitable rule for both sexes from childhood to old age.[1] Hence it is supremely important that women should be presented to the boy and youth only in fair and noble and dignified forms ; that he should learn, before his sex impulse attains its full strength, to regard women with respect as personalities.

We may enforce this point by imagining a normal boy subjected to influences of either of two extreme types. On the one hand, he may at an early age be led to regard woman as an animal endowed with a strong sex impulse, always seeking its gratification, and ever ready to co-operate with him in obtaining sensual pleasures. There could be no " long-circuiting " or sublimation of the sex energy in such a case. On the other hand, the boy who knows women, and who knows of them, only as beings superior to himself that deserve his profoundest respect and admiration, and who, when he learns the facts of sex and feels the powerful and mysterious attraction of a woman's body, believes that he cannot approach any one woman with the least hope of intimacy, unless he preserves an attitude of the utmost delicacy and respect, and then only by way of a long course of devoted service by which he may show his worth and his superiority to rival suitors ; in such a boy the repression of the immediate promptings

[1] It has often been maintained, and not improbably with justice, that the backward condition of so many branches of the negro race is in the main determined by the prevalence among them of this state of affairs.

of the sex instinct is as inevitable as their free indulgence in the former case ; and the energy of its impulse will lend itself to reinforce all those activities which appear to him as the indispensable means towards the attainment of the natural end of this, the strongest tendency of his nature.

The alternatives may be stated still more crudely and forcibly. If a boy grew up in a society in which he might obtain possession of any female by knocking her down with a club, or by making a lewd gesture before her, his sex energy would inevitably expend itself in the main in crude sexual acts. On the other hand, in a society in which all women were noble and beautiful and chaste, there would be no sexual problem and dis-order ; for the development of the sex impulse of men would be compelled to follow the higher course. But the truth about women lies somewhere between the extremes we have imagined, and women, like men, differ widely in these respects.

Here we may see a warning against the extreme policy of sex enlightenment in youth. There is coming into fashion a strong tendency to carry this policy too far. It is too often assumed that mere knowledge of the facts of sex and of what is most desirable and admir-able in the conduct of the sex life is all-important and all-sufficient. But knowledge may be more dangerous than ignorance ; ignorance of some of the facts is a great and necessary safeguard of youth ; a second-hand famili-arity with the facts of sexual vice cannot fail to be injurious to youth, and even a full insight into the psychology of sex is highly dangerous.[1] Surely the boy should know only parts of the facts ! Surely it is permissible to lead him to believe that all women are more or less as we should have them be in an ideal world, and to allow men to appear to him as rather better in these respects than they actually are ! The tree of knowledge cannot be robbed

[1] Those who so grotesquely put their faith in the redeeming power of mere knowledge of the facts and of the evils that result from sexual laxity should remember that medical students are constantly con-fronted with such evils in all their naked horror, and that nevertheless they are not as a class distinguished above others by chastity, or even by prudence in these matters.

of its dangers, though it be draped in the driest of scientific jargon.

At puberty the child becomes the adolescent, and the transformation involves many profound changes of mind and body. In regard to puberty the great question of theoretical interest is—Are all or most of the characteristic mental changes to be regarded as direct and indirect effects of the maturing of the sex instinct and its organs, and of the increase of strength of its impulse ? Or must we infer that a number of other innate tendencies that have been latent throughout infancy and childhood become active at this time ? The second alternative has been widely taught or implied in writings on this topic.[1] But the former is the simpler hypothesis, and we ought to explain the facts as far as possible by means of it, before we go on to make the other assumption. And it will go a long way towards explaining the facts. But first, something may be said against the other view.

We know that extirpation of the sex glands in infancy prevents the development of all the characteristic bodily changes of puberty, and it seems, though here the facts cannot be so easily observed, that it prevents also the characteristic mental changes. We should hardly expect these effects, if these changes depend upon the maturing at puberty of a number of more or less independent innate tendencies.

Again, those who take this second view have never succeeded in defining the nature of these tendencies whose existence and operation they assume. There is no theoretical objection to be made against the assumption ; but as a principle of psychological method we must set our faces against the easy *ad hoc* postulation of innate tendencies, whenever we are confronted with a problem of conduct or of mental development.

The mental change most generally recognised as characteristic of puberty is, of course, an increased interest in the opposite sex and in one's own sex stirrings and sex characters. All this we may confidently attribute to the

---

[1] Notably in the *Adolescence* and in other works of President Stanley Hall.

increase of strength and excitability of the sex impulse. We have to recognise that, in respect of mental changes at puberty that go beyond these most constant and direct effects, individuals differ widely. These differences seem to be determined largely by differences of the degree to which the repressive or inhibitory influences are brought into effective play.

If we tried to imagine a case in which these influences were not effectively applied, we should, I think, expect, as the principal and perhaps the sole secondary result of the increase of strength of the sex impulse, an intensification of self-consciousness, which, as we have seen (Chapter VII.), is always at the same time a consciousness of the social setting and relations of the self. This intensification of self-consciousness may obviously be determined in two ways : (1) as a consequence of new and exciting bodily functions, and of more intense feelings and cravings than any before experienced ; (2) through an increase of interest in other persons, which results in part from the direct attraction exerted by persons of the opposite sex, and in part from the enrichment of one's conception of other personalities achieved by reading into them one's own new experiences.

This enrichment of consciousness of self and of the self-in-relation-to-others naturally increases the frequency and strength of excitation of the two great self-regarding impulses, those of self-display and self-abasement, and of those conflicts between them which we call states of bashfulness. That is to say, the adolescent becomes more sensitive to the regards of other persons ; he is more elated or depressed by them, according as they are favourable or unfavourable ; and his mind is more frequently and more intensely occupied with the process of self-display. This is evinced in the crudest way by his increased interest in his personal appearance, and, in girls more especially, perhaps, by attention to dress. In boys the self-display takes more varied forms, display of bodily strength and skill and achievement being, no doubt, the primary and fundamental form.

I see no reason to think that, in the absence of the

repressive influences that are brought to bear in some
degree on almost all adolescents, puberty would produce
any further mental changes of importance. I see no
evidence that any further changes occur in those communities and in those individuals (*e.g.* the savages of
our great cities) in which the repressive influences are
not brought to bear

Among true savages, measures, prescribed by custom
and rigidly enforced (often in the form of initiation
ceremonies), impress upon the adolescent, in the strongest
manner, the code of sexual prohibitions and penalties,
and serve as repressive influences. Among ourselves
the code is impressed in many ways (generally less direct
than those of savage peoples) which greatly reinforce
the repressive influence of modesty and that exerted by
the respect previously acquired for members of the opposite
sex (especially the mother) and, perhaps, for the sex in
general.

The result of the repression of the sex impulse effected
by these influences may be described in the most general
terms as an increase of seriousness and intensity in almost
all fields of thought, feeling, and action, especially in all
that concerns personal and social relations and the conduct
of life, and therefore in all questions of morality and
religion. This may be regarded as an effect of a generalised " sublimation " of the sex energy.

But, beside this, there often occur " sublimations " of
the more specialised kinds to which the term is more
usually applied. The intensification of thought and
feeling may affect principally the religious interests, and
then becomes a main condition of the conversion which
is so characteristic of adolescence. In this, no doubt,
the sex instinct plays its part in another way also, namely,
by giving rise to a " consciousness of sin," or an awareness
of a powerful temptation to wrong-doing, of a force
within one that one cannot control unaided. Or the
sublimation may result, most frequently and naturally
perhaps, in a quickening of interest in romance or poetry
or other form of art.

THE DERIVED EMOTIONS

IN the first part of this book I distinguished certain emotions as primary emotions, namely, fear, anger, tender-emotion, disgust, positive self-feeling, negative self-feeling, and wonder. The peculiarity of these emotions which gives them their position of primary importance is, I maintained, the fact that each one is the immediate inevitable result and subjective expression of the excitement of an instinct, an innate disposition specifically directed to some particular mode of action. It was not my intention to assert that no other than these seven emotions belong to this class. I recognised the fact that the innate constitution of man comprises other instinctive dispositions, and that the excitement of any one of these is accompanied by some subjective excitement or feeling which is of the same order as the primary emotions ; but, I said, the qualities of these states of feeling are obscure, are but little differentiated and therefore not easily recognisable introspectively.

Beside these primary emotions I described a number of well-recognised emotions as being essentially compounds or blends of the primary emotions, that is to say, emotional qualities which are experienced when two or more of the great instinctive tendencies are simultaneously excited. Examples of this class are awe, reverence, gratitude, admiration, scorn, envy. Some of these blended emotions, I said, are only aroused in virtue of the previous acquisition of sentiments, permanent or habitual emotional-conative attitudes towards particular objects or classes of things. As examples of this class, reproach, jealousy, vengeful emotion, and shame were analysed.

I then discussed joy and sorrow, arguing that neither of these is to be classed with the primary emotions; because each of them is a state of feeling or emotion which is not the immediate effect and expression of the excitement of any one instinct or disposition, but rather arises when any of the conative tendencies operate under certain conditions. They may therefore be distinguished as derived or secondary emotions. Joy and sorrow are not the only emotions of this class; there is a large number of emotional states, easily recognised and commonly distinguished by well-established names, which must be regarded as belonging to this class of derived emotions; for they arise only when the various active tendencies of our nature operate under special mental conditions. They seem to be connected with no special conative dispositions; but each of them rises to colour our whole consciousness when any one of these dispositions operates under the appropriate conditions.

I have felt that not only are these emotions of great interest and importance in themselves, but that a discussion of them and of the conditions under which they arise and of their relations to the primary emotions and tendencies will make clearer to the mind of my readers the distinctive position assigned to the primary emotions in the foregoing chapters of this book. I therefore add this chapter, and I propose to discuss these derived emotions in the light of, and largely in the form of a criticism of, Mr. Shand's treatment of them in his work on *The Foundations of Character*.[1] For Mr. Shand has given us a more elaborate and careful study of these emotions than any other that has been published; and the contrasting of my own view of them with his will, I think, aid in bringing clearly to mind some of the many interesting problems presented by them.

Mr. Shand has pointed out that the emotions of this class, of which the types are confidence, hope, disappointment, anxiety, despondency, and despair, always arise in the course of the operation of some continued desire, and he therefore treats of them under the head of the

---

[1] London, 1914.

prospective emotions of desire. With this I am in entire agreement, save that I would enlarge the class by including in it the retrospective as well as the prospective emotions of desire ; thus we should add regret, remorse, and sorrow. Joy, I submit, occupies a peculiar position, in that it belongs to both groups ; there are retrospective as well as prospective joys.

These emotions occur in all degrees of intensity ; but we may with advantage fix our attention upon their most intense manifestations, to the neglect of their fainter forms in which one or other of them is present to consciousness at almost all moments of our waking life, faithfully attending every movement of our conative tendencies.

The operation of some strong continued desire is, then, the essential condition of the rise to consciousness of the emotions of this class ; and, since such desire commonly arises from some strongly organised sentiment, these emotions arise most frequently in connection with the operation of such sentiments ; but this is not necessarily or always the case. For example, a desire for food may spring from the simple primary hunger tendency ; and, if such a simple primary instinctive desire or appetite is sufficiently strong, it may generate most, though perhaps not all, of these prospective and retrospective emotions of desire.

Shand regards desire itself as an emotional system, and these emotions of desire as comparable with those I have distinguished as the primary emotions ; that is to say he regards each of these qualities of emotion as being rooted in or dependent upon the activity of a specific disposition, one which has its own conative tendency and proper end ; and the system of desire is for him a complex disposition given in the innate constitution and composed of the postulated dispositions of all these emotions of desire.[1] He is committed to this

---

[1] He writes : " Desire is then a very complex emotional system, which includes actually or potentially the six prospective emotions of hope, anxiety, disappointment, despondency, confidence, and despair " (p. 463). And he tells us that " desire . . . is essentially an organisation of those emotional dispositions which are characteristic of its process." Shand thus describes " desire " as a complex dis-

treatment of these emotions by his view that each emotion is not, as is my view, merely a specific affective tone or colouring of consciousness qualifying our mental activities, but is essentially a disposition having its own specific conative tendency; the instincts being merely dispositions to special modes of bodily movement, subordinated to and more or less organised within the emotional dispositions.

In opposition to this, I submit, that, while the primary emotions may loosely be said to have the specific tendencies of the instinctive dispositions in which they are rooted, these derived emotions have no such specific tendencies, for they are not attached to or rooted in any special dispositions; they are, therefore, not forces of character, and cannot be said in any true and significant meaning of the words to be organised within the sentiments or in the great hierarchy of sentiments which is the character of the individual.

Desire is the general name for that peculiar experience which arises in every mind (sufficiently developed intellectually to hold before itself the idea of an end) whenever any strong impulse or conative tendency cannot immediately attain or actively progress towards its natural end. If this be true, and I believe that some such statement of the nature of desire is generally acceptable to almost all psychologists, it is quite unnecessary to postulate some special disposition as the root of desire. If, following Shand, we did so, we should find ourselves involved in

position similar in nature to the complex sentiments of love or hate. Yet he is clearly aware that desire is not in the least comparable to either a sentiment or one of the primary emotions. For in another place (p. 519) he writes that desire is an abstraction, and that " it is a complete mistake to represent desire as an independent force, and to suppose that it can be co-ordinated either with the emotions or with the sentiments." This reveals very clearly the confusion into which he has fallen, a confusion which runs throughout the whole of his book, and which is largely due to his failure to hold fast to the very important distinction between facts of mental function and facts of mental structure. Desire, like the emotions, is a fact of mental function, a mode or aspect of mental activity, and may and does arise whenever any strong impulse or conative tendency cannot find immediate satisfaction. Dispositions within which, or from which, emotions and desires arise are facts of mental structure.

insoluble difficulties when we attempted to conceive the
relation of this special disposition to the other conative
dispositions, whether the primary instincts or the sentiments ; and if, like Shand, we further assumed that it is a
highly complex disposition, comprising the special dispositions of all the emotions of desire, our difficulties
would be very greatly and gratuitously increased.   Shand
seems to have reached this view through allowing himself
to be unduly influenced by the literary tradition, to which
he attaches great importance ; for in poetry and the
" belles-lettres " these emotions are commonly spoken of
as forces or agents, and are frequently personified.

This influence may be illustrated by citing Shand's
treatment of hope.   He regards hope as one of the greatest
forces that operate in the mind, as something that enters
into the structure of character ; and he attributes to it
a variety of effects upon conduct.   He points out that
the poets have generally attributed to it " a tendency of
supreme importance to desire and love."   Thus Shelley
wrote : " Hope still creates from its own wreck the thing
it contemplates."   Milton exclaimed :   " What reinforcement we may gain from hope ! " :   and Tennyson wrote
of " the mighty hope that makes us men."   Campbell,
addressing " Hope," said :

> " Thine is the charm of life's bewildered way,
>   That calls each slumbering passion into play " ;

and Amiel wrote : " At bottom everything depends on
the presence or absence of one single element in the soul
—hope.   All the activities of man . . . presuppose a
hope in him of attaining an end.   Once kill this hope,
and his movements become senseless, spasmodic, and
convulsive."   Shand, who cites these and other similar
remarks of the poets upon hope, adds : " No other emotion
has had such general tribute paid to it " ; and he regards
these poetic sayings as strong evidence of the truth of his
view of this emotion.   He proceeds to translate these
poetic expressions into sober scientific language, defining
the tendencies of hope as follows : " Hope increases the
activity of desire, aids it in resisting misfortune and the

influence of depressing emotions, and in both ways furthers the attainment of its end "; and " hope tends always to make the future appear better than the present," and thus also strengthens desire. We are told also that hope tends to give us courage, that it tends to conserve the direction of thought and effort, and that hope has this indispensable use and function for desire. He treats of the other emotions of this group in similar fashion, adducing the sayings of the poets in support of his view that they all are actual mental forces having their distinctive tendencies towards specific ends. Now we cannot put aside this literary evidence as of no account ; but Shand, I venture to think, attaches too much import ance to it. The poets speak with poetic licence and in metaphorical language, they are not concerned with scientific analysis, and do not attempt to use a scientific terminology ; and, when they speak of hope or despondency or despair as forces which impel to this or that form of behaviour, we do them no wrong and make no reflection upon their knowledge of human nature, if we abstain from taking their words in the most literal sense.

The principal objection to accepting these emotions as forces comparable to the great primary emotional conative tendencies, such as anger and fear, is that they always arise as incidents or phases of feeling in the course of the operation of some activity prompted by some other motive. Thus, hope is never an independent motive ; we hope always for the attainment of some end which we desire or aim at from some other motive than hope ; and the driving power which Shand attributes to hope itself may, without improbability or any distortion of the facts, be attributed to this primary motive or desire. Secondly, the ends assigned to these emotions are highly general and abstract ; it is difficult to suppose that any innate disposition can be directed to any specific end so highly abstract as " making the future appear better than the present." Thirdly, as we have already seen, desire itself is, by Shand's own admission, an abstraction, and these emotions of desire are equally abstractions ; they are so many distinguishable ways in which the desire

and emotion springing from any primary conative disposition, or from any sentiment, are modified by our
intellectual apprehension of the degree of success or
failure attending our efforts towards the end of our desire.
Fourthly, though these emotional states are sufficiently
distinct to be generally and intelligibly denoted by distinct
names, they do not differ one from another in the fundamental way in which anger differs from fear or disgust
or tender emotion ; rather they pass into one another by
insensible gradations, and the names we give them mark
merely points or regions in a continuous scale of feeling
If, then, we can account for them by a simpler hypothesis
than Shand's, and in so doing avoid the very great difficulties that arise on the acceptance of his view of them,
we are compelled by the principles of scientific method
to adopt the simpler hypothesis.

Let us see how the simpler view works when applied
to some one strong desire ; and, for simplicity's sake, let
us take a desire rooted in a strong and primitive tendency,
the tendency to seek food when hungry. Let us imagine
ourselves to be a party of polar explorers returning from
a dash for the Pole and making for a deposit of food a
few days' march away. We have exhausted the supplies
which we carried with us ; but the conditions of travelling
are good, we are all in vigorous health, and we know
exactly where to find the hidden store of food. Then,
though we all desire strongly to find this food, and though
our minds may be much occupied by the thought of it,
even tormented by ideas of succulent beefsteaks, we go
forward in confidence. We do not hope for the food ; we
confidently look forward to reaching it ; our line of
action lies clear before us ; nothing raises a doubt of our
success ; we are simply impelled to vigorous sustained
effort by our strong desire. Confidence has thus a negative
condition ; it is simply desire working towards its end
unobstructedly. Shand tells us that "Confidence tends to
relax the higher intellectual and voluntary processes and
to leave the accomplishment of desire to external events
or to processes that are automatic." It is easy to see in
the light of our illustration how he arrives at this view.

Our party of polar explorers needs to form no further plans ; it has only to persist in the one line of vigorous activity, and its end will be reached. But, though it needs no further deliberation, its efforts will hardly be relaxed by confidence. The true statement seems to be that, when our purpose and plan of action are in no way obstructed by any imagined possibility of failure, we work on simply without further planning along the line of action that lies plain before us ; our impulse or desire carries us on with full force and concentration of energy, because it is untroubled and unobstructed.[1]

But suppose that the sky becomes overcast, threatening a blizzard ; or that the snow underfoot becomes so soft as greatly to impede our progress ; or let any other difficulty arise that renders us a little doubtful of attaining our end. At once we begin to hope : we hope the weather will hold good ; we hope the snow will harden ; we trudge on, no longer confident, but full of hope, contemplating the desired end, enjoying in anticipation the food we desire and seek. But the threat, however faint, of some cause of failure leads us to concentrate our efforts a little more, keeps our minds more constantly occupied with the one all-important end, restrains us from all unnecessary dispersion of our energies. That is a fundamental law of all impulse, all conation ; obstruction leads to more explicit definition of the end and of the means to it, brings the conative process more vividly into consciousness. Hope, then, is not a new force added to our desire ; it is merely a new way in which the desire operates when confidence is no longer complete. So long as the threat is slight or distant, our desire continues to carry with it a pleasurable anticipation of attainment ; that is characteristic of the state of hope.

But let the difficulties loom larger ; the snow begins to fall and the wind rises against us. Then hope gives place to anxiety, or alternates with it ; and there is no sharp line of transition between the two states. In anxiety our attention becomes still further concentrated upon the task in hand, but especially upon the means, rather than

[1] See p. 385.

upon the end. We think of every possibility ; we try to think out new means to meet the hitherto unforeseen difficulty. We consider whether it might not be wiser to leave the less vigorous members of the party in some sheltered spot, while the stronger push on with all possible speed to find the much desired store of food. The pleasurable anticipation of success, which coloured our state of hope, gives place to the painful thought of failure and its consequences ; we begin to think, not so much of the meal we shall enjoy, but rather of our state if we should fail to attain the end of our desire ; we picture ourselves camping once more without food ; we think of the night of troubled dreams and continued anxiety, and of ourselves setting out once more in a weakened condition. This is not the effect of a new force ; it is the same force, the desire for food, working under changed intellectual conditions. Shand says : " Anxiety is a constant stimulus, sustaining attention and thought and the bodily processes subservient to desire. . . . Anxiety counteracts the extravagant anticipations of hope—it counteracts by watchfulness and forethought the careless attitude into which we are apt to fall through the influence of hope." [1] I submit that anxiety is the name by which we denote our state when the means we are taking towards the desired end begin to seem inadequate, when we cast about for possible alternatives and begin to anticipate the pains of failure. I suggest that, if in such case any new conative force enters into the process, it is the impulse of fear awakened by the thought of the consequences of failure, or that of anger roused, according to the general law of anger,[2] by obstruction to the course of conation. I maintain that anxiety in itself is not a conative force distant from, and capable of being added to, the original desire.

As confidence passes into hope, when difficulties arise ; and as hope passes into anxiety when the difficulties grow more serious and threatening ; so anxiety passes into despondency, as we begin to feel that our difficulties are too great to be overcome by any effort. When hope fades away and becomes faint, we begin to despond ; or in

[1] *Op. cit.* p. 482. [2] See p. 51.

poetical language we might say that despondency drives out hope ; and in similar language we might describe anxiety as a conflict between hope and despondency, each of the antagonists gaining in turn the upper hand. But this would be metaphorical language. When in an earlier chapter I wrote of conflict between the impulses of fear and curiosity, or of fear and anger, or of positive and negative self-feeling, that was not the language of metaphor. For in each of those cases there are at work two impulses of opposed tendency which really conflict ; as we see in the hesitating alternating behaviour of the animal or the child that is at once fearful and curious, or angry and yet afraid—" Willing to wound, and yet afraid to strike." But in hope and despondency, and when they alternate in anxiety, the motive or conative tendency and the end are the same throughout. The states differ only in that in hope the desire of the end is qualified and supported by pleasant anticipation of attainment; while in despondency our desire is coloured and checked by the painful anticipation of failure. In despondency we trudge on, but with lowered heads and drooping shoulders ; we have to reinforce our desire by volition, by calling up all our resolution ; that is to say, by holding up our idea of self, evoking our self-assertive tendency. We say : " No matter how hopeless our effort, we will not give in ; if we must die, we will die gamely, struggling to the end as Englishmen should." In so far as in despondency our efforts are less vigorous than in hope, the difference is sufficiently accounted for by the most general law of feeling, namely, that pleasure reinforces and sustains the activities it qualifies, while pain tends to weaken and suppress them. And in anxiety we have no true conflict of opposed impulses of hope and despondency ; we have merely the one desire or conative tendency, working under such conditions that pleasurable anticipation of success and painful anticipation of failure are about equally balanced ; the probabilities seem to be about equal, and we alternate between the two states. Shand, attempting to define the tendency of despondency and its biological function, says : " Despondency weakens desire, just as hope strengthens it " ; and then he is hard put to it to find a use, a biological justification and *raison d'être*, for such an impulse It serves, he suggests, to turn us from the particular line of action we are pursuing as means to the desired end, and to make us look about for other means. But this is just the function of pain as we see it at work all down the scale of life from the protozoon to man.

Now imagine our polar party overwhelmed by a blizzard, or arriving at the place where the food was stored and finding that the store has been broken open and everything eaten by bears. No possibility of success remains ; our strength is exhausted ; the most hopeful has to face the certainty of death from cold and starvation. Despondency gives place to despair ; we resign all hope, our efforts relax, and we lie down to die. Or, if we are resolute men, we do first whatever seems worth doing ; we write a letter of farewell to our friends or bring the log-book faithfully up to date, in the one hope that is still possible, the hope that our remains will be found by other explorers. If we are weak, we give way to the impulse of distress [1] and cry aloud for help, until we realise the utter futility of that impulse also, and complete despair overwhelms us.

Shand finds great difficulty in attempting to define the tendency and end of despair. In literature he finds many statements to the effect that despair imparts a new and desperate energy to our efforts, and he formulates four laws of despair : (1) " Despair tends to evoke an energy in desire and a resolution capable of attempting the most dangerous and uncertain actions " ; (2) " Despair excludes all hope from desire, and only arises after all hope is excluded " ; [2] (3) " Despair tends to weaken and discourage desire." But the first law states that despair evokes an energy in desire, and therefore a fourth law is needed to reconcile these contradictory statements, and

[1] See p. 378.

[2] This sentence illustrates very well the dangers of admitting to scientific discourse the looseness of language permissible in poetry. How is despair to exclude hope, if it only arises after all hope has already been excluded ?

we read : (4) " Despair tends to weaken the desire which submits to its influence, and to strengthen the desire which triumphs over it." This goes a long way in the personification of desires and the emotions of desire. We are asked to regard despair as a new force with which the primary desire (of whose system it is said to be a part) enters into a conflict like that of two persons ; the primary desire struggles against this new force, and either absorbs it and adds it to itself, or succumbs to it in despair ; and we are left to imagine the emotion of despair triumphant and exulting over the prostrate desire.

The true explanation of those forms of conduct which justify such phrases as " the courage of despair " is, I think, as follows : So long as there appears any possibility of attaining our desired end, we carefully follow out our adopted plan, adapting our actions in detail at each stage by taking anxious thought. But, when we see that all our carefully thought-out plans are of no avail, we may lose our self-control, relax our intellectual efforts, and abandon ourselves to the crude instinctive impulses which underlay all our deliberate efforts ; and then we strive blindly, wildly, purely instinctively, like animals. Our polar party, arrived at the crisis we have imagined, might throw aside all its equipment, all its cohesion and organisations and plans, and break up into its units ; each man might rush blindly on with, as we say, the blind courage of despair. But if this is courage, it is the courage of an animal impelled to struggle to the end by purely instinctive fear or anger.

Hume formulated a fundamental law of desire, which explains the attitude of despair, when he wrote : " We are no sooner acquainted with the impossibility of satisfying any desire, than the desire itself vanishes." This statement goes perhaps too far ; it is an exaggeration of the truth. The truth seems to be that the intellectual apprehension of the impossibility of attaining the desired end terminates all our efforts after it ; we cease to look forward to the end or to strive towards it. Our attitude becomes wholly retrospective ; but the desire lives on in the peculiar form of regret. Suppose that you have desired to help a friend in difficulties, but have delayed too long or have taken insufficiently active steps to prevent his dying, overwhelmed by his misfortune. Your desire is not entirely extinguished. In a sense it may become more acute than ever before. You say : " Oh, how I wish that I had done more or acted more promptly ! " expressing clearly the persistence of your desire ; and, though nothing can be done, you think of all the things you might have done, if you only had understood the urgency of his need ; and every such thought in which your desire now expresses itself is coloured with the pain of a baffled and thwarted desire that cannot achieve its end. That is regret ; and, if self-reproach enters into the state, it is one of remorse.

Despair, then, is the turning-point at which we cease to look forward, and, instead, look back with the finally thwarted desire which is regret. Our polar explorers, sitting in their tent awaiting death, will, if they are not utterly prostrated, be filled with regret—regret that they did not take this or that step, that they did not start out earlier on their return journey, regret that they did not make their stores of food at shorter intervals, regret for all the many things that might have made the difference between success and failure. But regret is no more a new force added to the primary desire than is confidence or hope, anxiety, despondency, or despair.

We have hitherto considered the derived emotions as they attend the operation of a desire of great intensity ; but it must be recognised that in fainter forms the same states of feeling accompany and qualify our most trivial efforts. For example, you set out in good time, as you believe, to catch your morning train to town. Having plenty of time, you walk in confidence, never doubting your catching it. Then you remember that your watch has been irregular of late, and you notice other persons hurrying towards the railway station ; hope replaces confidence Or shall we say, in poetical language, that hope drives out confidence ? You ask the time of a passer-by, and, according to his statement, your watch is slow ; hope passes into anxiety, and you begin to look for a cab or bus or other means of accelerating your passage.

The church clock confirms the opinion of the passer-by, and anxiety passes into despondency ; it seems hardly worth while to hurry on, your chance of catching the train is so small. From a distance you see the train arrive, and despondency becomes despair ; and, as it steams away, despair passes into regret. Just in proportion to the intensity of your desire to catch the train will be the intensity of these emotions.

In the light of the foregoing discussion I would add a few words to what was said in Chapter V., of joy and sorrow ; for these two emotions are closely allied to the emotions discussed in the foregoing pages.

Shand regards sorrow as one of the primary emotions and as one of the great forces of character. I maintain that it is rather a derived emotion, one of the retrospective emotions of desire ; that, in short, it is a special form of regret, essentially a regret that springs from the sentiment of love, and therefore a tender regret. The most frequent and typical occasion of sorrow is the death of one we love. Consider the sequence of emotions we experience during the fatal sickness of a much-loved child. While the child is in perfect health, love's desire to cherish and protect its object attains an ever renewed and progressive satisfaction in loving services rendered and in marks of love returned. The actions prompted by the desire of the sentiment of love are performed with confidence. Such confidence is, I submit, a variety of confidence properly called joy. It is a joyful activity attended by a joyful tender emotion. Its peculiarity is that desire is progressively satisfied while it continues unabated. Let the child show some slight indisposition, and we hope he will soon be well ; our tender care is redoubled. He grows worse rather than better, and we become anxious, hope alternating with despondency, and yielding place to it more and more as the little patient's strength ebbs away and the symptoms grow more serious. It becomes clear that he cannot live, and we despair. He dies, and despair gives place to sorrow : for our attitude is no longer prospective, but wholly retrospective. Desire no longer prompts to action ; the conative tendencies of the sentiment, especially the protective impulse, still prompt us to occupy our minds with its object ; we cannot dismiss it, and would not if we could ; we hug our sorrow ; for the sentiment is alive, and its impulses working constantly within us are baffled and painful just because they can attain no satisfaction ; we regret that we did not do this or that, take this or that precaution, act earlier or more energetically. Sorrow is, then, a tender regret. It seems to me clear that we never experience an emotion that can properly be called sorrow, save in connection with a sentiment of love and the complete thwarting of its impulses, which can hardly be brought about in any other way than by the destruction of its object.

If this be true, then clearly sorrow is not a primary but a derived emotion ; and, like those other emotions of desire, prospective and retrospective, it springs from no specific conative disposition, has no impulse or tendency of its own, is not a force in itself ; and, having no disposition, it cannot be organised within the sentiment of love nor yet within that of hate (as Shand maintains). Shand describes sorrow as having three distinct tendencies or impulses : (1) To cry out for aid and comfort ; (2) to cling to its object and to resist consolation ; (3) to restore its object. Of these alleged tendencies the first and second are contradictory or incompatibles ; the tendency to cling to the object and to restore it is the tendency of the tender emotion organised in the sentiment of love. The tendency to cry out for aid and comfort when our powers are completely baffled no doubt does often enter into sorrow ; but I submit that it does not essentially belong to it. It seems to be the expression of a primary instinctive disposition which I have neglected to distinguish in the earlier chapters. This tendency seems to manifest itself whenever our strength proves wholly insufficient to achieve the end that we keenly strive after, no matter what may be the nature of the conation at work in us. The working of this impulse to cry out for aid and comfort seems to be accompanied by a true primary emotion which, perhaps, is best called "distress." This is the emotion displayed so freely and frequently by the infant when he wails aloud,

We learn to suppress its outward marks ; but, though we can suppress our cries and sobs or transmute them to a mere sigh, we cannot so easily prevent the watering of the eyes, which is a part of this instinctive expression ; and even the strong man, when he has reached the utmost limit of his strength in the pursuit of any strongly desired end, may break down completely, sobbing, freely shedding tears, or crying aloud to God for help.

Shand speaks of the sorrow of a child when we forcibly take away from him his toy. But this emotion, where it is not predominantly anger, is, I submit, the emotion of distress ; and the common sequence upon such an occasion is an outburst of anger, followed by the tears and cries of distress, when the child finds that his angry efforts are unavailing.

Shand maintains that hate, equally with love, may generate sorrow, when its object is seen to be healthy and prosperous. This seems to me to be a misuse of, or at least a laxity in the use of, the term, which we should strive to avoid ; for only by the strictest care in our terminology can we hope to attain to further understanding and general agreement in this difficult province of psychology. And it is the business of scientific writers to specialise the terms by which in popular speech our emotional states are denoted with little discrimination of their finer differences, rather than to ignore the finer shades of difference in wellnigh synonymous words.

I submit, then, that our state of feeling on witnessing the success and prosperity of a hated person should not be called sorrow, but rather chagrin. This feeling is also one of the retrospective emotions of desire, but of the desire of hate, the desire to destroy, to bring down, or in any way thwart the hated object. It also is a form of regret, a regret having no element of tender emotion, but only the bitterness of thwarted anger and increased fear. And, if we have been striving against the hated object with all our powers and find our utmost efforts brought to naught, this feeling will include an element of distress, manifested perhaps by tears and sobs or even wild cries for help.

I turn now to consider an objection that may be raised

against this simplified view of these emotions of desire. In an earlier chapter it was said that we properly speak of a man as having a timid or fearful, an irascible, an inquisitive, a humble, or a self-assertive disposition. The word " disposition " is here used in the larger sense, namely, to denote the sum total of the person's natural dispositions ; and the qualifying adjective denotes the predominance in the total disposition of some one of the primary affective-conative dispositions. Surely, it may be said, we may with equal propriety speak of a hopeful, an anxious, or a despondent disposition. And, it may be asked, if that is a proper use of language, does it not justify Shand's assumption that each of these emotions springs from its own innate disposition, and is a primary emotion in the same sense as fear, anger, disgust, tenderness, curiosity, or positive and negative self-feeling ? If a man of timid or irascible disposition owes this peculiarity to the great strength or easy excitability of the disposition of fear or of anger, must we not assume that a man of hopeful or of despondent disposition owes this peculiarity in the same way to the native strength or excitability of a disposition of hope or despondency ?

It must be admitted that the common use of language does seem to justify this assumption of parallelism of the emotions of desire with the primary emotions. But, again, we must not allow ourselves to attach undue importance to the common forms of speech. If the facts can be more simply explained, we may disregard this evidence of common speech and accept the simpler explanation. First, I submit that the individual peculiarities which we are now considering, such as hopefulness and anxious-ness, may be more properly spoken of as peculiarities of temper rather than of disposition. I suggest that we should speak of a man as having an irascible or timid disposition, but a confident or hopeful or despondent temper. Now, if these emotions and the corresponding peculiarities of temper were rooted each in its own innate disposition, as are the primary emotions, we should expect to find that they are independent variables. The primary emotions are independently variable—that is to say, the native intensity and excitability of each of them varies from man to man, independently of the intensity and excitability of the rest of them; but obviously the derived emotions are not. The hopeful temper is a lesser degree of the confident temper; the despondent temper is closely allied to the despairing temper, and related to it as a lesser degree of the same tendency; while the anxious temper lies between the hopeful and the despondent; and every gradation occurs between the extremes of the confident and the despairing tempers.

But there are other forms of temper: there is the steadfast temper, and the fickle or variable temper; and there seems to be a range of native varieties of temper of which the extremes are denoted by the terms violent and equable or placid temper. It seems clear that these peculiarities of temper, which in the main are native endowments, are very important as determinants of character, exerting considerable influence upon the course of development of each man's character throughout his life, but especially in youth. How then are we to account for them? I presume that even Mr. Shand would not attribute fickleness of temper to a special innate disposition of fickleness, nor steadfastness nor violence nor placidity to corresponding special dispositions. Consider a number of men, all of well-balanced innate disposition—that is to say, endowed with dispositions in which no one of the primary affective-conative dispositions is disproportionately strong. These men may nevertheless differ widely in respect of temper.

The principal factors of temper seem to be of three kinds. First, the conative tendencies, though well balanced, may all be strong or all weak; or any or all of them may stand in some intermediate position in a weak-strong scale. Secondly, independently of their intensity, they may be either extremely persistent or but little persistent. That is to say, each man is natively endowed with conative tendencies (a will, if one uses that word in the widest sense as denoting the general power of striving, as distinct from the will in the more special sense in which it is identical with, or is the expression of, the developed character) which have two independently variable attributes, namely, intensity and persistence ; they may be low or high in either scale independently of their position in the other. Thirdly, a great factor of temper, also independently variable, is the native susceptibility of conation to the influences of pleasure and of pain. There are some men whose desires and strivings seem to be very easily and strongly influenced by pleasure and by pain. Pleasure greatly strengthens, supports, and confirms their conative tendencies ; and pain works powerfully in the opposite way, strongly checking, depressing, and diverting their strivings and desires. These are the people of whom we say that they have very sensitive feelings. Some men, on the other hand, are comparatively indifferent to pleasure and to pain. They are not easily turned aside by pain, nor strongly led on by pleasure. Their feelings are not very sensitive, we say. It is impossible to know whether this difference is more properly described by saying that the strivings of men of the former class are more strongly affected by a given degree of pleasure or of pain, or by the statement that the pleasure and the pain they experience are more acute, and therefore exert greater influence upon conation. But that men do differ widely by native constitution in this way seems clear ; and the differences are no doubt most obvious in respect of the influence of bodily pleasures and pains.

If it is true, as I suggest, that the conative endowment of individuals varies in these three ways, in respect of these three attributes, namely, intensity, persistence, and affectability, we can, I think, explain all the varieties of temper as being conjunctions of different degrees of these three attributes. There will be eight well-marked types, corresponding to the eight possible combinations : (1) The most steadfast and confident temper is that which results from the conjunction of high intensity and persistency with low affectability. (2) The most fickle and shallow temper results from the opposite conjunction, namely, high affectability with low intensity and persistence. (3) The conjunction of high affectability and high intensity with low persistence gives a violent, unstable

temper: the sort of man who alternates between confidence or hope and despondency or despair. (4) The
despondent temper is that which combines low affectability
and persistency with high intensity. (5) Great affectability combined with great persistency and low intensity
gives the anxious temper. (6) The hopeful temper results
from the conjunction of all three attributes in high degree.
(7) The placid temper combines high persistency with low
intensity and affectability; and (8) the conjunction of all
three attributes in low degree gives the sluggish temper.
It is possible that we ought to recognise two further motive
peculiarities: the one consisting in greater liability to the
influence of pleasure than of pain, and the other the
converse of this; these would account more adequately
perhaps for the hopeful and the despondent tempers, and
are perhaps required for their explanation.

If the foregoing account of the peculiarities of temper is
approximately correct, the argument from the usage of
common speech, when it refers to hopeful, anxious, or
despondent dispositions, need carry no serious weight
against the view of the nature of the derived emotions
which is suggested in this chapter.

An objection of a different kind may be raised to this
view. It may be asked—If hope and despair and despondency and the other derived emotions are not conative
forces sustaining thought and controlling action, what
function have they to discharge? Of what use are they
to us? This is a form of a wider question which may be
asked of all the emotions, considered as modes of experience. And, of course, the question has been asked, in a
still more general form, of experience or consciousness in
general. Leaving that widest form of the question, I will
attempt only to suggest an answer to the question which is
applicable both to the primary emotions and to the derived
emotions. I suggest that those qualitatively distinct modes
of feeling which we call the primary emotions have the
specific function of enabling the creature that experiences
them to recognise its own state and tendency at the
moment of experience, and also the state and tendency
of other creatures of its own species. We may see the

value for the control of behaviour of such qualitatively distinct modes of feeling, if we imagine a man or an animal whose instinctive reactions were evoked without any such accompaniment, one in which the various instinctive modes of behaviour were excited without any change of feeling, or in which all the instinctive reactions were accompanied by the same quality of feeling, a perfectly general feeling of emotional excitement without specific varieties of quality. Is it not obvious that such a creature would be greatly handicapped in comparison with one in which the excitement of each instinctive mode of behaviour is reflected in consciousness by a specific quality of feeling ? For the latter learns to recognise each of these qualities of feeling, and through them becomes aware of the tendency of its action ; and this is the necessary first step towards intelligent control of action. The other creature would find itself carrying out each step of the train of instinctive behaviour without having any power of foreseeing the coming phase, and therefore without any possibility of preventing, controlling, or modifying its actions. The qualities of the primary emotions serve, I suggest, to enable mind or intelligence to get a grip upon instinct, and so begin to establish the control which in the well-developed character becomes wellnigh complete. It seems obvious that the emotion-qualities subserve this function, and are indispensable to it in ourselves. One feels the awakening of, say, anger or fear within one as the behaviour of another man becomes insulting or threatening, and says to oneself—Now I must keep a tight hold on myself. Because the quality of the emotion implies the kind of actions which we shall be liable instinctively to display, we are enabled in some measure to counteract and control the tendencies to such actions. And, though it is more difficult to describe or to imagine the working of a similar process in the animal mind, we may fairly presume that on its lower plane and in simpler fashion the emotional experience of the animal subserves this same function. Further, if we consider how widespread and important among men and all the gregarious animals are the reactions due to the primitive sympathetic tendency, we shall see that the emotional qualities play an essential part in enabling each of us to understand the state of mind of our fellows, and therefore to some extent to foresee and adapt ourselves to the actions they are about to display. It is difficult to see how we could ever achieve any sympathetic insight into the minds and hearts of our fellow-men, if we were not equipped with these capacities for the specific qualities of emotion and the primitive tendency to experience them when we witness their outward manifestations in our fellows.

The derived emotions may be supposed to subserve a similar function in human life, although in the animal world they seem to occur only in the most rudimentary forms.

Note to p. 371.—It is perhaps worth while to point out that this view of the nature and condition of " confidence " points the way to a more satisfactory account of " belief " than any that we as yet have. It has been generally recognised that action, or readiness to act, upon belief is the best, if not the sole objective, evidence of its reality. It is perhaps less generally recognised that belief is always determined by conation, that there is no belief without desire ; yet such seem to be the fact. Propositions about things that awake in us no desire, no conation, are neither believed, not disbelieved, nor doubted ; in face of them we remain merely neutral. It has also been widely recognised that belief is a state of an emotional nature, or at least allied to the emotions. I suggest that " belief " is essentially the same emotional state as " confidence," and is accordingly a member of the continuous series of derived emotions of desire. The only essential difference between " confidence " and " belief " is that the former feeling qualifies our active striving towards a desired end, while " belief " is the feeling which qualifies processes on the plane of intellectual activity which cannot issue forthwith in action. If I have good evidence that a desired object is at a certain place, I go with confidence to find it ; but if I also know that there is no possibility of access to that place, I merely believe that the desired object is there. Doubt bears the same relation to belief that anxiety bears to confidence ; it is anxiety on the plane of intellectual activity when action is necessarily postponed or suspended. (See article in *Psychological Review* for 1921, " Belief as a Derived Emotion.")

NOTES ON CHAPTERS III. TO IX.

THE critics of the instinct theory find much comfort in the fact that the exponents of the theory do not agree as to the number and the definition of the human instincts, pointing to the long lists of some authors and the short lists of others, with the implication that a theory whose exponents disagree so widely in detail must be wholly false. They seem to demand that any theory of instincts must, if it is to be acceptable, spring full-blown and perfect from the brain of its propounder. As well might they reject the theory of the chemical elements on the ground that when John Dalton first expounded it, the theory was incomplete and has since undergone many changes in the way of improvements and refinements. The oft-repeated jibes at the lists of human instincts are as out of place as would be similar jibes at the constantly changing list of chemical elements. It would be presumptuous to pretend to draw up a final and completed list of the human instincts. But it is, perhaps, worth while to attempt to make the list as complete as the present state of knowledge allows. The instincts defined in the first edition of this book have, I venture to think, withstood the fires of criticism remarkably well. They have been accepted uncritically, if provisionally, by a great many authors ; and more or less critically, with some few proposed modifications, by many others. They may even be said, I think, to have been incorporated in orthodox British psychology. Further observation and reflection has led me to add to the list several instincts which perhaps are of minor importance for social psychology, but of which one at least, the instinct of laughter, is of great theoretical interest.

The Instinct of Laughter [1]

Under certain circumstances presently to be defined, the normal human being laughs, or experiences an impulse, a tendency, to laugh, which often it is difficult or impossible to control or suppress. If he attempts to suppress it, he feels the impulse surging up or bubbling up within him and threatening to overpower his best efforts to suppress its outward manifestation. These outward manifestations are highly complex, but specific; that is to say, they are constant in general form for all members of the human species.[2] The principal features are the spasmodic action of the diaphragm and other respiratory muscles, with an interrupted closure of the glottis, which results in the peculiar cachinnation. This behaviour, which to a Martian observer might well seem wholly useless and utterly absurd and (if he were endowed with a propensity to laughter of a quite different kind) ridiculous, bears most, though not quite all, the usual marks of an instinctive reaction. First, it is common to all members of the species. Secondly, it is unquestionably inborn, unlearnt, or provided for in the innate constitution of the race and the individual. Thirdly, it is actuated by a felt impulse, and is more or less subject to voluntary control, and can be partially but not perfectly imitated by voluntary effort. Fourthly, it tends to inhibit all

---

[1] A fuller exposition of the view of laughter here stated may be found in an article in *Psyche*, vol. ii., " A New Theory of Laughter," and in my *Outline of Psychology*, London and New York, 1923.

[2] It is commonly said that laughter is peculiar to the human species. But Dr. R. Yerkes has recently demonstrated to me the fact that his two domesticated chimpanzees can be provoked by tickling about the neck to a reaction which remarkably resembles human laughter, including the emission of spasmodically interrupted voice sounds. The gibbon also emits an interrupted musical cry remarkably suggestive of laughter, as I have repeatedly observed in wandering through the forests of Borneo.

other forms of bodily and mental activity of a voluntary or impulsive nature, all other conations ; and this inhibitory power is peculiarly strong in the case of the impulse to laughter. Fifthly, the outward expressions are accompanied, not only by a felt impulse which is apt to grow more intense the more we attempt to suppress it, but also by a peculiar emotional experience best described by the words " merriment " or " amusement " or " gaiety." Sixthly, the reaction is elicited, not by any merely physical stimulation, but only through the perception or intellectual appreciation of some complex situation of a specific nature. Seventhly, laughter, like all other instinctive expressions, illustrates (and in a peculiarly striking way) the principle of primitive passive sympathy : when we merely see or hear the laughter of others, without perceiving, or in any way knowing, the object that provokes their laughter, the laughter impulse is directly stirred within us.

In an important respect laughter differs from typical instinctive behaviour ; namely, it does not tend to produce any specific change in the circumstances that provoke it ; it seems to have no outward goal towards which the laughter-shaken subject strives and by the attainmenc of which his impulse is allayed or satisfied. The goal of the impulse remains for the most part extremely ill-defined in the mind of the subject, and can only be objectively defined in terms of the bodily and mental changes which result from the laughter. These bodily and mental changes are in the main of a stimulating nature. Laughter seems to be a physiological stimulus of a general kind ; it seems to quicken the respiratory and circulatory processes, and in these, and perhaps also in other, ways to produce a general sense of well-being or euphoria.

Most of the many eminent authors who have discussed laughter have been wholly or chiefly concerned to define in general terms the nature of the ridiculous. Some such general definition must be a part of any theory of laughter. But we can with advantage approach that problem indirectly, by first asking what is the biological function of laughter.   In the light of the theory of evolution we may confidently assume that a highly complex function such as laughter, involving as it does the nice co-ordination of a multitude of nervous and muscular processes, and a function which is provided ready-made in the innate constitution of all members of a species, we may assume that such a function is of biological value, that it is useful or beneficial, either to the individual or to the species ;   in fact we may assume that, like all other instincts, it has what the biologists call " survival value." What then is the value or utility of laughter ?   The answer to this, the most fundamental question, would seem to be that the essential and primary function of laughter is the production of those bodily and mental effects mentioned in the foregoing paragraph, namely, a promotion of the respiratory and circulatory processes and perhaps of other vital processes, a general stirring up of the basal metabolic processes which is reflected in consciousness as euphoria, or the sense of increased well-being.   The opposite of euphoria is the sense of depression which accompanies a depressed condition of the fundamental vital functions ;   laughter removes this depression by exerting a generally stimulating effect throughout the organism.   But it does more than this, it diverts us ;   that is to say, it has a quite peculiar power of arresting the stream of thought and inhibiting all other bodily functions. Even such automatised or deeply habitual bodily activities as walking and standing are apt to be interrupted by laughter.   We stand still while we rock to and fro ;   and, if the laughter impulse is excited in maximal intensity, we are apt to sink down, our knees loosened, and to roll and shake helplessly upon the ground.

What, then, are the circumstances under which this very peculiar inhibitory but stimulating behaviour may be advantageous ?   Here we see how this way of approaching the problem of the ridiculous enables us to avoid the error into which almost all writers on laughter have fallen. Almost without exception they have assumed, without question, that laughter is the expression of pleasure and that the ridiculous object or event or situation provokes

our laughter because it pleases us ; and they have devoted
all their ingenuity to the impossible task of discovering
what element or aspect of the ridiculous it is that pleases
us. Thus Thomas Hobbes, discerning truly enough,
that the ridiculous is almost always of the nature of some
mishap or shortcoming of some human being, some
failure or disappointment, some miscarriage or clumsiness
of action, some stupidity or grotesque defect, cynically
suggested that these things please us because they make
us feel superior to the person or persons who suffer or
display them ; thus he arrived at the famous theory that
laughter is due to a " sudden glory."

But when, approaching the problem from the biological standpoint, we ask—Why should we laugh when
we are pleased ? We can find no answer. If we accept
the common assumption that we laugh because we are
pleased, laughter must appear to be otiose, entirely without
utility, rendering no service to the organism that laughs.

Professor Bergson, starting from the same facts, has
attempted to remedy this radical defect of the Hobbesian
theory by assigning to laughter a social function and
utility. He sees no benefit to the laugher, but suggests
that in laughing we are performing a socially advantageous
function in disciplining the person who is ridiculous by
reason of his clumsy or inefficient activities or his bizarre
appearance. Now it is true that in highly civilised communities, and especially perhaps among the French,
laughter is, more or less, deliberately made to subserve
the ends of social discipline. But we can hardly suppose
that this was its primary function and utility for the sake
of which the laughter instinct was evolved in the species.
Social discipline is rather a secondary and late application of the instinctive tendency, arising only in a highly
developed and conventionalised society.

Let us then free our minds from the quite groundless
assumption that we laugh because we are pleased, and
let us look at the facts with fresh eyes. We then see that
the objects, events, and situations that are universally
ridiculous are such as in themselves are displeasing to us ;
they are such that, if we did not laugh at them, if they did

not provoke us to this mysterious reaction, they would displease us or be in some degree painful or distressing to us; for they are essentially the minor misfortunes and defects of our fellow-creatures. Mankind is a social species, and, like all the social animals, the species is endowed with the primitive sympathetic tendencies.[1] We have seen in Chapters IV. and XV. that to experience the emotions and feelings we see expressed by our fellows is natural to all men, though in some persons such sympathetic induction of emotion seems to occur much more readily than in others. And we have seen that such emotional contagion is the very cement of society at all levels, from that of the most simple animal groups to that of the most elaborated human communities. Without such primitive passive sympathy no effective social life would be possible. And, since man's evolution beyond the animal level has been essentially a social evolution, it was rendered possible only by the delicacy or readiness of these primitive sympathetic responses in the human species. But, as the social life of mankind developed, as men gathered in larger groups, and as the imaginative powers of primitive man grew stronger,[2] primitive sympathy, though indispensable as a social bond securing uniformity of feeling and co-operative action throughout the group, must have involved a certain grave disadvantage. This world, as we are often told, is a vale of tears; and this was true for primitive man in a higher degree than for us. Think of his situation, an almost defenceless naked savage, with little knowledge and only the crudest of material possessions, shivering and cowering in a world full of dangers and hardships. Imagine a community of such creatures, each so constituted by nature as sympathetically to respond to all the emotional expressions of his fellows, both upon direct perception of them and imaginatively. It is obvious that primitive sympathy, indispensable as it was for the life of the group, must have involved a heavy burden upon each member:

[1] Cp. p. 79.
[2] The development of imaginative power was one of the chief, perhaps the chief, step that raised men above the animals.

for he had not only to bear his own mishaps and disappointments and failures, but also to share the distresses and pains of his companions. Is it fantastic to suppose that the burden thus imposed was too heavy to be borne ; that primitive sympathy, which alone rendered possible a higher social development, threatened to destroy the individuals through depressing their vitality by excess of sympathetic distresses ? Some remedy was needed, some antidote to primitive sympathy, an antidote which, while leaving men delicately responsive to all the more intense emotional expressions about them, should spare them the unnecessary suffering involved in sympathetically sharing all the minor pains and distresses which were the daily lot of each member of the group. The problem of devising such an antidote might well seem insoluble ; yet Nature seems to have solved it by inventing laughter, by implanting in each member of the race the tendency to laugh when confronted by the spectacle of any of the minor mishaps and distresses of his fellows. And by thus inventing laughter she created the ridiculous.

The laughter-apparatus seems to be so placed in our constitution that every weaker impulse to sympathetic distress or pain is at once short-circuited into this most recently evolved and most specifically human of the instinctive dispositions ; and the instinctive reaction thus provoked then prevents our dwelling upon the ridiculous object, the mildly distressful situation, and stimulates our organic processes in a way which not only prevents our suffering the depression of sympathetic distress, but also exhilarates us and brings us to the condition of euphoria. The endowment of the species with the instinct of laughter has in short converted what in its absence would have been a depressing burden of frequent though minor sympathetic pains into occasions of refreshment and recreation.

The capacity for laughter, once acquired, men learnt, as with other instinctive tendencies, to make use of it in a more or less intentional fashion ; in other words, men learnt to joke, for to joke is to create by artifice the ridiculous or laughter-provoking situation. At first the practical joke, beloved of children and primitive minds of all times and places, was the standard agent for the provocation of laughter: a man was tripped up, or his cup dashed from his lips, or his meaty bone was tumbled in the mud of the cave's floor. Later came the more refined joke and the funny story at the expense of some member of the group. And, with the growth of civilisation, appeared the professional jester, the clown who, for the value of pay or social esteem, voluntarily makes himself ridiculous by his antics and stupidities. And, because we know that the distresses of the clown are self-induced and can be terminated at will, he must resort to a show of the extreme forms of pain and distress, he must submit to violent blows and heavy falls and make a great show of distress and disappointment such as, if they were real, would provoke in us sympathetic suffering.

We laugh when a man hits his thumb with his hammer; but we shrink in sympathetic pain if his hand is crushed in a machine. If a man clumsily lets fall the tasty morsel which he was contemplating with gusto, we laugh, we enjoy his discomfiture; but, when we see the same man suddenly deprived of that which is most dear to him, we suffer a sympathetic pain that may be wellnigh intolerable, and we look out on the world with sadder eyes, depressed and discouraged. And if we had not the capacity to laugh at our fellows' minor misfortunes, to find their lesser failures and disappointments ridiculous, we should on those occasions suffer in some degree the depression and discouragement that come with the sympathetic pain evoked by their major misfortunes.

The theory of laughter which I have now concisely propounded is capable, I submit, of being successfully applied to the interpretation of every instance of laughter. It is worth while to dwell briefly on some facts which at first sight may seem to offer difficulty. There is little room for doubt that smiling is the natural expression of pleasure. Now the smile is closely associated with laughter; so much so that it is commonly regarded as incipient laughter, or identified with laughter as a part of the total reaction. But there are good grounds for believing that they are distinct modes of reaction and that the association between them is secondary and acquired. We do not always smile as we laugh; there are many forms of laughter, all the hard and bitter forms, which are not accompanied by smiling. In the infant the smile appears some two months earlier than the laugh—a difference of date which marks them as innately distinct. The intimate association that grows up between these two distinct reactions, smiling and laughter, may well be attributed to the fact that, when we have laughed, we commonly experience in some degree its pleasing euphoric effects ; we are pleased, and our laughter, as it dies away, gives place to smiling.

Sometimes we laugh at hearing of great disasters ; and the more the horrors are piled up, the more we laugh, although we may feel a little ashamed of ourselves for so doing. In such instances the disaster is one affecting persons remote in time or place, and the recital of their suffering brings them but faintly before our minds ; hence these remote though severe sufferings work upon us in the same way as the minor distresses of persons closer to us.

There is a form of laughter, chiefly displayed by young children, when they sport and gambol in fulness of health and energy. Like their other bodily movements at such times, it is a mere bubbling over of exuberant nervous energy. They are not laughing *at* anything, though the slightest touch of the ridiculous may redouble their laughter ; they are merely finding vent through various motor mechanisms for the excess of energy within them.

Humour

One strong feature of this new theory of laughter is the fact that it renders possible for the first time an intelligible account of the nature of humour. It is clear that to possess a " sense of the ridiculous " is not the same thing as to be humorous. When we say that a man " possesses a sense of the ridiculous " we mean merely that he readily laughs at whatever is comic, absurd, or ridiculous. Many a man is very ready to laugh at the minor troubles of his neighbours and yet is not at all humorous.   To be humorous or " to have a sense of humour " is to be capable of laughing at one's own minor misfortunes, and thus to be able to make of them occasions for that stimulating refreshing activity we call merriment.   The egoistic humorist goes about the world perpetually drawing attention to, and, making fun of, his own deficiencies. But there is also the larger humour which finds occasion for laughter in those defects and shortcomings which are common to all men ;   such humour, including in its object the laugher himself, does not wound, as does the lower, simpler form of laughter ;   for it brings a bond of fellowship between him who laughs and all his fellows, inviting all men, without discrimination, to share in the genial exercise.   Humorous laughter is thus a higher form which implies the attainment in some degree of the power of viewing ourselves objectively, of seeing ourselves as others see us.

There is a peculiar condition of laughter which might well have served as the cue to the true theory, and is the touchstone which may be applied to all theories ;   namely, laughter on being tickled.   It is obvious that tickle-sensation is not in itself pleasing, but is rather annoying.   When a fly settles on our face and tickles us, we brush it away with slight annoyance ;   one can tickle oneself with a feather without provoking the least tendency to laugh ;   and, if we are persistently tickled in spite of our efforts to escape from the situation, we may be driven frantic.   In order to provoke by tickling the laughter-reaction, it is necessary to tickle in a playful, humorous manner.   If you tickle a child without making clear to him that you are playful and well disposed, he will merely struggle to escape, and will then avoid you.   But if you attack him playfully, you provoke his laughter ;   he then enjoys the game and returns again and again to renew it.   Laughter on being tickled is, then, the most primitive form of humour ;   it implies an appreciation of the ridiculous nature of one's own situation.   Children learn to laugh on being tickled only through tactful and playful repetition of the process ; it is their initiation to the humorous attitude.

In this connection the fact mentioned above that apes may be provoked by tickling to something like laughter is of quite peculiar interest. At first sight it might seem that the fact is fatal to the view here propounded. But Professor Yerkes, who has made a prolonged and intimate study of apes, assures me that what I have written above about children's laughter-reaction to tickling is true also of the ape. If you merely tickle him, he merely shows signs of discomfort and endeavours to escape. You can provoke in him this rudimentary laughter-reaction only by approaching him playfully, making of the tickling a game in which he takes part.

Laughter, then, is according to the theory here propounded a protective reaction, an instinctive endowment which protects us from the depressing influences inseparable from the social existence of a creature in whom the sympathetic reactions are delicately responsive. A man lacking completely the instinct of laughter, but normally endowed with the primitive sympathetic response-tendencies, would very frequently suffer depression of his energies through witnessing and sharing the minor distresses of all his fellows. The possession of the laughter-instinct spares him from these frequent though minor distresses, and actually converts what in its absence would be the occasions of them into occasions of stimulation and recreation. We do not laugh because we are pleased, as so many authors have uncritically assumed ; rather, we laugh because it is our nature to laugh when we witness the minor distresses of our fellows ; and, laughing, we enjoy a pleasant euphoria. After repeatedly experiencing these pleasing effects, we learn, as in the case of all other types of pleasing experiences, to seek the occasions that provoke them. When we feel out of sorts and depressed, we go to the pantomime or to the burlesque drama, where the antics of the clown and the misadventures of the fool may provoke us to health-giving laughter. Or, if we have attained to the level of humorousness, we may prefer the less crude stimulus of refined comedy, which presents the foibles and weaknesses of human nature in their universal aspect, and so evokes that touch of fellow-feeling which makes the whole world kin   For in laughing at the comedy we all laugh together at our common human nature.

Some Minor Instincts

The human species displays some minor reaction-tendencies which seem to occupy a position between the reflexes on the one hand and the instinctive responses on the other. They have commonly been described as " sensation-reflexes." The chief of them are the tendency to scratch an itching spot, coughing, sneezing, yawning, urination, and defecation. All these have in common the following peculiarities : First, the reaction is evolved by some stimulation of sensory nerves ; but, unlike the true reflexes, the reaction does not occur unless the stimulation evokes sensation, makes itself felt by the subject. The corneal reflex, the light reflex of the pupil, the knee-jerk, the plantar and the abdominal reflex, and all the true reflexes may be provoked while we are so intensely occupied as to remain entirely unaware of the provoking stimulations, or when we are surgically anæsthetised by ether or chloroform. But, under such conditions of concentrated attention or of anæsthesia, the so-called sensation-reflexes do not occur. Secondly, the stimulus provokes not only sensory effects in consciousness, but also a felt impulse to action. The itching spot evokes a felt impulse to scratch it ; the tickling in nose or throat evokes a felt impulse to sneeze or cough. And the impulse, though it may be controllable by voluntary effort if it is weak, may grow so strong, if we attempt to inhibit it, as to cause us much discomfort ; and it may prove too strong for our control, so that we break out with a sneeze or a cough in spite of our best effort to suppress the tendency. Thirdly, as with other instinctive reactions, we can imitate these reactions volitionally, but we cannot at will evoke the impulse, except by applying to the sensory nerves the appropriate stimulation. Fourthly, when the impulse is evoked, we can voluntarily reinforce or strengthen it ; as when the spontaneous cough fails to remove the irritating particle.

The impulsive and, at times, compulsive nature of these reactions is the principal ground for regarding them as instinctive rather than merely reflex. In the case of the scratching tendency we have a further ground, namely, that the tendency is perfectly general and may express itself, not in any one movement or particular combination of muscular contractions, but in a multitude of different movements all directed towards the one goal, the removal of the irritating object. We see this clearly in the animals, as well as in ourselves ; the dog or the horse, as well as the man, that has an obstinately itching spot, may resort in turn to a variety of movements for the alleviation of the discomfort ; he may scratch with fore or hind limb, or may bite, or may rub the spot against a post in varied contortions that employ a multitude of muscles and efferent nerve-paths. Further, all such efforts are directed, not by mere sensation, but by intelligent perception of the locality of the itching spot.

If we class these reactions as expressions of very simple instincts, as I think we should, we must recognise that in certain respects they are anomalous, that they do not conform in all ways to the type of instinctive action. Especially they are peculiar in that, like laughter, they do not impel to any activity directed upon the external world ; they do not seek goals external to the organism. Rather, the changes which they impel us to effect and in which they attain their satisfactions are intrinsic to the organism. With the exception of the scratching tendency, all these minor instincts express themselves very constantly through some one system of motor mechanisms, with but little variation in detail upon successive occasions. This peculiarity is due to the fact that in each case the exciting sense-impressions are confined to one locality, and the natural end of the instinct, the change of the condition of the organs affected, can be attained only by the employment of a particular set of muscles.

We should, perhaps, add one more to this list of obscure minor instincts, namely, an instinct to relaxa-

tion, rest, and sleep.   In recognising this tendency as
instinctive, I am following the lead of Professor Claparède,
who strongly urged this view twenty years ago.   Perhaps
the strongest argument in its favour adduced by him is
the analogy between our normal falling asleep and the
hibernating sleep of various animal species, to which it is
difficult to refuse the status of an instinctive process.   But
there are other good grounds for this view.   Fatigue-
sensations seem to provoke a tendency to relaxation and
rest of the organs through which they are evoked.   And
the fatigue-sensations about the eyes and eyelids seem to
have a quite specific influence of this kind tending to
induce closure of the lids, general relaxation, and sleep.
This fact is commonly made use of by the hypnotist in
inducing the hypnotic sleep.   Further, the fact that we
have in various degrees the power of sleeping and of
waking at will, and that this power can be cultivated, goes
to support Professor Claparède's theory.

Supplementary Remarks on Play and Suggestion

Of the topics discussed in Chapter IV., under the head
of " Some General or Non-Specific Innate Tendencies,"
I have little to say in the way of modification or addition.
What was there written of primitive passive sympathy or
the sympathetic induction of the primary emotions seem
to me to stand good and to be of the first importance
for the interpretation of the phenomena of group life,
as I have shown in my *Group Mind*; yet very few
psychologists have accepted the principle or recognised
its importance.

Play remains to me somewhat mysterious.   In the
section on " Play " in Chapter IV., I accepted with some
modification the theory of play propounded by Professor
Groos, namely, that play is the expression of instincts
prematurely and partially developed for the sake of
affording the young creature exercise in the bodily movements which it will later need for the serious conduct of
life.   I am not prepared to reject that view entirely, but
I feel now that it by no means covers the whole ground.

I am disposed to distinguish between pure play and those forms of play, notably organised games and sport, in which various instinctive impulses, especially the self-assertive impulse and impulses derived from various group-sentiments, give to play something of the nature of serious striving towards definite goals. In purely playful activity, I suggest, there is no such factor, no striving towards a goal, no impulse seeking satisfaction in attainment. The distinction drawn in the earlier part of this chapter between instinctive dispositions and motor mechanisms (a distinction which I had not clearly grasped when writing Chapter IV.) enables us to give a more satisfactory account of purely playful activity. The gambollings of lambs, of puppies, and of young children seem to be instances of pure play, bodily activity directed to no goal and sustained by no specific impulse. I suggest that such gambolling is merely the activation of the various motor mechanisms with which the young creature is innately endowed. Two young dogs gambolling together may make many of the movements and assume many of the postures appropriate to fighting; but they are not fighting; and they exhibit also many other movements and postures, bringing into play almost all their repertoire of motor mechanisms. The same is true of young rats and of the gambols of many young animals. Whence comes the energy that sustains such activities ? What relation does it bear to the instinctive energies ? The following answer may be, I suggest, an approximation to the truth. There is some reason to suppose that all the instincts draw their energies from a common source, the special function of each instinct being to give specific direction of such energy towards its own special goal. And we may suppose that the store of hormic energy in the young creature is in excess of its needs, its needs being mainly provided for by parental care, which also wards off from the young many of the impressions that might excite its instincts. Hence in the well-fed and well-rested young creature the hormic energy overflows directly into the various motor mechanisms, actuating them to the aimless activities which constitute pure play or gambolling. This is but another more technical statement of the popular view of such play, namely, the view that it is a mere working off of an excess of " animal spirits."

In the section on " Suggestion," I distinguished as the most important form of suggestion what I called "prestige-suggestion "; and I put forward the view that the success of prestige-suggestion depends upon the bringing into play of the impulse of the submissive instinct.   In subsequent articles and in my *Outline of Abnormal Psychology*, I have developed this view and generalised it, arguing that it is true of all forms of personal influence to which the term " suggestion " can properly be applied. A greatly extended experience in the use of hypnotism, for both experimental and therapeutic purposes, has convinced me of the truth of this view, which at the time of writing this book I had put forward very tentatively.

It is worth while to point out that Professor Freud has recently arrived at a very similar view of the nature of suggestion.   In his earlier writings, in accordance with his unfortunate pan-sexual tendency, he had taught that the energy at work in all suggestion, the energy which produces conviction and expresses itself in the compulsion to perform every suggested act, such as post-hypnotic actions and the forced actions and inhibitions and contractures of the hypnotic state, is the *libido*, the energy of the sex instinct.   And this view quickly became the accepted doctrine of the psycho-analysts.   In putting forward this view, Freud was making a great step in the right direction.   Previous writers had failed to define, much more to solve, the essential problem of suggestion, namely, What is the nature and source of the hormic energy at work in suggestion—that energy which the hypnotist's suggestions evoke and direct within the hypnotic subject ?   In accordance with his sound fundamental principle, Freud brushed aside as worthless all the current intellectualistic and mechanical theories of suggestion and sought the source of the energy manifested in the working of suggestion in the instinctive constitution. But, preoccupied too exclusively with the sexual instinct and its energy, the *libido*, he erred in deriving the energy of suggestion from that source. In a recent work, Freud [1] has improved upon his earlier theory and has come nearer to the theory propounded in this book. He now regards the suggestible attitude as due to the working of a special innate disposition or instinct developed in the males of the human race by many generations of life in the primitive human horde; for he believes that during a long period primitive society took the form of a horde, the leader of which horde, the horde-father, actuated by his sexual jealousy, habitually treated his sons with extreme brutality, and that such treatment induced and impressed upon the race (or the male half of it) the docile, submissive, or suggestible attitude.

To me it seems unnecessary to give any such extremely speculative, not to say fantastic, account of the genesis in the race of this instinctive tendency. Freud's account of this genesis not only postulates a condition of primitive society which is very hypothetical, but also assumes the truth of the Lamarckian theory of transmission of acquired modifications. And it is further rendered very improbable by the fact that, like other instinctive tendencies of the human species, the submissive tendency is clearly manifested both by the anthropoid apes and by many other species of mammals, and, therefore, was in all probability evolved long before the human species became differentiated. Freud's speculative account of the genesis of docility, of the submissive tendency, merely illustrates once more the ill effects of neglecting the comparative method in psychology. We may and must recognise and attempt to define the various instinctive tendencies of man, even though we may be unable to give any satisfactory account of their genesis in the race. The psychologist may legitimately speculate on the problems of phylogenesis; but he is under no obligation to offer any phylogenetic theory before accepting as racial endowments the innate tendencies manifested in human and animal

---

[1] *Group Psychology and the Analysis of the Ego.* In an article in *Problems of Personality, Essays in Honour of Morton Prince,* I have examined at some length this new attempt of Freud to solve the problem of suggestion.

behaviour. As well might the anatomist refuse to recognise the existence of the liver or the spleen until he may be able to account for their phylogenesis.

Freud's new theory of suggestion, stripped of the speculative phylogenetic hypothesis, is, then, essentially the same as that put forward in the first edition of this book; and I am glad to acknowledge this identity and find in it fresh ground for confidence in the truth of the theory.

The Theory of the Sentiments and of the Development of Character

In conclusion, I would add a few words about the account of the sentiments and of the growth of character contained in Chapters V. to IX. This account was the most novel, original, and, in my view, the most important part of the book. But, while my preliminary account of the instincts and the primary emotions has been very widely discussed and, in many quarters, accepted as substantially correct, most of my professional colleagues seem to have failed to notice that the book presents the only intelligible and consistent account of the nature and growth of character and volition that has hitherto been propounded. I wish, therefore, to draw attention to that account, and to point out that recent great advances in the field of psycho-pathology have gone far to substantiate my account. Especially studies of the disintegration of personality, such as those of Dr. Morton Prince, Dr. T. W. Mitchell, and Professor E. C. Cory, have clearly shown that what we call personality or character is a highly complex product of a long integrative process, a process which may go wrong and may be largely undone at any stage ; a process which seldom, if ever, is carried to an ideal completion. The same studies, as well as the general trend of the psycho-analytic movement, has shown also that the functional units which enter into the integration we call character are the sentiments, the so-called complexes, of the psycho-analysts.[1] And the same studies

[1] As I have elsewhere shown, the psycho-analysts use the term " complex " to cover both the normal sentiments and the morbidly

have shown that my account of character was essentially correct in assigning a dominant and all-important rôle in character formation and in volition to the master-sentiment of self-regard. The Freudians have recognised the importance of this rôle in all that they have written of the function of the " ego-complex " and the " ego instincts " in inhibiting, controlling, conflicting with, and repressing the sexual tendencies. And all these studies converge to support the view that the harmonious integration of the instinctive tendencies in sentiments, and of the sentiments in a hierarchy dominated by the sentiment of self-regard and an ideal of character, is the supreme goal of individual development and the only route by which an efficient and stable personality may be developed. As I wrote in Chapter IX., " In this way the self comes to rule supreme over conduct, the individual is raised above moral conflict ; he attains character in the fullest sense and a completely generalised will, and exhibits to the world that finest flower of moral growth, serenity."

repressed sentiments. I have urged that by restricting the term " complex " to the latter, and using the term " sentiment " for the former, we usefully differentiate our terminology.

INSTINCTS OF MAN IN THE LIGHT OF RECENT DISCUSSION

The Present State of Opinion on Instinct

IN writing this book many years ago, I did not know that I was helping to bring to a head a division of opinion and a controversy which had long been shaping themselves somewhat obscurely. I had supposed that I was merely rendering more definite and precise a view of human nature that was generally held. But it has now become clear that the instinct-problem is one that stands at the parting of the ways in psychology, the way of mechanical explanation on the one hand, and on the other hand, the way which, in the broadest sense of the word "vitalism," may be called vitalistic. Vitalism is a word of bad odour to a great number of men of science, many of whom incline to the view that any vitalistic view is the very negation of science. I would explain, therefore, that I use the word "vitalism" to cover all views which reject the belief that the facts of biology, the facts of life and mind, can be adequately and completely interpreted in terms of the conceptions and principles with which at the present time the physical sciences operate. Up to a very recent date those conceptions and principles were strictly mechanistic, or determinist; they assumed that the present is wholly determined by the past, and that the future course of events is in principle strictly predictable from a knowledge of its past and present course. They, therefore, when applied to human action, left no room for belief in the reality and effectiveness of our efforts, our strivings toward goals or ideals. Yet in practice all men assume such reality and effectiveness; we adopt the belief as a working hypothesis and we find that it works ; it is thereby pragmatically justified. It is, then, in no spirit of opposition to science that the enlightened vitalist seeks to describe human nature in terms which shall avoid a deadlock between scientific principles and the pragmatically justified belief in our limited power of self-determination, our power, however slight, to create novelties in the way of thought and action. And, since the continuity of human with animal evolution is so well established, he inclines to credit the animals also with some slight germ of this power of effective striving towards natural goals.

There is only one way in which we can in any sense understand or interpret such effective striving towards a goal, and that is in terms of our own experience of such striving. We know what it is to desire to attain a goal, to feel impelled to seek and to strive towards a goal—a goal which we may conceive either clearly and definitely or with various degrees of vagueness, down to the extreme vagueness of those instances in which we merely know that we want something but cannot say what it is we want. And, when we observe an infant or an animal behaving as though it wants something, and, especially, when it seems to strive persistently towards some object or goal, refusing to rest, to be satisfied or content, until it attains that goal, we seem justified in interpreting such behaviour in terms of our own experience during similar behaviour on our own part.

Now, we find that our own strongest strivings, our most vivid desires, our most powerful urges to action, spring up within us in relation to goals that are prescribed for us in our common human nature. Every man is so constituted as to seek, to strive for, and to desire, certain goals which are common to the species, and the attainment of which goals satisfies and allays the urge or craving or desire that moves us. These goals and these modes of striving towards them are not only common to all men, but also in a general way are common to men and their nearer relatives of the animal world ; such goals as food, shelter from danger, the company of our fellows, intimacy with the opposite sex, triumph over our opponents, and leadership among our companions. These are the facts on which the theory of human instincts is based.

If we believe that all such forms of human and animal behaviour can be adequately interpreted in mechanistic terms, as sequences of strictly determined causes and effects, then we have no need and no use for the conception of instinct. All that is called instinctive action can then be more properly described as reflex action of more or less complexity, reflex action being mechanistically regarded as action wholly predetermined by the mechanical structure of the organism.

If, on the other hand, we believe that such modes of behaviour cannot be adequately interpreted in such terms, if we believe that the conceptions of present-day physics and chemistry are not adequate to the interpretation of them, then we are, provisionally at least, vitalists, and we are prepared to accept the theory of instincts. For instinct is the conception we form for the interpretation of such modes of behaviour and such modes of experience as accompany them. The word " instinct " indicates that we regard the urge to action, the impulsion to strive towards a goal, as something *sui generis* in nature, something without parallel in the inorganic world, or, if there paralleled, paralleled only by some aspect of inorganic happenings so subtle as to have escaped hitherto the observation of physical science.

Any psychologist who recognises the urge to action and the strivings in which it expresses itself as other than a mechanical compulsion, thereby defines his position in respect of the most fundamental of all the issues that divide psychologists ; he places himself on the side of purposive psychology over against mechanistic psychology. For all the strivings to which we are impelled by the urging of our instinctive constitution are of the same nature as those strivings which are purposive in the fullest and most unmistakable sense, those in which our activity is guided by our thinking of a goal which we desire to attain and of the course of action by which we hope to attain it.

In the more primitive forms of striving, the goal of

action is not clearly envisaged, but there is nevertheless some conscious reference to some goal, there is some germ of desire directed to the future ; and since the strivings we experience range in a series without breaks or sharp difference in kind from those that are purposeful or purposive in the fullest sense to those that have only this vague direction towards a goal scarcely defined in consciousness, we may validly extend the term "purposive striving" to cover the whole series. In this extended or wide sense of the word "purposive," then, the simplest instinctive actions of men and of animals seem to be purposive. And it is only by recognising the continuity of the series, and the essential similarity of type between the higher or explicitly purposive forms of striving and the lower and simpler forms, that we can understand the development of the higher out of the lower forms of striving in course both of individual development and of racial evolution.

This division between those who regard all human and animal action as purely mechanical and those who recognise purposive activity as something radically distinct from mechanistic causation is, I say, the deepest, most significant, division between the schools of psychologists. In contemporary thought it takes the place of the older divisions between materialists and spiritualists or idealists, between psycho-physical monists and dualists, between parallelists and interactionists. I do not assert that these several oppositions of opinion or theory are identical with one another, but that the opposition of purposive to mechanical interpretation of human action is the form taken in contemporary thought by a fundamental opposition which at different periods has assumed these various forms.

And the modern formulation of this opposition, as that between purposive and mechanical psychology, differs from the older formulations in that it makes no claim to metaphysical or ultimate validity; rather, it remains upon the plane of science and leaves to metaphysics the task of deciding whether the distinction between purposive and mechanical processes is ultimate and final, or one that may be resolved by showing that one

of them is more fundamental than the other, or, by showing that both are imperfect and provisional formulations,
which will eventually be resumed within a single formula.
The psychology that finds in our instinctive constitution
the foundation or source of all our activities may then
be identified with purposive psychology as opposed to
mechanistic psychology; for the latter, if it makes any use
of the term " instinctive," does so only to imply the more
complex forms of reflex action mechanically conceived.
Of late years an old Greek word has been given currency
as the most convenient term to denote all psychology
that is vitalistic, purposive, or instinctive, in the sense
defined above. It is proposed to use the word " hormé "
(derived from the Greek noun ὁρμή = an urge to action,
and the verb ὁρμάω = I strive, I am impelled or suffer
impulsion) to denote the energy that seems to find expression in purposive striving, in conation of every kind;
and the adjective " hormic " to denote such strivings or
activities and also the psychology which, in opposition
to the mechanical psychology, regards this conception of
hormic striving as its most fundamental category.[1]

[1] Two authors share the responsibility for the introduction of this
useful word into our psychological vocabulary, namely, Professor T. P.
Nunn and Dr. C. G. Jung. The latter, writing of that energy which is
expressed in instinctive strivings, says : " I postulate a hypothetical
fundamental striving which I designate *libido*. In the classical use
of the word, *libido* never had an exclusively sexual connotation as
it has in medicine. The word interest, as Claparède once suggested
to me, could be used in this special sense, if this expression had to-day
a less extensive application. Bergson's concept, *élan vital*, would also
serve if this expression were less biological and more psychological.
Libido is intended to be an energising expression for *psychological
values*. The psychological value is something active and determining;
hence it can be regarded from the energic standpoint without any
pretence of exact measurement." And, in a footnote, Jung adds :
" This energy may also be designated as hormé. Hormé is a Greek
word, ὁρμή—force, attack, press, impetuosity, violence, urgency, zeal.
It is related to Bergson's ' élan vital.' The concept hormé is an
energic expression for psychological values " (*Analytical Psychology*,
p. 347).
    Professor Nunn, in his *Education, its Data and First Principles*,
writes : " We need a name for the fundamental property expressed in
the incessant adjustments and adventures that make up the tissue of
life. We are directly aware of that property in our conscious activities
as an element of ' drive,' ' urge,' or felt tendency toward an end.
Psychologists call it *conation*, and give the name conative process to

The issue between the hormic or purposive and the mechanical psychology is only in process of being defined. At the time when this book was first published (1908) the view that human nature comprises some instinctive foundations was widely, I think one may fairly say generally, accepted. It was supported by the great authority of William James and of Wilhelm Wundt. But this book, by its attempt to define more nearly the nature and rôle of instincts in human life, has done much to bring to a head the issue between the hormic and the mechanical psychology. Many authors have criticised adversely the theory of human instincts propounded in this volume on the ground that it implies that instinctive activity is something that cannot be wholly interpreted in mechanistic terms.[1]

The essence of the reasonings of these deniers of instinct, however varied and copious their expositions, may be stated succinctly in a single syllogism : All events

any train of conscious activity which is dominated by such a drive—for instance, the reader's endeavour to understand the present sentence s a conative process in which a relatively complex system of mental acts moves towards a more or less clearly envisaged end. While the reader's mind is pursuing the printed argument, his neuro-muscular mechanisms are keeping with his head aloft upon his shoulders, his digestive glands are dealing with his latest meal. None of these purposive processes may be called conative, for they lie below, even far below, the conscious level ; yet a suprahuman spectator, who could watch our mental behaviour in the same direct way as we can observe physical events, would see them all as instances of the same class, variant in detail but alike in general plan. In other words, he would see that they all differ from purely mechanical processes by the presence of an internal ' drive ' . . . to this element of drive or urge, whether it occurs in the conscious life of men and the higher animals or in the unconscious behaviour of lower animals, we propose to give a simple name—hormé (ὁρμή). In accordance with this proposal all the purposive processes of the organism are hormic processes, conative processes being the subclass whose members have the special mark of being conscious."

According, then, to the usage proposed by these two eminent authors, hormé means purposive energy, or energy that manifests itself to us objectively as well as subjectively in our immediate experience as making for or striving towards a goal of some kind.

[1] This reaction against the conception of instinct has been most marked in America. Most of the authors who have taken up this attitude of negation belong to the school of Behaviourists. The reasoning and conclusions of this movement are well represented by Professor L. L. Bernard's recent volume, *Instinct*.

are mechanically explicable; the alleged instinctive actions are not mechanically explicable: therefore there are no instinctive actions and no instincts. In this reasoning the major premise lacks solid foundation; it expresses merely a prejudice which has been much favoured by the course of modern science; for the adoption of this major premise as a guiding principle in the physical sciences has been very fruitful. But we have no guarantee that it will prove equally fruitful in biology. That is a question which only the future can solve. There is much ground for the view that at the present time the dogmatic acceptance of this principle in biology by so many men of science is blocking the path of progress. It behoves us to keep an open mind on such a fundamental question. To pretend to know the answer to such a question is merely a mark of scientific incompetence. It is rather the part of scientific wisdom to observe accurately the phenomena and to classify them and to interpret them by the aid of suitable general conceptions. Instinct is such a general conception to which we are led in our endeavour to interpret by a common principle the various forms of unlearned activity displayed by man and animals.

When we array these forms of activity and seek their common objective characters, we find seven which seem to mark them as distinct in kind from all processes of the inorganic world and as expressive of mind, of hormic, or, in the widest sense, purposive action or striving. These objective marks of purpose may be enumerated as follows: First, a certain spontaneity of movement, a power of initiative. Secondly, a tendency to persistence, whether the movement concerned is apparently spontaneous or is initiated by some physical stimulus falling on the organism from without. Thirdly, variation of kind or of direction of the persistent movements. Fourthly, the cessation of the movements when, and not until, they result in the attainment of the goal, in effecting a change of situation of a particular kind. Fifthly, the movements commonly seem to anticipate, or to prepare in some manner for, the new situation which they themselves tend to bring about. Sixthly, repetition of the situation that has evoked the train of movements, evokes again a similar train of movements, but the movements so evoked commonly show, as compared with those of the former occasion, some degree of improvement in respect of efficiency, *i.e.*, in respect of speed, accuracy, or nicety of adjustment. Seventhly, the purposive action is in a sense a total reaction, that is to say, it is an activity in which the whole organism takes part so far as necessary ; the energies of the whole organism seem to be bent towards the one end, all other concurrent processes within it being subordinated to the major or dominant system of hormic activity. It may perhaps be questioned whether this last character can properly be asserted of all hormic processes, but it seems to be true of those which are conative in the sense defined by Professor Nunn, or truly purposive in that they involve or imply foresight of the goal to be achieved.

These seven objective characters of hormic bodily activity are not found in, or displayed by, the indisputably reflex actions ; but they are found in all cases of instinctive action which we have the opportunity to observe in detail. Further, when we ourselves exhibit reflex actions, we do not experience any urge or impulse towards, or any desire for, a goal ; but, when we act instinctively, we do experience such an " internal drive," some urge, impulse, or desire, no matter how vaguely we may conceive the goal or end of our action. The reflex action seems (though this may be illusory) to be evoked in the body as a mechanical response to a stimulus, a response in the production of which we, as conscious personalities, have no part and no concern ; whereas in instinctive action or striving or conation of any kind, we commonly feel that we take an active part, are actively concerned, even though the action may be one to which we do not positively assent or even one which we strive to avoid or inhibit.

All these facts, then, justify us in regarding instinctive action as other than a purely mechanical sequence of events, as a mode of action that expresses in some degree the mental or psychical nature of the organism. But all these facts are set aside or ignored by those who profess themselves incapable of discerning any difference between instinctive activity and mechanical reflex action.

Of the facts enumerated one is of peculiar importance and deserves some more special consideration, namely, the third of the seven characters of hormic activity defined above. If an instinctive action were merely the mechanical response to a sense-impression or stimulus, the nature of which is wholly determined by pre-existing channels of conduction in the nervous system of a certain pattern, we should expect to find that a sense-impression or stimulus of a particular kind should evoke from any particular organism one particular response in the form of a certain movement or train of movements. This we find to be the rule with reflex actions ; though reflex action may be inhibited or otherwise modified by the incidence of other stimuli. But we find that in this respect instinctive action differs profoundly from purely reflex action. In simple situations in which the organism (man or animal) easily and immediately attains its natural goal, instinctive action often proceeds in a routine fashion, repeating itself without obvious variation on repetition of the exciting impression or situation. It is when the instinctive action cannot attain its goal in the simplest most direct fashion that its peculiar nature and its profound difference from mechanical reflex action clearly appear. All down the scale of animal life we find that under such circumstances the instinctive striving is apt to display a surprising variability. The animal, baffled in its first effort, changes its line of action and tries another. In the simpler instances of instinctive locomotion, whether movements of appetition or aversion, whether a striving to reach an object, such as food, or a striving away from an object, as in striving to escape, the variations may take the simple form of changes of direction of locomotion. But in a multitude of instances the variations are less simple ; the animal may bring into play successively a great range of motor capacities. Thus a hungry dog, or cat, confronted with food which it cannot reach (because either the animal or the food is shut in a cage) may first try to attain its goal, the food, by squeezing through some aperture ; failing in this, he prowls round and seeks other apertures ; still failing, he bites and claws at the obstructing bars, or turns the cage over and shoves it hither and thither. In all the instinctive actions of the higher animals such variation of movement is the rule rather than the exception. Thus when two dogs (or any birds or mammals) fight, they exhibit movements and attitudes which in a general way are those characteristic of the species and of the situation ; but in detail the movements are infinitely varied. In the course of the struggle each animal may bring into play almost the whole of its repertoire of movements ; it crouches, leaps, runs, growls, bites, scratches, tears ; all these many kinds of bodily activity being activated by the one instinctive impulse. In the courtship of animals, which is one of the undeniably unlearnt forms of behaviour, that is to say, instinctive behaviour, we observe a similar variety of movement. In many species the coyness of the female necessitates on the part of the male a prolonged courtship. Thus the male pigeon of the domestic species, under the impulse of the mating instinct, may execute a multitude of movements that bring into play almost all his varied powers of movement ; he struts and bows and spreads his tail, he coos now loudly, now softly, he pursues the object of his attentions assiduously from place to place on foot and on wing, he pecks her now violently, now caressingly.

Now in such instances of instinctive behaviour the animal makes use of a large number of inborn motor mechanisms, nervous arrangements or patterns, each of which gradually takes the shape common to all members of the species, by a process of maturation which is but little influenced by the circumstances of the animal and little by the animal's own activities. Thus the nestling bird on attaining a certain age spreads its wings and flies almost as well at its first attempt as it will ever do. Such improvement as it may later show is probably due almost wholly to further maturation that would go on even though the first flight were postponed, or may be due in part to a mere strengthening of the muscles through exercise.   That is to say, the precision of the bird's flight which enables it to catch the midge on the wing is almost wholly due to an inborn or inherited nervous organisation which works automatically, and which may fairly be called a motor mechanism of the nervous system.   The same is true of the movements by means of which the bird or the mammal walks, runs, swims, eats, utters his specific calls or cries, mates, attacks or defends himself. That is to say, each animal species possesses, as part of its hereditary equipment common to all its members, an array of such motor mechanisms.   If each instinct could be identified with some particular motor mechanism, the fact would go far to justify the mechanistic view of instinct and the description of an instinctive act as merely a somewhat complex reflex response.   Now this identification is commonly made by the deniers of instinct, by those who take the mechanistic view of instinctive action. But that such identification is erroneous is clearly shown by facts of two orders.   First, as I have already pointed out, one instinct may impel an animal to a series of activities in which it employs in turn two or more such motive mechanisms or, in some cases, wellnigh its entire array of such mechanisms.   Secondly, two or more instincts may in turn impel the animal to use the same motor mechanisms.   Especially is this true of those motor mechanisms which subserve locomotion.   The bird may use his powers of flight in the course of migration, of mating, of fighting, of escape from danger, of building his nest, of pursuing his prey.   And the mammals of the various species illustrate the same truth, although perhaps in a less vivid manner than the birds.   How absurd, then, to pretend that an instinctive action is nothing more than the activation of a preformed motor mechanism of particular pattern !   The adaptability of instinctive action to the circumstances of the moment is of its very essence ; and this adaptability consists mainly in bringing into action first one, then another, motor mechanism, according as the circumstances of each moment require.

The critic of instinct may reply to this reasoning as follows : If your alleged instinct impels the animal to a varied sequence of movements in which it employs first this motor mechanism then that, and presently another, by what right do you attribute all these different activities to one instinct ? The reply is easy. An instinct is not defined by the kind or kinds of bodily activity to which it impels the animal, but rather by the nature of the objects and situations that evoke it and, more especially, by the nature of the goal, the change in the situation, in the object or in the animal's relation to it, to which the instinct impels. And, if it be asked—How do we ascertain the nature of the goal ? we reply that, though in any particular instance we may be in doubt during observation of the train of action, repeated observation of animals of the same species in similar situations enables us to define the goal. Thus by observing the courtship actions of many male pigeons, we learn the nature of the goal of that kind of activity evoked by that kind of object and situation. Or, after observing the nest-building activities of many birds of a particular species, we know the kind of goal, the specific form of nest, towards the production of which all the varied movements are directed. And we observe not only that these activities tend to continue, or to be renewed again and again, until that goal is accomplished ; but also, we observe, that as soon as that goal is attained, the activities of this general kind cease, to give place to a new cycle, directed towards a different goal. It is not any one kind of movement that defines the instinct, but the general tendency of many different and variously combined movements to bring about a result of a kind common to the species and of a nature to contribute to the welfare of the individual, or of the group, or of the species.

And observation of the animal affords in many cases yet another clue to the nature of the instinct at work in it, namely, the signs or expressions of emotion which, though we may observe them very imperfectly and interpret them but crudely, are seldom lacking altogether. The animal which is pairing, or escaping, or fighting, or hunting, gives signs of an emotional excitement which are peculiar, more or less, to each such form of striving, no matter how varied may be the bodily movements primarily concerned in achieving the goal.[1]

Those who are concerned to deny or belittle the rôle of instinct in human and animal life commonly are content to imply that they can explain alleged instinctive behaviour by postulating in vague general terms a " reaction pattern " in the nervous system corresponding to every movement and attitude displayed, and by assuming that every such " action pattern " is brought into play by a specific combination of sensory stimuli. But they have never succeeded in demonstrating the validity of such interpretation in any single case of instinctive behaviour. Some such attempt has been made to show that the assumption of a gregarious instinct is unnecessary and therefore invalid. And gregarious behaviour is perhaps the most favourable to the attempt ; for there is little in it that is highly specific, whether in the gross bodily movements or in the finer emotional expressions. The gregarious instinct expresses itself in the main very simply by means of the motor mechanism of locomotion. All that is specific is the direction of the locomotory movements. The gregarious animal, isolated from his herd or flock, is apt to move about in a restless and

---

[1] These bodily signs of emotions not only are constant in the individual and common to all members of the species, but also are, in many instances, common to all members of many allied species— a fact which indicates a common evolutionary origin and the quantity and remarkable persistence of such constitutional peculiarities. It must be millions of years since the domestic cat and the African leopard diverged from a common ancestral stock ; yet the cat and the leopard display almost identical bodily signs of emotion ; when angry, both crouch with belly touching the ground, snarling and growling, with tail lashing, hairs bristling. Recently I saw in a cage a leopard making a friendly approach to his keeper. His emotional expressions were as nearly as possible identical with those of a domestic cat when he rubs himself in friendly fashion against one's leg. The legs were straight, the back slightly arched, the tail held straight and vertically, except the tip which was slightly bent over. In view of such facts, the present endeavour of some biologists and psychologists to abolish the mystery of heredity by denying it all but a very slight influence on human and animal behaviour seems to me ridiculous. If we could describe in full the bodily signs of emotion in two such animals as the cat and the leopard, we should in all probability find that the similarity runs throughout, even to details of chemical changes, such as the composition of special hormones secreted.

apparently random fashion ; but, as soon as he comes
within sensory reach (by sight, or sound, or smell) of his
company, his movements are at once directed towards it.
It has been attempted to explain this comparatively
simple instinctive behaviour by assuming that the gregarious animal is so constituted as to respond reflexly with an
avoiding or retreating movement to all sense impressions
other than those which come to him from the herd.   This
ingenious assumption (which is founded not at all on
fact, but only in the needs of the mechanical theorist)
interprets the behaviour of the animal rejoining the herd
as the consequence of a multitude of mechanical re-
pulsions ; it regards the movements which eventually
being him back into the herd as expressing, not in any
sense a striving of the animal towards the herd, but as
being merely a multitude of reflex movements which
bring about in the end the restoration of the individual
to the herd, because the herd is the only object from which
proceed no stimuli provoking aversive reflex movements.
Such theorising is best refuted by the observation of
simple instances of animal behaviour.   Observe a horse,
or an ox, turned into a meadow where a herd is grazing ;
see how he is at once interested in the distant herd and
directs his movements towards it.   Or note the behaviour
of a horse solitary in an enclosed meadow when a troop
of cavalry passes down the road, his excited calls, his
lively approach, his endeavours to break out and join
the herd.

I recently had the opportunity to observe continuously,
for more than half an hour, a migrating flock of geese.
They were travelling southward, and my car was running
at the same speed and in the same direction   The flock
preserved the familiar arrowhead formation ; the shape
of it varied from moment to moment, always returning
towards the typical symmetrical form after each disturbance.   This formation is in itself a profoundly interesting
problem.   But I was especially interested in the behaviour
of those birds which from time to time became detached
from the flock, singly or in twos and threes.   In some
cases they would rejoin the flock very soon ; in others,

one or two birds would become more widely separated and continue to fly behind the flock and to one side of its path for some minutes. Two birds, who kept close together, became separated from the flock by a distance which I judged to be at least two miles ; they were a little behind and far to the eastward of the flock. I felt sure that they were lost ; it seemed impossible that they should regain the flock save by happy chance. But, after flying thus widely separated for some ten minutes, they began to close the gap, and soon were merged once more in the flock. The stragglers must have been guided by vision or hearing. Their visual power is known to be excellent ; and no calls were audible to me. The guiding impressions were presumably visual. That sense-impressions from the flock guided the impulse to rejoin it cannot be doubted. Far aloft in the blue of the sky there were no other visible objects to repel them. The flock itself was for them but a distant speck subtending a very small visual angle.

The mechanist, confronted with such facts, inclines to fall back on the theory of tropisms. Admitting that guiding sense-impressions come from the flock, he argues that these, falling on the sense-organs of the stragglers, provoke, by way of a mechanical reflex, such action of the muscles concerned in flight as to turn the animal's path towards the flock. If we grant that this is conceivable, there remains the problem of the pace. The stragglers could only rejoin the flock by accelerating their pace ; for they, having followed a divergent course, were distinctly behind the flock. The difference between the tropic theory and the instinct theory is, in this relatively simple instance, reduced to its simplest terms. Both theories postulate the guiding-sense impressions : the tropic theory assumes that they work by modifying the action of the muscles of flight in a mechanical reflex process. The instinct theory, on the other hand, assumes that the isolated situation of the straggler provokes in him an uneasiness, excitement, and urge, a felt tendency to rejoin the flock, and that, when sense-impressions come to him from the flock, they are utilised by him in the way we call intelligent, at however low and simple a level of intelligence; they serve as the basis of an act of recognition, and this recognition guides and perhaps intensifies the urge, the hormic impulse already at work in him, until this impulse attains its goal and is satisfied and allayed by the new situation, the near presence of the flock.

Even if we were to admit provisionally the plausibility of the mechanistic interpretation of the birds' behaviour in rejoining the flock, we should still have on our hands in a rather different form the same problem. For how are we to understand the fact that the flock of geese flies steadily southward, maintaining its course over thousands of miles, resting here and there perhaps at long intervals and resuming its southward flight after each pause? Here no external compulsion by sense-impressions evoking reflexes will explain the facts; and so the mechanist falls back on internal sense-impressions. Now we certainly must postulate some cyclic organic change, dependent perhaps in some degree on climatic conditions, which is a necessary condition of the impulse to migration; and we must assume that sense-impressions from the outer world play some part in enabling the birds to maintain the direction of their migratory flight. But their internal and external impressions only serve to awaken and guide the impulse to migrate which sustains the immense output of energy displayed.

It is in respect of such simple facts of animal behaviour as the rejoining of the herd or the return home from a distance, that the mechanical theory, which would deny all instinctive activity, should most easily achieve some plausible explanations. The capacity of "homing," of returning from a distance to the nest or lair or hole, is displayed by a great number of animal species; it presents a crucial problem to the mechanical theorisers; and some of them have attempted to deal with it on the basis of the tropic theory, there being no other line that offers them the least prospect of success. In my *Outline of Psychology* I have examined these attempts in some detail and have shown that they break down hopelessly; and have shown further that the only way in which we can interpret or in any sense understand such behaviour on the part of animals is to interpret it in the light of our own experience and behaviour in similar situations. In short, we are compelled to regard the return home of the animal as a train of activity sustained by an impulse or desire and guided by intelligent recognition of various landmarks previously perceived in their spatial relations to the home.

The consideration of homing is especially instructive, not only because it reveals clearly the inadequacy of all attempts at mechanical explanation of the facts, but also because it illustrates another fact of fundamental importance, namely, the intimate co-operation and mutual dependence of what we call instinct and intelligence, respectively. By an intellectual process of abstraction we distinguish instinct and intelligence as two functions or faculties; and some authors, notably Professor Bergson, go so far as to regard them as radically different and in a sense opposed functions; alleging that, while the insects have evolved along the line of increasing specialisation of instinct, the mammals have evolved along a very different line, namely, one of supersession of instinct by intelligence. But this separation of instinct and intelligence is effected by a misleading process of abstraction. In reality, instinctive action everywhere displays that adaptability to special circumstances which is the mark of intelligence; instinct is everywhere shot through with intelligence, no matter how constantly, in how routine a fashion, a particular mode of instinctive behaviour may be repeated. Where the routine-specialised behaviour suffices, there no special adaptation of the inborn mode of action is made; but where the inborn mode of action does not suffice for the attainment of the natural goal of the instinct, there some adaptation, or some effort at adaptation, is made. And intelligence, on the other hand, works always in the service of some conation, some tendency, some desire, or intention, rooted in and springing from our instinctive constitution.

The foregoing discussion has been directed against the attempt to discredit the theory of instinct by showing that all animal and human behaviour may be adequately interpreted mechanistically, *i.e.*, solely by reference to physical and chemical causes of movement, without making use of the conception of a goal or of an impulse directed to a goal.　This mechanistic endeavour has been made in the main by the members of the school of Behaviourists, that school which, in endeavouring to interpret human and animal behaviour, perversely refuses to make use of such aid as we can obtain by reflection upon our own experience, our own introspective observations, and the introspective reports of other men.　But there are members of this school who see that the conceptions of a goal and of striving towards a goal are useful, and that, in the present state of science, they are indispensable. Professor E. C. Tolman classes himself as a member of the behaviourist school, because he harbours this strange prejudice, observes this perverse self-denying ordinance, against making use of introspection.　It is interesting, therefore, to find that, in a series of papers dealing with this problem, he frankly avows the inadequacy of the mechanistic categories, and admits the propriety and the advantage of using the teleological conceptions of goal, end, and purposive striving.　In a recent article [1] he carefully examines the various arguments against the conception of instinct, and finds them to be invalid ; shows the inadequacy of the mechanical reflex theory, and concludes that instinct is a useful conception and that any instinct is to be defined in terms of the end or goal towards which the instinctive action tends.　Countless observations of the variability and adaptability of instinctive behaviour have, he says, " given the pure reflex pattern theory its final *coup de grâce*."　And he quotes with approval Professor Hocking, who says, " It may be admitted at once that the explanation of instinctive behaviour by the chain-reflex pattern has definitely broken down."

The contention that instinctive behaviour is nothing more than a train or chain of reflex actions of mechanical responses to physical stimuli, is the principal objection

[1] " The Nature of Instinct," *Psychological Bulletin,* 1923.

to the theory of instincts brought forward by its critics. But many of them insist also on another objection which may at first sight seem to have a certain plausibility. The psychology of instinct, they say, is merely the old fallacious faculty psychology served up in a different form. And they point to the usage of numerous authors who, in the course of literary or social studies, inevitably come upon psychological problems and who proceed to solve them by the easy method of postulating corresponding instincts in the human race or in the particular individuals concerned. And they support this charge, somewhat irrelevantly, by pointing out that the various authors who have attempted to deal with the problems of instinct in a more scientific manner are not agreed as to what instincts are common to the human race, some postulating few and others many human instincts. I have examined this and various other criticisms at some length elsewhere.[1] Here it may suffice to cite the concise refutation of this criticism made by Professor Tolman. " The assumption of instincts, it is said, is similar to the now discredited assumption of mental faculties. For the ' instincts ' are mere class names which the instinct psychologists have elevated to the rank of potencies. The charge is levelled most directly at the teleological theories. These theories are said to assume mystical drives or forces behind the actual responses. But the assumption of such forces adds nothing to a causal and descriptive explanation of the phenomena. Is the indictment sound? Are the teleological definitions, in any serious sense, a return to faulty psychology? It would hardly seem so. For how else can we so *simply and easily describe* such empirical facts as that, with constant environmental conditions, one and the same external stimulus will, in the same individual on one occasion arouse one response and on another occasion a quite different response, and that one and the same stimulus will arouse two quite different

---

[1] In two articles published in the *Journal of Abnormal and Social Psychology*, " The Use and Abuse of Instinct in Social Psychology " (1922), and " Can Sociology and Social Psychology dispense with Instincts ? " (1924).

responses in two different individuals, except by assum·
ing varying degrees of instinctive proclivity. For, as
McDougall points out : ' The correct ascription of an
action, or a phase of behaviour, to a particular instinct
enables us to forecast the further course of behaviour.'
It is because there *are* observable functional interde-
pendencies, common wakings and warnings, common
references to preceding causal excitement, that we find
the concept of instincts a simple and useful descriptive
tool. In one individual, we say, a given instinct is relatively weak, in another relatively strong ; and in the
case of one and the same individual, we say that it is
easily touched off by such and such a set of conditions,
but not by such and such another set of conditions. Or,
again, we discover that for the species as a whole its
liveliness is thus and thus functionally dependent upon
such general conditions as age, internal physiological
conditions, etc."

We see, then, that even the behaviourist (provided that
he is not committed to that form of the doctrine which
Professor Tolman contemptuously refers to as " a mere
Muscle Twitchism of the Watsonian variety ") finds that
the conception of instinct is indispensable.

Instinct in Psycho-Analytic Theory

The instinct theory propounded in this book as the
most fundamental part of human psychology finds
stronger support in the successes of another modern
development, namely, the psycho-analytic movement.
This book was written at a time when Professor Freud's
doctrines were only just beginning to make a noise in the
world, and it was written in entire independence, and
almost complete ignorance, of Freud's works. It is,
therefore, very satisfactory to find that the psycho-analysts,
approaching the problem of human nature exclusively
by way of the study of mental and nervous disorders in
the human subject, have arrived at the same fundamental
theory of human nature as that reached in these pages by
wav of a comparative psychology based upon the hypo-

thesis of the continuity of human with animal evolution. For, however little one may incline to accept the more detailed and speculative hypotheses of the psycho-analysts, there is no room for question that the psycho-analytic movement has achieved striking successes, has been productive of very great and rapid progress in the sphere of mental medicine, and has established, as lasting contributions to psychology, a number of conceptions of the greatest value—conceptions such as conflict, repression, regression, sublimation, and rationalisation.[1]

The psycho-analysts are now divided into several schools ; but all the schools retain those features of the parent school of Freud, to which it has chiefly owed its success. Those features are the following: First, the full recognition of the hormic or purposive nature of man ; the recognition that all his activities, even his dreams and his neurotic symptoms, are in a sense products of a purposive activity, a striving towards goals, however obscure or ill-defined in consciousness those goals may be. Secondly, all the psycho-analytic schools recognise that the strivings, the active tendencies, the desires, and impulses of men, are rooted in instincts common to the race.

It is true that the psycho-analysts have made little attempt to define the human instincts. But that has been due to their unfortunate neglect of the comparative method and to Professor Freud's undue extension of the sphere of influence of a single instinct, namely, the sex instinct. Impressed by the immense strength and influence in human life of the sex instinct, his attention became concentrated upon it ; and, as he found it necessary to recognise various other instinctive tendencies, such as curiosity, disgust, self-assertion, submission, and acquisitiveness, he has endeavoured to exhibit them as in some sense derivatives from, or components of, the sex instinct. However, even Freud does not carry this tendency to the extreme of denying all other human

---

[1] For a critical evaluation of the contribution of the psycho-analytic schools, I may refer the reader to my *Outline of Abnormal Psychology*, and to my *Psycho-analysis* and *Social Psychology*.

instincts ; he recognises, however vaguely and inadequately, a group of instincts which he calls "the ego
instincts," and which he regards as perpetually conflicting
with the sex instinct or group of sex instincts. In a
recent publication Freud has declared that the most
satisfactory way of approaching the problems of human
nature, if such a way were practicable, would have been
to study and define as nearly as possible the array of
human instincts : thus indirectly admitting the truth of
the charge that his own psychology has been seriously
handicapped and led astray through his neglect to make
any such preliminary study.[1] And one of the leading
British exponents of the Freudian psychology has recently
formulated the foundations of that psychology in words
which are a paraphrase of the much-quoted statement of
the rôle of instinct in human life, contained in the con-
cluding paragraphs of Chapter II. of this book (p. 38).
Dr. James Glover writes as follows : "What might be
called the raw material of the individual, namely, those
inherited instincts which, in spite of subsequent complex
changes, remain throughout life the hidden sources of all
his manifold activities." And on another page he writes :
"Psycho-analysis has demonstrated a firm genetic
continuity between the earliest nascent manifestations
of these instincts and their most complicated and remote
end-products. This range of indirect expression is
especially marked in the case of energy derived from the
sexual instincts." [2]

Recent Developments of German Psychology— The Gestalt School

It seems worth while to draw attention to the fact
that a new and very influential school of German psychologists is just now very actively developing a type of

---

[1] In his recent work, *Beyond the Pleasure Principle*, Freud has
written : "No knowledge would have been so important for the
establishment of a sound psychology as some approximate understanding of the common nature and possible differences of the
instincts."

[2] *Social Aspects of Psycho-Analysis.* London, 1924.

psychology which stands much closer to the teachings of this book than did the psychology predominant in Germany under the leadership of Wundt, Ebbinghaus, and Müller. I refer to the school of *Gestalt*, or configuration psychology, led by Professors Koehler, Wertheimer, and Koffka. The essential novelty (for German psychology) of the teaching of this school is the repudiation of atomistic sensationism, the recognition that our mental life and the course of experience cannot be adequately or usefully described as a streaming and clustering of atoms of consciousness called sensations or images or feelings or by any other name. It is claimed that any cross-section of experience is a structural whole, the distinguishable features of which are not entities capable of independent existence, like the bricks of a wall or the pieces of a mosaic picture, but rather are parts of a whole of which each part is organically related to all the rest ; and it is insisted that the whole is more than the sum of its parts. I venture to think that this school, when it shall have fully developed its doctrine and applied it to the temporal succession of experience as well as to the co-existent parts of the cross sections of experience, must advance to the position which I have long held and taught ; namely, that that which has a definite *Gestalt* or configuration is not the pattern of experience, taken either in cross-section or longitudinally or in both ways, but rather the structure of the mind, the mental dispositions whose activity and interplay underlie and express themselves both in the introspectively observable facts and in behaviour. At present the *Gestalt* or configuration has, to my thinking, too much of the flavour of the entities out of which the older psychologies composed their " consciousness," namely, sensations, images, and ideas, and what not. It is, it is true, a vast improvement upon them, but it retains something in common with them, as one of a number of similar units by the juxtaposition of which " consciousness " is supposed to be compounded.

More important from the point of view of the present discussion is the fact that the *Gestalt* psychology frankly rejects the mechanical accounts of human and animal behaviour based upon the conception of the mechanical reflex. The leaders of this new school rightly point out that it is impossible to interpret the complexities and niceties of behaviour as achieved by the mechanical co-ordination of a multitude of mechanical reflexes, and that the life of the organism cannot be conceived as merely the working of a vast number of linked machines. They aim at establishing in biology and psychology a position midway between the old mechanistic theory and the vitalistic views. As regards the ultimate nature of the processes of the body, and especially those of the nervous system, they are open minded. They admit that these processes may perhaps be more truly described as of the purposive than as of the mechanistic or strictly causal type. They reserve judgment on this deep question. But they do not, like the dogmatic mechanists, insist that we must put aside and ignore as illusory our experience of activity, of active purposive striving. Rather they recognise that our life is fundamentally a series of such strivings. It is true that they are somewhat chary of using the language of common sense. What German philosopher is not ? But they recognise the facts of striving towards goals and the fact that we cannot begin to describe human or animal life in any terminology that does not provide words for taking account of such facts. And so they make use of a new terminology for this purpose. Professor Koffka, for example, uses the expression " closure," and says that the psycho-physical process tends to " closure," a new way of saying that it tends towards a natural end or goal. And they have devised ingenious experiments which show that animals do not act like machines, that their learning is not subject only to the so-called laws of habit formation, and of association, the laws of frequency and recency, but that the animals solve their problems by intelligently appreciating the situation confronting them and adapting their behaviour accordingly.

In his extremely important study, *The Mentality of Apes*, Professor Koehler completely demolishes the attempts at mechanical explanations in terms of habits and associations of chance reactions. After describing

the behaviour of chimpanzees under a variety of in-
geniously devised situations, devised not to show how
little but rather how much the animal can achieve, he
writes : " It would be simply nonsense to assert that the
animal has gone through special combinations of accidental impulses for all these different cases and variations.
Success is supposed [*i.e.*, by the mechanical theorisers he
is criticising] to have selected and joined together the
objectively suitable combinations out of all those that
occurred. But the animals produce complete methods of
solution quite suddenly, and *as complete wholes which
may, in a certain sense, be absolutely appropriate to the
situation, and yet cannot be carried out. They can never
have had any success with them,* and, therefore, such
methods were certainly never practised formerly (as they
would have had to be, according to the theory). . . .
After all this, as far as I can see, even an adherent of the
theory must recognise that the reports of experiments
here given do not support his explanation. The more
he tries to advance more valuable data than the general
scheme of his theory, and really thinks out and shows
how he would explain and interpret all the experiments in
detail, the more will he realise that he is attempting something impossible." In short, Koehler shows very clearly
that the animals' behaviour can only be validly interpreted by attributing to them in some degree insight and
understanding of the situations they have to deal with,
or, in other words, intelligence.

I would especially draw the reader's attention to the
Appendix to Professor Koehler's book, in which he has
briefly reported a number of observations on the emotional
and impulsive life of the chimpanzees. His descriptions
show very clearly that these animals display all, or almost
all, of the emotions and instinctive impulses attributed
in this book to the human species, and that these emotions
and impulses are called forth by just such situations as
have been stated in these pages. This is especially clear
as regards anger, fear, especially fear of the uncanny,
self-assertion, submission, the tender emotion and protective impulse, gregariousness, curiosity, sex, distress,

and the acquisitive impulse. He describes instances of behaviour which illustrate in the most vivid manner the working of the principle of primitive passive sympathy. And his description and discussion of imitative acts bears out entirely the view of imitation taken in these pages, namely, that there is no instinct of imitation, but that rather such slight general capacity of imitation as these animals display implies intelligent appreciation of actions as means to the ends they desire to attain.

THE STRUCTURE OF CHARACTER

R ECENT years have brought great increase of interest in the study of character. In Germany recent books and articles on characterology are numerous. In America many efforts have been made to bring traits of character within the reach of laboratory methods and of mental tests. On all hands it is recognised that, during the period dominated by the development of laboratory experiment, the study of the personality as a whole has been unduly neglected, while psychologists have concentrated their attention on details abstracted from the concrete whole of mental life. A recently published bibliography of Character and Personality lists 3341 titles, a large proportion of which are of the last few years ; and a comprehensive review of the literature by the same learned and assiduous student [1] has shown how great is the confusion still prevailing in this field, how little progress we have made towards agreement as to what we mean by " character."

It is generally agreed that character is an important part of personality, and that the word stands in some sense for the organisation of the affective and conative constituents of personality. But the distinctions drawn in this volume between character, disposition, and temperament are by no means generally accepted or grasped ; while the factors of personality distinguished (in Supplementary Chapter III.) under the head of temper have been noticed by very few authors.

Although this book has now been before the public for nearly twenty years, and has been widely read and used, the fact that it contains a sketch of a complete

[1] *The Psychology of Character*, by A. A. Roback, London, 1927.

theory of character seems to have gone unnoticed until very recently. And when in a popular book [1] I used this theory as the basis of my discussion of the ways in which the growth of character may be promoted and guided, some of my critics, while admitting that I had said something about character, complained that I had not analysed character. Yet lately there have been indications that these distinctions may prove acceptable, and that the theory of character outlined is obtaining some recognition and proving itself useful. The educational authorities of one State of the American Union (Nebraska) have given me much encouragement by " lifting " the whole theory (without public acknowledgment) and making of it a foundation stone of their educational system. My friend Dr. Roback has recognised, and, in part, has accepted the theory. Dr. R. G. Gordon in his recent book [2] has incorporated it in his exposition. Still more encouraging is the fact that the most influential group of academic psychologists in Germany (those of the *Gestalt* school) are now working actively in the laboratory along the general lines which I have long advocated, and that one of the most active of them [3] is arriving by way of laboratory studies at an account of the conative organisation of personality very similar to my own.

In view of this state of affairs it has seemed to me worth while to add to this volume a very bald and concise statement of what in my view character is, leaving unchanged in the text my account of the growth of character ; for, brief as that account is, it seems to me substantially correct, though in need of supplementation of the kind given in my new book just now mentioned. I have not found anything in the voluminous literature of recent date that impairs my confidence in that account. My studies in the field of abnormal psychology and of neurotic and mental disorder, made for the most part since

---

[1] *Character and the Conduct of Life,* London and New York, 1927.

[2] *Personality,* London, 1926.

[3] Dr. Kurt Lewin, in various articles, but especially in a most interesting booklet—*Vorsatz, Wille u. Bedürfnis, mit Vorbemerkungen über die psychischen Kräfte und Energien und die Struktur der Seele,* Berlin, 1926.

the publication of this volume, have shown me that the account of character contained in it, and arrived at by way of the study of normal personality, is borne out by such studies of the abnormal ; for, as I have shown in my *Outline of Abnormal Psychology*, the scheme suggests promising hypotheses for the interpretation of the facts of manic-deprensive insanity and of *dementia prœcox*, as well as of some of the severer forms of neurotic disorder.

Well-developed character, I would say, is an integrated system of sentiments, a system that is a hierarchy dominated by a single master-sentiment and integrated by that dominance.

Before explicating this definition, let me say something in defence and further clarification of the sentiment as I conceive it.   I have found that many psychologists are extremely slow to grasp this conception and to realise its importance.   Some of them, misinterpreting my account of it, have proceeded to criticise it adversely and to suggest improvements.

The first difficulty is part of the more general difficulty in persuading psychologists of the validity and usefulness of the distinction between mental process and mental structure.   Objection to this distinction seems to be found by both the more physiologically and the more philosophically minded psychologists.   The former are ready to dabble to any extent in extremely speculative physiology, and to describe purely hypothetical neural structure and mechanism underlying and expressing itself in our mental processes and our behaviour ; but they are slow to admit that, in the absence of all but the most uncertain guesses at the nature of the cerebral organisation underlying our mental life, we do better frankly to recognise our ignorance, and to build up our account of the structure which thus expresses itself by inference from the observed facts of mental life and of behaviour, guided by such indications as neurology affords, but not relying wholly or mainly on such guidance.

The more philosophically minded seem to be under the spell of the long-standing but unfortunate identifications of mind with consciousness. Though they are willing to discuss " the structure of consciousness," they seem to feel that to postulate or infer a mental structure that lies behind, and partially reveals its nature in, our conscious activities, is an act of disloyalty to this traditionally accepted but misleading identification. Yet nothing is more certain than that we cannot hope to explain the flow of consciousness in terms only of consciousness, to formulate adequate laws of mental process in terms only of introspectively observable events, their concurrences and successions. The full richness of mental process is revealed only very partially to introspection ; much of it can be reached only by inference ; and by inference only can we achieve any useful account of the enduring conditions of our intellectual and affective life, which we may properly call the structure of the intellect and of character respectively. Let me illustrate with a crude analogy. When a gramophone recites a poem, the sounds or the air-waves emitted reveal order and system ; but no amount of study of such air-waves would enable us to explain their conjunctions and sequences in terms of air-waves alone. In order to understand or explain their occurrence we must learn to understand the structure of the gramophone and its recording disc. In similar fashion, when I silently recite a poem, the sequence of words and their meanings flows by as a stream of consciousness ; but no amount of study of such streams will enable us to understand and explain them in terms of conscious events alone. As the complex sound-waves from the gramophone are conditioned only very partially by the interplay of the constituent waves, and chiefly by the structure of the gramophone and its disc, so the waves of consciousness are conditioned only partially by their interplay with one another, and chiefly by the underlying structure of the mind. In both cases the stream of events elapses, passes away, and is gone; the structure endures and may, after intervals long or short, play the same essential part in the repetition of similar events.

In this connection I will venture a critical remark on

the admirable work of the *Gestalt* or Configuration school, that has excited so much attention in the last few years. They seem to me to err in that they attempt to describe the configuration of mental process in terms of introspectively observable facts ; whereas the complete configuration must in all cases be a field of energy whose complexity is only partially revealed in consciousness, and whose configuration is determined largely by the mental structure concerned. In other words, they seem to be repeating, in an improved form, the error of those who in the past have attempted to describe and explain the stream of consciousness in terms of consciousness alone.

Accepting, then, as valid and important the distinction between mental structures and mental process, we regard a sentiment as a fact of mental structure, an organisation that endures, though it is susceptible of growth, development, or decay, and, like any other living organisation, can hardly cease to undergo such changes so long as it lives. Emotions, on the other hand, are events or partial aspects of conscious events, and in very many instances our emotion is an event in the life-history of a sentiment ; that is to say, the nature of the emotion is conditioned by the nature of the sentiment from which it springs.

Two men may be closely alike in respect of the instinctive basis of their personalities—that is to say, in disposition—and alike in intellectual equipment, yet through differing circumstances they may have acquired very different sentiments for the same object : one may have learnt to love a person whom the other has learnt to hate. Thenceforward every event in the life of that person will evoke very different emotions in the two men. Where the one is tender and full of solicitude, the other is angered ; where the one hopes, the other despairs ; where the one sorrows, the other rejoices : all these and many other differences of their emotional reactions to the one object are to be understood only in terms of their diverse enduring sentiments. And either sentiment never displays its nature completely in any one emotional

event ; only by observing the various emotional reactions to the loved or hated object on many successive
occasions and under diverse circumstances are we able
to infer the structure of the sentiment.

The sentiment and the emotion, thus, more clearly
than any other constituents of personality and than any
other experiences, illustrate the validity and necessity
of the distinction between mental structure and mental
process or activity. Let me say again, a sentiment
is an enduring structure within the total structure of the
mind or mental organisation, while emotion is a passing
phase or, more strictly, an aspect of a phase of mental
process.

Perhaps a main source of the difficulty in securing
recognition of the distinction between emotions and
sentiments is the ambiguous usage of the term " sentiment " in common speech, the usage of it to denote
feelings or emotions as well as sentiments ; and, still
more, the fact that in certain cases the same name may
properly, and is perhaps inevitably, given to some particular kind of emotional experience or reaction, and also
to some sentiment. For example, in common speech
we speak of the emotion of hate or hatred, yet hatred
is also the general name of all sentiments in the structure
of which the affective dispositions of anger and of fear
are incorporated. We speak of the emotion of love,
meaning an emotion in which is prominent the quality
I have called in these pages " tender emotion " ; yet
love is also the name of all sentiments in which the disposition of this tender emotion is incorporated. We
speak of the emotion of admiration, meaning, as I have
suggested (p. 111), an emotional experience in which the
qualities of wonder and negative self-feeling or submission are blended ; but we cannot refuse the same name
to a sentiment in which the dispositions of these two
tendencies are principal constituents—disposing us to
react with these emotions in the presence of the object
of the sentiment.

These ambiguities of language we cannot hope to
avoid or remove ; and yet they should not be, I suggest,

an insuperable bar to clear thinking, either for psychologists or for the plain man.

A few words now about the commonest misinterpretation of my view of the sentiment. On p. 105 a sentiment was described as "an organised system of emotional tendencies centred about some object." And on p. 106 occurs, "the system of emotional dispositions that constitutes the sentiment of love." I have to admit that this language gives scope for the misinterpretation of which I complain ; namely, that I am said to conceive the sentiment as consisting of emotional dispositions only, and as comprising no cognitive system. Now this, as I have pointed out,[1] is true of Mr. Shand's conception of the sentiment, but is not true of mine. In saying that "a sentiment is an organised system of emotional tendencies centred about an object," I used a loose expression in order to avoid disagreeable technicality of language. I should have written : "A sentiment is a system in which a cognitive disposition is linked with one or more emotional or affective conative dispositions to form a structural unit that functions as one whole system (or, in more recent terminology, as one configuration or *Gestalt*)." I trusted that the crude diagram on p. 108 would make clear that the system which is the sentiment, in my view, comprises (as its essential centre that links together the group of emotional dispositions) a cognitive disposition corresponding to the object of the sentiment. And, though in my diagram the cognitive disposition is indicated merely by a small circle, it was, I supposed, clear that such a cognitive disposition might be one of very great complexity. If a man has a sentiment of love for his country, it is surely clear that the cognitive disposition corresponding to or representing in the structure of his mind that object, his country, must be one of great extent and complexity, one built up by a multitude of experiences, perhaps by long and arduous study of the history of that country. And the same is true of any important sentiment ; for, just because

[1] Cp. "Symposium on Instinct and Emotion," by Shand, Stout, and McDougall, *Proceedings of the Aristotelian Society*, 1915.

the possession of the sentiment gives the man a strong interest in its object, his mind can hardly fail to be much occupied with that object, and therefore to build up some rich system of knowledge about it—that is to say, a large differentiated cognitive system.

The relation between the cognitive disposition and the emotional dispositions comprised within a sentiment is that the latter remain the conative-affective root of the whole system, no matter how large its cognitive division may become, furnishing to it the energy, " drive," conative force or interest by which all thinking of the object is sustained, and yielding the wide range of primary, blended, and derived emotions that colour all such thinking.

Each sentiment may then be likened to a tree or bush which, springing from a few roots (among which a single tap-root often predominates in importance), may grow very large and complex, sending out many branches, twigs, and leaves. No matter how large and complex the stem and branches above ground may become, their life and activity continue to be dependent upon the hidden root ; as, in the sentiment, the many parts of the growing cognitive system remain dependent upon the conative-affective root buried deeply in the instinctive levels of the personality.

Another and less pardonable misinterpretation of my view, which I often find carelessly thrown out as a passing remark, consists in asserting that I ascribe every human action to some instinct, or regard it as the direct expression of some instinct. This is to ignore the whole scheme of sentiment and character for which my sketch of the instinctive nature of man furnishes merely the foundation, but a foundation that is in my opinion absolutely indispensable. It is for lack of such foundation that so much of present-day discussion of character remains sterile. In the man of developed character very few actions proceed directly from his instinctive foundations: perhaps an occasional start of fear or sudden gesture of anger ; but all others proceed from his sentiments, that is to say, from the complex interplay of the impulses and desires springing (as regards their energy) from the conative dispositions incorporated in his sentiments, and guided (as regards the lines of their expression and action in striving towards their goals) by the whole system of acquired knowledge both of the object of the sentiment and of its relation to the world in general. Thus the ardent patriot may sustain through fifty years an unceasing round of patriotic activities in war and peace, on the fields of battle and the halls of legislation, in the press and on the platform ; but when he dies at last, clasping in his arms his country's flag, and pressing its folds to his lips, he reveals in this moment the instinctive sources of the energy that he has poured out so freely in the service of his beloved country, in protecting it, in promoting its interests, in exalting it, in striving to render it nearer in reality to the ideal which he cherishes—an ideal which is perhaps more truly the object of his sentiment than the reality seen by any unimpassioned observer.

Returning now to the actual structure of character, I venture to submit a diagram*which, although it inevitably must be a wooden and wholly inadequate representation of the facts, may be of some service in making clear the nature of the complex whole as I conceive it.

In the diagram are represented four levels, corresponding roughly to the four main periods of development of character sketched on p. 156. The lowest level is the instinctive level, and the circles stand for the affective-conative dispositions or cores of the several instincts.

In the second level are represented the cognitive systems, corresponding to the objects of the leading concrete sentiments peculiar to the particular individual. Each is joined to one or more of the dispositions of the first level by lines the thickness of each of which indicates the strength or intimacy of the connection of the two dispositions thus joined.

In the third level are represented the cognitive dispositions corresponding to various moral qualities ; and the fact that each of these is the cognitive centre of a senti-

* See pages 526–527.

ment is indicated by the lines joining it to the dispositions of the first level. They are arranged in two groups, representing the negative and the positive moral sentiments—sentiments of dislike, of hate, of contempt, and sentiments of liking, of love, and of admiration. Some of the latter are enclosed within a line to represent the fact that the qualities so indicated are those which the man has brought together to form his ideal of character, that group of qualities which the man desires to realise in his own life and person and in his own character.

The single circle of the fourth level stands for that complex disposition or system which is self-knowledge, active in all thinking of the self ; and that it is the centre of the sentiment of self-respect is indicated by the lines connecting it with the dispositions of self-assertion and submission—the two principal conative roots of the sentiment. Other lines join it to the qualities of the ideal, indicating the close functional connections between these dispositions, connections so intimate that these qualities may be said to be incorporated in the cognitive system of the self, and the sentiments of which they are the centres to be incorporated in the dominant sentiment of self-respect.

The four levels of the diagram represent the historical order of development of the structures and foundations ; they represent also the relations of dominance, each level dominating those below it. The fact of relative dominance thus symbolised in the diagram is of the first importance, though very difficult to understand. We may concentrate on the problem of the dominance of the sentiment of self-respect. No doubt the self-assertive impulse becomes very strong through much exercise ; but that is not, I think, the whole of the story. Dominance depends, in part at least, on the richness of development of the cognitive aspect of each sentiment and on the richness of its connections with other cognitive systems ; and in this respect the self-sentiment in a well-developed personality takes the lead, and to this owes in part its dominance.

The problem may be related to the parallel neurological problem. It is an established fact that the higher levels of the nervous system constantly exert inhibitory influences on the lower; but physiologists have not been able to find any explanation of the fact. Now in the interplay of impulses and desires that takes place within the system of the sentiments, the conflict between two incompatible or opposed tendencies is not merely a brute conflict, obeying some such principles as the parallelogram of forces; the effective energy of action does not represent the mere surplus of the strength of the stronger impulse over that of the weaker. We see the same or an analogous principle exemplified at the lowest level in the play of the antagonistic muscles of our limbs. When the arm is bent, the flexor muscles do not merely overcome the pull of the extensor muscles by exerting a stronger pull: rather, at the moment of the innervation of the flexors, the extensors are relaxed by inhibition of the nerve currents flowing to them (according to the principle of reciprocal innervation so brilliantly revealed by Sir Charles Sherrington). And it would seem that a similar principle of reciprocal inhibition is constantly exhibited in the interplay of the sentiments and their impulses or desires. A stronger impulse (or a conjunction of concordant impulses) does not merely overcome an opposed impulse; rather, it inhibits it. And there is ground for believing that, in inhibiting the opposing impulse, the inhibitor gains at the expense of the inhibited, takes over, absorbs into itself some at least of the energy of the other.[1] I suggest that this is the essential principle at work in the process of sublimation, the process now widely recognised (but obscure in its *modus operandi*) by which the energies of our instinctive nature are utilised on higher planes of action than the instinctive.

So important is the process of inhibition within the system of sentiments which is character that Dr. Roback

[1] I have reported experiments which seem to show that this is true of the reciprocal inhibitions that occur on the sensory levels, and have suggested that these give support to the hypothesis of inhibition of drainage.

in his recent volume proposes to regard it as the essential mark and work of character, and proposes to measure the degree of the development of character by the range and power of inhibition displayed. I cannot go so far in this direction as Dr. Roback. In my view, inhibition is always only a negative supplementary aspect of positive activity ; we inhibit our output of energy in one direction, along one line of action, by adopting another line of action (even though it have no explicit outcome in muscular innervation) and by concentrating our energies along that line, as when, under sudden pain, we grind our teeth and clench our fists in order to inhibit the impulse to cry out.

These inhibitory processes are possible only in so far as the whole personality is integrated. Integration and the inhibitions in which it manifests itself are functions of the relations between the cognitive (or higher cortical) dispositions of the various sentiments ; for it is only through their cognitive parts that unlike sentiments are functionally related. Thus, as regards their conative-affective dispositions, a sentiment of hatred and one of love have nothing in common ; but if you hate a certain man, and understand that he is dear to another whom you love, you may inhibit the impulse of your sentiment of hatred. And, on the higher plane, you may inhibit those impulses, if you understand that their free play is inconsistent with the ideal of conduct which, in the form of moral sentiments, you have incorporated in your character. And if you pursue this line of conduct consistently, constantly inhibiting the impulses of your sentiment of hatred, you drain it of its energies and reduce it in the end to a state of innocuous desuetude.

If, on the other hand, you fail or refuse to recognise your hatred for what it is, fail to establish adequate cognitive relations between its system and the rest of your personality, then you suffer from the state technically known as repression ; and the system of hatred works in relative detachment from the rest of your personality in obscure fashion, determining bizarre, uncontrolled phases of emotion and behaviour. You become the seat of a brute conflict of impulses, having no voluntary control of your repressed sentiment of hatred, the cognitive connections through which alone control might be exercised, not having been established.

Thus vaguely we may conceive of the way in which the cognitive system that grows up from instinctive roots serves to direct the energies that spring from those roots ; the way in which adequate conception of the relations of the self to other persons and objects enables the sentiment of self-respect, with its incorporated ideal, to integrate our whole personality, inhibiting and sublimating the tendencies that are inconsistent with its own tendencies and rendering these dominant in all processes of deliberation.

Dr. Kurt Lewin, in the very interesting work to which reference was made above, distinguishes between directive forces (*Kräfte*) and the fundamental energies of the mind, identifying the former with our cognitive systems, and insisting that the former must be regarded as very much smaller or slighter than the latter. I do not understand how we can validly distinguish between forces and energies in this way ; but I think we may validly regard our cognitive systems as directive agencies, though we must, I think, regard them all, higher and lower alike, as activated by the same fundamental energies, namely, those which spring from the conative dispositions of our instincts, and are manifested most directly in crude displays of the primary emotions.

THE HORMIC PSYCHOLOGY

IN the volume *Psychologies of 1925* I took the field as an exponent of *purposive psychology*. Anticipating a little the course of history, I shall here assume that the purposive nature of human action is no longer in dispute, and in this article shall endeavour to define and to justify that special form of purposive psychology which is now pretty widely known as *hormic psychology*. But first a few words in justification of this assumption.

Fifteen years ago American psychologists displayed almost without exception a complete blindness to the most peculiar, characteristic, and important feature of human and animal activity, namely, its goal-seeking. All bodily actions and all phases of experience were mechanical reactions to stimuli, and all learning was the modification of such reactions by the addition of one reaction to another according to the mechanical principles of association. The laws of learning were the laws of frequency, of recency, and of effect; and, though the law of effect as formulated by Thorndike may have suggested to some few minds that the mechanical principles involved were not so clear as might be wished, the laws of frequency and recency could give rise to no such misgivings. The law of effect, with its uncomfortable suggestion of an effect that somehow causes its cause, was pretty generally regarded as something to be got rid of by the substitution of some less ambiguous and more clearly mechanical formula.

Now, happily, all this is changed; the animal psychologists have begun to realise that any description of animal behaviour which ignores its goal-seeking nature is futile, any " explanation " which leaves it out of account, fictitious, and any experimentation which ignores motivation, grossly misleading ; they are busy with the study of " drives," " sets," and " incentives." It is true that their recognition of goal-seeking is in general partial and grudging ; they do not explicitly recognise that a " set " is a set toward an end, that " a drive " is an active striving toward a goal, that an " incentive " is something that provokes such active striving. The terms " striving " and " conation " are still foreign to their vocabularies.

Much the same state of affairs prevails in current American writings on human psychology. Its problems are no longer discussed, experiments are no longer made with total and bland disregard for the purposive nature of human activity. The terms " set," " drive," and " incentive," having been found indispensable in animal psychology, are allowed to appear in discussions of human problems, in spite of their anthropomorphic implications ; " prepotent reflexes," " motives," " drives," " preponderant propensities," " impulses toward ends," " fundamental urges," and even " purposes " now figure in the texts. In the final chapter on personality of a thoroughly mechanical text (1), in which the word " purpose " has been conspicuous by its absence, a rôle of first importance is assigned to " dominant purposes." Motivation, after being almost ignored, has become a problem of central interest. Yet, as was said above, we are in a transition period ; and all this recognition of the purposive nature of human activity is partial and grudging. The author (Dr. H. A. Carr), who tells us on one page that " Man attempts to transform his environment to suit his own purposes," nowhere tells us what he means by the word " purposes " and is careful to tell us on a later page that " We must avoid the naïve assumption that the ulterior consequences of an act either motivate that act or serve as its objective." Almost without exception the authors who make any recognition of the goal-seeking or purposive nature of human and animal activities fall into one of the three following classes : (a) they imply that, if only we knew a little more about the nervous system, we should be able to explain such activities mechanically ; or (*b*) they explicitly make this assertion ; (*c*) more rarely, they proceed to attempt some such explanation.

Partial, half-hearted, reluctant as is still the recognition of purposive activity, it may, I think, fairly be said that only the crude behaviourists now ignore it completely ; that, with that exception, American psychology has become purposive, in the sense that it no longer ignores or denies the goal-seeking nature of human and animal action, but accepts it as a problem to be faced.

It would, then, be otiose in this year of grace to defend or advocate purposive psychology in the vague sense of all psychology that recognises purposiveness, takes account of foresight and of urges, impulses, cravings, desires, as motives of action.

My task is the more difficult one of justifying the far more radically purposive psychology denoted by the adjective " hormic," a psychology which claims to be autonomous ; which refuses to be bound to and limited by the principles current in the physical sciences ; which asserts that active striving towards a goal is a fundamental category of psychology, and is a process of a type that cannot be mechanistically explained or resolved into mechanistic sequences ; which leaves it to the future development of the sciences to decide whether the physical sciences shall continue to be mechanistic or shall find it necessary to adopt hormic interpretations of physical events, and whether we are to have ultimately one science of nature, or two, the mechanistic and the teleological. For hormic psychology is not afraid to use teleological description and explantion. Rather, it insists that those of our activities which we can at all adequately describe are unmistakably and undeniably teleological, are activities which we undertake in the pursuit of some goal, for the sake of some result which we foresee and desire to achieve. And it holds that such activities are the true type of all mental activities and of all truly vital activities, and that, when we seek to interpret more obscure instances of human activity and when we observe on the part of animals actions that clearly are goal-seeking, we are well justified in regarding them as of the same order as our own explicitly teleological or purposive actions.

While the academic psychologies of the recent past have sought to explain the higher types of activity from below upward, taking simple physical and chemical events as their starting-point, hormic pyschology begins by accepting the higher activities, those which are clearly and explicitly purposive and into the nature of which we have the most insight, and seeks to extend such insight downwards to the simpler but more obscure types of action.

Teleology, Intrinsic and Extrinsic

I introduce the term " teleological " early in the exposition because I do not wish to seem to smuggle it in at a later stage after betraying the innocent reader into acceptance of a position which commits him unwittingly to teleology. Modern science has shown an aversion to all teleology ; one might almost say that it has a " complex " on that subject. The origin and development of this unreasoning and unreasonable aversion is intelligible enough. It developed in the course of the conflict of science with religion. The favourite explanation of all obscure natural processes offered by the theologians was that they expressed and were governed by the purpose of the Creator, who had designed and constructed the various objects of the natural world in order that, as parts of one grand system, they might exhibit and fulfil His purposes. Whether the theologians conceived natural objects as having been once and for all designed and created in such a way that natural events would run their courses, fulfilling God's purpose without further intervention on His part, or believed that the finger of God still actively directs the course of natural events, these teleological explanations were, in either case, utterly repugnant to the spirit of modern science : for science had found it possible to explain many events as the effects of natural causes, and it had become the accepted programme of science to extend such explanations as widely as possible.

It has become usual to speak of the explanations offered by science as naturalistic, and to oppose them to the supernatural explanations of the theologians. Now, to explain an event is to assign the causes of it, the play of antecedent events of which the event in question is the consequence. Early scientists inclined to interpret many events after the model of our own experience of causation. We foresee a particular event as a possibility ; we desire to see this possibility realised ; we take action in accordance with our desire, and we seem to guide the course of events in such a way that the foreseen and desired event results. To explain an event as caused in this way was to invoke teleological causation, not the extrinsic supernatural teleology of the theologians, but a natural teleological causation, a causal activity thoroughly familiar to each man through his own repeated experiences of successful action for the attainment of desired goals. Primitive man applied explanation of this type to many natural events, regarding anthropomorphically many natural objects which modern science has taught us to regard as utterly devoid of any such affinity with ourselves. The early students of physical nature did not entirely discard explanations of this type. They regarded natural events more analytically than primitive men had done ; but they still inclined to regard the elements into which they analysed the given natural objects as acting teleologically, as moved by desire, and as striving to achieve the effects they naturally desired. The Newtonian mechanics put an end to explanation of this type in the physical sciences. For it appeared that very many physical events, more especially various astronomical events, could be adequately explained in terms of mass, motion, momentum, attraction, and repulsion, all exactly measurable ; and many such events became strictly predictable from such principles of causation. From such causal explanations all reference to foresight of something, to desire for something, to striving for that something, in fact all reference to the *future* course of events, was wholly excluded. The explanation of any event was given in terms only of other events *antecedent* to it; all reference to possible or probable consequences proved to be unnecessary; explanation was purged of all taint of teleology. Explanation of this type was so successful in the physical sciences that, although the hope of strictly mechanical explanation of all events of the inanimate world is now seen to have been illusory, such ateleological explanation has become established as the type and model to which naturalistic explanation should conform. Such ateleological explanation is what is meant by mechanistic explanation in the broad sense.[1] The mechanistic or ateleological explanations of science were dubbed naturalistic and were accepted in place of the supernatural teleological explanations of theology. So far all was well; the procedure was entirely justified. But at this point an unfortunate confusion of thought became very general. The confusion consisted in falling victim to the compelling force of words and in regarding as supernatural, not only the external teleological causation of the theologians, but also the internal teleological causation or causal activity of men.

This, I say, was an unfortunate and unwarranted confusion; and it still pervades the thinking of most men of science when they approach the problems of psychology and biology. Any proposal to take seriously the teleological causation which seems to be revealed in human activities, to regard such causation as real and effective, they repudiate as trafficking in supernatural causes; for, in learning to repudiate the external supernatural teleology of theology, they have come to regard as also supernatural the internal teleological causation of the human organism. Yet there is no good ground for so regarding it. To desire, to strive, and to attain our goal is as natural as falling off a log, and with such

---

[1] As I have shown in my *Modern Materialism and Emergent Evolution* (21), there is no other way of defining the meaning of the word " mechanistic," no other way than this negative way which defines it by excluding all trace of teleology, all reference to the future; mechanistic means ateleological.

teleological causation we are entirely familiar ; we have more intimate understanding of it than of mechanistic causation.

During the nineteenth century, under the prevalence of the faith that strictly mechanical or Newtonian causation was adequate to the explanation of all events of the inanimate world, it was natural enough to regard such causation as the one and only type of naturalistic causation, and, therefore, to class intrinsic teleological causation with the extrinsic teleological causation of the theologians, as supernatural. But now, when it has become clear that that faith or hope was illusory and that we have no insight into the nature of mechanistic causation, this ground for repudiating intrinsic teleological causation has been taken away—and none remains.

It is probable that the remaining prejudice against it is more than a hang-over from the days of belief in strictly mechanical or Newtonian causation. To accept the teleological causation of human agents is to believe in the causal efficacy of psychical events ; and it seems to be widely felt that to do this is necessarily to commit one's self to psychophysical dualism or animism, and thus to offend against the common preference for a monistic world-view and against the theory of continuity of evolution of the organic from the inorganic. But this is an error which a little clear thinking should quickly dispel. Two monistic theories, both implying continuity of evolution, are now enjoying considerable vogue among both philosophers and men of science, namely, psychic monism and the emergent theory.

Psychic monism, as expounded by Paulsen, Morton Prince, C. A. Strong, Durant Drake, and L. T. Troland, has no ground for doubting the causal efficacy of psychic events ; for its teaching is that all events are psychic Morton Prince, with his ever youthful mind, saw this clearly enough and hence did not hesitate to figure as an exponent of purposive psychology in the volume *Psychologies of 1925* (27). Dr. Troland, curiously enough, seems to cast aside in the most gratuitous fashion the opportunity afforded by his espousal of psychic monism to lift psychology above the sterile plane of mechanistic explanation.

The emergent theory [1] is equally compatible with, and in fact asserts, the causal efficacy of psychic events and the continuity of organic with inorganic evolution ; and it is a monistic theory. Hence it fulfils all the requirements of the psychologist who cannot blind himself to the reality of goal-seeking behaviour and purposive activity, and yet holds fast to monism and continuity of evolution. And it is a theory now in excellent standing, sponsored by such outstanding thinkers as S. Alexander, L. T. Hobhouse, Lloyd Morgan, H. S. Jennings, R. B. Perry, W. M. Wheeler.

With these alternatives open to the choice of the psychologist, he has no valid ground for denying the causal efficacy of psychic activity in the natural world, no ground for continuing to regard intrinsic teleological causation as supernatural, and therefore no ground for blinding himself to the purposive nature of human activity. One suspects that the prevalent reluctance to recognise fully and freely the purposive nature of human activity and the goal-seeking nature of animal activities is mainly due to the fact that most of us were brought up to believe in epiphenomenalism or psychophysical parallelism, those equally illogical, profoundly unsatisfactory, and now discredited makeshifts of a generation dominated by mechanical materialism and imbued with an ill-founded prejudice in favour of regarding all causation as mechanistic. Or perhaps the common case is simpler : throughout a considerable period the physical sciences have worked very successfully in terms of purely mechanistic or ateleological causation ; therefore psychology and all the biological sciences must do likewise. To this contention the answer is obvious : this policy is running psychology and biology in general into a blind alley. Weismannism, the only purely mechanistic theory of biological evolution, has broken down ; and vague theories of creative evolu-

---

[1] Cf. Lloyd Morgan's two volumes of Gifford Lectures, *Emergent Evolution* (24) and *Life, Mind, and Spirit* (25), also my *Modern Materialism and Emergent Evolution* (21) for exposition of the emergent theory.

tion or orthogenesis are the order of the day. There is renewed interest in the possibility of Lamarckian transmission. Physiologists are breaking away from the mechanistic tradition. Dr. K. S. Lashley, in his presidential address to the American Psychological Association, speaking in the light of his own very extensive researches, has thrown all the prevailing views on cerebral action back into the melting-pot without offering a substitute. Three at least of the leaders of biology in America, Lillie, Herrick, and Jennings, are calling aloud for recognition of the causal efficacy in nature of psychical activities.[1] In Great Britain, Drs. J. S. Haldane and E. S. Russell are building up the psychobiological school, which utterly denies the adequacy of mechanistic principles of explantion in biology. (The former bluntly denounces as " clap-trap " the claim, so often repeated " parrot-like," that physiology is revealing the mechanism of life.) The German thinkers interested in the various human sciences, impatient of the failure of the " strictly scientific " psychology taught in the universities to furnish any psychological basis for those sciences, are turning away to construct a psychology of the kind they need, a *geistes-*

[1] Dr. R. S. Lillie (11) writes : " What we agree to call the spiritual appears at times to act directly as a transformer of the physical, as in artistic or other creation. Such experiences cannot be accounted for on physical grounds, for one reason because it is in the very nature of physical abstraction to rule out as irrelevant all factors of a volitional or other ' psychic ' kind. To trace the course of the physiological processes accompanying an act of intellectual creation would undoubtedly give us curious information, of a kind, but would throw little if any light on the essential nature of the reality underlying."

Dr. C. J. Herrick (5) writes : " No abyss of ignorance of what consciousness really is, no futilities of introspective analysis, no dialectic, destroy the simple datum that I have conscious experience and that this experience is a controlling factor in my behaviour. . . . The prevision of possible future consequences of action is a real causative factor in determining which course of action will actually be chosen." Cf. also (6).

H. S. Jennings is no less emphatic. He writes (9) of " that monstrous absurdity that has so long been a reproach to biological science ; the doctrine that ideas, ideals, purposes have no effect on behaviour. The mental determines what happens as does any other determiner. . . . The desires and aspirations of humanity are determiners in the operation of the universe on the same footing with physical determiners."

wissenschaftliche Psychologie, which frankly throws aside the mechanistic principles and recognises the teleological nature of human activity. The Gestalt school of psychology protests against mechanistic interpretations.

Clearly the dominance of biology by the mechanistic ideal of the physical sciences is passing ; while physical science itself is giving up strict determinism and exact predictability. Where, then, is to be found any justification for the old-fashioned prejudice against psychical causation, which, if admitted at all, can be only teleological causation ? Why should not we psychologists, whose business is with the psychical, boldly claim that here is the indeterminate and creative element in nature, rather than leave it to physicists and physiologists to show the way and force us to recognise the fact ? To admit the efficacy of psychical activity in nature is not, as so many seem to imagine, to deny causation.[1] Science must

---

[1] *E.g.*, Professor R. S. Woodworth (33) writes : " Some authors, as especially McDougall, appear to teach that any thorough-going causal interpretation of human behaviour and experience implies shutting one's eyes to the facts of purpose and striving. There is certainly some confusion here. There can be no contradiction between the purposiveness of a sequence of action and its being a causal sequence. A purpose is certainly a cause : if it had no effect, it would be without significance." There is confusion here ; but I suggest it is Woodworth's thinking, rather than mine, that is confused. Both in this essay and in his *Psychology* (34), Woodworth professes to give full recognition to " purpose " and even says, as in the passage cited, that a purpose is a cause. To me it seems very misleading to speak either of " a purpose " or of " a cause." And the sentence, " a purpose is a cause," is ambiguous and confused ; it leaves the reader in doubt of the author's meaning. We go in search of passages which will tell what the author means by " a purpose." We find in the same essay that " Your purpose would be futile if it had no effects, it would be incredible if it had no causes. It is a link in a causal chain, but it is as fine a purpose for all that." Now, in the same essay, Woodworth characteristically refuses to face the question of what he calls " the philosophy of purpose and striving and their place in the world-process as a whole," as also the question of the validity of the mechanistic conception of life. He will not commit himself for or against the mechanistic conception. He seeks to give the impression that his psychology takes full account of the purposive striving of men and animals. He would like to run with the hare and hunt with the hounds ; he desires both to eat his cake and to have it. He is too clear-sighted to ignore the facts of goal-seeking ; but his thinking is too timid to allow him to see and to say that here is a parting of the ways, a crucial question to which one of two answers is right and the other wrong, the question, namely—Is

hold fast to causation, if not to strict determination. Psychical events, though teleological, have their conditions and their causal antecedents; but in them the foreseeing activity is a real factor which makes, not the future event foreseen, but the foreseeing of it as possible and as desirable or repugnant a co-operating factor in the total configuration of the present moment. To put it in other words, valuation is a psychical function which is rooted in the past history of the individual and of the race; and it is an activity that makes a difference; applied to the foreseen possibility, it inclines our activity this way or that, to seek or accept, avoid or reject.

human mental activity mechanistic or is it teleological? However these two terms be defined (and as I have said, the only satisfactory way of defining "mechanistic process" is the negative one of defining it as the ateleological), they are by common consent mutually exclusive: if a process is mechanistic, it is not teleological; and if it is teleological, it is not mechanistic. But in spite of Woodworth's careful non-committal ambiguity, and in spite of his air of giving full recognition to the causal efficacy of purposive striving, it seems that he remains mechanistic; that he means by cause and causation always and only the mechanistic type, and means to repudiate all teleological causation. This comes to light in one passage: he writes of a "need" as "the controlling factor in the activity"; and immediately adds: "Whether the concept of 'need' is a useful dynamic concept is perhaps open to doubt; it smacks considerably of the sort of teleology that we do well to leave aside." Even here he suggests vaguely that there is teleology of some sort that he would not leave aside; but that is merely one more expression of his inveterate tendency to sit on the fence. When we discover finally his definition of "a purpose," it confirms our suspicion that, in spite of all his well-sounding camouflage, Woodworth is on the side of the mechanists: "Conscious purpose is an adjustment still in the making or just being tuned up, and specially an adjustment that is broad and still precise. . . . Purpose is the activity itself, initiated but not completed. It is an activity in progress." Again: "A purpose is a set for a certain activity with foresight of the result of that activity." But does the foresight play any part, or is it merely an accompaniment? Woodworth refuses to commit himself. "How can a conscious purpose have any effect on the brain and muscles anyway? Thus one of the old puzzles of philosophy is injected into our peaceful psychological study, muddling our heads and threatening to wreck our intellectual honesty. We cannot deal with this metaphysical question here" (34). Woodworth would like to explain human action teleologically; but he sees that to do so would be to admit the causal efficacy of psychical activity, and, as he cannot bring himself to take that step, his intellectual "honesty" compels him to put the responsibility on the metaphysicians until such time as the push from his scientific colleagues of the other sciences shall leave him and his fellow-psychologists no option in the matter.

Surely, a future age, looking back upon the vagaries of our own, will record with astonishment the fact that in this early stage of the development of the biological sciences, men of science, while perceiving clearly that the power of foreseeing, of anticipating the future course of events, has developed steadily in the race until in man it has become his most striking characteristic, yet persistently deny that this wonderful capacity is of any service in our struggle for existence.[1]

Two Forms of Teleological or Purposive Psychology, the Hedonistic and the Hormic

The psychologist who can summon enough courage to follow the lead of physicists and biologists and to accept the causal efficacy of psychical activity, of foresight and desire, is confronted with a choice between two theories of the ground of all desire, of all striving or conation, the hedonistic and the hormic.

Psychological hedonism enjoyed a great vogue in the

---

[1] Many eminent physicists have insisted on the control and direction of energy transformations by human agency as something that will not fit with the physicists' scheme of things. Why, then, should psychologists fear to follow them ? I cite a very recent instance. Commenting on Eddington's discussion of the law of entropy as universally valid in the physical realm, Sir O. Lodge (12) writes : " This has long been known, but Eddington illustrates it very luminously by what he calls the operation of ' shuffling.' Given an orderly pack of cards, it may be hopelessly disorganised by shuffling, and no amount of shuffling will bring it back into order. [It is pointless to say, as does a recent reviewer of Eddington's book, that, if you continue to shuffle for an infinite time, the order will be restored ; for the order may be restored by human activity many times in a brief period.] Many of the processes in nature thus result in greater disorganisation ; and, according to Eddington, the irreversible disorganisation measures the entropy. Entropy is disorganisation. It is easy to break an orderly arrangement down, but not so easy to build it up. Yet it can be built up. Not by random and unintelligent processes truly : a mob of monkeys playing on a million typewriters will not compose a volume of poems. The only way to restore order is to apply the activity of mind. . . . Shuffling, as Eddington luminously says, is ' an absent-minded operation.' . . . Mind is essential to organisation, and organisation or reorganisation is a *natural result of mental activity consciously directed to a present end*."

nineteenth century and is not yet dead ; for it embodies some truth. Not every theory of action that assigns a rôle to pleasure and pain is teleological. Two prominent American psychologists, Drs. E. L. Thorndike and L. T. Troland, have elaborated a theory which remains strictly mechanistic, though it assigns a rôle to pleasure and pain. In this theory, pleasure accompanying any form of activity " stamps in " that activity, affects the brain structures in such a way that similar activity is the more likely to recur under similar conditions ; and pain has the opposite effect. It is clear that there is nothing teleological in this form of hedonic theory ; it is a hedonism of the past. It is a striking evidence of the strength of the prejudice against teleological causation, that Dr. Troland, who believes that all things and events are in reality psychical, should thus choose to elaborate his psychical theory in terms of purely mechanistic causation.[1]

A second form of hedonism may be called " hedonism of the present." It asserts that all action is to be regarded as prompted by the pleasure or the pain of the moment of experience. Its position in relation to mechanism and teleology is ambiguous. It can be held and stated in a mechanistic form : the feeling accompanying present process is a factor of causal efficacy in the total configuration, one that prolongs and modifies the total process. It can be stated in a teleological form : the pleasure of the moment prompts efforts to prolong the pleasurable activity and secure more pleasure ; the pain of the present moment prompts an effort to get rid of the pain and secure ease.

---

[1] Cf. (31). Dr. C. J. Herrick (7) follows the same strange procedure. He stoutly asserts the causal efficacy of psychical events, especially of ideals, but just as decidedly proclaims the all-sufficiency of mechanistic principles in biology and psychology. Like Woodworth (cf. footnote 4), he seems to believe that to admit the teleological causation involved in the working of an ideal would be to give up causation. His unexamined postulate is that the natural is the mechanistic, and any non-mechanistic or teleological causation is *ipso facto* non-natural or supernatural. He accepts emergent evolution and asserts that the human brain is a creative agent; yet asserts also that it works purely mechanistically. He does not see that these two assertions are in flat contradiction, that a strictly mechanistic event cannot be creative of novelties ; that to assert it to be so is to make a self-contradictory statement, since " mechanistic " excludes " creation of novelty " in its definition.

In this second form the rôle assigned to foresight renders the formulation teleological.

This second variety of hedonism embodies truth. But it is false if put forward as a general theory of all action. We do seek to prolong pleasant activities and to get rid of pain. But it is not true that all, or indeed any large proportion, of our activities can be explained in this way. Our seeking of a goal, our pursuit of an end, is an activity that commonly incurs pleasure or pain ; but these are incidental consequences. Our striving after food, or a mate, or power, knowledge, revenge, or relief of others' suffering is commonly but little influenced by the hedonic effects incident to our striving. The conation is prior to, and not dependent upon, its hedonic accompaniments, though these may and do modify its course.

The traditional psychological hedonism is thoroughly teleological. It asserts that all human action is performed for the sake of attaining a foreseen pleasure or of avoiding foreseen pain. It is, however, inacceptable, and for two reasons chiefly. First, it is in gross contradiction with clear instances of human action initiated and sustained, not only without anticipation of resulting pleasure or of resulting avoidance of pain, but with clear anticipation of a resulting excess of pain. Secondly, it cannot be applied to the interpretation of animal action (unless, possibly, to some actions of the highest animals) ; and thus would make between human and animal action a radical difference of principle, inconsistent with the well-founded theory of continuity of human with animal evolution.[1]

The hopeless inadequacy of psychological hedonism appears very clearly when it is attempted to apply it to the explanation of our valuations. J. S. Mill attempted to

[1] The fallacy that hedonism can explain both human and animal actions involves, I suggest, a confusion of teleological hedonism, the theory that we act for the sake of attaining pleasure or of avoiding pain, with mechanistic hedonism, the theory that pleasures and pains leave after-effects which play their parts in the determination of subsequent actions, and with hedonism-of-the-present, the theory that pleasure sustains present action and pain checks or turns it aside. The first is used to explain human action; the second or third, or both, to explain animal action.

extricate the doctrine from its predicament in face of the problem of values by recognising lower and higher pleasures ; but it is generally conceded that in so doing he saved his moral theory at the cost of making an indefensible psychological distinction.

It should be sufficient answer to point to that sphere of human experience which the hedonists most commonly adduce in illustration of their theory, namely, the sexual. When we reflect on the profound influence of the sex urge in human life, its vast range, its immeasurable strength that so often drives men to the most reckless adventures and the most tragic disasters or sustains them through immense and prolonged labours, its frenzies of passionate desire, its lofty exaltations and its deep depressions, we must surely conclude that he who would see the ground of all these phenomena in the pleasurable tone of certain cutaneous sensations must lack all personal experience of any but the most trivial manifestations of sex.

The Hormic Theory of Action

We are thus driven to the hormic theory as the only alternative teleological theory of action. The essence of it may be stated very simply. To the question—Why does a certain animal or man seek this or that goal ?—it replies : Because it is his nature to do so. This answer, simple as it may seem, has deep significance.

Observation of animals of any one species shows that all members of the species seek and strive toward a limited number of goals of certain types, certain kinds of food and of shelter, their mates, the company of their fellows, certain geographical areas at certain seasons, escape to cover in presence of certain definable circumstances, dominance over their fellows, the welfare of their young, and so on. For any one species the kinds of goals sought are characteristic and specific ; and all members of the species seek these goals independently of example and of prior experience of attainment of them, though the course of action pursued in the course of striving towards the goal may vary much and may be profoundly modified by experience. We are justified, then, in inferring that each member of the species inherits the tendencies of the species to seek goals of these several types.

Man also is a member of an animal species. And this species also has its natural goals, or its inborn tendencies to seek goals of certain types. This fact is not only indicated very clearly by any comparison of human with animal behaviour, but it is so obvious a fact that no psychologist of the least intelligence fails to recognise it, however inadequately, not even if he obstinately reduces their number to a minimum of three and dubs them the " prepotent reflexes " of sex, fear, and rage. Others write of " primary desires," or of " dominant urges," or of " unconditioned reflexes," or of appetites, or of cravings, or of congenital drives, or of motor sets, or of inherited tendencies or propensities ; lastly, some, bolder than the · rest, write of " so-called instincts." For instincts are out of fashion just now with American psychologists ; and to write of instincts without some such qualification as " so-called " betrays a reckless indifference to fashion amounting almost to indecency. Yet the word " instinct " is too good to be lost to our science. Better than any other word it points to the facts and the problems with which I am here concerned.

The hormic psychology imperatively requires recognition not only of instinctive action but of instincts. Primarily and traditionally the words " instinct " and " instinctive " point to those types of animal action which are complex activities of the whole organism ; which lead the creature to the attainment of one or other of the goals natural to the species ; which are in their general nature manifested by all members of the species under appropriate circumstances ; which exhibit nice adaptation to circumstances ; and which, though often suggesting intelligent appreciation of the end to be gained and the means to be adopted, yet owe little or nothing to the individual's prior experience.[1]

[1] Two very different prejudices have co-operated to give currency in recent psychology to a very perverted and misleading view of instinctive

The words as thus traditionally used point to a problem. The word " instinctive " describes actions of this type. The word " instinct " implies that unknown something which expresses itself in the train of instinctive action directed towards a particular natural goal. What is the nature of that x to which the word " instinct " points ? The problem has provoked much speculation all down the ages ; the answers ranging from " the finger of God " to " a rigid bit of reflex nervous mechanism."

It is characteristic of the hormic theory that it does not presume to give a final and complete answer to this question in terms of entities or types of events that enjoy well-established scientific status.

Hormic activity is an energy manifestation ; but the hormic theory does not presume to say just what form or forms of energy or transformations of energy are ·involved. It seems to involve liberation of energy potential or latent in chemical form in the tissues ; and hormic theory welcomes any information about such transformations that physiological chemistry can furnish. But it refuses to go beyond the facts and to be bound by current

action. On the one hand are those observers of animal life (of whom Fabre and Wasmann are the most distinguished) whose religious philosophy forbids them to admit the essential and close similarities between human and animal actions. Thus prejudiced, they select and emphasise in all their observations and reports of animal, and especially of insect, behaviour the stereotyped unvarying instances, those which seem to imply lack of all individual adaptation to unusual situations. Thus they emphasise the quasi-mechanical character of instinctive behaviour.

On the other hand, the mechanists, moved by the desire to find instinctive actions mechanically explicable, also select and emphasise these same instances and aspects, neglecting to notice the very numerous and striking evidences of adaptability of instinctive action in ways that can only be called intelligent. Thus both parties are led into regarding instinctive behaviour as always a train of action precisely predetermined in the innate constitution of the animal. And this view, of course, readily lends itself to interpretation of all instinctive action as the mechanistic play of chains of reflexes, the touching-off by stimuli of so-called " action-patterns " congenitally formed in the nervous system.

Yet any impartial review of instinctive behaviour [an excellent example is Major R. W. G. Hingston's recent book (8)] shows clearly the falsity of this view, shows beyond dispute that instinctive action (even among the insects) does not consist in any rigidly prescribed sequence of movements, and that any particular type of instinctive hypotheses of physical science; and it refuses to be blinded to the essential facts. And the most essential facts are (*a*) that the energy manifestation is guided into channels such that the organism approaches its goal; (*b*) that this guidance is effected through a cognitive activity, an awareness, however vague, of the present situation and of the goal; (*c*) that the activity, once initiated and set on its path through cognitive activity, tends to continue until the goal is attained; (*d*) that, when the goal is attained, the activity terminates; (*e*) that progress towards and attainment of the goal are pleasurable experiences, and thwarting and failure are painful or disagreeable experiences.

These statements imply that hormic activity is essentially mental activity, involving always cognition or awareness, striving initiated and governed by such cognition, and accruing satisfaction or dissatisfaction. The theory holds that these are three fundamental aspects of all hormic activity, distinguishable by abstraction, but not separable or capable of occurring in nature as separate

behaviour cannot be characterised by the particular movements and sequences of movements but only by the type of goal towards which the action is directed. Any such review reveals clearly two much neglected facts: (1) that very different instincts of the one animal may express themselves in very similar trains of movement; (2) that one instinct may express itself in a great variety of movements. A dog racing along with utmost concentration of energy in the effort of speedy locomotion may be pursuing his prey; he may be fleeing from a larger pursuing dog or leopard; or he may be rushing to join a concourse of dogs. On the other hand, in either fighting or pursuing and seizing his prey, he may bring into play a very large proportion of his total capacities for co-ordinated movement, his native motor mechanisms; and many of the motor mechanisms which he brings into play are identical in the two cases. Or consider the male pigeon in the two very different instinctive activities of fighting and courting; the forms of bodily activity he displays are in many respects so similar that an inexperienced observer may be unable to infer which instinct is at work in him. In both, all the motor mechanisms of locomotion and of self-display, of flying, strutting, walking, running, and vocalisation, are in turn brought into action; few, if any, of the many motor manifestations are peculiar to the expression of either instinct. These facts are very difficult to interpret in terms of neurology; but that difficulty does not justify us in denying or ignoring them. The tendency to deny or ignore the many facts of behaviour that present this difficulty has long been dominant in American psychology and is a bar to progress of the first magnitude.

events.　Thus it necessarily holds that hormic activity can be exhibited only by organisms or natural entities that have a certain complexity of organisation, such entities as have been traditionally called monads.　And it inclines to the view that the simplest form under which such monads appear to us as sensible phenomena is that of the single living cell.　The theory does not seek to explain the genesis of such complex organisations by the coming together of simpler entities.　It inclines to regard any attempt at such a genetic account (such, for example, as has been attempted by various exponents of emergent evolution) as inevitably fruitless : for it regards with extreme scepticism the common assumption that every thing and event can in principle be analysed into some complex of ultimately simple things and events ; and it is especially sceptical of the emergentists' assumption that a conjunction of purely mechanistic events can result in the emergence of teleological events.[1]

The theory is ready to welcome and accept any evidence which physical science can furnish of hormic activity, however lowly, in the inorganic sphere, and is ready to use such evidence to build a bridge between the organic and the inorganic realms ; but it is content to await the verdict of the physicists, confident that its own facts and formulations will stand fast whether that verdict prove to be positive or negative.　In short, the hormic theory holds that where there is life there is mind ; and that, if there has been continuity of evolution of the organic from the inorganic, there must have been something of mind, some trace of mental nature and activity in the inorganic from which such emergence took place.

The Adequacy of the Hormic Theory

The question arises : Is the hormic theory as here stated adequate to the interpretation of all forms of animal and human activity ?　And the question takes two forms : First, can the hormic theory be carried over from psychol-

[1] Cf. my *Modern Materialism and Emergent Evolution* (21).

ogy into physiology ?   Can it be profitably applied to the interpretation of the activities of the several organs and tissues ? This is a very deep question which only the future course of science can answer.   But we notice that biologists are becoming increasingly conscious of the inadequacy of mechanistic principles to their problems, especially the problems of evolution, of heredity, of self-regulation, of the maintenance of organic equilibrium, of the restitution of forms and functions after disturbance of the normal state of affairs in the organism, and are seeing that, as Dr. E. S. Russell (29) emphatically insists, " the essential difference between the inorganic unit and the living individual is that the activities of all living things tend toward some end and are not easily diverted from achieving this end . . . all goes on in the organic world as if living beings strove actively towards an end . . . what differentiates a living thing from all inorganic objects or units is this persistence of striving, this effort towards the expression of deep-lying distinctive tendencies." We therefore are well disposed to agree with this physiologist when he writes : " We must interpret all organic activities as in some sense the actions of a psycho-physical individual."[1]   That is to say, we may reasonably hope that it may become increasingly possible to extend

[1] Dr. J. S. Haldane (3), distinguished as one of the most exact of experimental physiologists, referring to the notion that life and mind may have emerged from a lifeless and mindless, strictly mechanistic realm, writes : " I must frankly confess that to me it seems that such ideas are not clearly thought out.   In fact they convey to me no meaning whatever.   It is very different, however, if we conclude that in spite of superficial appearances something of conscious behaviour must in reality be present behind what appears to us as the mere blind organic behaviour of lower organisms or plants," to which he adds, though on very different grounds—behind also " what appears to be the mere mechanical behaviour of the inorganic world."   In the same volume he rightly insists : " The knowledge represented in the psychological or humanistic group of sciences is not only differentiated clearly from other kinds of scientific knowledge, but is the most fundamental variety of scientific knowledge."   He adds : " I am thoroughly convinced of the limitations attached to physiological interpretation of human behaviour.   At present there is what seems to me an exaggerated idea among the general public, not of the importance of psychological knowledge, for its importance can hardly be overestimated, but of the importance of mere physiological or even physical treatment of human behaviour."

the hormic principle to the elucidation of fundamental problems of physiology and of general biology.

Secondly, are the inborn impulses (*die Triebe*) the only sources of motive power ? For this is the thesis of the hormic theory in the pure form as propounded in my *Social Psychology* in 1908 (13). Let me cite a restatement of it by Professor James Drever of Edinburgh (2). " The basis of the developed mind and character of man must be sought in the original and inborn tendencies of his nature. From these all development and education must start, and with these all human control, for the purposes of education and development, as for the purposes of social and community life, must operate. These are more or less truisms, but they are truisms which have been ignored in much of the educational practice of the past, and in many of the best intentioned efforts at social reorganisation and reform. The original human nature, with which the psychologist is concerned, consists, first of all, of capacities, such as the capacity to have sensations, to perceive, to reason, to learn, and the like, and, secondly, of conscious impulses, the driving forces to those activities without which the capacities would be meaningless." And " though control of primitive impulses becomes more and more complex, it is always a control by that which draws its controlling force, ultimately and fundamentally, from primitive impulses, never a control *ab extra.*" Yet again : " Educationally the most important fact to keep in mind with regard to these specific ' emotional ' tendencies is that in them we have . . . the original, and ultimately the sole important, motive forces determining an individual's behaviour, the sole original determinants of the ends he will seek to attain, as of the interests which crave satisfaction."

If my knowledge of contemporary thought is not gravely at fault, four and only four attempts to supplement the pure hormic theory as here concisely stated call for consideration.

First, we have to consider a view maintained by Professor Drever himself, inconsistently as it seems to me, with his statements cited in the foregoing paragraphs.

He writes in the same treatise : " It must be granted that, in the human being, in addition to the instinctive springs of action, or motive forces which determine behaviour prior to individual experience, pleasure and pain are also motive forces depending upon individual experience " (2, p. 149). To admit this is to combine hedonism with hormism ; and in such combination Dr. Drever does not stand alone ; he is in the good company of Professor S. Freud and all his many disciples.

I take Dr. Drever's statement to mean that man learns to anticipate pain or pleasure from this or that form of activity and in consequence to turn away from the former and to choose the latter. Now, in so far as we have in view the modes of activity adopted or followed as means to our goals, this is certainly true doctrine. Past experiences of pain and pleasure attending our activities are remembered ; they determine our anticipations of pain and pleasure ; and we choose our forms of activity, our lines of approach to our goals, in accordance with such anticipations. But more than this is implied in the statement that " pleasure and pain are also motive forces," as also in Freud's " pleasure principle." It is implied that desire of pleasure and the aversion from pain are motive forces which impel us to goals independently of the hormic impulses. It is a mixed theory of action, which supplements the hormic theory with a measure of hedonism. Is this true ? Does the hormic theory require this admixture ? The answer seems clear in the case of pain. The anticipation of pain from a certain course of action can only deter from that line of activity ; it turns us not from the goal of that activity, but only from the form of activity previously followed in pursuit of that goal ; and, if we can find no other line of activity that promises attainment, we may in the end cease to strive toward that goal ; but the anticipation of the pain is not in itself a motive to action. Pain in the proper sense is always the accompaniment or consequence of thwarting of desire, of failure of impulse or effort ; and, if we desire nothing, if we strive after no goals, we·shall suffer no pains.   This is the great truth underlying the Buddhist philosophy of renunciation.

There is one seeming exception that arises from the ambiguity of language ;   the word " pain " is applied not only to feeling that results from thwarting and failure but also to a specific quality or qualities of sensation. And we are accustomed to regard " pain-sensation " as a spur to action, and also the aversion from anticipated " pain-sensation " as a motive to activity the goal of which is the avoidance of such " pain."   Here is a grand source of confusion ;   which, however, is cleared away forthwith when we recognise the fact that pain-sensation from any part of the body is a specific excitant of fear, and fear is or involves a powerful hormic impulse.

It is notorious that threats of physical punishment, if they are to spur the unwilling child or man to activity, must be pushed to the point of exciting fear in him ; short of that they are of no avail.   The case might be argued at great length ;   but the citation of this one fact may suffice.   The activity prompted by physical pain is an activity of one of the most deeply rooted and powerful of the hormic impulses, the impulse of fear.

If the hormic impulse excited by impressions that involve pain-sensation is not in every case the impulse of the fear instinct, then we can interpret the facts only by postulating a specific impulse of avoidance or withdrawal rooted in a correspondingly specific and simple instinct, closely comparable to the instinct to scratch an itching spot.

The case for desire of pleasure as a motive force is less easily disposed of, the problem is more subtle (18).

Let us note first that pleasure is an abstraction, not a concrete entity or situation ;   it is a feeling qualifying activity.   Hence we find that " pleasures " we are alleged to pursue are pleasurable forms of activity.   In every case the activity in question is sustained by some impulse or desire of other nature and origin than a pure desire for pleasure, namely, some hormic impulse.   Take the simplest instances, most confidently cited by the hedonist —the pleasures of the table and of sex.   A man is said to seek the pleasures of the table.   What in reality he does is to satisfy his appetite for food, his hormic urge to eat, in the most pleasurable manner, choosing those food-substances which, in the light of past experience, he knows will most effectively stimulate and satisfy this impulse. But without the appetite, the hormic urge, there is no pleasure. So also of the man alleged to pursue the pleasures of sex. Moved or motivated by the sex urge he chooses those ways of indulging it which experience has shown him to be most effective in stimulating and satisfying the urge. But without the hormic urge there is no pleasure to be had.

These instances seem to be typical of all the multitude of cases in which men are said to seek pleasure as their goal. Take the complex case of the man who is said to pursue the pleasure of fame or of power. In pursuit of fame or power many a man shuns delights and lives laborious days. But he is moved, his efforts are sustained, by the desire of fame or power, not by the desire of pleasure. If there were not within him the hormic urge to figure in the eyes of the world or to exert power over others, he could find no pleasure in pursuing and in attaining these goals, and he would not in fact pursue them. You may paint the delights of fame or of power in the most glowing colours to the boy or man who is by nature meek and humble ; and your eloquence will fail to stir within him any responsive chord, for in his composition the chord is lacking. On the other hand, in the man in whom the self-assertive impulse is naturally strong, this impulse readily becomes the desire of fame or of power ; and, under the driving power of such desire, he may sacrifice all " pleasures," perhaps with full recognition that fame can come only after his death, or that the attainment of power will involve him in most burdensome and exacting responsibilities. Without the hormic urge which sets his goal, neither will be pursue those goals nor would he find any pleasure in the possession of fame or power, if these came to him as a free gift of the gods. These surely are simple truths illustrated by countless instances in fiction and in real life.

Take one more instance Revenge, it is said, is

sweet ; and men are said to seek the pleasures of revenge. But, if the injured man is a meek and humble creature, if the injury does not evoke in him a burning desire to humble his adversary, to get even with him, to assert his power over him, the statement that revenge is sweet will have no meaning for him, he will have no impulse to avenge his injury, and the imagining of injury to the adversary will neither afford nor promise him pleasure. On the other hand, injury to the proud self-assertive man provokes in him the vengeful impulse, and in planning his revenge he may well gloat upon the prospect of hurting his adversary ; and, if he is a peculiarly sophisticated and ruthless person, he may choose such means to that goal as experience leads him to believe will be most gratifying, most pleasurable.

It is needless to multiply alleged instances of pleasure-seeking ; all alike fall under this one formula : the pleasure is not an end in itself ; it is incidental to the pursuit and attainment of some goal towards which some hormic impulse sets.

Perhaps a word should be added concerning beauty Surely, it may be urged, we seek to attain the beautiful and we value the beautiful object for the sake of the pleasure it gives us ! Here again hedonist æsthetic inverts the true relations. The foundations of all æsthetic theory are here in question. It must suffice to say that the beauty of an object consists not in its power to excite in us a complex of sensations of pleasurable feeling-tone (if it were so, a patchwork quilt should be as beautiful as a Turner landscape) ; it consists rather in the power of the object to evoke in us a multitude of conations that work together in delicately balanced harmony to attain satisfaction in a rich and full appreciation of the significance of the object.[1]

---

[1] This topic is closely connected with the much neglected problem of the acquirement of "tastes," a problem I have dealt with in my *Character and the Conduct of Life* (20).

Since this article was put in print the International Library of Psychology has published a volume (*Pleasure and Instinct : A Study in the Psychology of Human Actions.* London and New York : Harcourt, Brace, 1930) wholly devoted to the examination of the question

A second widely accepted supplementation of the hormic theory is that best represented by the thesis of Dr. R. S. Woodworth's little book, *Dynamic Psychology* (32). I have criticised this at length elsewhere (15) and can therefore deal with it briefly.

Woodworth's thesis may be briefly stated by adopting the language of the passage cited above from Dr. Drever, in which he distinguishes between " capacities " for activities, on the one hand, and, on the other, " conscious impulses, the driving forces to those activities without which the capacities would be meaningless."

The " capacities " that are inborn become immensely differentiated and multiplied in the growing child ; all these may be divided roughly into two great classes, capacities of thinking (of ideation) and capacities of acting, of skilled movement. Now Woodworth's contention is that every such capacity is intrinsically not only a capacity but also a spring of energy, a source of impulsive or motive power ; it is implied that every capacity to think or to act in a certain way is also *ipso facto* a tendency or impulse to think or to act in that way. To put it concretely—if I have acquired the capacity to recite the alphabet, I have acquired also a tendency to repeat it ; if I have acquired the capacity to solve quadratic equations, I have acquired a tendency to solve them ; and so on of all the multitude of specific capacities of thinking and acting which all of us acquire.

This is the modern form of the old intellectualistic doctrine that ideas are forces ; and its long sway proves that it has its allure, if no solid foundation. The hormic

discussed in the foregoing section. The author, A. H. Burlton Allen, after carefully examining the question from every point of view and in the light of all available evidence arrives at the conclusion that the pure hormic theory as defined in this article and in my various books is the only tenable theory of human action. The writer says on p. 273 : " Thus it is no doubt true that there is in the feelings no original force that leads to action. The source of all movement and action lies in the driving force of the main instincts, that is to say, in the inherent energy of the organism striving towards outlet in the forms prescribed by its inherited structure. The feelings of pleasure and unpleasure are secondary results dependant on the successful or unsuccessful working of these instincts."

theory contends that there is no truth, or, if any truth, then but the very smallest modicum in this doctrine. It asks : If each one of the immense array of capacities possessed by a man is also intrinsically a tendency to exercise itself, what determines that at any moment only a certain very small number of them come into action ? The old answer was given in the theory of the association of ideas. Its defects, its utter inadequacy, have been expounded again and again. Yet it rears its head again in this disguised modern form. The hormic answer to the question is that the " capacities " are but so much latent machinery, functional units of differentiated structure ; and that the hormic impulses, working largely through the system of associative links between " capacities," bring into play in turn such capacities as are adapted for service in the pursuit of the natural goals of those impulses. In other words, it maintains that the whole of the machinery of capacities and associative links is dominated by the " interest " of the moment, by conation, by the prevalent desires and active impulses at work in the organism.

It points to " capacities," simple or complex, that remain latent and unused for years, and then (when " the interest " in whose service they were developed is revived, is awakened once more by some change in the man's circumstances) are brought back into action in the service of the renewed interest ; as when a man, having become a parent, recites once more for his children the nursery rhymes and the fairy stories he has learned in childhood.

It may be suggested that the current psychoanalytic treatment of the " complex " is in harmony with Woodworth's principle ; that in this special case " ideas " or " capacities," are validly treated as possessing, in their own right, motive power or conative energy.

It is true that much of the language of Professor Freud and other psychoanalysts seems to countenance this interpretation of the facts. But it must be remembered that the energy of the complex is regarded as in some sense derived from some instinct, generally the sex instinct ; it is *libido*. And though these authors speak of emotion-

ally charged ideas, or ideas *besetzt* with emotional energy
(as though each complex owed its power to a charge of
libido imparted once for all to it), yet it is, I think, in
line with Freud's general treatment to say that such a
" complex " is a " capacity," a structural unit, which has
acquired such connections with the sex (or other) instinct
that the *libido*, or hormic energy of the instinct, readily
flows into it and works through it, and thus is determined
to modes of expression recognisable as due to the influence
of the complex. Consider a fear complex, say a phobia
for running water. There has been acquired a peculiar
formation which leads to a paroxysm of fear with great
expenditure of energy upon the perception of running
water, a reaction which may be repeated at long intervals
through many years. Are we to suppose that this formation, the complex, contains as an integral part of itself
all the energy and all the complex structural organisation
which every manifestation of fear implies, that each fear
complex involves a duplication of the fear organisation
peculiar to itself ? Surely not ! The essence of the new
formation is such a functional relation between the perceptual system concerned in the recognition of running
water and the whole apparatus of fear, that the perception
becomes one of the various afferent channels through
which the fear system may be excited. In this connection
it is to be remembered that a sufficient mass of evidence
points to the thalamic region as the principal seat of the
great affective systems or centres of instinctive excitement.
In neurological terms, the perception of running water
is in the main a cortical event, while the manifestation of
fear is in the main a subcortical or thalamic event ; and
the essential neural ground of the complex-manifestation
is a special acquired cortico-thalamic connection between
the two events, or, more strictly, between the two neuron
systems concerned in the two events and respectively
located in cortex and in thalamus.

The hormist can find no clear instances that support
Woodworth's thesis and can point to a multitude of
instances which indicate an absence of all driving power
in the " capacities " as such He maintains therefore

that the burden of proof lies upon his opponents ; and, though he cannot conclusively prove the negative thesis, that no " capacity " has driving power, he sees no ground for accepting this supplement to the hormic theory.

There remain for brief consideration two very modern theories which claim to find the hormic theory in need of supplementation and to supply such supplement.

I refer first to the psychology of Dr. Ludwig Klages and of his able disciple, Dr. Hans Prinzhorn.[1] According to this teaching (I write subject to correction, for it is not easy to grasp), the hormic theory is true of the life of animals and of the lower functions of the human organism, of all the life of instinct and perceptual activity ; but the life of man is complicated by the co-operation of two factors of a different order, *Geist* and *Wille*, spirit and will, two aspects of a higher purely spiritual principle which is not only of an order different from that of the hormic impulses but is in many respects antagonistic to them, a disturbing influence that threatens to pervert and even destroy the instinctive basis of human life.

I know not what to say of this doctrine. To me it seems to involve a radical dualism not easily to be accepted. It seems to contain echoes of old ways of thinking, of the old opposition of the instinct of animals to the reason of man, of Hegel's objectified spirit, even of Descartes' dualism, the animal body a machine complicated in man by the intervention of reason, although, it is true, these authors repudiate whole-heartedly the mechanical physiology. I suggest that the *Geist* and *Wille* which, as these authors rightly insist, make human life so widely different from the life of even the highest animals, are to be regarded not as some mysterious principles of a radically different order from any displayed in animal life ; that they are rather to be identified with what the Germans call *objectiver Geist*, objectified spirit of humanity, the system of intellectual processes and of cultural values which has been slowly built up as the traditional possession of each

[1] Set forth in numerous works of which one only, Klages' *Psychology of Character* (10) has been translated into English. Prinzhorn's *Leibseele Einheit* (28) gives the best brief approach to this system.

civilisation and largely fixed in the material forms of art and science, in architecture, in tools, in written and printed words, in enduring institutions of many kinds. Each human being absorbs from his social environment some large part of this objectified spirit ; and it is this, working within him, that gives rise to the higher manifestations of human life which in Klages' doctrine are ascribed to *Geist* and *Wille*. Until this interpretation of the facts shall have been shown to be inadequate, there would seem to be no sufficient foundation for the new dualism of Klages and Prinzhorn.

Lastly, I mention an interesting supplement to the hormic theory offered in a recent book by Mr. Olaf Stapledon (30). The author begins by accepting the hormic theory in a thoroughgoing teleological sense. But he goes on to say : " A human being's inheritance would seem to include a capacity for discovering and conating tendencies beyond the inherited nature of his own organism, or his own biological needs." And he chooses, as the clearest illustrations of what he means, instances of love of one person for another. Criticising my view that in sex love we have a sentiment in which the principal motive powers are the impulses of the sexual and of the parental instincts in reciprocal interplay, he writes : " But this theory ignores an important difference between parental behaviour and love, and between the tender emotions and love. Parents do, as a matter of fact, often love their children ; but they do also often merely behave parentally toward them, and feel tender emotion toward them. The love of a parent for a child may be said to be ' derived ' from the parental tendency, in the sense that this tendency first directed attention to the child, and made possible the subsequent *discovery of the child* as itself a living centre of tendencies. And it may well be that in all love there is something of this instinctive parental behaviour. But genuine love, for whatever kind of object, is very different from the tender emotion and from all strictly instinctive parental behaviour. . . . Genuine love . . entails the espousal of the other's needs in the same direct manner in which one espouses one's own private needs.

Merely instinctive behaviour is, so to speak, the conation of a tendency or complex of tendencies of the agent's own body or person. Genuine love is the conation of tendencies of another person . . if love occurs, or in so far as it occurs, the other is regarded, not as a stimulus, but as a centre of tendencies demanding conation in their own right."

Referring to the patriotic sentiment of Joan of Arc, Stapledon writes : " That sentiment certainly did become the ruling factor of her life. And, further, whatever its instinctive sources, her cognition of her social environment turned it into something essentially different from any mere blend of instinctive impulses. The chief weakness of instinct psychology is that it fails, in spite of all efforts to the contrary, to do justice to the part played in behaviour by environment. And this failure is most obvious in human behaviour." He adds that the " instinct psychologists . . . have left out the really distinctive feature of human behaviour."

What, then, is this distinctive feature ? Here is a new challenge to the hormic theory ; a denial not of its truth, up to a certain point, but of its adequacy to cover all the facts and especially the facts of distinctively human activity.

The " distinctive feature," this alleged source of conations not derived from native impulses, is defined as follows : " I am suggesting, then, that the essential basis of conation is not that some tendency of the organism, or of a simple inherited mental structure, is the source (direct or indirect) of every conative act, but that *every* cognition of tendency *may* give rise to a conative act. Every tendency which is an element in the mental content suggests a conation, and is the ground of at least incipient conation. If the tendency does not conflict with other and well-established conative ends, its fulfilment will be desired."

Now, obviously, if this doctrine be true, it is very important. For among tendencies the cognition of any one of which gives rise to corresponding conation, the desire of its fulfilment, Mr. Stapledon includes not only all human and animal tendencies, but also all physical tendencies, *e.g.* the tendency of a stream of water to run downhill, of a stone to fall to the ground, of a needle to fly to the magnet. Of every tendency he asserts : " In the mere act of apprehending *it*, we desire its fulfilment." And " if we ask—' How does the primitive self expand into the developed self ? ' we find the answer is that the most important way of expanding is by the cognition of a wider field of objective tendencies and the conative espousal of those tendencies " ; for " any objective tendency may enter the mental content and influence the will in its own right."

I find this theory very intriguing. But I find also the grounds advanced as its foundation quite unconvincing. They are two : first, the alleged inadequacy of the instinct theory ; secondly, the assertion that every cognition of any tendency tends to evoke corresponding or congruent conation. As regards the former ground, I am, no doubt, a prejudiced witness, yet, in Stapledon's chosen instance of love, I cannot admit the inadequacy. I admit that Joan of Arc's patriotic behaviour was " different from any mere blend of instinctive impulses." Here Stapledon has failed, I think, to grasp the implication of the theory of the sentiments. In the working of a developed sentiment, whether love of country, love of parent for child, or of man for woman, we have to do not merely with a blending and conflicting of primitive impulses. Such a sentiment is a most complex organisation comprising much elaborated cognitive structure as well as instinctive dispositions, and its working can only properly be viewed in the light of the principles of emergence and Gestalt.

Further, Stapledon seems to neglect to take account of the principles of passive and of active sympathy. It is true, I think, that the cognition of a tendency at work in another person tends to evoke or bring into activity the corresponding tendency in the observer ; and in very sympathetic personalities this sympathetic induction works strongly and frequently. When we recognise fully these facts, we cover, I suggest, the manifestation of such complex sentiments as love, which Stapledon chooses to illustrate the inadequacy of the hormic principles. As to his essential novelty, his claim that cognition of any tendency, even merely physical tendency, gives rise to conation similarly directed, I remain entirely unconvinced. There are two parts of this thesis, the second depending on the former ; and both seem to me highly questionable. First, he assumes that the conation rooted in the instinctive nature arises through cognition of an active tendency at work in oneself. This is to make a two- or three-stage affair of the simplest impulsive action. First, the tendency is aroused into activity, presumably by cognition of some object or situation ; secondly, it is cognised ; thirdly, this cognition gives rise to conation. Is not this pure mythology ? Is it correct to say that we strive only when we " espouse " a tendency which we cognise as at work within us ? Is it not rather true that the activity of the tendency primarily aroused by cognition of some object or situation is the conation which proceeds under guidance of further cognition. It seems clear that the instinctive impulse may and often does work subconsciously, that is, without being cognised ; and in any case, its working is so obscure to cognition that the majority of psychologists, failing to cognise or recognise it in any form, deny the reality of such experience of active tendency.

Admitting the wide range in human life of the sym-pathetic principle, admitting that, in virtue of this principle, cognition of desire in others evokes similar desire in ourselves, or a tendency towards the same goal, or a tendency to co-operate with or promote the striving cognised in the other, I cannot find sufficient ground for believing that cognition of tendency in physical objects also directly evokes in us congruent tendency or conation. I would maintain that only when in the mood of poetry or primitive animism we personify natural objects and events, only then do we feel sympathy, or antagonism ; and on the whole we are as liable to feel antagonism as sympathy. When I contemplate the flow of a river, I may murmur with the poet " Even the weariest river winds

somewhere safe to sea," and may feel a sympathetic
inclination to glide with the current ; but I may equally
well (especially if a resident of the lower Mississippi
valley) regard the flowing river as a hostile force against
which I incline to struggle, or (if I am a thrifty Scot) as a
distressing waste of energy ; and, if it is a mountain
stream, I may even be moved to try to dam its course.
Immersed in the water, I am equally ready to enjoy
swimming with the current or struggling up-stream, letting
myself be rushed along with the breaker or hurling myself
against it.   If I contemplate the wind gently moving the
branches of a tree or caressing my face, I may feel it to
be a friendly power and exclaim, " O Wild West Wind,
thou breath of autumn's being " ; or I may observe with
delight the little breezes that " dusk and shiver."   But if I
apprehend the wind as tearing at a tree, buffeting the
ship, or lashing the waves to fury, I am all against it as a
fierce and cruel power to be fought and withstood ;   I
sympathise with the straining tree, the labouring ship,
or the rock or stout building that stands foursquare to all
the winds that blow.   In short, my reaction to the wind
varies as it seems to whisper, to whistle, to sing, to murmur,
to sigh, to moan, to roar, to bluster, to shriek, to rage, to
tear, to storm.   Such sympathies and antagonisms provoked by the forces of nature are the very breath of nature
poetry ;   but they seem to me to afford no support to
Mr. Stapledon's thesis.   The primitive animistic tendency is, I submit, an extension of primitive or passive
sympathy ;   an imaginative extension to inanimate nature
of the emotional stirrings we directly or intuitively discern
in our fellow-creatures, rather than an immediate and
fundamental reaction to all cognition of physical agency,
as Mr. Stapledon maintains.   In gentle highly sympathetic natures, such as Wordsworth's, it works chiefly
in the form of sympathy with natural forces ;   but more
pugnacious and self-assertive natures are more readily
stirred to antagonism and opposition than to congruent
conation.   It would seem that, as is commonly the case
when writers on ethics undertake to construct their own
psychology, Stapledon's supplementation of the hormic

psychology is determined by the needs of his ethical theory rather than by consideration of the observable facts of experience and activity.

I conclude, then, that the hormic theory is adequate and requires no such supplementations as those examined in this section and found to be ill-based and otiose.

The Advantages of the Hormic Theory

One advantage of the hormic theory over all others is that it enables us to sketch in outline an intelligible, consistent, and tenable story of continuous organic evolution, evolution of bodily forms and mental functions in intelligible relation to one another ; and this is something which no other theory can achieve. It does not attempt the impossible task of describing the genesis of experience out of the purely physical and of teleological activity out of purely mechanistic events. It does not make the illegitimate assumption that experience can be analysed into and regarded as compounded out of simple particles or entities. It insists that experience, or each phase of it, is always a unitary whole having aspects that are distinguishable but not separable. It finds good reason to believe that the life of the simplest creature involves such experience, however utterly vague and undifferentiated it may be. It regards the story of organic evolution as one of progressive differentiation and specialisation of structure, of experience and of activity from the most rudimentary and simplest forms. It regards the striving capacities, the hormic tendencies, of each species as having been differentiated out of a primal urge to live, to be active, to seek, to assimilate, to build up, to energise, to counteract the forces of dissolution. Such differentiations of striving involve parallel differentiations of the cognitive function subserving the discrimination of goals. And still further differentiation of it for the discernment and adaptation of means results in longer and more varied chains of activity through which remoter and more difficult goals are attained. The theory recognises that only in the human species does cognitive differentiation attain such a level that detailed foresight of remote goals becomes possible, with such definite hormic fixation on the goal as characterises action properly called purposive in the fullest sense of the word. But it claims that, though the foresight of even the higher animals is but of short range, envisaging only the result to be attained by the next step of action, and that perhaps very vaguely, the cognitive dispositions of the animal are often linked in such fashion as to lead on the hormic urge from step to step, until finally the biological goal is attained and the train of action terminates in satisfaction. It finds in human activity and experience parallels to all the simpler forms of activity displayed and of experience implied in the animals. It sees in the growing infant signs of development from almost blind striving with very short-range and vague foresight (when its cognitive powers are still but slightly differentiated) to increasingly long-range and more adequate foresight enriched by the growing wealth and variety of memory. It insists that memory is for the sake of foresight, and foresight for the sake of action ; and that neither can be validly conceived other than as the working of a forward urge that seeks always something more behind and beyond that which is given in sense-presentation, a something more that will satisfy the hormic urge and bring it for the time being to rest, or permit it to be turned by new sense-impressions to some new goal.

If we turn from the descriptive account of evolution to the problem of the dynamics of the process, the hormic theory again is the only one that can offer an intelligible and self-consistent scheme. It notes how the human creature, through constant striving with infinitely varied circumstances, carries the differentiation of both cognitive and striving powers far beyond the point to which the hereditary momentum will carry them, the point common to the species, how it develops new discriminations, modified goals of appetition and aversion, modified trains of activity for pursuit or retreat. It notes that these modifications are achieved under the guidance of the pleasure and the pain, the satisfaction and dissatisfaction, that attend success and failure respectively ; it inclines to view the evolution or rather the epigenesis of the individual creature's adaptations as the model in the light of which we may interpret the epigenesis of racial adaptations. Such interpretation implies acceptance of Lamarckian transmission ; but, since the only serious ground for rejecting this is the assumption that mechanistic categories are sufficient in biology, an assumption which the hormic psychology rejects, this implication is in its eyes no objection. Rather it points to the increasing weight of evidence of the reality of Lamarckian transmission.[1]

The hormic theory insists that the differentiation of instinctive tendencies has been, throughout the scale of animal evolution, the primary or leading feature of each step. Bodily organs cannot be supposed to have acquired new forms and functional capacities that remained functionless until some congruent variation of instinctive tendency brought them into play. Rather, it is necessary to believe that, in the case of every new development of form or function, the first step was the variation of the instinctive nature of the species toward such activities as required for their efficient exercise the peculiarities of form and function in question. Given such variation, we can understand how natural selection may have brought about the development in the species of the peculiarities of bodily form and function best suited to subserve such modified or new instinctive tendency. Thus the theory overcomes the greatest difficulty of the neo-Darwinian theory, the difficulty, namely, that, if novelties of form and function are to be established in a species, very many of the members must have varied in the same direction at the same time and in such a wide degree as will give survival value to the variation. For, given some changed environmental conditions of a species (*e.g.* a growing

[1] Since 1920 I have conducted an experiment on strictly Lamarckian principles and have found clear-cut evidence of increasing facility in successive generations of animals trained to execute a particular task. This very great increase of facility seems explicable in no other way than by transmission of the modifications acquired by the efforts of the individuals. Cf. two reports in the *British Journal of Psychology* (19, 22).

scarcity of animal food for the carnivorous land ancestor of the seal), the intelligence common to all members might well lead all of them to pursue prey by a new method (the method of swimming and diving). And if this relatively new mode of behaviour became fixed, if the tendency to adopt it became stronger through repeated successful efforts to secure prey in this fashion, natural selection might well perpetuate all congruent bodily variations and might eliminate variations of an opposite kind ; and thus convert the legs of the species into flippers. This is the principle that has been named " organic selection," rendered effective by the recognition of the causal efficacy of hormic striving and the reality of Lamarckian transmission, a principle which without such recognition remains of very dubious value.[1]

The hormic theory thus renders possible a workable theory of animal evolution, one under which the mind, or the mental function of cognition-conation, is the growing point of the organism and of the species, a theory under which the intelligent striving of the organism is the creative activity to which evolution is due. Surely such a theory is more acceptable than any that pretends to illuminate the mystery of evolution by such utterly vague terms as " orthogenesis " or " *élan vital* " or " the momentum of life."

The hormic theory is radically opposed to intellectualism and all its errors, the errors that have been the chief bane of psychology (and of European culture in general) all down the ages. It does not set out with some analytic description of purely cognitive experience, and then find itself at a loss for any intelligible functional relation between this and bodily activities. It recognises fully the conative nature of all activity and regards the cognitive power as everywhere the servant and the guide of striving. Thus it is fundamentally dynamic and leads to a psychology well adapted for application to the sciences and practical problems of human life, those of education, of hygiene, of therapy, of social activity, of religion, of

---

[1] As formulated many years ago by the neo-Darwinians, E. B Poulton, J. M. Baldwin, and Lloyd Morgan.

mythology, of æsthetics, of economics, of politics, and the rest.[1]

Of all forms of psychology the hormic is the only one that can give to philosophy the psychological basis essential to it. Philosophy is properly concerned with values, with evaluation and with standards and scales of value ; it seeks to establish the relative values of the goals men seek, of their ideals, of the forms of character and types of conduct. All such valuation is relative to human nature ; a scale of values formulated with reference, not to man as he is or may be, but to some creature of radically different constitution would obviously be of little value to men ; and philosophy can advance towards a true scale of values only in proportion as it founds itself upon a true account of human nature, its realities and its potentialities. The claim, then, that hormic psychology is the psychology needed by philosophy may seem merely a repetition of the claim that it is true. But it is more than this ; for a glance at the history of philosophy shows that the hormic psychology is the only one with which philosophy can work, the only one on which it can establish a scale of values that does not break to pieces under the slightest examination.

The intellectualist philosophy, adopting an intellectualist psychology of ideas, finds its source and criterion of all values in logical consistency of its system ; and surely it is plain that men do not and will not bear the ills they have, still less struggle heroically against them, supported only by the satisfaction of knowing themselves to be part of a perfectly logical system.

The mechanistic psychology can recognise no values ; can give no account of the process of valuation. At the best it can but (as in Mr. B. Russell's essay, " A Free

---

[1] When a young man I was invited to dine with a distinguished economist and a leading psychologist of that period. It was mentioned that I was taking up psychology. " Ah ! " said the economist, " Psychology ! Yes, very important, very important ! Association of ideas and all that sort of thing. What ! " It was obvious to me that he did not attach the slightest importance to psychology and had neither the faintest inkling of any bearing of it on economics, nor any intention of seeking any such relation. From that moment dates my revulsion against the traditional intellectualistic psychology.

Man's Worship ") hurl defiance at a universe without meaning and without value which man is powerless to alter.

The hedonist psychology consorts only with a hedonist philosophy, which can save itself from being a philosophy of the pig-trough only by postulating with J. S. Mill, in defiance of clarity and of logic, a profound difference of value between higher and lower pleasures.

The hormic psychology alone offers an intelligible and consistent account of human valuations and at the same time offers to philosophy a scientific foundation in which freedom of the rational will of man, the power of creating real novelties, actual and ideal, and the power of self-development towards the ideal both of the individual and of the race, can find their proper place consistently with its fundamental postulates. It is thus the only foundation for a philosophy of meliorism.

The hormic theory, holding fast to the fact that cognition and conation are inseparable aspects of all mental life, does not elaborate a scheme of the cognitive life, a plan of the structure and functioning of the intellect, and leave to some other discipline (be it called ethology or praxiology or ethics) the task of giving some account of character. For it understands that intellect and character are, as structures, just as inseparable as the functions of cognition and conation, are but two aspects, distinguishable only in abstraction, of the structure of personality.

Recognising that introspection can seize and fix in verbal report only the elaborated outcome of a vast and complex interplay of psychophysical events, it avoids the common error of setting over against one another two minds, or two parts of one mind or personality, under such heads as " the Conscious " and " the Unconscious," and steadily sets its face against this mystification, which, though it appeals so strongly to the popular taste for the mysterious and the bizarre, is profoundly misleading.

It recognises that the fundamental nature of the hormic impulse is to work towards its natural goal and to terminate or cease to operate only when and in so far as its natural goal is attained; that the impulse which, in the absence of conflicting impulses, works toward its goal in trains, long or short, of conscious activity (activity, that is, which we can introspectively observe and report with very various degrees of clearness and adequacy) is apt to be driven from the field of conscious activity by conflicting impulses; that, when thus driven from the conscious field, it is not necessarily (perhaps not in any instance) arrested, terminated, brought to zero; that, rather, any impulse, if it is driven from the conscious field before its goal is attained, continues to work subterraneously, subconsciously, and, so working, may obtain partial expressions in the conscious field and in action, expressions which often take the form of not easily interpretable distortions of conscious thinking and of bodily action; that such subconscious activity (but presumably not in any strict sense unconscious activity, far removed though it be from the possibility of introspective observation and report) is a normal feature of the complex life of man, in whom so many natural impulses are checked and repressed by those evoked through the demands of society; that in this way we are to interpret the phenomena now attracting the attention of experimental psychologists under the heads of " perseveration " and " secondary function," as well as all the many morbid and quasi-morbid phenomena of dream life, hallucinations, delusions, compulsions, obsessions, and all the multitudinous bodily and mental symptoms of functional disorder.

The principles of the hormic theory are capable of extension downwards from the conscious life of man, not only to the more explicitly teleological actions of animals, but also to the problems of physiology, the problems of the regulation and interaction of the functioning of all the tissues. It is thus the truly physiological psychology, the psychology that can assimilate and apply the findings of physiology, and in turn can illuminate the problems of physiology, and thus lead to a comprehensive science of the organism; a science which will not regard the organism as a machine with conscious processes somehow mysteriously tacked on to it as " epiphenomena," but a science which will regard the organism as a true organic unity all parts of which are in reciprocal interplay with all other parts and with the whole ; a whole which is not merely the sum of the parts, but a synthetic unity maintained by the systematic reciprocal interaction of all the parts, a unity of integration, a colonial system of lesser units, whose unity is maintained by the harmonious hormic activity of its members in due subordination to the whole.

The hormic psychology has the advantage that it does not pretend to know the answers to the great unsolved riddles of the universe. It leaves to the future the solution of such problems as the relation of the organic to the inorganic realm, the origin or advent of life in our world, the place and destiny of the individual and of the race in the universe, the possibility of powers and potentialities of the race not yet recognised by science. In short, it does not assume any particular cosmology ; it recognises the littleness of man's present understanding ; it makes for the open mind and stimulates the spirit of inquiry, and is hospitable to all empirical evidences and all legitimate speculations.[1]

It is impossible to set forth here the many advantages of the theory in its detailed application to all the special problems of psychology. It must suffice to point out that, unlike the psychologies which begin by accepting such artificial entities of abstraction as reflexes,[2] sensations, ideas, concepts, feelings, in mechanistic interplay accord-

---

[1] Hence it does not close the mind to the much disputed field of alleged phenomena investigated by the Societies for Psychical Research, but makes for a truly scientific attitude towards them, an attitude so conspicuous by its absence in most men of science and especially in academic psychologists.

[2] It is of interest to note that from the purely physiological side protests against the mechanical atomising tendency multiply apace. One of the latest and most important of these is a paper read before the International Congress of Psychology in September 1929, by Dr. G. E. Coghill, who showed good embryological grounds for refusing to regard the spinal reflexes as functional units that first take shape independently and later are brought into some kind of relation with one another. He showed reason to believe that each reflex unit develops by differentiation within the total nervous system of which it never ceases to be a functional part in reciprocal influence with all other parts.

ing to laws of association, fusion, reproduction, and what-not, it regards all experience as expressive of a total activity that is everywhere hormic, selective, teleological. Thus its recognition of the selective goal-seeking nature of our activity, of all the facts implied by the words " desire," " motivation," " attention," and " will," is not reluctant, grudging, and inadequate, added under compulsion of the facts to a mechanical system into which they refuse to fit. It recognises these aspects as fundamental, and traces the genesis of desire, attention, and rational volition irom their germs in the hormic impulses of primitive organisms.

The hormic theory projects a completely systematic and self-consistent psychology on the basis of its recognition of the whole of the organised mind of the adult as a structure elaborated in the service of the hormic urge to more and fuller life. Every part of this vastly complex structure it regards as serving to differentiate the hormic impulses, and to direct them with ever-increasing efficiency towards their natural goals in a world of infinite complexity that offers a multitude of possible routes to any goal, possibilities among which the organism chooses wisely according to the richness of its apparatus of sensory apprehension and its span of synthetic integration of many relations, the effective organisation of its memory, the nicety of its discriminatory judgments, and its sagacity in seizing, out of a multitude of possibilities offered by sense-presentation and memory, the possibilities most relevant to its purposes.

Especially clearly appears the advantage of the hormic psychology in that it is able to render intelligible account of the organisation of the affective or emotional-conative side of the mental structure, a relatively independent part or aspect of the whole of vast importance which remains a closed book to all psychologies of the intellectualistic mechanistic types. This side of the mental structure, which the latter psychologies ignore or recognise most inadequately with such words as " attitudes " and " sets," is treated a little less cavalierly by the psychoanalytic school under the all-inclusive term—" the Unconscious,"

and a little more analytically under the heads of " complexes " and " emotionally toned ideas." But the treatment remains very confused and inadequate, confining
itself almost exclusively to the manifestations of conflict
and disorder in this part of the mind. The hormic
psychology, on the other hand, insists that the elucidation
of this part of the mental organisation is theoretically no
less important, and practically far more important, than
that of the intellectual structure and functions, and is an
integral part of the task of psychology, not a task to be
handed over to some other science, be it called ethics, or
characterology, or ethology, or praxiology, or by any
other name ; for it insists that we cannot understand the
intellectual processes without some comprehension of the
organisation and working of the affective processes whose
servants they are.

Towards the elucidation of this part of the problem of
psychology it offers the doctrine of the sentiments, the
true functional systems of the developed mind, through
the development of which in the growing individual the
native hormic impulses become further differentiated and
directed to a multitude of new and specialised goals, a
process which obscurely and profoundly modifies the
nature of these native tendencies ; for in these new and
individually acquired systems, the sentiments, the native
tendencies are brought into various co-operations, form
new dynamic syntheses in which their individuality is
lost and from which true novelties of desire, of emotion,
and of action emerge.

Further, it aims to show how these fundamental
functional systems, the sentiments, tend to become
organised in one comprehensive system, character, which,
when it is harmoniously integrated, can override all the
crude promptings of instinctive impulse however strong,
can repress, redirect, or sublimate them on every occasion,
and thus, in intimate co-operation with the intellectual
organisation, engender that highest manifestation of
personality, rational volition.

Lastly, the hormic theory is ready to welcome and is
capable of assimilating all that is sound and useful in

the newer schools of psychology. Unlike the various psychologies currently taught in the American colleges, it does not find itself indifferent or positively hostile to these newer movements because incapable of assimilating what is of value in them. Rather it finds something of truth and value in the rival psychoanalytic doctrines of Freud, of Jung, and of Adler, in the allied doctrines of Gestalt and Emergence, in the *verstehende* psychology of the *Geisteswissenschaftler*, in the teachings of Spranger, of Erismann, of Jaspers, in the *personalistische* psychology of Stern, in the *Charackterologie* of Klages and Prinzhorn, in the child studies of the Bühlers, in the correlational studies and conclusions of Spearman, and in the quite peculiar system of dynamic interpretation which Dr. Kurt Lewin is developing. This catholicity, this power of comprehensive assimilation of new truth from widely differing systems of psychological thinking is, perhaps, the best proof of the fundamental rightness of the hormic psychology.

Origins of the Hormic Psychology

The psychology of Aristotle is thoroughly teleological ; but it can hardly be claimed that it was purely hormic. In his time the distinction between mechanistic and teleological explanations and that between hedonist and hormic explanations had not been sharply defined. As with most of the later authors who approximate a hormic psychology, his hormic theory is infected with hedonism.[1] But it may at least be said that in Greek thought there were already established two broadly contrasting views of the world, the Apollinian and the

---

[1] Professor W. A. Hammond summarises Aristotle's theory of action as follows : " Desire, as Aristotle employs it, is not a purely pathic or affective element. Feeling as such (theoretically) is completely passive —mere enjoyment of the pleasant or mere suffering of the painful. Aristotle, however, describes desire as an effort towards the attainment of the pleasant ; *i.e.* he includes in it an activity or a conative element. It is feeling with an added quality of impulse (*Trieb*)." Here we see the cloven hoof of hedonism. The hormic theory would say rather that desire is impulse (*Trieb*) with an added quality of feeling.

Dionysian, and that Aristotle was on the Dionysian side.[1]

The Apollinian view was the parent of European intellectualism, of which the keynote has been Socrates' identification of virtue with knowledge. It has generated the allied, though superficially so different, systems of absolute idealism and of Newtonian mechanism; and modern psychology, from Descartes and Locke onward, has reflected in the main the influence of these two systems, with their fundamental postulates of the idea and the atom (or mass-point) in motion.

The inadequacy of the Apollinian view, the misleading nature of its ideal of perfect intelligibility, of complete explanation of all events by deduction from first principles or transparent postulates, has now been manifested in the collapse of pure idealism and of the strictly mechanistic physics; and no less clearly in the culmination of centuries of effort to reconcile the Apollinian ideal with the facts of nature in the doctrine of psychophysical parallelism; a doctrine so unsatisfactory, so obviously a makeshift, so unintelligible, so obstructive to all deeper understanding of nature, that although it was, in one form or another, very widely accepted at the close of the nineteenth century, the century dominated by the Apollinian tradition, it has now been almost universally abandoned, even by those who have nothing to put in its place.

The Dionysian tradition has lived in the main outside the academies. European thought, though it was dominated by Aristotle until the end of the mediæval period, was more concerned with reason than with action, and yielded more and more to Apollinian tradition; and, with the triumph of intellectualism at and after the Renaissance, the Dionysian tradition was represented only by the poets and came near to exclusion from their pages

---

[1] Nietzsche seems to have been the first to point clearly to these contrasting and rival world-views. I have attempted elsewhere (23) to show how these two currents have been represented in psychology all down the stream of European thought and how the distinction affords the best clue to a useful classification of psychological theories, since it distinguishes them in respect to their most fundamental features, their inclination towards intellectualism or towards voluntarism.

also in the great age of Reason, the eighteenth century
The early years of the nineteenth century saw its revival
in the works of the nature poets and of such philosophers
as Oken, Schelling, and Fichte. And in the Scottish
school of mental philosophy it began to find definite
expression in psychology, especially in the works of
Hutcheson and Dugald Stewart, a movement which was
well-nigh extinguished by Bain's capitulation to the
intellectualism of the English association school.

On the continent of Europe, Schopenhauer revived it
with his doctrine of the primacy of will ; and von Hartmann, his disciple, may be said to have first written
psychology on a purely hormic basis,[1] but marred by the
extravagance of his speculations on the unconscious.
Nietzsche's scattered contributions to psychology are
thoroughly hormic ; and Bergson's vague doctrine of the
" *élan vital* " can be classed only under the same heading.
Freud's psychology would be thoroughly hormic, if he
had not spoilt it in his earlier writings by his inclusion
of the hedonist fallacy in the shape of his " pleasure
principle." My *Introduction to Social Psychology* (13)
was, so far as I have learned, the first attempt to construct
a foundation for psychology in strict accordance with the
hormic principle ; and my two *Outlines* (16, 17) represent
the first attempt to sketch a complete psychology (normal
and abnormal) built on the hormic foundation. It was
unfortunate for the hormic theory that my *Social Psychology* was shortly followed by my *Body and Mind* (14).
For my defence of animism in that book created in many
minds the impression that hormism stands or falls with
animism ; an impression that has been, I judge, largely
responsible for the waning of the influence of the former
book in American academic psychology. But the two
theories do not necessarily hang together, as is clearly
shown by Sir P. T. Nunn, that wisest of professors of
education, distinguished as mathematician, philosopher,
and psychologist, who founds his educational theory on a
thoroughly hormic psychology, while repudiating animism.
In his *Education, its Data and First Principles* (26), he

[1] Cf. his *Die Moderne Psychologie* (4).

has given the most lucid and persuasive statement of the hormic principles. In this statement he makes what is, I believe, the first definite proposal to use the terms *horme* and *hormic* in the sense in which they are used in this essay.

It is fitting, then, that this essay should conclude with citations from Dr. Nunn's book, citations that may serve further to clarify and fix the meaning of the terms *horme* and *hormic* and the implications of the theory.

" We need a name," writes Dr. Nunn, " for the fundamental property expressed in the incessant adjustments and adventures that make up the tissue of life. We are directly aware of that property in our conscious activities as an element of " drive," " urge," or felt tendency towards an end. Psychologists call it *conation* and give the name *conative process* to any train of conscious activity which is dominated by such a drive and receives from it the character of unity in diversity." Referring then to instances of the many subconscious activities that find expression in action, he writes : " None of these purposive processes may be called conative, for they lie below, and even far below, the conscious level ; yet a superhuman spectator, who could watch our mental behaviour in the same direct way as we can observe physical events, would see them all as instances of the same class, variant in detail but alike (as we have said) in general plan. In other words, he would see that they all differ from purely mechanical processes by the presence of an internal " drive," and differ from one another only in the material in which the drive works and the character of the ends towards which it is directed. To this element of drive or urge, whether it occurs in the conscious life of man and the higher animals, or in the unconscious activities of their bodies and the (presumably) unconscious behaviour of lower animals, we propose to give a single name—horme (ὅρμη). In accordance with this proposal all the purposive processes of the organism are hormic processes, conative processes being the subclass whose members have the special mark of being conscious.
. . Horme . . . is the basis of the activities that

differentiate the living animal from dead matter, and, therefore, of what we have described as the animal's characteristic attitude of independence towards its world."

Accepting this admirable statement, I will add only one comment. In my recent *Modern Materialism and Emergent Evolution* (21), I have argued that we can interpret the subconscious hormic processes (which Dr. Nunn agrees to regard as purposive or teleological), we can begin to gain some understanding of them, however vague, only if we regard them not as entirely blind but rather as involving, however dimly, something of that foresight (however vague and short-ranging) which is of the essence of our most clearly purposive activities ; that therefore we must regard every hormic process as of the same fundamental nature as our mental activity, even if that interpretation involves us in a provisional dualism, held as a working hypothesis the final verdict upon which can come only with the progress of both the biological and the physical sciences.

REFERENCES

1. CARR, H. A. *Psychology*. London : Longmans, Green, 1925. P. 226.

2. DREVER, J. *Instinct in Man*. Cambridge : Cambridge Univ. Press, 1917. Pp. x + 293.

3. HALDANE, J. S. *The Sciences and Philosophy*. London : Hodder & Stoughton, 1929. P. 344.

4. HARTMANN, E. v. *Die Moderne Psychologie*. Leipzig : Haacke, 1901. Pp. vii + 474.

5. HERRICK, C. J. "The Natural History of Purpose." *Psychol. Rev.*, 1925, **32**, 417–430.

6. ———. "Biological Determinism and Human Freedom." *Int. J. Ethics*, 1926, **37**, 36–52.

7. ———. "Behaviour and Mechanism." *Soc. Forces*, 1928, **7**, 1–11.

8. HINGSTON, R. W. G. *Problems of Instinct and Intelligence*. London : Arnold, 1928. Pp. viii + 296.

9. JENNINGS, H. S. "Diverse Doctrines of Evolution, their Relation to the Practice of Science and of Life." *Science*, 1927, **65**, 19–25.

10. KLAGES, L. *The Science of Character*. (Trans. by W. H. Johnson.) London : Allen & Unwin, 1929. P. 308.

11. LILLIE, R. S. "The Nature of the Vitalistic Dilemma." *J. Phil.*, 1926, **23**, 673–682.

12. LODGE, O. "Beyond Physics." *J. Phil. Stud.*, 1929, **4**, 516–546.

13. MCDOUGALL, W. *An Introduction to Social Psychology*. London : Methuen. Enlarged Edition, 1928. Pp. xxvi + 455.

14. ———. *Body and Mind*. London : Methuen, 1911. Pp. xix + 384.

15. ———. "Motives in the Light of Recent Discussion." *Mind*, 1920, **29**, 277–293.

16. ———. *Outline of Psychology*. London : Methuen. Revised Edition, 1928. Pp. xxii + 456.

17. ———. *Outline of Abnormal Psychology*. London : Methuen, 1926. Pp. xvi + 572.

18. ———. "Pleasure, Pain, and Conation." *Brit. J. Psychol.*, 1926, **17**, 171–180.

19. ———. "An Experiment for the Testing of the Hypothesis of Lamarck." *Brit. J. Psychol.*, 1927, **17**, 267–304.

20. ———. *Character and the Conduct of Life*. London : Methuen, 1927. Pp. xiv + 287.

21. ———. *Modern Materialism and Emergent Evolution*. London : Methuen, 1929. Pp. xi + 296.

22. ———. "Second Report on a Lamarckian Experiment." *Brit. J. Psychol.*, *J. Phil. Stud.*, 1930, **4**, No. 17.

23. ———. "The Present Chaos in Psychology and the Way Out." *J. Phil. Stud.*

24. MORGAN, C. L. *Emergent Evolution*. London : Williams & Norgate, 1923. Pp. xii + 313.

25. ———. *Life, Mind, and Spirit*. London : Williams & Norgate, 1926. P. 356.

26. NUNN, P. T. *Education : its Data and First Principles*. London : Arnold, 1920. P. 224.

27. PRINCE, M. "Three Fundamental Errors of the Behaviourists and the Reconciliation of the Purposive and Mechanistic Concepts." Chap. 9 in *Psychologies of 1925*. Worcester, Mass. : Clark Univ. Press, 1926. Pp. 199–220.

28. PRINZHORN, H. *Leib-seele Einheit*. Potsdam : Müller & Kripenhauer, 1927. P. 201.

29. RUSSELL, E. S. *The Study of Living Things*. London : Methuen, 1924. P. 294.

30. STAPLEDON, W. O. *A Modern Theory of Ethics : A Study of the Relations of Ethics and Psychology.* London : Methuen, 1929. P. 278.

31. TROLAND, L. T. *The Fundamentals of Human Motivation.* New York : Van Nostrand, 1928. P. xiv + 521.

32. WOODWORTH, R. S. *Dynamic Psychology.* New York : Columbia Univ. Press, 1918. P. 210.

33. WOODWORTH, R. S. " Dynamic Psychology." Chap. 5 in *Psychologies of 1925.* Worcester, Mass : Clark Univ. Press, 1926. Pp. 111–126.

34. ———. *Psychology.* London : Methuen. Revised Edition, 1930. Pp. xiv + 590.

SUPPLEMENTARY CHAPTER VIII

A RECTIFICATION, A DIFFICULTY, AND AN ADDITION

IN the foregoing seven supplementary chapters of this book, I have endeavoured to keep it abreast with the progress of psychology in general and of my own thinking. This chapter, which seems likely to be my last attempt in this direction, concisely reports a modification of my treatment of instinct and one novelty, namely, a discussion of a topic entirely overlooked in the body of the book, but one which is intimately related with the main theme, namely, the individually acquired tastes. Of the importance of the theory of tastes, as supplementing the theory of the sentiments, I become increasingly convinced.

In my more recent discussions of instinct I have recognised that the treatment of that fundamental topic in the body of this book may be improved in one respect. The improvement is of minor importance, involving no radical change of view ; but it diminishes some of the difficulties of the hormic theory felt by some readers and, more especially, by its opponents.

I have become convinced that, in describing a typical instinctive disposition as consisting of three distinguishable parts (as on p. 28) I was in error in one respect, namely, in drawing the line of separation between the second and third parts. As I now see, there is no sufficient ground for regarding a conative part as distinguishable from the emotional or affective part. In so far as a motor or efferent part may validly be recognised (and in the most typical forms of instinctive action involving complex nicely co-ordinated movements common to all members of the species, such a motor part

495

can be inferred with certainty) this motor part may properly be regarded as a purely neural apparatus, or motor mechanism, through which the instinctive excitement discharges itself. Now such a system of well-organised pathways of innervation, of motor discharge of the instinctive excitement, such an innate motor mechanism, is, as I say, validly inferred in many of the most typically instinctive actions ; namely, wherever all the members of a species execute an instinctive action independently of prior learning in some one highly stereotyped fashion. Nevertheless, the process of motor innervation in such cases is posterior to, and consequential upon, the truly instinctive mental process, with its cognitive, conative, and affective aspects.

On what grounds do I make this assertion ? On the ground that, when an animal which possesses such innate motor mechanism for the service of an instinct is prevented (as, for example, by some bodily injury or by some experimentally designed conditions of the environment) from attaining the natural goal of the instinct in the usual manner common to the species, it will, (apparently in all cases) to a degree proportional to its position in the scale of intelligence, find other ways, other movements, by means of which to work towards its goal. In the lower insects this power of adapting instinctive movement to special circumstances is very slight : that is the mark of their low position in the scale of intelligence ; and it is because many insects and some other lower animals, such as the spiders, exhibit highly complex stereotyped instinctive movements and very little power of adapting those movements to unusual circumstances, that they have been so widely regarded as manifesting instinct in its pure form, and indeed, by some authors, as the sole exponents of instinctive activity.[1] Yet there is good ground for believing that some adaptability is always potentially present ; even though we may fail to observe the evidence of it in

[1] Professor Bergson's famous separation of instinct from intelligence is based upon the neglect of the adaptability of instinctive action, as presented in its minimum degree in these most purely instinctive actions

particular cases, and may not be sufficiently ingenious to evoke such evidence by experimental interference. And when we turn to the higher insects, such evidence is abundant and may be multiplied indefinitely by judicious and patient experiment.[1]

At the higher level of the birds, the instinctive nature of most of their activities is still obvious ; for, although in the attaining of any one natural goal, such as the completed nest, a pair of birds may use almost every form of co-ordinated movement of which they are capable, and in the most varied combinations and sequences, no observer, other than the psychologist brought up in the atmosphere of the mechanistic dogma, can fail to recognise that such activities are instinctively inspired ; that is, that they are sustained by some native impulse, some propensity common to all members of the species which determines the goal and the goal-seeking. And, when we turn to the higher mammals, the variety of movement and the influence of individual experience in shaping the modes of activity, and still more in determining what objects and situations shall evoke the creature's activities ; and also in determining what means it will employ in striving towards its goals ; this variety and this influence become so large that it is difficult to discern and distinguish the instinctive sources

Just such complications become so abundant and so pronounced in human activities that the layman and nearly half the psychologists are still unable to understand that, here also, the same principles of action, the hormic principles, are manifested ; and even so enlightened a biologist as the late Sir Arthur Thomson can deny that the human mother is moved by a maternal instinct.

I mention the case of Sir Arthur Thomson, because some seven years ago he publicly reproached me with misleading the public in asserting the reality of a maternal instinct in the human species   And it was then I decided

---

[1] I refer the reader to the account of the experiments of my son, Kenneth, with the clay-building wasps (reported in my *Energies of Men*) and to G. W. R. Hingston's *Problems of Instinct and Intelligence*, for numerous illustrations of my point   Also cp. p. 413 *et seq* of this volume.

to try to develop a terminology which would not encounter the resistance which the application of the term " instinct " in human psychology seems inevitably to meet with, even in a biologist so enlightened as Sir Arthur Thomson.

It seems clear that this resistance is founded in the traditional but erroneous view of instinct ; the view, namely, which took form in the days when it was said and commonly accepted that man is governed and activated by reason, while the animals are moved by instinct ; a view which was shaped by a too exclusive attention to the more striking and wonderful examples of instinctive action provided by the lower animals, the insects and spiders and crustaceans more especially. For, under the influence of such one-sided partial and external (*i.e.* non-psychological) interest in instinctive actions (the kind of interest taken by the naturalist and the layman), the most striking and therefore the most distinctive feature of instinctive action appears to be the stereotyped unvarying repetition of trains of complex and commonly advantageous movements whenever the creatures of a given species encounter particular things or circumstances.[1]

Now it cannot be too much insisted upon that this acceptance of the stereotypic quality of action as the essential mark of instinct is, though so widely accepted,

---

[1] The acceptance of such stereotyped activity as the essential mark of instinct, which naturally resulted from such one-sided observation by the impartial layman, was further spread and confirmed by two groups of less naïve observers and writers, as I have pointed out elsewhere. First, there were those who, like the great French observer of insect-life, Henri Fabre, accepted the theological interpretation of instinct, seeing the finger of God at work directly guiding the animal in all its instinctive activities, and who, in the interests of enforcing this view, or under this bias, selected their cases and coloured their descriptions in such a way as to emphasise the stereotypic quality and to hide from sight the variable adaptive quality of instinctive actions. Secondly, the mechanists among the scientists, observing and describing under the influence of the opposite bias, the desire to exhibit all instinctive action as reflex and mechanical, emphasised and selected the same features and ignored the same features as their opponents, the theologians : a most unfortunate instance of two opposite false theories converging to determine the same errors of observation and description.

even by naturalists as famous as Sir Arthur Thomson, an error. The stereotypic quality is the mark, not of the instinctive nature of an action, but rather of the lack of intelligence of the actor. And by " lack of intelligence," I mean, not total, but relative, lack, a low level of intelligence, either natively prescribed or due to special circumstances. Thus the averagely intelligent human being, when half-asleep from fatigue, or under the influence of drugs (such as alcohol) that partially paralyse his " intelligence," and in certain states of disease, falls back in the scale of intelligence and tends to manifest the stereotypic quality of action.

The true outward mark of the instinctive nature of any activity (a mark which cannot always be observed by a single glance nor even by a careful inspection of a single instance, but, in some cases, only by careful comparative study of many instances) is that, independently of prior experience that might conduce to such activity, under particular circumstances the animal strives towards a goal common to its species and in ways more or less common to the species.

Now, as we review the scale of increasing intelligence from insect to man, we see activities inspired and sustained by instinct become less and less stereotyped and more and more varied in adaptation to special circumstances. There is no point in this scale at which we can say that the activities of that level can no longer be said to be instinctive in some sense and degree. We can only say that the share of inborn disposition or of racial constitution and tendency in shaping action becomes more and more overlaid and obscured by intelligent adaptation in the light of individual experience. And, in the case of the average adult human being, this overlaying and obscuring goes so far that we cannot appropriately describe the bulk of his actions as instinctive.

The hormic psychology does not assert, and I have never asserted (at least, to the best of my recollection) that all human actions are instinctive. Rather I have asserted that in all human activities there is a dynamic factor, a sustaining or driving energy, which derives from the instinctive basis common to the human species and, further, that this instinct-derived urge or goal-directed energy is an essential factor without which no such activity would occur. Again, taking any particular kind of outward behaviour, I do not assert that such behaviour is, in all instances, the expression of some one instinct or of the same co-operating instincts. Different motives or impulsions may prompt and sustain outwardly similar behaviours

Let us examine the matter more concretely by going back to the question of a maternal instinct in the human species. This is of very special interest ; because the maternal instinct of the human species is not only denied by Sir Arthur Thomson (and on similar grounds doubted, I suppose, by a multitude of laymen), but is ignored and (by implication) denied by the psycho-analysts who for a third of a century have been trying to construct their psychology on the hormic basis, that is to say, on the postulate of human instincts as the dynamic basis of all human activity. It is denied also by many "behaviorists"; not merely by the more obtuse of them who deny even the sex instinct of our species, but also by the more intelligent, like Dr J. B. Watson ; he, the Arch-behaviourist, mocks at the notion of a maternal instinct in the human species, and refutes it by pointing out that many human mothers require to learn how to bathe their babies (and, I add, do not even know without instruction what is the best kind of soap to use for this purpose) Could any demonstration be more complete or more silly !

I, on the other hand, against all this formidable opposition, continue to maintain the view of the maternal instinct put forward in the first edition of this book, at a time when, as I supposed, there stood in its way nothing more serious than the pompous, confused, and didactic pronouncements of Alexander Bain ; that is to say, I ascribe to it a rôle in human life of the utmost importance. Let me try once more to make clear my view of the rôle of this one instinct, as illustrative of the rôle of human instincts in general   I do not mean that every mother executes upon or about her child some stereotyped series of movements, precisely alike on all occasions and in all human mothers ; nor do I mean that the normal mother, when she cherishes her child in normal fashion, acts without the least comprehension of what she is doing, without consciously aiming at relieving the needs or the distress of the child or at contributing to its well-being.

I do mean that the vast majority of women are naturally moved to respond to any young child's cry of distress with some effort to relieve that distress ; and that such active response is accompanied by the experience of what can most properly be called tender emotion, a quality of experience that cannot be adequately described in words that would make clear the nature of that quality to any one who has never been the subject of it ; yet an experience, the outward signs of which are familiar enough to every observant person and which have been depicted in words, in stone, and in paint by ten thousand artists of all ages.

Further, I mean that the vast majority of women, in thus responding, attain a satisfaction that rises to the level of delight in so far as their efforts are successful ; and that they experience distress, or anxiety or some unpleasant feeling, in so far as their efforts are unsuccessful. I mean also that the tendency to such activity and such experience is rooted in a disposition (at once conative and affective) which is a part or feature of the native constitution, which matures as naturally and spontaneously as, say, the liver or the spleen or any other organ of the organism ; though its full development may be promoted, and perhaps hastened, by appropriate exercise evoked by appropriate objects and situations ; as by a little girl's play with her doll. I mean that, if this particular psycho-physical disposition were completely absent from the constitution of any woman, that woman would never be moved in this fashion by the child's cry of distress ; she would never experience the impulse to aid and relieve such distress, nor the tender emotion that normally accompanies it ; and no other object or situation could evoke in her this impulse or this emotion at any time in her life

I do not mean that such a woman could never execute actions consciously directed to relieve the distress of a child. She might, under the influence of quite other motives (perhaps the desire to earn praise or her daily bread) achieve a fairly good imitation of maternal behaviour. She might even become a professional children's nurse, though that would be very improbable ; and if she did adopt that calling, she would in all probability never achieve any high degree of success and never find much satisfaction in it. Further, if by some strange sport of nature, this particular native disposition were suddenly omitted from the constitution of all members of some branch of the human race, one which had entered upon our contra-ceptive stage of civilisation, then, even though the sexual instinct remained unaffected, that branch of the race would very quickly become extinct ; and the decline in numbers would be far more rapid than it is among our actual contra-ceptive communities, which, if they shall continue to propagate themselves and to survive, will owe that survival, neither to reason nor to the sexual instinct, but predominantly to the maternal instinct, the main ground of the delight which women find in their children and of their desire for the possession of children of their own.

Now let us return to the constitution of the instinctive disposition In the light of the foregoing discussion it seems clear that we should regard the second or central part of it as both affective and conative in function, as responsible both for the emotional or feeling quality of the instinctive response (with the corresponding system of visceral and other innervations which determine what we call the expressions of the emotion) and for the conative experience, with the setting of the goal, with the continued direction of the striving towards that goal, no matter what forms of bodily movement may be used in the course of such striving

It is this central part of the instinct, both affective and conative in function, which we need to distinguish and define as clearly as possible ; and since we can properly and very advantageously regard it as a functional unit of structure, we need for it some special designation. I have, therefore, proposed to speak of this central part of the innate disposition which is an instinct as a *propensity*, making use of a good English word used by many of the older authors in almost this sense.

Under this terminology we recognise in any instinct of the typical and fully developed kind, a central core, the propensity (more technically to be called the conative-affective disposition or, more shortly, the affective disposition, or affective core of the instinct), as well as, on the motor side, some motor mechanism (or complex system of motor mechanisms in the highly complex chain-instincts, such as that of the famous Yucca moth [1]) through which the conative tendency most readily expresses itself; and, on the afferent or receptive side, some one or more cognitive dispositions by means of which the animal is able to perceive the objects that evoke and guide its instinctive striving. The cognitive disposition like the motor mechanism, is in some cases very simple, and in others very complex and multiple. And it is of the first importance, for the understanding of the formation of the sentiments and of all the organisation of our affective life, that the propensity (the central affective-conative core of each instinct) seems capable of functioning in relative independence of both the cognitive and the motor parts of the total instinctive disposition ; readily acquiring functional relations with other cognitive dispositions and with other motor mechanisms than those with which it is innately and directly linked in the racial constitution.

And this central core or propensity, having once attained its full development by a process of spontaneous maturation, seems to maintain its native properties and functions relatively unchanged throughout the life of the creature ; while the cognitive disposition may undergo very great elaboration and differentiation ; and the motor mechanisms may (in man to an unlimited extent, but in

[1] Cp. the account of the very elaborate chain of processes by means of which this moth lays its eggs and provides for the nutrition of its grubs, in my *Outline of Psychology*.

the animals to a very small extent only) undergo that kind of development which we call the acquisition of skills.

The Objection that Emotion results only from Arrest of Tendency

The view here elaborated and rendered more definite, namely, that both the affective and the conative functions of an instinct are functions of one central disposition which functions as one whole (even though we may and do legitimately distinguish in abstraction between the affective and the conative aspects of that functioning) has been widely criticised and opposed by some of the authorities who agree in other respects with the general theory of instinct and its rôle in human life set forth in this book (who, in short, accept the hormic principle of human activity). The ground and the principal ground of such opposition is that the objectors seem to find reason for asserting that the emotions proper (or the primary emotions, regarded as peculiar qualities of experience) are not evoked on every occasion on which the instincts come into operation ; that, rather, the typical instinctive activity, so long as it runs its course smoothly and attains its goal without difficulty or serious obstruction, is not accompanied by emotion ; and that emotion is evoked when, and only when, activity is in some degree obstructed. To the best of my knowledge the first author to put forward this general proposition was F. Paulhan in his *The Laws of Feeling.*[1]

[1] The first edition was published in 1884. Paulhan makes no reference to any earlier statement of the proposition and I can think of none. Using feeling and emotion as nearly synonymous terms, Paulhan's first chapter is devoted to stating " The General Law of the Production of Feeling." And the law proposed is that feeling is in every instance the consequence of the arrest or inhibition of some tendency. The term " tendency " is used in an extremely vague and general and abstract sense. The only attempt to define the term tendency is not very illuminating ; it runs : " We designate as a tendency the first part of the elements of one of these systems, those which, considered in relation to time, appear before the last and which consist in general of a certain activity of the nervous elements." And the word " systems " is illuminated only by the statement that " in man we have a systematisation or a juxtaposition of various small systems more or less bound together." However vague his terms, Paulhan is

Paulhan asserts that : " In hunger, in thirst, in all organic needs which are manifested to consciousness by affective phenomena, we find arrested tendencies." And : " If we ascend in the hierarchy of human needs and deal with desires of a higher order, we still find that they only give rise to affective phenomena when the tendency awakened undergoes inhibition." It seems that, in his view, his law applies equally to all forms of pleasant and unpleasant feeling : " The phenomenon of arrest is especially well illustrated by painful emotions, but we have reason to believe that agreeable impressions are also due to the arrest of motor impulses."

Nowhere does Paulhan adduce a convincing concrete instance to illustrate his general law. He seems to have arrived at this most general law of feeling, not by empirical generalisation, but rather by deduction from a vague highly general speculation to the effect that conscious activity is always in some sense the making of an adjustment and, thus, the overcoming of some lack of adjustment, some difficulty in the way of action ; that, in short, if any organism were so perfectly adapted to its environment that its every physiological need were satisfied by perfectly automatic reflex actions carried out by reflex mechanisms innately given in its nervous constitution, such an organism would never execute any conscious activities, would never become conscious.

Now this speculative assumption has considerable plausibility.[1] But, if Paulhan's general law of emotion means nothing more than the application of this speculative proposition concerning all consciousness to the special

plentifully dogmatic in the assertion of his most general law. " Whatever affective phenomenon we take, we can observe the same fact : the arrest of a tendency. From the most ordinary emotions to the highest and most complex feelings, we can always verify this law." What is meant by arrest of a tendency is illuminated only by the statements that " the production of the affect is brought about by the arrest of a tendency, by an impediment to the systematisation of certain psychical or physical elements," and that " by an arrested tendency I understand a more or less complicated reflex action which cannot terminate as it would if the organisation of the phenomena were complete, if there were full harmony between the organism or its parts and their conditions of existence."

[1] I have propounded it myself in my first published article. *Mind*, 1897

case of emotion, it has no significance as an objection to my theory that the primary emotional qualities are aspects of instinctive activities.

Other authors who make similar objection to my view of the relation of emotion to instinct and who claim to found it empirically would seem to mean that activities sustained by innate or instinctive impulses involve cognitive consciousness, but no affective consciousness whatsoever, unless obstructed ; that, if not obstructed, mental activity is purely intellectual. Others again seem to mean that activity, though it may be pleasantly or unpleasantly toned, is not accompanied by the specific qualities of emotion such as fear or disgust, unless obstructed or inhibited in some degree.

The answer to the objection in both these forms is, I think, that our introspective powers are very inadequate to the task of analysing all our experiences, and especially they are inadequate to the task of introspectively recognising the subtler and feebler shades of affective consciousness. Further, that a general proposition of this kind, asserting a general correlation (in this case, the correlation between emotional experience and instinctive activity) cannot be refuted by pointing to instances in which it is difficult to establish the coincidence of both factors alleged to be correlated, instances that remain disputable for lack of clear evidence of their nature While, on the other hand, the contrary generalisation (to the effect that no emotional quality accompanies instinctive activity unless the activity be obstructed) is refuted, if we can point to a single indisputable instance in which the emotional quality accompanies the unobstructed activity. And I submit and assert that in my own experience and (according to the statements of many men) in the experience of others also, such instances abound. The quality of affective experience we call "fear" seems to afford the clearest possible evidence of this kind. I allege that on many occasions I have experienced instantaneous and unmistakable fear on starting back, recoiling in perfectly unimpeded fashion, from some sudden alarming impression, in many instances an impression of a very trivial kind. Further, many soldiers have related to me how, at the explosion of a shell, or the fall beside them of a shell which failed to explode, they have instantaneously fled away from the spot under an uncontrollable impulse, experiencing as they fled the horrible soul-shaking emotion we call fear.

To cite in support of the opposite view and in refutation of mine (as Rivers did and as Professor Koffka has again recently done) the unquestionable fact that some men have extricated themselves from dangerous situations, coolly and calmly, without experiencing fear, is entirely illogical and ineffective. There are many possible motives, besides fear, for the avoidance of injury or annihilation.

In parallel fashion, there are other motives than the impulse of disgust for refusing to swallow poisonous substances ; but that fact does not prove that the impulse of disgust to spew out an evil-tasting substance can be evoked and can operate without any tinge of the emotional quality of disgust. Similarly, there are many motives that may prompt a man to careful inspection of an unfamiliar object ; but that fact does not prove that the impulse of curiosity can work without any faintest tinge of the emotional quality proper and peculiar to it. Again, one may administer physical punishment in cold blood, from a " stern sense of duty," or with reluctance and shrinking from the act ; or may overcome stupid opposition with tolerant good humour or cool ridicule : but such instances do not prove that the aggressive destructive anger-impulse can work without any faintest accompaniment of angry feeling. Unless psychologists are prepared to observe the more elementary laws of logic, I cannot see that these difficult questions can be profitably discussed.

My difficulty in rebutting this doctrine of " arrest of tendency," as the one essential condition of all emotion, is that, although so many authors have maintained it, and have put it forward as a reason for refuting my view, no one of them has offered any substantial argu-

ment in its support ; and to attack it is, therefore, like
trying to cut a smoke wreathe with a sword

Acquired Tastes and Distastes

The word " taste " is used in common speech in
several senses : we speak of the sense of taste ; of a man
as showing " good taste " ; of another as having " ex-
pensive tastes," or " simple tastes." It is in this last
sense that the word is used in this paragraph   I propose
to discuss very briefly the nature and acquisition and
rôle of the tastes for this and that and the other form
of activity which every man normally acquires.

The most familiar, simple, and transparent instances
of tastes are the tastes for various games and sports
or other forms of active recreation, such as horseback-
riding or sailing.   There are few men who have no
tastes in this sense of the word ; and some tastes, such
as a taste for gardening or farming, become very complex
and intimately bound up with sentiments of various
kinds ; as, for example, a taste for gardening with a
sentiment for a particular garden, one's own home and
garden.   What is commonly called a " hobby " is perhaps
in all cases a taste for some particular form of activity
working in the service of some sentiment   But, in
principle, a taste is something distinct from a sentiment.

In the great majority of people, tastes play a rôle,
though a subordinate rôle, in determining the modes of
activity which they display ; and it may seem, at first
sight, that tastes are in themselves sources of motives
that prompt and sustain activities.

Consider such a taste as that for figure-skating   A
youth begins to skate, moved, perhaps, by the desire to
emulate his companions   He rapidly acquires skill in
this art, practises it with increasing zest, and presently
finds that he has a strong taste for it ; the taste is a
new factor acquired in the course of acquiring skill,
enduring, perhaps, for many years, and manifesting its
existence by prompting him to prefer to spend his leisure
in the exercise of this taste whenever opportunity offers.

Considering such a simple instance, one might incline to say that a taste is a skill, and the acquisition of a skill is *ipso facto* the acquisition of a taste.

But a taste is more than an acquired skill ; as we see at once if we consider the not infrequent cases in which some form of skill is acquired under compulsion   In such cases the subject may, and in some cases does, acquire a taste for the exercise of that form of skill ; but in other cases, the subject, in spite of acquiring under compulsion a certain degree, even a very considerable degree, of skill, acquires at the same time a very strong distaste for the exercise of it. Thousands of children have been compelled by parental pressure to acquire some skill in piano-playing, and at the same time have acquired a distaste, rather than a taste, for such activity. More common are the cases in which a skill is voluntarily acquired for some definite purpose, such as wage-earning ; and the subject remains without either positive taste or distaste for the exercise of that skill.

Distastes, then, are positive acquisitions, no less than tastes ; and both are enduring acquisitions over and above the skill which they may qualify. Consideration of the conditions of acquisition of taste and of distaste for any mode of activity reveals the essential conditions of both processes of acquisition.

Putting aside complicating factors which may favour or make against the acquirement of tastes and distastes (such as compulsion, external rewards and punishments, prizes, glory, reputation, disgrace, social success or failure), I submit that the conditions of formation of a taste or a distaste for any particular mode of activity, bodily or purely mental (such as mathematical activity), may be defined very simply. For any repeated activity in which we are consistently successful we acquire a taste ; and for any repeated activity in which we are more often unsuccessful than successful we acquire a distaste. And in both cases the effect seems to follow from the hedonic law, the law, namely, that success in any activity renders it pleasant, and the pleasure accruing from the activity sustains and re-enforces that activity and accentuates the tendency to repeat it ; while failure or lack of success in any activity is unpleasant, and the displeasure accruing from the activity tends to discourage it, weaken it, and divert us from it, and to leave us disinclined to repeat it.

An additional factor, closely allied but distinguishable, is that successful repetition commonly brings increasing facility or skill ; and the consciousness of this increasing facility or mastery is in itself pleasant, an additional source of pleasure which is founded in the sentiment of self-regard ; while failure to improve, or relative failure as compared with the improvement shown by other persons, is an additional ground of displeasure which assists the formation of a distaste.

There remains the question whether a taste, once acquired and strongly established, can properly be regarded as an independent source of motivation, as a disposition that may engender desire for the exercise of the taste.   This is a very difficult and subtle question I am inclined to answer it in the negative ; although at first sight it may seem obvious that a man does indulge a taste simply for its own sake, or for the sake of the pleasure he expects from such indulgence.   Such cases seem to be the last stronghold of psychological hedonism.

Something must, I think, be conceded to the hedonic principle, namely, that tastes and distastes, once acquired, play a considerable rôle in determining our choice of the means, the modes of activity, through which we work towards our goals.   But that the most pronounced taste ever engenders an independent motive, a desire for a goal, seems to me open to question ; and indeed I would provisionally reject that view and would say that tastes work always and only in the service of motives (desires) springing either from our sentiments or, in some cases, perhaps, directly from our propensities.

I found this verdict chiefly on consideration of cases which seem at first sight most favourable to the opposite view—the cases of pronounced tastes for games, sports, or other forms of recreation   The motives which prompt us to take up such activities are many : obviously, it is not the taste itself that supplies the motive ; for the taste is acquired in the course of practising the particular activity. And the decisive fact seems to be that, when the original motive (such as the desire to make friends or acquaintances, or to establish oneself in a social set, or to benefit one's health, or to distinguish oneself, or to avoid boredom) falls away, the taste that has been acquired may lie latent indefinitely and, perhaps, fade gradually away. We see a similar state of affairs in the case of tastes acquired in the service of more serious motives, such as the tastes acquired in the course of exercising professional skill. The surgeon or the dentist or the professional player of games may acquire a positive taste for the exercise of this or that form of skill ; and yet, if and when he no longer is moved by the desire to earn his living, having perhaps inherited a fortune, he may be well content to take up some other mode of life and to cease to indulge that particular taste.

Finally, let us note that when strong tastes are developed in the service of a strong sentiment, the system of the sentiment becomes consolidated and of correspondingly increased power, efficiency, and stability. The mother who has a strong love for her children, but is inefficient and unsuccessful in her efforts to control and educate them, and generally to promote their welfare, will be apt to find all such activities a burden and even to acquire positive distaste for them. It is such persons that bring sentiments into disrepute ; so that we speak of them disparagingly as mere creatures of sentiment. Whereas the mother who acquires tastes for these forms of activity will find her happiness in the exercise of them ; for they enable and promote the effective operation of the motives springing from her maternal sentiment. Similarly, the patriot who has found no ways in which he can serve his country and has acquired no tastes for such activities remains a somewhat pathetic figure, even if not justly an object of derision   But, in the patriot who has found ways of effectively serving his country and has acquired strong tastes for such activities, the patriotic sentiment, incorporating such tastes, may well become the dominant factor of a life of public-spirited endeavour.

Our likings and dislikings are, then, founded both in our sentiments and in our tastes. Our sentiments determine our likes and dislikes for objects, for persons, places, and things (including such abstract things as justice, generosity, cruelty, and dishonesty) ; our tastes and distastes determine our likes and dislikes for various modes of activity Our sentiments determine our goals and purposes, and sustain our efforts in pursuit of such goals ; our tastes and distastes largely determine our choice of means, of the particular modes of activity to be used in the service of such efforts

INDEX

STRUCTURE OF THE CHARACTER
OF JOHN DOE

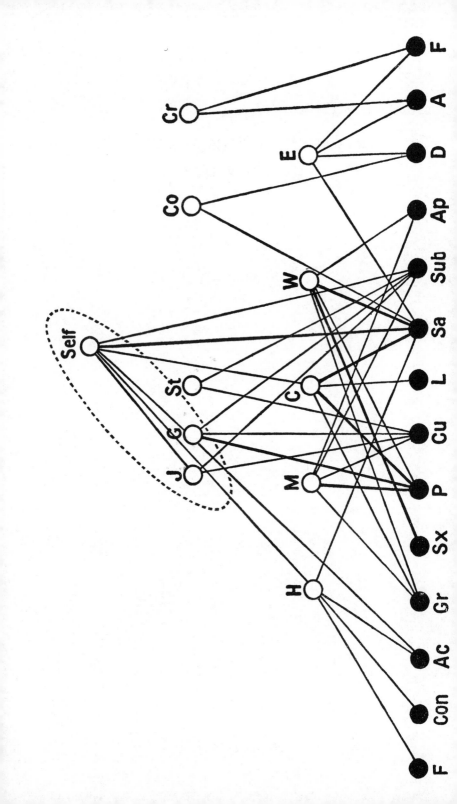

Diagram to illustrate the structure of the character of John Doe, a man who loves his mother, child and wife (M, C, W), hates his enemy (E), and is proud of his home (H) ; who dislikes Cowardice and Cruelty (Co, Cr), admires Strength (St) and Justice (J), lovingly admires Generosity (G) ; who has strong self-respect, has incorporated his sentiments for Justice and Generosity within his self-regarding sentiment, and has extended it to include also his home (H) and his child (C).

The hollow circles of the three higher levels represent the cognitive dispositions corresponding to the objects indicated by the letters attached to them. These are not to be thought of as simple structures, but rather as highly complex and connected in multitudinous fashion with one another ; each one stands for a system of knowledge and belief about the corresponding object. The filled circles of the lowest level stand for the conative-emotional cores of the several instinctive dispositions. The lines connecting them with the circles of the upper levels represent their functional connexions with the cognitive dispositions or systems, the strength or intimacy of each connexion being indicated by the thickness of each line. Any one Sentiment is represented by one cognitive disposition or system, together with the conative-emotional dispositions with which it is connected in the way indicated by the lines of the diagram ; thus John Doe's sentiment for his child consists of the system of which C is the centre, and of which the dispositions Gr, P, L, Sa are the principal conative roots. The key to the conative-emotional dispositions runs as follows : F =food-seeking, Con =construction, Ac =acquisition, Cu =curiosity, L =laughter, Sa =self-assertion, Sx =sex, P =parental or protective tendency, Gr =gregariousness, Ap =appeal, D =disgust, A =anger, F =fear, Sub =submission or self-abasement.

A CATALOG OF SELECTED
DOVER BOOKS
IN ALL FIELDS OF INTEREST

A CATALOG OF SELECTED DOVER
BOOKS IN ALL FIELDS OF INTEREST

CONCERNING THE SPIRITUAL IN ART, Wassily Kandinsky. Pioneering work by father of abstract art. Thoughts on color theory, nature of art. Analysis of earlier masters. 12 illustrations. 80pp. of text. 5⅜ x 8½.   23411-8

ANIMALS: 1,419 Copyright-Free Illustrations of Mammals, Birds, Fish, Insects, etc., Jim Harter (ed.). Clear wood engravings present, in extremely lifelike poses, over 1,000 species of animals. One of the most extensive pictorial sourcebooks of its kind. Captions. Index. 284pp. 9 x 12.   23766-4

CELTIC ART: The Methods of Construction, George Bain. Simple geometric techniques for making Celtic interlacements, spirals, Kells-type initials, animals, humans, etc. Over 500 illustrations. 160pp. 9 x 12. (Available in U.S. only.)   22923-8

AN ATLAS OF ANATOMY FOR ARTISTS, Fritz Schider. Most thorough reference work on art anatomy in the world. Hundreds of illustrations, including selections from works by Vesalius, Leonardo, Goya, Ingres, Michelangelo, others. 593 illustrations. 192pp. 7⅛ x 10¼.   20241-0

CELTIC HAND STROKE-BY-STROKE (Irish Half-Uncial from "The Book of Kells"): An Arthur Baker Calligraphy Manual, Arthur Baker. Complete guide to creating each letter of the alphabet in distinctive Celtic manner. Covers hand position, strokes, pens, inks, paper, more. Illustrated. 48pp. 8¼ x 11.   24336-2

EASY ORIGAMI, John Montroll. Charming collection of 32 projects (hat, cup, pelican, piano, swan, many more) specially designed for the novice origami hobbyist. Clearly illustrated easy-to-follow instructions insure that even beginning papercrafters will achieve successful results. 48pp. 8¼ x 11.   27298-2

THE COMPLETE BOOK OF BIRDHOUSE CONSTRUCTION FOR WOOD-WORKERS, Scott D. Campbell. Detailed instructions, illustrations, tables. Also data on bird habitat and instinct patterns. Bibliography. 3 tables. 63 illustrations in 15 figures. 48pp. 5¼ x 8½.   24407-5

BLOOMINGDALE'S ILLUSTRATED 1886 CATALOG: Fashions, Dry Goods and Housewares, Bloomingdale Brothers. Famed merchants' extremely rare catalog depicting about 1,700 products: clothing, housewares, firearms, dry goods, jewelry, more. Invaluable for dating, identifying vintage items. Also, copyright-free graphics for artists, designers. Co-published with Henry Ford Museum & Greenfield Village. 160pp. 8¼ x 11.   25780-0

HISTORIC COSTUME IN PICTURES, Braun & Schneider. Over 1,450 costumed figures in clearly detailed engravings–from dawn of civilization to end of 19th century. Captions. Many folk costumes. 256pp. 8⅜ x 11¾.   23150-X

STICKLEY CRAFTSMAN FURNITURE CATALOGS, Gustav Stickley and L. & J. G. Stickley. Beautiful, functional furniture in two authentic catalogs from 1910. 594 illustrations, including 277 photos, show settles, rockers, armchairs, reclining chairs, bookcases, desks, tables. 183pp. 6½ x 9¼. 23838-5

AMERICAN LOCOMOTIVES IN HISTORIC PHOTOGRAPHS: 1858 to 1949, Ron Ziel (ed.). A rare collection of 126 meticulously detailed official photographs, called "builder portraits," of American locomotives that majestically chronicle the rise of steam locomotive power in America. Introduction. Detailed captions. xi+ 129pp. 9 x 12. 27393-8

AMERICA'S LIGHTHOUSES: An Illustrated History, Francis Ross Holland, Jr. Delightfully written, profusely illustrated fact-filled survey of over 200 American lighthouses since 1716. History, anecdotes, technological advances, more. 240pp. 8 x 10¾. 25576-X

TOWARDS A NEW ARCHITECTURE, Le Corbusier. Pioneering manifesto by founder of "International School." Technical and aesthetic theories, views of industry, economics, relation of form to function, "mass-production split" and much more. Profusely illustrated. 320pp. 6⅛ x 9¼. (Available in U.S. only.) 25023-7

HOW THE OTHER HALF LIVES, Jacob Riis. Famous journalistic record, exposing poverty and degradation of New York slums around 1900, by major social reformer. 100 striking and influential photographs. 233pp. 10 x 7⅞. 22012-5

FRUIT KEY AND TWIG KEY TO TREES AND SHRUBS, William M. Harlow. One of the handiest and most widely used identification aids. Fruit key covers 120 deciduous and evergreen species; twig key 160 deciduous species. Easily used. Over 300 photographs. 126pp. 5⅜ x 8½. 20511-8

COMMON BIRD SONGS, Dr. Donald J. Borror. Songs of 60 most common U.S. birds: robins, sparrows, cardinals, bluejays, finches, more–arranged in order of increasing complexity. Up to 9 variations of songs of each species.

Cassette and manual 99911-4

ORCHIDS AS HOUSE PLANTS, Rebecca Tyson Northen. Grow cattleyas and many other kinds of orchids–in a window, in a case, or under artificial light. 63 illustrations. 148pp. 5⅜ x 8½. 23261-1

MONSTER MAZES, Dave Phillips. Masterful mazes at four levels of difficulty. Avoid deadly perils and evil creatures to find magical treasures. Solutions for all 32 exciting illustrated puzzles. 48pp. 8¼ x 11. 26005-4

MOZART'S DON GIOVANNI (DOVER OPERA LIBRETTO SERIES), Wolfgang Amadeus Mozart. Introduced and translated by Ellen H. Bleiler. Standard Italian libretto, with complete English translation. Convenient and thoroughly portable–an ideal companion for reading along with a recording or the performance itself. Introduction. List of characters. Plot summary. 121pp. 5¼ x 8½. 24944-1

TECHNICAL MANUAL AND DICTIONARY OF CLASSICAL BALLET, Gail Grant. Defines, explains, comments on steps, movements, poses and concepts. 15-page pictorial section. Basic book for student, viewer. 127pp. 5⅜ x 8½. 21843-0

THE CLARINET AND CLARINET PLAYING, David Pino. Lively, comprehensive work features suggestions about technique, musicianship, and musical interpretation, as well as guidelines for teaching, making your own reeds, and preparing for public performance. Includes an intriguing look at clarinet history. "A godsend," *The Clarinet,* Journal of the International Clarinet Society. Appendixes. 7 illus. 320pp. 5⅜ x 8½. 40270-3

HOLLYWOOD GLAMOR PORTRAITS, John Kobal (ed.). 145 photos from 1926-49. Harlow, Gable, Bogart, Bacall; 94 stars in all. Full background on photographers, technical aspects. 160pp. 8⅜ x 11¼. 23352-9

THE ANNOTATED CASEY AT THE BAT: A Collection of Ballads about the Mighty Casey/Third, Revised Edition, Martin Gardner (ed.). Amusing sequels and parodies of one of America's best-loved poems: Casey's Revenge, Why Casey Whiffed, Casey's Sister at the Bat, others. 256pp. 5⅜ x 8½. 28598-7

THE RAVEN AND OTHER FAVORITE POEMS, Edgar Allan Poe. Over 40 of the author's most memorable poems: "The Bells," "Ulalume," "Israfel," "To Helen," "The Conqueror Worm," "Eldorado," "Annabel Lee," many more. Alphabetic lists of titles and first lines. 64pp. 5$\frac{3}{16}$ x 8¼. 26685-0

PERSONAL MEMOIRS OF U. S. GRANT, Ulysses Simpson Grant. Intelligent, deeply moving firsthand account of Civil War campaigns, considered by many the finest military memoirs ever written. Includes letters, historic photographs, maps and more. 528pp. 6⅛ x 9¼. 28587-1

ANCIENT EGYPTIAN MATERIALS AND INDUSTRIES, A. Lucas and J. Harris. Fascinating, comprehensive, thoroughly documented text describes this ancient civilization's vast resources and the processes that incorporated them in daily life, including the use of animal products, building materials, cosmetics, perfumes and incense, fibers, glazed ware, glass and its manufacture, materials used in the mummification process, and much more. 544pp. 6⅛ x 9¼. (Available in U.S. only.) 40446-3

RUSSIAN STORIES/RUSSKIE RASSKAZY: A Dual-Language Book, edited by Gleb Struve. Twelve tales by such masters as Chekhov, Tolstoy, Dostoevsky, Pushkin, others. Excellent word-for-word English translations on facing pages, plus teaching and study aids, Russian/English vocabulary, biographical/critical introductions, more. 416pp. 5⅜ x 8½. 26244-8

PHILADELPHIA THEN AND NOW: 60 Sites Photographed in the Past and Present, Kenneth Finkel and Susan Oyama. Rare photographs of City Hall, Logan Square, Independence Hall, Betsy Ross House, other landmarks juxtaposed with contemporary views. Captures changing face of historic city. Introduction. Captions. 128pp. 8¼ x 11. 25790-8

AIA ARCHITECTURAL GUIDE TO NASSAU AND SUFFOLK COUNTIES, LONG ISLAND, The American Institute of Architects, Long Island Chapter, and the Society for the Preservation of Long Island Antiquities. Comprehensive, well-researched and generously illustrated volume brings to life over three centuries of Long Island's great architectural heritage. More than 240 photographs with authoritative, extensively detailed captions. 176pp. 8¼ x 11. 26946-9

NORTH AMERICAN INDIAN LIFE: Customs and Traditions of 23 Tribes, Elsie Clews Parsons (ed.). 27 fictionalized essays by noted anthropologists examine religion, customs, government, additional facets of life among the Winnebago, Crow, Zuni, Eskimo, other tribes. 480pp. 6⅛ x 9¼. 27377-6

FRANK LLOYD WRIGHT'S DANA HOUSE, Donald Hoffmann. Pictorial essay of residential masterpiece with over 160 interior and exterior photos, plans, elevations, sketches and studies. 128pp. 9¼ x 10¾. 29120-0

THE MALE AND FEMALE FIGURE IN MOTION: 60 Classic Photographic Sequences, Eadweard Muybridge. 60 true-action photographs of men and women walking, running, climbing, bending, turning, etc., reproduced from rare 19th-century masterpiece. vi + 121pp. 9 x 12. 24745-7

1001 QUESTIONS ANSWERED ABOUT THE SEASHORE, N. J. Berrill and Jacquelyn Berrill. Queries answered about dolphins, sea snails, sponges, starfish, fishes, shore birds, many others. Covers appearance, breeding, growth, feeding, much more. 305pp. 5¼ x 8¼. 23366-9

ATTRACTING BIRDS TO YOUR YARD, William J. Weber. Easy-to-follow guide offers advice on how to attract the greatest diversity of birds: birdhouses, feeders, water and waterers, much more. 96pp. 5³⁄₁₆ x 8¼. 28927-3

MEDICINAL AND OTHER USES OF NORTH AMERICAN PLANTS: A Historical Survey with Special Reference to the Eastern Indian Tribes, Charlotte Erichsen-Brown. Chronological historical citations document 500 years of usage of plants, trees, shrubs native to eastern Canada, northeastern U.S. Also complete identifying information. 343 illustrations. 544pp. 6½ x 9¼. 25951-X

STORYBOOK MAZES, Dave Phillips. 23 stories and mazes on two-page spreads: Wizard of Oz, Treasure Island, Robin Hood, etc. Solutions. 64pp. 8¼ x 11. 23628-5

AMERICAN NEGRO SONGS: 230 Folk Songs and Spirituals, Religious and Secular, John W. Work. This authoritative study traces the African influences of songs sung and played by black Americans at work, in church, and as entertainment. The author discusses the lyric significance of such songs as "Swing Low, Sweet Chariot," "John Henry," and others and offers the words and music for 230 songs. Bibliography. Index of Song Titles. 272pp. 6½ x 9¼. 40271-1

MOVIE-STAR PORTRAITS OF THE FORTIES, John Kobal (ed.). 163 glamor, studio photos of 106 stars of the 1940s: Rita Hayworth, Ava Gardner, Marlon Brando, Clark Gable, many more. 176pp. 8⅜ x 11¼. 23546-7

BENCHLEY LOST AND FOUND, Robert Benchley. Finest humor from early 30s, about pet peeves, child psychologists, post office and others. Mostly unavailable elsewhere. 73 illustrations by Peter Arno and others. 183pp. 5⅜ x 8½. 22410-4

YEKL and THE IMPORTED BRIDEGROOM AND OTHER STORIES OF YIDDISH NEW YORK, Abraham Cahan. Film Hester Street based on *Yekl* (1896). Novel, other stories among first about Jewish immigrants on N.Y.'s East Side. 240pp. 5⅜ x 8½. 22427-9

SELECTED POEMS, Walt Whitman. Generous sampling from *Leaves of Grass*. Twenty-four poems include "I Hear America Singing," "Song of the Open Road," "I Sing the Body Electric," "When Lilacs Last in the Dooryard Bloom'd," "O Captain! My Captain!"–all reprinted from an authoritative edition. Lists of titles and first lines. 128pp. 5³⁄₁₆ x 8¼. 26878-0

THE BEST TALES OF HOFFMANN, E. T. A. Hoffmann. 10 of Hoffmann's most important stories: "Nutcracker and the King of Mice," "The Golden Flowerpot," etc. 458pp. 5⅜ x 8½.   21793-0

FROM FETISH TO GOD IN ANCIENT EGYPT, E. A. Wallis Budge. Rich detailed survey of Egyptian conception of "God" and gods, magic, cult of animals, Osiris, more. Also, superb English translations of hymns and legends. 240 illustrations. 545pp. 5⅜ x 8½.   25803-3

FRENCH STORIES/CONTES FRANÇAIS: A Dual-Language Book, Wallace Fowlie. Ten stories by French masters, Voltaire to Camus: "Micromegas" by Voltaire; "The Atheist's Mass" by Balzac; "Minuet" by de Maupassant; "The Guest" by Camus, six more. Excellent English translations on facing pages. Also French-English vocabulary list, exercises, more. 352pp. 5⅜ x 8½.   26443-2

CHICAGO AT THE TURN OF THE CENTURY IN PHOTOGRAPHS: 122 Historic Views from the Collections of the Chicago Historical Society, Larry A. Viskochil. Rare large-format prints offer detailed views of City Hall, State Street, the Loop, Hull House, Union Station, many other landmarks, circa 1904-1913. Introduction. Captions. Maps. 144pp. 9⅜ x 12¼.   24656-6

OLD BROOKLYN IN EARLY PHOTOGRAPHS, 1865-1929, William Lee Younger. Luna Park, Gravesend race track, construction of Grand Army Plaza, moving of Hotel Brighton, etc. 157 previously unpublished photographs. 165pp. 8⅞ x 11¾.   23587-4

THE MYTHS OF THE NORTH AMERICAN INDIANS, Lewis Spence. Rich anthology of the myths and legends of the Algonquins, Iroquois, Pawnees and Sioux, prefaced by an extensive historical and ethnological commentary. 36 illustrations. 480pp. 5⅜ x 8½.   25967-6

AN ENCYCLOPEDIA OF BATTLES: Accounts of Over 1,560 Battles from 1479 B.C. to the Present, David Eggenberger. Essential details of every major battle in recorded history from the first battle of Megiddo in 1479 B.C. to Grenada in 1984. List of Battle Maps. New Appendix covering the years 1967-1984. Index. 99 illustrations. 544pp. 6½ x 9¼.   24913-1

SAILING ALONE AROUND THE WORLD, Captain Joshua Slocum. First man to sail around the world, alone, in small boat. One of great feats of seamanship told in delightful manner. 67 illustrations. 294pp. 5⅜ x 8½.   20326-3

ANARCHISM AND OTHER ESSAYS, Emma Goldman. Powerful, penetrating, prophetic essays on direct action, role of minorities, prison reform, puritan hypocrisy, violence, etc. 271pp. 5⅜ x 8½.   22484-8

MYTHS OF THE HINDUS AND BUDDHISTS, Ananda K. Coomaraswamy and Sister Nivedita. Great stories of the epics; deeds of Krishna, Shiva, taken from puranas, Vedas, folk tales; etc. 32 illustrations. 400pp. 5⅜ x 8½.   21759-0

THE TRAUMA OF BIRTH, Otto Rank. Rank's controversial thesis that anxiety neurosis is caused by profound psychological trauma which occurs at birth. 256pp. 5⅜ x 8½.   27974-X

A THEOLOGICO-POLITICAL TREATISE, Benedict Spinoza. Also contains unfinished Political Treatise. Great classic on religious liberty, theory of government on common consent. R. Elwes translation. Total of 421pp. 5⅜ x 8½.   20249-6

MY BONDAGE AND MY FREEDOM, Frederick Douglass. Born a slave, Douglass became outspoken force in antislavery movement. The best of Douglass' autobiographies. Graphic description of slave life. 464pp. 5⅜ x 8½. 22457-0

FOLLOWING THE EQUATOR: A Journey Around the World, Mark Twain. Fascinating humorous account of 1897 voyage to Hawaii, Australia, India, New Zealand, etc. Ironic, bemused reports on peoples, customs, climate, flora and fauna, politics, much more. 197 illustrations. 720pp. 5⅜ x 8½. 26113-1

THE PEOPLE CALLED SHAKERS, Edward D. Andrews. Definitive study of Shakers: origins, beliefs, practices, dances, social organization, furniture and crafts, etc. 33 illustrations. 351pp. 5⅜ x 8½. 21081-2

THE MYTHS OF GREECE AND ROME, H. A. Guerber. A classic of mythology, generously illustrated, long prized for its simple, graphic, accurate retelling of the principal myths of Greece and Rome, and for its commentary on their origins and significance. With 64 illustrations by Michelangelo, Raphael, Titian, Rubens, Canova, Bernini and others. 480pp. 5⅜ x 8½. 27584-1

PSYCHOLOGY OF MUSIC, Carl E. Seashore. Classic work discusses music as a medium from psychological viewpoint. Clear treatment of physical acoustics, auditory apparatus, sound perception, development of musical skills, nature of musical feeling, host of other topics. 88 figures. 408pp. 5⅜ x 8½. 21851-1

THE PHILOSOPHY OF HISTORY, Georg W. Hegel. Great classic of Western thought develops concept that history is not chance but rational process, the evolution of freedom. 457pp. 5⅜ x 8½. 20112-0

THE BOOK OF TEA, Kakuzo Okakura. Minor classic of the Orient: entertaining, charming explanation, interpretation of traditional Japanese culture in terms of tea ceremony. 94pp. 5⅜ x 8½. 20070-1

LIFE IN ANCIENT EGYPT, Adolf Erman. Fullest, most thorough, detailed older account with much not in more recent books, domestic life, religion, magic, medicine, commerce, much more. Many illustrations reproduce tomb paintings, carvings, hieroglyphs, etc. 597pp. 5⅜ x 8½. 22632-8

SUNDIALS, Their Theory and Construction, Albert Waugh. Far and away the best, most thorough coverage of ideas, mathematics concerned, types, construction, adjusting anywhere. Simple, nontechnical treatment allows even children to build several of these dials. Over 100 illustrations. 230pp. 5⅜ x 8½. 22947-5

THEORETICAL HYDRODYNAMICS, L. M. Milne-Thomson. Classic exposition of the mathematical theory of fluid motion, applicable to both hydrodynamics and aerodynamics. Over 600 exercises. 768pp. 6⅛ x 9¼. 68970-0

SONGS OF EXPERIENCE: Facsimile Reproduction with 26 Plates in Full Color, William Blake. 26 full-color plates from a rare 1826 edition. Includes "The Tyger," "London," "Holy Thursday," and other poems. Printed text of poems. 48pp. 5¼ x 7. 24636-1

OLD-TIME VIGNETTES IN FULL COLOR, Carol Belanger Grafton (ed.). Over 390 charming, often sentimental illustrations, selected from archives of Victorian graphics–pretty women posing, children playing, food, flowers, kittens and puppies, smiling cherubs, birds and butterflies, much more. All copyright-free. 48pp. 9¼ x 12¼. 27269-9

PERSPECTIVE FOR ARTISTS, Rex Vicat Cole. Depth, perspective of sky and sea, shadows, much more, not usually covered. 391 diagrams, 81 reproductions of drawings and paintings. 279pp. 5⅜ x 8½. 22487-2

DRAWING THE LIVING FIGURE, Joseph Sheppard. Innovative approach to artistic anatomy focuses on specifics of surface anatomy, rather than muscles and bones. Over 170 drawings of live models in front, back and side views, and in widely varying poses. Accompanying diagrams. 177 illustrations. Introduction. Index. 144pp. 8⅜ x11¼. 26723-7

GOTHIC AND OLD ENGLISH ALPHABETS: 100 Complete Fonts, Dan X. Solo. Add power, elegance to posters, signs, other graphics with 100 stunning copyright-free alphabets: Blackstone, Dolbey, Germania, 97 more–including many lower-case, numerals, punctuation marks. 104pp. 8⅛ x 11. 24695-7

HOW TO DO BEADWORK, Mary White. Fundamental book on craft from simple projects to five-bead chains and woven works. 106 illustrations. 142pp. 5⅜ x 8. 20697-1

THE BOOK OF WOOD CARVING, Charles Marshall Sayers. Finest book for beginners discusses fundamentals and offers 34 designs. "Absolutely first rate . . . well thought out and well executed."–E. J. Tangerman. 118pp. 7¾ x 10⅝. 23654-4

ILLUSTRATED CATALOG OF CIVIL WAR MILITARY GOODS: Union Army Weapons, Insignia, Uniform Accessories, and Other Equipment, Schuyler, Hartley, and Graham. Rare, profusely illustrated 1846 catalog includes Union Army uniform and dress regulations, arms and ammunition, coats, insignia, flags, swords, rifles, etc. 226 illustrations. 160pp. 9 x 12. 24939-5

WOMEN'S FASHIONS OF THE EARLY 1900s: An Unabridged Republication of "New York Fashions, 1909," National Cloak & Suit Co. Rare catalog of mail-order fashions documents women's and children's clothing styles shortly after the turn of the century. Captions offer full descriptions, prices. Invaluable resource for fashion, costume historians. Approximately 725 illustrations. 128pp. 8⅜ x 11¼. 27276-1

THE 1912 AND 1915 GUSTAV STICKLEY FURNITURE CATALOGS, Gustav Stickley. With over 200 detailed illustrations and descriptions, these two catalogs are essential reading and reference materials and identification guides for Stickley furniture. Captions cite materials, dimensions and prices. 112pp. 6½ x 9¼. 26676-1

EARLY AMERICAN LOCOMOTIVES, John H. White, Jr. Finest locomotive engravings from early 19th century: historical (1804–74), main-line (after 1870), special, foreign, etc. 147 plates. 142pp. 11⅜ x 8¼. 22772-3

THE TALL SHIPS OF TODAY IN PHOTOGRAPHS, Frank O. Braynard. Lavishly illustrated tribute to nearly 100 majestic contemporary sailing vessels: Amerigo Vespucci, Clearwater, Constitution, Eagle, Mayflower, Sea Cloud, Victory, many more. Authoritative captions provide statistics, background on each ship. 190 black-and-white photographs and illustrations. Introduction. 128pp. 8⅞ x 11¾. 27163-3

LITTLE BOOK OF EARLY AMERICAN CRAFTS AND TRADES, Peter Stockham (ed.). 1807 children's book explains crafts and trades: baker, hatter, cooper, potter, and many others. 23 copperplate illustrations. 140pp. 4⅝ x 6. 23336-7

VICTORIAN FASHIONS AND COSTUMES FROM HARPER'S BAZAR, 1867–1898, Stella Blum (ed.). Day costumes, evening wear, sports clothes, shoes, hats, other accessories in over 1,000 detailed engravings. 320pp. 9⅜ x 12¼. 22990-4

GUSTAV STICKLEY, THE CRAFTSMAN, Mary Ann Smith. Superb study surveys broad scope of Stickley's achievement, especially in architecture. Design philosophy, rise and fall of the Craftsman empire, descriptions and floor plans for many Craftsman houses, more. 86 black-and-white halftones. 31 line illustrations. Introduction 208pp. 6½ x 9¼. 27210-9

THE LONG ISLAND RAIL ROAD IN EARLY PHOTOGRAPHS, Ron Ziel. Over 220 rare photos, informative text document origin (1844) and development of rail service on Long Island. Vintage views of early trains, locomotives, stations, passengers, crews, much more. Captions. 8⅞ x 11¾. 26301-0

VOYAGE OF THE LIBERDADE, Joshua Slocum. Great 19th-century mariner's thrilling, first-hand account of the wreck of his ship off South America, the 35-foot boat he built from the wreckage, and its remarkable voyage home. 128pp. 5⅜ x 8½. 40022-0

TEN BOOKS ON ARCHITECTURE, Vitruvius. The most important book ever written on architecture. Early Roman aesthetics, technology, classical orders, site selection, all other aspects. Morgan translation. 331pp. 5⅜ x 8½. 20645-9

THE HUMAN FIGURE IN MOTION, Eadweard Muybridge. More than 4,500 stopped-action photos, in action series, showing undraped men, women, children jumping, lying down, throwing, sitting, wrestling, carrying, etc. 390pp. 7⅞ x 10⅝. 20204-6 Clothbd.

TREES OF THE EASTERN AND CENTRAL UNITED STATES AND CANADA, William M. Harlow. Best one-volume guide to 140 trees. Full descriptions, woodlore, range, etc. Over 600 illustrations. Handy size. 288pp. 4½ x 6⅜. 20395-6

SONGS OF WESTERN BIRDS, Dr. Donald J. Borror. Complete song and call repertoire of 60 western species, including flycatchers, juncoes, cactus wrens, many more–includes fully illustrated booklet. Cassette and manual 99913-0

GROWING AND USING HERBS AND SPICES, Milo Miloradovich. Versatile handbook provides all the information needed for cultivation and use of all the herbs and spices available in North America. 4 illustrations. Index. Glossary. 236pp. 5⅜ x 8½. 25058-X

BIG BOOK OF MAZES AND LABYRINTHS, Walter Shepherd. 50 mazes and labyrinths in all–classical, solid, ripple, and more–in one great volume. Perfect inexpensive puzzler for clever youngsters. Full solutions. 112pp. 8⅛ x 11. 22951-3

PIANO TUNING, J. Cree Fischer. Clearest, best book for beginner, amateur. Simple repairs, raising dropped notes, tuning by easy method of flattened fifths. No previous skills needed. 4 illustrations. 201pp. 5⅜ x 8½. 23267-0

HINTS TO SINGERS, Lillian Nordica. Selecting the right teacher, developing confidence, overcoming stage fright, and many other important skills receive thoughtful discussion in this indispensible guide, written by a world-famous diva of four decades' experience. 96pp. 5⅜ x 8½. 40094-8

THE COMPLETE NONSENSE OF EDWARD LEAR, Edward Lear. All nonsense limericks, zany alphabets, Owl and Pussycat, songs, nonsense botany, etc., illustrated by Lear. Total of 320pp. 5⅜ x 8½. (Available in U.S. only.) 20167-8

VICTORIAN PARLOUR POETRY: An Annotated Anthology, Michael R. Turner. 117 gems by Longfellow, Tennyson, Browning, many lesser-known poets. "The Village Blacksmith," "Curfew Must Not Ring Tonight," "Only a Baby Small," dozens more, often difficult to find elsewhere. Index of poets, titles, first lines. xxiii + 325pp. 5⅜ x 8¼. 27044-0

DUBLINERS, James Joyce. Fifteen stories offer vivid, tightly focused observations of the lives of Dublin's poorer classes. At least one, "The Dead," is considered a masterpiece. Reprinted complete and unabridged from standard edition. 160pp. 5³⁄₁₆ x 8¼. 26870-5

GREAT WEIRD TALES: 14 Stories by Lovecraft, Blackwood, Machen and Others, S. T. Joshi (ed.). 14 spellbinding tales, including "The Sin Eater," by Fiona McLeod, "The Eye Above the Mantel," by Frank Belknap Long, as well as renowned works by R. H. Barlow, Lord Dunsany, Arthur Machen, W. C. Morrow and eight other masters of the genre. 256pp. 5⅜ x 8½. (Available in U.S. only.) 40436-6

THE BOOK OF THE SACRED MAGIC OF ABRAMELIN THE MAGE, translated by S. MacGregor Mathers. Medieval manuscript of ceremonial magic. Basic document in Aleister Crowley, Golden Dawn groups. 268pp. 5⅜ x 8½. 23211-5

NEW RUSSIAN-ENGLISH AND ENGLISH-RUSSIAN DICTIONARY, M. A. O'Brien. This is a remarkably handy Russian dictionary, containing a surprising amount of information, including over 70,000 entries. 366pp. 4½ x 6⅛. 20208-9

HISTORIC HOMES OF THE AMERICAN PRESIDENTS, Second, Revised Edition, Irvin Haas. A traveler's guide to American Presidential homes, most open to the public, depicting and describing homes occupied by every American President from George Washington to George Bush. With visiting hours, admission charges, travel routes. 175 photographs. Index. 160pp. 8¼ x 11. 26751-2

NEW YORK IN THE FORTIES, Andreas Feininger. 162 brilliant photographs by the well-known photographer, formerly with *Life* magazine. Commuters, shoppers, Times Square at night, much else from city at its peak. Captions by John von Hartz. 181pp. 9¼ x 10¾. 23585-8

INDIAN SIGN LANGUAGE, William Tomkins. Over 525 signs developed by Sioux and other tribes. Written instructions and diagrams. Also 290 pictographs. 111pp. 6⅛ x 9¼. 22029-X

ANATOMY: A Complete Guide for Artists, Joseph Sheppard. A master of figure drawing shows artists how to render human anatomy convincingly. Over 460 illustrations. 224pp. 8⅜ x 11¼. 27279-6

MEDIEVAL CALLIGRAPHY: Its History and Technique, Marc Drogin. Spirited history, comprehensive instruction manual covers 13 styles (ca. 4th century through 15th). Excellent photographs; directions for duplicating medieval techniques with modern tools. 224pp. 8⅜ x 11¼. 26142-5

DRIED FLOWERS: How to Prepare Them, Sarah Whitlock and Martha Rankin. Complete instructions on how to use silica gel, meal and borax, perlite aggregate, sand and borax, glycerine and water to create attractive permanent flower arrangements. 12 illustrations. 32pp. 5⅜ x 8½. 21802-3

EASY-TO-MAKE BIRD FEEDERS FOR WOODWORKERS, Scott D. Campbell. Detailed, simple-to-use guide for designing, constructing, caring for and using feeders. Text, illustrations for 12 classic and contemporary designs. 96pp. 5⅜ x 8½. 25847-5

SCOTTISH WONDER TALES FROM MYTH AND LEGEND, Donald A. Mackenzie. 16 lively tales tell of giants rumbling down mountainsides, of a magic wand that turns stone pillars into warriors, of gods and goddesses, evil hags, powerful forces and more. 240pp. 5⅜ x 8½. 29677-6

THE HISTORY OF UNDERCLOTHES, C. Willett Cunnington and Phyllis Cunnington. Fascinating, well-documented survey covering six centuries of English undergarments, enhanced with over 100 illustrations: 12th-century laced-up bodice, footed long drawers (1795), 19th-century bustles, l9th-century corsets for men, Victorian "bust improvers," much more. 272pp. 5⅜ x 8¼. 27124-2

ARTS AND CRAFTS FURNITURE: The Complete Brooks Catalog of 1912, Brooks Manufacturing Co. Photos and detailed descriptions of more than 150 now very collectible furniture designs from the Arts and Crafts movement depict davenports, settees, buffets, desks, tables, chairs, bedsteads, dressers and more, all built of solid, quarter-sawed oak. Invaluable for students and enthusiasts of antiques, Americana and the decorative arts. 80pp. 6½ x 9¼. 27471-3

WILBUR AND ORVILLE: A Biography of the Wright Brothers, Fred Howard. Definitive, crisply written study tells the full story of the brothers' lives and work. A vividly written biography, unparalleled in scope and color, that also captures the spirit of an extraordinary era. 560pp. 6⅛ x 9¼. 40297-5

THE ARTS OF THE SAILOR: Knotting, Splicing and Ropework, Hervey Garrett Smith. Indispensable shipboard reference covers tools, basic knots and useful hitches; handsewing and canvas work, more. Over 100 illustrations. Delightful reading for sea lovers. 256pp. 5⅜ x 8½. 26440-8

FRANK LLOYD WRIGHT'S FALLINGWATER: The House and Its History, Second, Revised Edition, Donald Hoffmann. A total revision—both in text and illustrations—of the standard document on Fallingwater, the boldest, most personal architectural statement of Wright's mature years, updated with valuable new material from the recently opened Frank Lloyd Wright Archives. "Fascinating"—*The New York Times*. 116 illustrations. 128pp. 9¼ x 10¾. 27430-6

PHOTOGRAPHIC SKETCHBOOK OF THE CIVIL WAR, Alexander Gardner. 100 photos taken on field during the Civil War. Famous shots of Manassas Harper's Ferry, Lincoln, Richmond, slave pens, etc. 244pp. 10⅝ x 8¼. 22731-6

FIVE ACRES AND INDEPENDENCE, Maurice G. Kains. Great back-to-the-land classic explains basics of self-sufficient farming. The one book to get. 95 illustrations. 397pp. 5⅜ x 8½. 20974-1

SONGS OF EASTERN BIRDS, Dr. Donald J. Borror. Songs and calls of 60 species most common to eastern U.S.: warblers, woodpeckers, flycatchers, thrushes, larks, many more in high-quality recording. Cassette and manual 99912-2

A MODERN HERBAL, Margaret Grieve. Much the fullest, most exact, most useful compilation of herbal material. Gigantic alphabetical encyclopedia, from aconite to zedoary, gives botanical information, medical properties, folklore, economic uses, much else. Indispensable to serious reader. 161 illustrations. 888pp. 6½ x 9¼. 2-vol. set. (Available in U.S. only.) Vol. I: 22798-7
Vol. II: 22799-5

HIDDEN TREASURE MAZE BOOK, Dave Phillips. Solve 34 challenging mazes accompanied by heroic tales of adventure. Evil dragons, people-eating plants, blood-thirsty giants, many more dangerous adversaries lurk at every twist and turn. 34 mazes, stories, solutions. 48pp. 8¼ x 11. 24566-7

LETTERS OF W. A. MOZART, Wolfgang A. Mozart. Remarkable letters show bawdy wit, humor, imagination, musical insights, contemporary musical world; includes some letters from Leopold Mozart. 276pp. 5⅜ x 8½. 22859-2

BASIC PRINCIPLES OF CLASSICAL BALLET, Agrippina Vaganova. Great Russian theoretician, teacher explains methods for teaching classical ballet. 118 illustrations. 175pp. 5⅜ x 8½. 22036-2

THE JUMPING FROG, Mark Twain. Revenge edition. The original story of The Celebrated Jumping Frog of Calaveras County, a hapless French translation, and Twain's hilarious "retranslation" from the French. 12 illustrations. 66pp. 5⅜ x 8½. 22686-7

BEST REMEMBERED POEMS, Martin Gardner (ed.). The 126 poems in this superb collection of 19th- and 20th-century British and American verse range from Shelley's "To a Skylark" to the impassioned "Renascence" of Edna St. Vincent Millay and to Edward Lear's whimsical "The Owl and the Pussycat." 224pp. 5⅜ x 8½. 27165-X

COMPLETE SONNETS, William Shakespeare. Over 150 exquisite poems deal with love, friendship, the tyranny of time, beauty's evanescence, death and other themes in language of remarkable power, precision and beauty. Glossary of archaic terms. 80pp. 5³⁄₁₆ x 8¼. 26686-9

THE BATTLES THAT CHANGED HISTORY, Fletcher Pratt. Eminent historian profiles 16 crucial conflicts, ancient to modern, that changed the course of civilization. 352pp. 5⅜ x 8½. 41129-X

THE WIT AND HUMOR OF OSCAR WILDE, Alvin Redman (ed.). More than 1,000 ripostes, paradoxes, wisecracks: Work is the curse of the drinking classes; I can resist everything except temptation; etc. 258pp. 5⅜ x 8½. 20602-5

SHAKESPEARE LEXICON AND QUOTATION DICTIONARY, Alexander Schmidt. Full definitions, locations, shades of meaning in every word in plays and poems. More than 50,000 exact quotations. 1,485pp. 6½ x 9¼. 2-vol. set.
Vol. 1: 22726-X
Vol. 2: 22727-8

SELECTED POEMS, Emily Dickinson. Over 100 best-known, best-loved poems by one of America's foremost poets, reprinted from authoritative early editions. No comparable edition at this price. Index of first lines. 64pp. 5³⁄₁₆ x 8¼. 26466-1

THE INSIDIOUS DR. FU-MANCHU, Sax Rohmer. The first of the popular mystery series introduces a pair of English detectives to their archnemesis, the diabolical Dr. Fu-Manchu. Flavorful atmosphere, fast-paced action, and colorful characters enliven this classic of the genre. 208pp. 5³⁄₁₆ x 8¼. 29898-1

THE MALLEUS MALEFICARUM OF KRAMER AND SPRENGER, translated by Montague Summers. Full text of most important witchhunter's "bible," used by both Catholics and Protestants. 278pp. 6⅝ x 10. 22802-9

SPANISH STORIES/CUENTOS ESPAÑOLES: A Dual-Language Book, Angel Flores (ed.). Unique format offers 13 great stories in Spanish by Cervantes, Borges, others. Faithful English translations on facing pages. 352pp. 5⅜ x 8½. 25399-6

GARDEN CITY, LONG ISLAND, IN EARLY PHOTOGRAPHS, 1869–1919, Mildred H. Smith. Handsome treasury of 118 vintage pictures, accompanied by carefully researched captions, document the Garden City Hotel fire (1899), the Vanderbilt Cup Race (1908), the first airmail flight departing from the Nassau Boulevard Aerodrome (1911), and much more. 96pp. 8⅞ x 11¾. 40669-5

OLD QUEENS, N.Y., IN EARLY PHOTOGRAPHS, Vincent F. Seyfried and William Asadorian. Over 160 rare photographs of Maspeth, Jamaica, Jackson Heights, and other areas. Vintage views of DeWitt Clinton mansion, 1939 World's Fair and more. Captions. 192pp. 8⅞ x 11. 26358-4

CAPTURED BY THE INDIANS: 15 Firsthand Accounts, 1750-1870, Frederick Drimmer. Astounding true historical accounts of grisly torture, bloody conflicts, relentless pursuits, miraculous escapes and more, by people who lived to tell the tale. 384pp. 5⅜ x 8½. 24901-8

THE WORLD'S GREAT SPEECHES (Fourth Enlarged Edition), Lewis Copeland, Lawrence W. Lamm, and Stephen J. McKenna. Nearly 300 speeches provide public speakers with a wealth of updated quotes and inspiration–from Pericles' funeral oration and William Jennings Bryan's "Cross of Gold Speech" to Malcolm X's powerful words on the Black Revolution and Earl of Spenser's tribute to his sister, Diana, Princess of Wales. 944pp. 5⅜ x 8⅜. 40903-1

THE BOOK OF THE SWORD, Sir Richard F. Burton. Great Victorian scholar/adventurer's eloquent, erudite history of the "queen of weapons"–from prehistory to early Roman Empire. Evolution and development of early swords, variations (sabre, broadsword, cutlass, scimitar, etc.), much more. 336pp. 6⅛ x 9¼. 25434-8

CATALOG OF DOVER BOOKS

AUTOBIOGRAPHY: The Story of My Experiments with Truth, Mohandas K. Gandhi. Boyhood, legal studies, purification, the growth of the Satyagraha (nonviolent protest) movement. Critical, inspiring work of the man responsible for the freedom of India. 480pp. 5⅜ x 8½. (Available in U.S. only.) 24593-4

CELTIC MYTHS AND LEGENDS, T. W. Rolleston. Masterful retelling of Irish and Welsh stories and tales. Cuchulain, King Arthur, Deirdre, the Grail, many more. First paperback edition. 58 full-page illustrations. 512pp. 5⅜ x 8½. 26507-2

THE PRINCIPLES OF PSYCHOLOGY, William James. Famous long course complete, unabridged. Stream of thought, time perception, memory, experimental methods; great work decades ahead of its time. 94 figures. 1,391pp. 5⅜ x 8½. 2-vol. set.
Vol. I: 20381-6   Vol. II: 20382-4

THE WORLD AS WILL AND REPRESENTATION, Arthur Schopenhauer. Definitive English translation of Schopenhauer's life work, correcting more than 1,000 errors, omissions in earlier translations. Translated by E. F. J. Payne. Total of 1,269pp. 5⅜ x 8½. 2-vol. set.
Vol. 1: 21761-2   Vol. 2: 21762-0

MAGIC AND MYSTERY IN TIBET, Madame Alexandra David-Neel. Experiences among lamas, magicians, sages, sorcerers, Bonpa wizards. A true psychic discovery. 32 illustrations. 321pp. 5⅜ x 8½. (Available in U.S. only.) 22682-4

THE EGYPTIAN BOOK OF THE DEAD, E. A. Wallis Budge. Complete reproduction of Ani's papyrus, finest ever found. Full hieroglyphic text, interlinear transliteration, word-for-word translation, smooth translation. 533pp. 6½ x 9¼. 21866-X

MATHEMATICS FOR THE NONMATHEMATICIAN, Morris Kline. Detailed, college-level treatment of mathematics in cultural and historical context, with numerous exercises. Recommended Reading Lists. Tables. Numerous figures. 641pp. 5⅜ x 8½. 24823-2

PROBABILISTIC METHODS IN THE THEORY OF STRUCTURES, Isaac Elishakoff. Well-written introduction covers the elements of the theory of probability from two or more random variables, the reliability of such multivariable structures, the theory of random function, Monte Carlo methods of treating problems incapable of exact solution, and more. Examples. 502pp. 5⅜ x 8½. 40691-1

THE RIME OF THE ANCIENT MARINER, Gustave Doré, S. T. Coleridge. Doré's finest work; 34 plates capture moods, subtleties of poem. Flawless full-size reproductions printed on facing pages with authoritative text of poem. "Beautiful. Simply beautiful."–*Publisher's Weekly*. 77pp. 9¼ x 12. 22305-1

NORTH AMERICAN INDIAN DESIGNS FOR ARTISTS AND CRAFTSPEOPLE, Eva Wilson. Over 360 authentic copyright-free designs adapted from Navajo blankets, Hopi pottery, Sioux buffalo hides, more. Geometrics, symbolic figures, plant and animal motifs, etc. 128pp. 8⅜ x 11. (Not for sale in the United Kingdom.) 25341-4

SCULPTURE: Principles and Practice, Louis Slobodkin. Step-by-step approach to clay, plaster, metals, stone; classical and modern. 253 drawings, photos. 255pp. 8⅛ x 11. 22960-2

THE INFLUENCE OF SEA POWER UPON HISTORY, 1660–1783, A. T. Mahan. Influential classic of naval history and tactics still used as text in war colleges. First paperback edition. 4 maps. 24 battle plans. 640pp. 5⅜ x 8½. 25509-3

CATALOG OF DOVER BOOKS

THE STORY OF THE TITANIC AS TOLD BY ITS SURVIVORS, Jack Winocour (ed.). What it was really like. Panic, despair, shocking inefficiency, and a little heroism. More thrilling than any fictional account. 26 illustrations. 320pp. 5⅜ x 8½.
20610-6

FAIRY AND FOLK TALES OF THE IRISH PEASANTRY, William Butler Yeats (ed.). Treasury of 64 tales from the twilight world of Celtic myth and legend: "The Soul Cages," "The Kildare Pooka," "King O'Toole and his Goose," many more. Introduction and Notes by W. B. Yeats. 352pp. 5⅜ x 8½.
26941-8

BUDDHIST MAHAYANA TEXTS, E. B. Cowell and others (eds.). Superb, accurate translations of basic documents in Mahayana Buddhism, highly important in history of religions. The Buddha-karita of Asvaghosha, Larger Sukhavativyuha, more. 448pp. 5⅜ x 8½.
25552-2

ONE TWO THREE . . . INFINITY: Facts and Speculations of Science, George Gamow. Great physicist's fascinating, readable overview of contemporary science: number theory, relativity, fourth dimension, entropy, genes, atomic structure, much more. 128 illustrations. Index. 352pp. 5⅜ x 8½.
25664-2

EXPERIMENTATION AND MEASUREMENT, W. J. Youden. Introductory manual explains laws of measurement in simple terms and offers tips for achieving accuracy and minimizing errors. Mathematics of measurement, use of instruments, experimenting with machines. 1994 edition. Foreword. Preface. Introduction. Epilogue. Selected Readings. Glossary. Index. Tables and figures. 128pp. 5⅜ x 8½.
40451-X

DALÍ ON MODERN ART: The Cuckolds of Antiquated Modern Art, Salvador Dalí. Influential painter skewers modern art and its practitioners. Outrageous evaluations of Picasso, Cézanne, Turner, more. 15 renderings of paintings discussed. 44 calligraphic decorations by Dalí. 96pp. 5⅜ x 8½. (Available in U.S. only.)
29220-7

ANTIQUE PLAYING CARDS: A Pictorial History, Henry René D'Allemagne. Over 900 elaborate, decorative images from rare playing cards (14th–20th centuries): Bacchus, death, dancing dogs, hunting scenes, royal coats of arms, players cheating, much more. 96pp. 9¼ x 12¼.
29265-7

MAKING FURNITURE MASTERPIECES: 30 Projects with Measured Drawings, Franklin H. Gottshall. Step-by-step instructions, illustrations for constructing handsome, useful pieces, among them a Sheraton desk, Chippendale chair, Spanish desk, Queen Anne table and a William and Mary dressing mirror. 224pp. 8⅛ x 11¼.
29338-6

THE FOSSIL BOOK: A Record of Prehistoric Life, Patricia V. Rich et al. Profusely illustrated definitive guide covers everything from single-celled organisms and dinosaurs to birds and mammals and the interplay between climate and man. Over 1,500 illustrations. 760pp. 7½ x 10⅛.
29371-8

Paperbound unless otherwise indicated. Available at your book dealer, online at **www.doverpublications.com**, or by writing to Dept. GI, Dover Publications, Inc., 31 East 2nd Street, Mineola, NY 11501. For current price information or for free catalogues (please indicate field of interest), write to Dover Publications or log on to **www.doverpublications.com** and see every Dover book in print. Dover publishes more than 500 books each year on science, elementary and advanced mathematics, biology, music, art, literary history, social sciences, and other areas.